Vietnam and the Chinese Model

D1534961

Harvard East Asian Monographs, 140

Vietnam and the Chinese Model

A Comparative Study of Vietnamese and Chinese Government in the First Half of the Nineteenth Century

Alexander Barton Woodside

Published by
the Council on East Asian Studies,
Harvard University,
and distributed by
the Harvard University Press,
Cambridge (Massachusetts) and London
1988

Preparation of this volume has been aided by
a grant from the Ford Foundation

The Council on East Asian Studies at Harvard University publishes a
monograph series and, through the Fairbank Center for East Asian
Research and the Reischauer Institute of Japanese Studies, administers
research projects designed to further scholarly understanding of China,
Japan, Korea, Vietnam, Inner Asia, and adjacent areas.

Library of Congress Cataloging-in-Publication Data

Woodside, Alexander.
  Vietnam and the Chinese model : a comparative study of Vietnamese
and Chinese government in the first half of the nineteenth century /
Alexander Barton Woodside.
    p. cm. — (Harvard East Asian monographs ; 140)
  Reprint. Originally published: Cambridge, Mass. : Harvard
University Press, 1971. (Harvard East Asian series ; 52) With new
pref.
    ISBN 0-674-93721-x
    1. Vietnam — Politics and government.   2. China — Politics and
government — 19th century.   I. Title.   II. Series.
JQ811.w66   1988
320.3 — dc19   88-22869
                                                         CIP

To my parents, Moffatt and Eleanor Woodside

Contents

Nguyễn Vietnam in 1835

This book was written during the second Indo-China War. The most formidable Western power was bombing the Vietnamese people but not understanding them, and it was almost impossible to find English-language translations anywhere of even the most beautiful and most widely read Vietnamese classical literature. (Since 1971, our lack of access to the poetry of one of the most literature-loving peoples on this planet has been remedied by, especially, the heroic efforts of Huynh Sanh Thong. See Thong's translation *Nguyen Du: The Tale of Kieu, a Bilingual Edition* (1983) and his *The Heritage of Vietnamese Poetry: An Anthology* (1979). The latter book contains more elegant and more authoritative translations of much of the poetry I first translated quite amateurishly in the pages that follow.)

The Western-language scholarship on Vietnam that has appeared between 1971 and 1988 has obviously improved our understanding of many aspects of Vietnamese history. But it cannot be said that we know very much more about Vietnam as the mature Confucian kingdom of the eighteenth and early-nineteenth centuries than we did when *Vietnam and the Chinese Model* was first published. Some Western scholars are, at the end of the 1980s, in the midst of an arresting and occasionally callow debate about the "post-Confucian challenge" offered to the West by the Asian societies whose historic adherence to Confucian values supposedly equipped them for great breakthroughs in economic growth and applied learning in our own age. Yet we still know less about the subtle variances between Vietnamese and Chinese Confucianism, or Vietnamese and Korean

Confucianism, than we do about the differences between Islam as it is practiced in Java and Islam as it is practiced in the Middle East. No doubt the postwar economic disasters that presently grip Vietnam make the study of Vietnamese thought and institutions seem unpromising to even the most uninhibited "post-Confucian-challenge" theorists. Yet no exposition of the philosophically vital Confucian civilization which once extended from Seoul to Saigon can ever be complete without a greater consideration of Vietnamese Confucianism and its politics, any more than the spread of Islam could ever be properly explored without reference to Indonesia. In this respect I hope that this book's reappearance is justifiable, even though no one is more aware than I that it presents an overly schematic and somewhat court-centered view of a hypnotically complex society. In the very brief compass of a new preface, I can only confess a few of my afterthoughts to what I wrote two decades ago.

First of all, the outstanding authority on "Vietnam and the Chinese model" is no modern scholar, but a Vietnamese Neo-Confucian philosopher who died two centuries ago, Le Quy Don (1726–1784). He appears far too infrequently in the pages that follow. Le Quy Don was a child prodigy who had read all the works of Chu Hsi by the time he entered his teens. One of his most important works, the *Kien van tieu luc* (A small chronicle of things seen and heard), completed in 1777, was a magisterial analysis and history in twelve parts (only eight of which have survived) of the literature, institutions, and religious practices both of Vietnam and of the wider Confucian classical world. His book makes it clear that the critical discourse in Vietnam about proper Confucian political and cultural arrangements had ramified well beyond rulers' courts by the eighteenth century, and that the Nguyen emperors' emphasis on a relatively narrow orthodoxy in the nineteenth century was much more reactionary, by existing Vietnamese cultural standards, than I originally suggested. What Le Quy Don's "chronicle" also makes clear is that the Vietnamese intellectual of the 1700s was perfectly aware that he belonged to a far-flung Confucian commonwealth which comprised, in time and space, something more than just the contemporary Chinese and Vietnamese governments.

This commonwealth increasingly shared geographic, literary, and technical knowledge. Soviet scholars have recently drawn our attention to the contacts between Vietnamese and Korean literati, encouraged by the overlapping of Vietnamese and Korean tribute embassies in Peking. But Le Quy Don himself also discusses, extensively, such Vietnamese contacts with Korea. Minh-mang's public salutation of Korea in the 1800s as a "civilized" country was merely an echo of what Le Quy Don had written in 1777. The first momentous Vietnamese-Korean dialogue probably occurred in 1597, when a friendship flourished in Peking between Phung Khac Khoan and Yi Su-gwang. Khoan, the Vietnamese envoy, was a Board president and learned Confucian scholar in his own right, and is famous for having brought new seeds for maize and bean crops back to Vietnam from Ming China. Yi Su-gwang was a notable reformer and historian who helped to found the *Sirhak* (Practical-Learning) movement in Korea, as an alternative to rarefied Neo-Confucian metaphysics. He wrote a preface to Phung Khac Khoan's poems (in which he courteously alluded to the pearls, ivory, tortoise shells, and other tropical wealth Vietnam was supposed to possess), and the two men may have exchanged broad ideas about books and politics. Another important Vietnamese-Korean encounter occurred in 1760. Le Quy Don became friends, during his two months at the Court of State Ceremonial in Peking, with some of the Korean reform scholars sent on a mission there, one of whom was later to participate in the creation of the famous Korean encyclopedia *Tongguk munhon pigo* (Reference compilation of documents on Korea).

I now suspect that such links with Korea gave Vietnamese thinkers a stronger awareness of the international variety of Asian attempts to reproduce the classical political ideals of the original Confucian philosophers, and a more confident inclination to distinguish such ideals from the Chinese politics of their own age. Discussing Korean history in his *Kien van tieu luc,* Le Quy Don even wrote that Korea's example of having had only two dynasties in the previous eight centuries — the Koryo dynasty and the Yi dynasty — ought to have caused shame to the more turmoil-ridden Chinese. The Emperor Minh-mang's tendentious China-bashing comparisons of his own Vietnam to the ancient Chou city-states, which I mention but do not stress sufficiently in Chapter 3 of this book, show at least a moderate tendency to greater independence in political thought which was almost certainly stimulated by Minh-mang's awareness that Vietnam did not share the stage with only one contemporary "Chinese model."

Second, if Confucian Vietnam in its final centuries had a stronger sense of membership in an international Confucian commonwealth than I suggested in 1971, it also was dominated more by its own medieval past, and by the many pockets of that past that survived, than I imply in the pages that follow. Le Quy Don pointed out in 1777 that the inhabitants of whole villages still preserved the thirteenth-century custom of shaving their heads like monks. Other northern villagers continued to celebrate the memory of tenth-century village "strongmen" (*tho hao,* a Sino-Vietnamese term with a significantly less unfavorable and more pre-Confucian flavor than its Chinese counterpart, *t'u-hao*). They did so not just by supporting temples that worshipped the legacy of someone like "Former Lord Khuc" (a village leader who had proclaimed himself "military commissioner" of his region in the last years of the T'ang protectorate) but even by widely sharing the surname of such long-dead medieval leaders.

From this one does not have to travel far to see interesting similarities between the Vietnamese monarchy itself, and medieval European kingships. Of course, the Vietnamese monarchy's "Chineseness" separated it from them by making it Caesaropapist: Vietnamese rulers performed, in European terms, the functions both of kings and of popes. Yet a similarity lay in Vietnamese rulers' efforts to combine two different political traditions. Just as European kings in the Middle Ages were a would-be combination of Teutonic warrior chief and Roman emperor, blending universal Latin and parochial German elements, Vietnamese rulers tried to combine the centralizing mandate of the Chinese "Son of Heaven" with the more indigenous, more parochial, less centralizing tradition of communal chieftainship, which remained very much alive. Keith Taylor has now shown us something of the early Vietnamese courts' attempted imperial consummation of the idea of heroic communal leadership: the greater importance of Taoism at Vietnamese courts (because it reinforced and systematized popular animist beliefs); the early medieval stress, more reminiscent of Cambodia than China and later abandoned under Confucian pressure, upon formal imperial polygamy, which could link a ruler with other local heroic families more equitably than would be true of mere concubinage; and the particular importance of the link between Vietnamese kingship and the powerful local legend of water spirits. (See Keith Weller Taylor, *The Birth of Vietnam,* 1983.) No doubt the hybridization of two political leadership traditions worked in Vietnam, at times, almost as well as it had for Charlemagne in Europe. A successful Vietnamese emperor, as a supreme communal chief, could command genuine popular support in a way more august Chinese emperors could not. But hybridization of this sort could not avoid sanctifying a peculiarly Vietnamese "bipolar" distribution of authority between the court and the villages, in which the Vietnamese emperor was not only more subject to challenge by other would-be imperialized chiefs (as the period of disunity between 1528 and 1802 suggested), but had to accept a greater degree of village-based communal authority than his Chinese counterpart.

Part of this acute bipolarity between the Vietnamese court and the villages was, of course, economically determined. By the end of the eighteenth century, Vietnam had begun to achieve a diversified tropical agriculture that was more complex than the fifteenth-century farm economy upon which the Le dynasty had originally depended, even if it still based itself upon two big rice harvests a year, as it had since at least the first century A.D. (See Nguyen Thanh Nha, *Tableau économique du Vietnam aux XVIIe et XVIIIe siècles,* 1970). Vietnamese peasants made distinctions among some seventy strains of rice, according to Le Quy Don. The south alone grew winter melons and musk melons in Ba Ria, maize and sweet potatoes in Bien Hoa, mangosteens in Bien Hoa and Vinh Long, peanuts in Gia Dinh, mangoes in Binh Dinh, pepper in Ha Tien, and internationally coveted sugar-cane crops in Quang Nam and Binh Thuan, if we follow the early-nineteenth-century inventory of Truong Quoc Dung. But such economic specialization never became impressive enough to disturb bipolarity, by creating big landlords (except in the south, and not until the late 1700s) or major cities. The provincial intelligentsia remained in the villages as schoolteachers, rather than becoming the associates of urban academies or salt merchants' libraries, separated from the peasants, like their Chinese counterparts.

Even so, rural communalism was a Vietnamese value, as well as a symptom of Vietnamese economic history. The great seventeenth-century Chinese philosopher Ku Yen-wu's attack upon China's over-concentration of people and assets in its cities and towns, and upon the excessive power of the Chinese emperor and of his more menial underlings and the relative powerlessness of non-menial local governments and communities, and Ku Yen-wu's desire to infuse a spirit of feudal localism into Chinese imperial administration by returning genuine authority to local social forces, were all quite irrelevant in the more bipolar Vietnam. Hence, the Chinese monarchy could more easily be captured by outside invaders, but was challenged by fewer village-based rebel intellectuals like Cao Ba Quat (a very Vietnamese figure in so many ways). The Vietnamese monarchy, on the other hand, was stronger—before 1800—against external threats, in ironic confirmation of Ku Yen-wu's theories, but was less able to preserve a domestic hegemony.

Third, the greater importance than I originally conceded of village-based medieval leadership traditions may shed a new light upon even the most seemingly "Chinese" of Vietnam's institutions. Both in the old Preface and in Chapter 4 of this book, I write that, by Chinese standards, the Vietnamese examination system was "underdeveloped." Yet Le Quy Don in 1777, in his discussion of the existing northern Vietnamese examinations, called not for their greater development but for their simplification. In particular, he attacked the proposed importation into Vietnam from China of the "eight-legged essay," arguing that, if the Vietnamese examinations were not simplified, the "people below" would "dissipate their resolution" and the "people above" would not have succeeded in creating a serviceable "ladder of advancement" for them. In his appeal for the further simplification of these supposedly "underdeveloped" examinations, Le Quy Don used a language of mutual obligations, implicitly: what the "people above" must do to choose talent, what the "people below" must do to be chosen. He was talking, clearly, about a process of political representation. Indeed Vietnamese, and Chinese, political theory is deeply concerned with the subject of non-democratic techniques of representation: the obligation of rulers to allow ordinary people to speak out, to validate with their critical comments the reputations of court officials, and to become officials themselves if they are capable. Western scholars underestimate this concern because such techniques have little in common with our traditions of parliamentary democracy, or with the earlier history behind those traditions of regarding the state as a combination of "estates" whose spheres of competence, being separate, needed constitutional or contractual representation. Also, the great but sometimes crippling inpiration of Max Weber has encouraged us to make the study of types of authority, not types of representation, the focus of our analysis of non-Western societies, as in the following pages.

But if we look at the Vietnamese examination system from Le Quy Don's angle, instead of from the angle of the refinement of hierarchical authority which I employed in 1971, we quickly see that the simpler Vietnamese examinations may have been designed to promote particular Vietnamese sorts of solidarity between "people above" and "people below." In one of the more remarkable passages in the *Kien van tieu luc,* Le Quy Don observed that Vietnamese courts conferred extraordinary prestige-enhancing favors upon senior graduates of the examination system, at the village level, which Chinese courts never conferred upon senior graduates in China. Such favors included mansions built by conscript labor at government direction, and "glorious return" (*vinh qui*) receptions in the villages, made spectacular by flags, fans, and drum performances. One may hypothesize that the Vietnamese Confucian state was more conscious of having to compete with a pre-Confucian past of heroic solidarity in its villages, and knew that the transition to a mature Confucian clerical officialdom required a government-sponsored replacement of such pre-Confucian heroic traditions by Confucian traditions of scholastic achievement which nevertheless had to be made to seem heroic too, by mansions and by drum playing, in their own right.

All this is another way of suggesting that Lord Acton's famous pronouncement in 1859, that "two great principles" of "antiquity" and the "Middle Ages" contributed to a dualism which ran through Western civilization, and contended for mastery over it, had a Vietnamese application. In the centuries-long battle to change the symbolic and practical representation of the villages in the polity, higher degree-holders had to stand in for the old village communal leaders both in fact and in memory. This Asian Confucian version of medieval Europe's conversion of pagan warriors into Christian knights was almost certainly more difficult in Vietnam than in China, given the greater formal and informal importance of village communalism. By extensive rituals, and by keeping the examinations more simple or "underdeveloped," Vietnamese courts did succeed in translating Confucian scholastic achievement into an accessible heroic ideal which would allow Confucian scholars to subsume older, potentially contrapuntal traditions of community leadership which were apparently closer to the surface in Vietnamese rural life than in rural China. But Vietnamese dynasts did so at the cost of themselves helping to consolidate a village intelligentsia which was relatively more powerful with respect to their rulers, and more closely linked to the peasants, than the gentry of Ch'ing China were.

One lives for the day when we shall know as much about Vietnamese Confucianism as we do about Thai Buddhism. But it is now clear to me that, by the 1700s, Vietnamese needs such as the ones I have mentioned had created a relatively more independent Vietnamese Confucianism than I acknowledged in 1971. We can see this even in high philosophy. As just one example, medieval Chinese Neo-Confucianism debated the necessary division between "moral-nature knowledge" and "empirical knowledge," with important philosophers arguing that sages had to escape from the fetters of empirical knowledge (Chang Tsai); or that moral-nature knowledge did not even need to make use of empirical knowledge (Ch'eng I); or that empirical knowledge was only secondary to "innate knowledge of the good" (Wang Yang-ming). By taking the medieval term for this supposedly inferior "empirical knowledge" (*kien van,* Chinese: *chien-wen*) and putting it in the title of one of his major works (the *Kien van tieu luc*), Le Quy Don showed his disdain for much Chinese Neo-Confucian metaphysics; and it is worth noting that, even in the far less metaphysical Ch'ing period, no major Chinese philosopher ever wrote a work of equivalent importance bearing such a title. Perhaps Vietnamese thinkers were less interested in men creating themselves anew by means of an intuitive sagely oneness with the world which transcended observable knowing, and more interested in self-recreation through an imaginative reconciliation of the scholastic with the locally venerated. Or, to put it more positively, Le Quy Don believed that self-recreation depended upon a self-knowledge that could be gained only from careful historical study, of the local as well as of the national. In that respect this very formidable Vietnamese thinker, though dead, continues to fight for something that is very much alive.

Apart from the people whose help I acknowledged in 1971, I should like to mention the steady inspiration I received from my father, Moffatt Woodside, who died just before this book was published, and whose first name I unaccountably misspelled in the original dedication.

ABW
June 1988

This book is concerned with the problem of Chinese cultural influences and their limitations in the politics, literature, education, and society of early nineteenth-century Vietnam. In it I attempt to make explicit point-by-point comparisons of certain Chinese and Vietnamese traditional institutions. One of the arts of Vietnamese studies lies in being able artificially to disentangle (for the sake of those heuristic purposes which every scholar invokes) the Chinese or Sino-Vietnamese characteristics of Vietnamese history and society from the Southeast Asian characteristics, while remaining perfectly aware at the same time that Vietnamese culture represents a combination of the two. Such a process of identification or disentanglement necessitates consideration of the implicit as well as the explicit cultural features of nineteenth-century Vietnamese life, no easy task for an outsider.

Within the existing patterns of any society there obviously lurk incapsulations of the past events of its history. This process of incapsulation has produced the standardized ideas about time and history, in varying social contexts, which the members of that society hold. The French colonial regime in Vietnam, which came to an end in 1954, lasted less than a century. It cannot remotely compare with the roughly ten centuries of Vietnamese cultural development under Chinese rule, from the Han through the T'ang, or with the nine centuries of Vietnam's more autonomous development, still within the cultural circle of the Chinese world, which succeeded them. Even today, in Vietnamese thought and politics, East Asian conceptual categories, new and old, are vastly more dominant than French ones. The question of the historical nature of the Chinese influence in recent Vietnamese history is, I think, a crucial one.

Although I examine Vietnamese traditional government only after 1802, it is important to consider the immediate historical background of the Nguyễn "restoration," which was one of disorder. After the golden age of Lê Thánh-tông (1460–1497), when one court ruled a unified Vietnam from the site of modern Hanoi, imperial sovereignty had informally crumbled. From the 1500's to the 1700's two groups of rulers competed for power in Vietnamese society, the *chúa* (lords) of the Trịnh family in the north and the *chúa* of the Nguyễn family in central Vietnam. The Lê emperors preserved their titles but, like Japanese emperors before 1868, enjoyed the trappings and not the substance of sovereignty. Then, in the 1700's, disunity was first compounded and then resolved by the Tây-sơn Rebellion.

The rebellion was a massive peasant upheaval, led by three brothers, which began in Bình Định province in 1771. By 1773 Qui-nhơn had fallen to the sonorous "roaring armies" (*quân ó*) of the Tây-sơns, whose soldiers hissed, shouted, and responded to each other as they moved through the countryside, sounding like waves breaking through a dike (according to Vietnamese tradition.) By 1778 the Tây-sơns were masters of much of the center and the south. The eldest brother even proclaimed himself emperor (*vua*) of Vietnam in this year, having already made himself "king" (*vương*) two years earlier. At this point, the end of the first phase of the Tây-sơn rebellion, Vietnamese political loyalties were divided among three groups of regional rulers, instead of just two as they had been only eight years before. The Trịnh family ruled the north and some of the center, the Tây-sơns ruled the center and briefly seized the south, and the last descendant of the old ruling Nguyễn house of central Vietnam, Nguyễn Phúc Ánh, now attempted to survive, in alliance with Siam, in the south and in the islands of the Gulf of Siam.

In 1786–87 Tây-sơn armies attacked the north. The Trịnh family collapsed. The incompetent Lê emperor requested assistance from China. Ch'ing armies invaded northern Vietnam in 1788, nominally to defend his throne. The defiant Vietnamese response was to proclaim the most gifted Tây-sơn brother Quang-trung emperor in December 1788. Quang-trung's armies defeated the Chinese invaders, who subsequently withdrew. The dynamic Quang-trung then embarked upon an unprecedented program of political and cultural experimentation which Vietnamese today look back upon as the "Tây-sơn revolution." It included the precedence of soldiers over civil bureaucrats and the overthrow of classical Chinese as a written court language, in favor of *nôm*. This remarkable man's premature death in 1792 ended the triumphant second phase of the Tây-sơn rebellion.

The third phase (1792–1802) of the Tây-sơn Rebellion was its political conservatism and military collapse. Quang-trung's son was young and ineffective. Nguyễn Phúc Ánh, whom the Tây-sơns had driven into exile in Bangkok, recaptured southern Vietnam while Tây-sơn armies were preoccupied with the north. When Ánh defeated Tây-sơn generals in central Vietnam in 1799–1801, the Tây-sơn dynasty fell apart. In 1802 Ánh easily recovered northern Vietnam. He could now claim to be emperor of the north, the center, and the south. Ánh's emergence as the Gia-long emperor of the "restored" Nguyễn house in 1802 is the point in time where this book begins.

The Tây-sơn Rebellion has not received the attention it deserves as one of the major episodes of eighteenth-century Southeast Asian and East Asian history. Yet it could be argued that this rebellion inaugurates modern Vietnamese history. First, it led to the extensive involvement of Westerners in Vietnamese politics for the first time. Gia-long was aided by a group of French sailors, soldiers, and ecclesiastics in his conquest of the Tây-sơns. Second, it summarized the socio-economic discontents of the Vietnamese peasantry in a more dramatic and large-scale fashion than ever before, for the first time making the peasant world the crucial battleground for Vietnamese rulers and would-be rulers that it would remain into the twentieth century. Third, it led to the political unification of Vietnam, after centuries of disunity. The memory of this fragile unity of the period 1788–1862 (or 1802–1862) became an important symbol and force in Vietnamese politics after French colonialists had administratively dismembered the country. Fourth, in addition to having a serious war with China for its climax, the rebellion also was the occasion for an expression of antipathies to the growing Chinese merchant class in Vietnam for the first time in a major way. In a sense, the

Tây-sơn troops who protested against the slowly germinating "plural society" in southern Vietnam by massacring thousands of Chinese traders there in 1782 were the spiritual ancestors of the Vietnamese who boycotted Chinese trade in Saigon in the 1920's. Fifth, Gia-long's victory over the Tây-sơns represented the shadowy beginnings of an integration of mainland Southeast Asian history, at least in military and diplomatic terms. Siamese troops participated in it, and both Cambodia and Burma felt its repercussions almost immediately. The new Nguyễn dynasty threatened the independence of the former country and wrongly seemed to the rulers of the latter to be a potential ally against Siam.

If modern Vietnamese history opens with the Tây-sơn Rebellion, the study of modern Vietnamese history must lead in two directions. Obviously it must add to our knowledge about Southeast Asia. It must also aid in the expansion of comparative historical analysis within the more or less perdurable framework of East Asian civilization. How did certain classical East Asian institutions—bureaucracy, or familism, or law, or merchant guilds—work out the implications of their archetypal rules and ideologies within the changing ecological and social environments of four very different countries? If a satisfactory typology of East Asian institutions proves elusive, it should still be possible to ascertain at a given moment in time which Chinese classical institutions truly were "universal" within traditional East Asia—in the sense that they were adopted also by the Koreans, the Vietnamese, and even the Japanese—and which ones were more parochially Chinese.

For example, in Chapter 4, I attempt to show that there were important differences between the Ch'ing and Nguyễn examination systems, given the fact that both the Chinese and Vietnamese bureaucracies depended upon this ingenious institution. There was slightly less institutionally guaranteed social mobility through geographical space in the Vietnamese system. More of the Vietnamese system's privileges and ceremonies were concentrated in the capital city. There were fewer bureaucratic control laws governing the Vietnamese examinations. There were also fewer achievement levels in the Vietnamese system between village and court, which in turn meant less standardization in depth of the professional training of Vietnamese bureaucrats. The Vietnamese printing industry was more highly controlled and centralized, and there were fewer libraries in Vietnamese provinces. Vietnamese examination sites were more informal and more highly improvised. There was less formal specialization among Vietnamese examiners. There was a proportionately greater bureaucratic demand for, and a smaller answering supply of, Confucian scholars in Vietnam; and considerations of a scholar's original place in the academic hierarchy had less impact upon long-range appointments strategy in the Vietnamese civil service. I attempt to show that the causes of these divergences were complex, involving different cultural emphases as well as the more obvious effects of the discrepancy in size between the two societies. In this book I merely hover on the outskirts of comparative institutional history. The future holds enormous possibilities, which wait to be explored.

Finally, I have attempted to present in translation a very tiny sample of the profusion of writings and poems that were produced by certain Vietnamese intellectuals of the early 1800's. My justification for doing this rests upon a significant irony. The brilliant nineteenth-century literary revolution in Vietnam, as represented most magistrally by Hô Xuân Hương, Cao Bá Quát, Nguyễn Công Trứ, Nguyễn Đình Chiểu, and others, sometimes revealed a historical trend perceptibly opposed to that of Minh-mạng's institutional borrowing from China, namely a trend away from Chinese literary and even cultural styles. For Southeast Asian specialists, concerned as they are with indigenous reactions to imported institutions, this literary revolution is one of the most rewarding topics of nineteenth-century Vietnamese history. To the twentieth-century Vietnamese people, it might be added, Minh-mạng's bureaucracy belongs to a fallen and forgotten world. Literature alone is the historically redemptive legacy the early Nguyễn era has bequeathed them.

The research for this book was largely accomplished in the period 1965–1967. Generous support from the Foreign Area Fellowship Program, which is not responsible for the book or the opinions expressed in it, enabled me to stay in Hong Kong, Tokyo, Saigon, and Paris during those two years of research. I must also record my very grateful appreciation of grants-in-aid from the East Asian Research Center of Harvard University and from the American Council of Learned Societies and the Social Science Research Council. I should also mention my gratitude for a Woodrow Wilson Fellowship during my first year of graduate school.

To proceed from institutions to individuals, I am indebted beyond repayment to a number of scholars and friends. Professor John K. Fairbank directed my thesis, tried to impose some clarity upon my literary style, and in general, over eight years, 'has given me that viatical endowment of learning and training every newcomer to Asian studies requires. I am also very indebted to Professor G. William Skinner, under whose direction and in whose Cornell anthropology seminar part of this book first germinated. I owe much as well to the advice and kindly hospitality of Professor Ch'en Ching-ho, of the New Asia Research Institute in Kowloon. And, over the years, I have received much sinological inspiration and wisdom from Professor W. A. C. H. Dobson of the University of Toronto.

For inspiration, scholarly training, counsel, and other forms of tangible and intangible help I would also like to acknowledge my gratitude to Professor Lien-sheng Yang, Professor Albert Feuerwerker, Professor Benjamin Schwartz, Professor Tatsuro Yamamoto, and Mrs. Daniel Southerland.

The Vietnamese people have seen many Westerners make fools of themselves writing about their country. Surprisingly, this has not dulled their kindness or exhausted their patience with the next Western scholar to come along. At different times a number of Vietnamese friends have watched me preparing this book. But I would particularly like to express my thanks to Miss Phan Mỹ Chương, under whose tutelage I began to learn the Vietnamese language at Cornell, and Mr. Ngô Vĩnh Long, whose profound knowledge and intelligent love of Vietnam and its culture have made him an incomparable adviser.

None of the people whom I have just listed are responsible for the shortcomings of this study, but many of them are more than slightly responsible for any merits it may possess.

ABW

One
Vietnam and China:
Acculturation's Apparitions
and Certain Realities
behind Them

For two thousand years or more, Vietnam, like Korea, Japan, and China, was a member of what might appropriately be called the East Asian classical civilization. At about the same time that the British Isles were first integrated into Roman Europe by Julius Caesar and his successors, the ancestors of the modern Vietnamese people, then living in the Red River delta of northern Vietnam, were conquered by Chinese armies and drawn into the ambit of the early Chinese empire.

From the first century to the tenth century, when it finally broke away and established its independence, northern Vietnam was a dependency of the Chinese empire. Over this span of nine hundred years, the Vietnamese people received a comprehensive initiation into the scholarship, political theories, familial organization patterns, bureaucratic practices, and even the religious orientations of Chinese culture. The consequences for Southeast Asian history were enormous. The Vietnamese people were sinicized centuries before Chinese culture had even been definitively consolidated in areas that are today considered part of China proper—for example, the province of Kweichow. One scholar has observed that ten centuries of Chinese rule over northern Vietnam destroyed all significant local aristocratic groups in Vietnamese society. Furthermore, Chinese rule gave the Vietnamese people—through the imposition of Chinese social, bureaucratic, and familial forms—a cohesion that guaranteed their permanence, on the eastern edge of a sub-continent where impermanent states were the rule rather than the exception.[1] Such cohesion enabled the Vietnamese to resist future Chinese invasions of their country successfully. It also enabled them to expand south to the Gulf of Siam at the expense of other Southeast Asian kingdoms.

But appearances have always been deceptive. How completely in any given century did Chinese culture in Vietnam subdue the Southeast Asian environment, the indigenous foundation or infrastructure of patterns of belief and action that lay so pervasively and mysteriously underneath acculturation? The question is important to Vietnamese history because Vietnamese emperors and bureaucrats privately hardly ever ceased asking it.

Some Vietnamese historians have been briefly tempted to argue against the existence of any qualitative cultural differences between China and Vietnam at all. One historian has asserted that when Vietnamese independence from China was indisputably established after centuries of Chinese rule, it was merely an instance of a fruit ripening and dropping from its mother tree in order to begin a related but geographically separate life.[2] In the first few centuries after independence was gained, Vietnamese political life was seemingly such a comfortable reflection of the Chinese experience that ambitious Chinese immigrants could easily come to Vietnam and win bureaucratic positions there. The lists of degree holders for the Vietnamese examination systems of the Lý (1010–1225) and Trần (1225–1400) dynasties reveal a large proportion of surnames that even now sound faintly Chinese to modern Vietnamese ears, like Châu, Dư, Vương.[3] The transition from life in south China to life in medieval Vietnam fell so far short of being rigorous or impossible that the not very remote ancestor of the thirteenth-century Trần rulers was a Chinese fisherman who had emigrated from Fukien.[4]

Yet some of this evidence loses its potency when other facts are remembered. The father of Phraya Tak (King Taksin), the man who ruled Siam from 1767 to 1782, was a Kwangtung merchant. His royal son did not hesitate to speak Chinese as well as Thai.[5] The problem of Vietnam's cultural interaction with China is, for better or for worse, associated with a fundamental feature of Southeast Asian societies in general. Culturally speaking, they were all of the "importing" rather than the "exporting" kind. And the relations of all of them, not just Vietnam, with the expansion-minded maritime communities of south China, ran deep. At the top of

Vietnamese society in the 1800's, the monarchy itself offered a revealing example of the ways in which East Asian or "Sino-Vietnamese" political conceptions could dominate but not monopolize a basic Vietnamese institution.

The Vietnamese Monarchy and Its Two Traditions

The first three emperors of the nineteenth-century Nguyễn dynasty, which was founded or, according to its own perspective, "restored" in 1802, were Gia-long, who ruled from 1802 to 1820; Minh-mạng, who succeeded him from 1820 to 1841; and Thiệu-trị, who ruled from 1841 to 1847. All three of them upheld Chinese concepts of empire and of the ways of ruling an empire. All three of them had themselves saluted at their courts as *hoàng-đế*. These two Sino-Vietnamese words had separately suggested divinity in ancient China until the imperial unifier of China, Ch'in Shih Huang-ti, had joined them together to refer to, and mean, a human "emperor." All three personally alluded to themselves by the august first person pronoun *trẫm*, which had been used exclusively by emperors in China, again since the time of Ch'in Shih Huang-ti. More significantly, the Nguyễn rulers invoked a more inveterate Chinese term for kingship. They called themselves "Sons of Heaven" or *thiên-tử*. This concept proposed that they were deputies of the natural forces of heaven. They ruled their people in heaven's place. They were therefore to be judged, not by the touchstone of how broadly popular their initial selection as power holders had been, but by the touchstone of how prosperous the "livelihood" (*dân sinh*) of the people under them was. This was considered to reflect the wisdom or unwisdom of their policies.

In traditional China and Vietnam it was commonly believed that men received their nature (*tính*; Chinese, *hsing*) or their endowment of abilities and aptitudes from heaven, which was the ultimate source of all things. This belief made the Son of Heaven the humanly incarnated source of education and economic sustenance, the "father and mother" of the people. His bureaucrats were supposed to model themselves after him. He was supposed to govern, by his intrinsic virtue, a strongly hierarchical society.

Nineteenth-century Vietnamese political theories, borrowed with elaborate fidelity from China, searched for a perfectly ordered society, stipulated that men were born unequal in talent, argued that education was more important than economic luxury (or progress), and stressed the value of elitist example in politics.

As a result, the imperial creed of Nguyễn emperors in Huế appeared to differ very little from that of Ch'ing emperors in Peking. In fact, however, a dual theory of sovereignty existed in Vietnam. Vietnamese rulers even had two sets of names. One of the Vietnamese terms for ruler was a domesticated Chinese name, *hoàng-đế*, mentioned above. But the other major term for ruler was an indigenous expression, *vua*, which could not be represented by a Chinese character but had to be written in *nôm*. The content of the word *vua*, the term for ruler used by the Vietnamese peasant, is difficult to expound. It had no equivalent in Chinese culture. Roughly, it suggested a protector figure (like the Vietnamese kitchen god or *vua bếp*), who was not or should not have been as aloof from his subjects as a Chinese-style emperor. Certainly Vietnamese peasants were far more inclined than Chinese peasants to look to their *vua* for leadership in daily life and to blame him directly for their misfortunes. Later in the century, a popular refrain would begin a summary of village social discontents by declaiming, "From the time I grew up to the present, grandfather ruler Tự-đức has made things worse and worse."[6] Nineteenth-century Chinese spectators of Vietnamese life, unaware of this dual theory of sovereignty, found the Vietnamese emperor's lack of remoteness from his officials and people incomprehensible. Hsü Chi-yü, the famous geographer, satirized it in his "world gazetteer" of the 1840's. He maliciously wrote that Vietnamese bureaucrats sat down in their emperor's presence and even felt free to search themselves for body lice during Huế court audiences.[7] Vietnamese emperors themselves could make fun of their own ambivalent role conception. Gia-long once did this when he told the son of J. B. Chaigneau, his French adviser, that use of the term Son of Heaven in Vietnam was an absurdity—at least in mixed Vietnamese-European company.[8]

It is not too much to say that the Vietnamese traditional monarchy's position was affected by two streams of thought, each concerned with social integration and each with its own symbolic forms. One

stream of thought was socio-political in nature. It was derived ①
wholly and directly from China. It stressed that the integration of
Vietnamese society could only come from the vertical accommodation of social differences, through application of Confucian principles of hierarchy. The most elementary form of such accommodation
was the submissiveness of pious children to their parents. Once
parental authority was exalted in this way, exaltation of the authority
of the ruler was merely a logical extension. The obligation of filial
piety, learned and "internalized" in early childhood, could be
transformed into political obedience to the throne after adulthood.

The outstanding literary text of this approach to the development
of authority in early nineteenth-century Vietnam was a primer
for children entitled *Twenty-four Stories of Filial Piety* (*Nhị Thập Tứ
Hiếu*). It was a book written by Lý Văn Phức (1785–1849), an
impoverished Hanoi scholar of recent (seventeenth-century) Chinese
ancestry. Phức entered the Nguyễn bureaucracy in 1819 and visited
Singapore, the Philippines, Macao, and China on official missions
in the 1830's. His book contained twenty-four stories about the lives
of great Chinese of the past. These exemplary figures had been
submissive to their parents to the point of martyrdom, for the sake
of a greater social good. In one of the twenty-four stories, for example,
a filial son, remembering that his dead mother had feared thunder,
went to sit upon the edge of her grave during storms, in order to
give her symbolic protection. In another story, a disciple of Confucius, Mẫn tử Khiên (Chinese, Min Tzu-ch'ien) suffered a tyranni-
cal stepmother for the sake of his two stepbrothers. (This latter story
is sometimes invoked even today in Vietnam for political reasons.)[9]

The source of this approach to the development of authority was,
as has been stated, entirely Chinese. In part, it descended from the
Chinese Yüan period scholarly movement to venerate Sung studies,
now transplanted to Vietnam centuries later to enjoy a Southeast
Asian renascence. Lý Văn Phức's *Twenty-four Stories of Filial Piety*
itself was merely a nineteenth-century Vietnamese translation of a
Chinese text that had been written about five centuries earlier.
The author of the Chinese text, Yüan scholar Kuo Chü-ching, thus
posthumously became one of the invisible architects of social authority in Nguyễn Vietnam.

The second stream of thought that affected the monarchy, and ② patterns of authority in Vietnam, was mythopoeic and religious in nature. It was stronger than any equivalent tradition in China. It was best represented by a fascinating and extremely popular work, the *Việt Điện U Linh Tập* (Anthology of the spirits of the departed of the Vietnamese domain). Although this book was apparently first written in 1329, in the next five centuries other authors added their own sections to it. Its organic growth through time revealed its importance in Vietnamese life. In the early 1800's Phan Huy Chú was the leader of what some Vietnamese historians have called the "literary movement" to expand this text. The book sets forth the life histories of famous Vietnamese rulers and their ministers who had sacrificed their own happiness in order to bring happiness to the Vietnamese people. Popular religion maintained that there was a connection between the spiritual and material worlds. These dead heroes were supposed to live on in the Vietnamese environment in superhuman form. In fact they did so as historical or mythical paragons, heavily idealized, of the virtues good contemporary Vietnamese rulers should possess. The hero rulers who were described in this fourteenth-century book included the Trưng sisters; the eighth-century Vietnamese rebel against T'ang Chinese rule who was canonized after his death as "the great king who was father and mother of his country" (*bố cái đại vương*);[10] the gods of land and grain, who were the spirits of agricultural fertility; and an early, autonomous Chinese governor of Vietnam and south China who had brought higher Chinese culture to the Vietnamese people.

These heterogeneous biographies emphasized three distinct qualities of kingship. The ideal Vietnamese ruler, by their reckoning, should be able to resist the political domination of the Chinese court. He should be able to preserve the people's livelihood and well-being. And he should be able to introduce and domesticate Chinese culture. He should be part rebel, part guardian of agricultural fertility, and part cultural innovator. This tradition was more vivid than the one of Kuo Chü-ching and Lý Văn Phức, which indirectly made the ruler a politically transcendental Confucian father. The tradition of the *Việt Điện U Linh Tập* stressed the creative obligations of the *vua*. The tradition of Kuo and Phức pointed to the moral obligations of the *hoàng-đế*.

In a superficial way such a dual theory of sovereignty is likely to remind scholars who enjoy the adventure of comparative institutional history of the double theoretical structure of Japanese kingship. After all, the Japanese term for emperor, *tennō*, was Sino-Japanese in origin and had referred both to a ruler and to the polar star in early China. Yet indigenous Shinto teachings in Japan stressed the non-Chinese doctrine that the Japanese ruler was sacrosanct, the representative of a divinely appointed unbroken imperial line. In Vietnam, the ruler could be considered a "hero of the people," a term that was rarely if ever applied to a Chinese emperor. A major qualification of this comparison, however, is that the Sino-Japanese word for ruler came to terms with its environment in a way that the Sino-Vietnamese phrase for ruler never did. In Japan, *tennō* successfully developed an indigenous content of meaning, causing the original native word for ruler to disappear. Perhaps because Korean diplomats of the state of Paekche appear to have been the first to apply this title to the Japanese emperor, no later than the sixth century, the essentially foreign background of the word never echoed too resoundingly in Japanese ears. It had come to Japan from China vaguely and indirectly.[11] In Vietnam, the Sino-Vietnamese title *hoàng-đế* was borrowed more directly and with more calculated premeditation from the Chinese. It certainly failed to achieve a decisive enough indigenous validity to justify the disappearance of the non-Chinese word for king. Heavy sinicization and heavy cultural resistance were both paradoxically but explicitly reflected in the persistence in Vietnam, to the end of the monarchy, of the two parallel titles for ruler.

However, at the court itself in the nineteenth century the two traditions coexisted without tension, behind a facade of Chinese classical symbols. The Vietnamese elite's sense of Chinese history was strong. Its faith in Chinese allusions, classical and historical, momentous and trivial, was romantic and unlimited. When soldiers digging at the site of the Zenith Gate (*Ngọ môn*) of the Huế imperial city in 1833 unearthed the dried bones of a skeleton, the skeleton was reburied properly at Minh-mạng's expense on the strength of a precedent set by King Wen of Chou. A performing elephant in Huế in the 1820's led one Nguyễn official to recall without the slightest effort an elephant that had held a goblet in its mouth at the T'ang court in Ch'ang-an in the eighth century.[12]

Minh-mạng was so conversant with Chinese history that he could retail anecdotes of more than three hundred words about the career of the first Ming emperor, complete with dialogue, at the slightest pretext.[13]

Furthermore, the Vietnamese emperor's performance of certain Chinese classical rituals became an act of continuity, expected and anticipated by his court, which enhanced his authority. Continuity implied propriety. The Vietnamese Son of Heaven, like his Chinese counterpart, surveyed the weather (heaven) for its political and economic omens. But the act meant little unless the tradition of the early Chinese Sons of Heaven, laid down thousands of years before in the Chinese *Book of Songs* (*Thi-kinh;* Chinese, *Shih-ching*) was consciously remembered. Minh-mạng said at the end of 1834: "On every winter solstice day the ancients ascended the Spirit Tower to examine the clouds . . . Today in the early dawn I saw that the color of the sun was radiant and the cloud ornaments were luxuriant, and I reflected that the peace and happiness of men next spring could be foretold."[14]

As an imperial prophet of nature in the tradition of the Chinese "Spirit Tower" (*linh-đài;* Chinese, *ling-t'ai*), Minh-mạng pretended to look at Vietnam's tropical skies half with the eyes of an ancient diviner of north China. This was not an unconditional pose. The coexistence of two traditions behind the Vietnamese monarchy ensured that it would be conditional. The Vietnamese emperor brought trophies of Chinese culture and classical institutions to his people. With the dexterity of a sociological clinician, he searched for ways to impose them permanently. But he also felt himself charged with the task of preventing his orthodox Sino-Vietnamese officials from going too far with Chinese ideas in Vietnam, to the point of meaninglessness or inappropriateness.

For example, tensions that were completely unknown in China arose in Huế between orthodox imitation of Chinese terminology and scholarly passions, derived from Chinese Sung neo-Confucianism, for accurate classification of Vietnamese natural objects. (Most members of the nineteenth-century Vietnamese elite were disciples of Chu Hsi.) Blameless Sino-Vietnamese concepts like "rectification of names" (*chính danh;* Chinese, *cheng-ming*) then began to twist and turn unpredictably in the hands of Vietnamese emperors. Undesired controversies and unwanted dilemmas rapidly crystallized. "Up until now our names for plants, birds, trees, and animals have all been obediently inherited appellations," Minh-mạng told his court in 1840. "Many are still not self-evident. We must at one stroke investigate them and apply 'rectification of names' to their appellations . . . Of the various plants and trees, each has its own suitabilities, and if you violate their soil nature then you cannot grow them . . . Our country's borders are situated in the southern region."[15]

This perfectly serious remark nonetheless had its place in a long tradition of satirical speculation in Vietnam over the inability of Confucian system builders to understand the natural laws of their environment. Perhaps one of the historical fountainheads of this satirical tradition in Vietnam was the 398-line poem *Truyện Trê Cóc* (The chronicle of the catfish and the frog), rich in character delineation, which was believed to date from the early thirteenth century. This medieval satire recounted the circumstances of a lawsuit between two frogs and a catfish. The female frog went to the pond of the catfish to give birth to some tadpoles, which the catfish saw and coveted. The catfish stole the tadpoles and called them its own offspring. The female frog returned to her husband and the two frogs launched a lawsuit against the catfish at the office of the nearest Confucian mandarin. The bureaucrat ordered the catfish imprisoned, but the wife of the catfish bribed an underling of the mandarin to have the affair examined. The mandarin's inspectors, after traveling to the pond, solemnly declared that the tadpoles were the true offspring of the catfish. The bureaucrat ordered his underlings to release the catfish and imprison the frog. Now the frog's wife appealed to a famous scholar who specialized in law. He advised her merely to wait until the tadpoles had shed their tails and appeared upon dry land. She did so, the tadpoles matured, and the catfish had to confess its crime, pay the expenses of the lawsuit, and submit to being exiled. Much of the wit of this famous satire was certainly directed not just against bureaucratic management of litigation but also against the Chinese-style mandarin's attempt to thwart the concrete realities of his environment. The simple natural law that tadpoles grow up into frogs, not into catfish, ultimately prevented his perversion of justice from going unnoticed and actually made a fool of him.

It is true, however, that such profane forces of satire and social commentary usually engaged in muffled but discriminating battle behind the scenes. On front stage center, the heavy if controversial dependence of the Vietnamese imperial tradition upon the Chinese classics and their ideas remained the preponderant theme of early nineteenth-century Vietnamese politics. It even explained a minor mystery of early nineteenth-century Vietnamese history. During the 1780's when he was a desperate refugee in Bangkok, a bizarre handful of French soldiers and priests had gathered under the banner of the future Gia-long emperor. After Gia-long had triumphed over the Tây-so'n armies and seized the Vietnamese throne in 1802, his French confederates had accompanied him to Huế. Why were they totally unable to inculcate European science and European political philosophies in Vietnam?

Before 1802 the future Gia-long had needed European support. He cultivated the French through a French bishop, Pigneau de Behaine (Bách Da Lộc). He also communicated with the Portuguese through their colony at Goa. He was carefully affable in his relations with French missionaries, whom he called *linh-mục*, "spiritual shepherds" or priests.[16] Probably nearly four hundred Frenchmen served Gia-long between the 1780's and 1820. They received Vietnamese names, mainly being enrolled as the emperor's personal servants. In that way they remained outside the regular bureaucracy and undertook no administrative or executive duties.[17] Their enduring achievement was the construction of "citadel" walls around Huế and assorted provincial towns. Victor Olivier usually directed this construction, working from plans drawn by Theodore Le Brun according to the methods of the renowned Vauban. Later under purely Vietnamese auspices French "citadel art" spread peacefully to northern Vietnam. Here it blended perfectly with Chinese administrative and geomantic concepts.[18]

Gia-long's employment of hundreds of foreigners in his efforts to defeat the Tây-so'ns has created controversy in Vietnam ever since. Some recent Vietnamese historians have argued that the Tây-so'ns had already unified Vietnam, after centuries of civil war, and that Gia-long's alliance with the French meant a cynical willingness to cede Vietnamese territory in order to protect the interests of the "feudal" community.[19] French missionaries in Vietnam in the early 1800's were confounded when imperial favor suddenly ceased to shine upon them in 1820, with the accession of Minh-mạng. Subsequently, nineteenth-century French accounts of Vietnamese society systematically traduced Minh-mạng's policies and capacities. Only an exhaustive examination of Vietnamese records reveals the historical truth. In the context of his times, Minh-mạng was the strongest and most creative of all the Nguyễn emperors.

In fact the importance of the role of the Chaigneaus and Oliviers and Behaines in Vietnamese history has been grossly exaggerated. Financial and judicial and political and administrative and educational matters in the Gia-long period never concerned the French. They were encouraged to live in Huế merely to give military advice and to serve as a shield against others of their kind who might come to Vietnam seeking trade. There were no Robert Harts or William Martins among them. Even in the building of fortified centers of government their influence was less than predominant. The citadel which foreshadowed modern Saigon and which began to rise in Gia Định after 1790 was even designed Chinese-style as an "eight-diagrams city" (*bát quái thành*), as an octagonal, lotus-shaped settlement with eight gates.[20]

Moreover, the French were far from being the only foreigners who helped Gia-long become Gia-long in 1802. The miscellany of others included Ho Hsi-wen, the infamous Szechwan-born pirate and member of the Triad Society, who first made contact with the Vietnamese leader when his illicit fleet anchored off Poulo Condore Island (better known to the Vietnamese as Côn Lôn Đảo). It included a former Cambodian palace slave who received, like the French, a Vietnamese name (Nguyễn Văn Tôn), joined Gia-long in Bangkok, and later recruited thousands of Cambodian soldiers for him. And it included a Thai rebel, Vinh Ma Ly (as he is known in Vietnamese records), who also added war junks to the Nguyễn cause. Based upon the shifting brigand populations of the Gulf of Siam and the South China Sea, Gia-long's forces at the lowest ebb of their fortunes exhibited a maritime heterogeneity which was typically Southeast Asian. If his French allies contributed military science, his Cambodian ones contributed troops, and his Thai and Chinese ones contributed (most important of all) junks. Gia-long became more novel to the French than the French were novel to Gia-long. The life histories of Pigneau de Behaine and Ho Hsi-wen appear only a few pages apart in the official biographies of the Nguyễn dynasty.[21]

The frustration of Gia-long's French advisers after 1802 dramatized the apparent indissolubility of Vietnam's membership in the traditional Chinese cultural world. More specifically, it dramatized the functional interdependence of the monarchy and Chinese classical political theories in Vietnam. Nguyễn emperors, beginning with Gia-long, preferred Confucian political orthodoxy to cultural change. The Chinese classics were not only familiar to all literate Vietnamese; they also stressed or supported, directly or indirectly, centralized government by one man whose moral persuasiveness was supposedly unparalleled. This made their cause the cause of the dynast at the top of the power structure. In the early 1800's, centralized government was clearly the cardinal concern of the Vietnamese court. It was all the more greatly desired because, under Gia-long, power was still essentially dispersed. One military overlord in Hanoi (known by its traditional name, Thăng-long, or as the "northern citadel," Bắc-thành, in the period 1803–1831) ruled most of the territory north from Ninh Bình. Another military overlord in the citadel of Gia Định (modern Saigon) ruled most of the territory south from Bình Thuận. The emperor's authority was unchallenged only in the center.[22] The centripetal forces of classical bureaucratization transcended this decentralization only in the more orthodox reign of Minh-mạng. This development was no accident.

Vietnamese Historiography and Vietnamese Interaction with China

The Vietnamese did not believe that it was an eccentricity for them to argue that a Son of Heaven in Huế could exemplify unique imperial virtues. But the price of consistent defense of this position was the artificial devaluation of China in the Vietnamese mind. In 1805 Gia-long referred to Vietnam as the "middle kingdom" or *trung-quốc*. The conventional Chinese term for China thus became, in Vietnamese hands, an abstraction devoid of any one geographic reference. It changed into a phrase capable of being used to refer to any kingdom, founded upon the principles of the Chinese classics, which felt itself surrounded by unread barbarians.[23]

The ordinary Sino-Vietnamese words for China and the Chinese people were intimate but hardly respectful. For the former they were the Northern Court (*Bắc triều*) or the Ch'ing country (*Thanh-quốc*). For the latter they were the northerners (*bắc-nhân*) or the Ch'ing people (*Thanh-nhân*). These patterns of reaction were so systematic that the Chinese empire could never be known in Vietnam as the imperial world (that is, "all under Heaven," *thiên-hạ*). Nor could the Chinese emperor ever commonly be distinguished as a competing or more powerful *thiên-tử*. Then as now the Vietnamese language responded to China's proximity and importance in Vietnamese life by developing a variety of terms for different areas of contact with China. Diversification of Vietnamese terms for China reflected Vietnamese distinctions among the universal culture whose geographical origins were in China; the Chinese people and the Chinese state; and the overseas Chinese in Vietnam. When Vietnamese is translated into English, this sophisticated variety of terms is completely lost (see Table 1).

The task of clarifying these orientations and extending the court's

Table 1. Vietnamese and English Terms for Things Chinese.

English	Nineteenth-century Vietnamese	Modern Vietnamese
China	*Thanh-quốc* or *Bắc-Triều*	*Nước Trung-quốc* or *Nước Trung-hoa*
The classical Chinese language	*Hán văn* or *chữ Nho*	*Hán văn*
Vernacular Chinese language	*Thanh-quốc ngữ* or *tiếng Tàu*	*Tiếng Tàu* or *tiếng Trung-quốc*
Chinese people in China	*Thanh nhân* or *Bắc nhân*	*Người Trung-quốc* or *người Tàu*
Chinese people in Vietnam	*Hoa kiều*	*Hoa kiều*

political ideology—ideology in the sense of a given culture's own explanations and justifications of its origins, premises, methods, and ultimate purposes—back into time fell to Vietnamese historiography, which was itself something of an affluent of the main stream of Chinese historiography. But it had a different viewpoint. Vietnamese court historians quite conscientiously attempted to distinguish history from superstition. Yet the fifteenth-century historian Ngô Sĩ Liên declared unabashedly of Vietnam's origins: "Our founding father sprang from the posterity of the Divine Farmer ruler [Shen-nung, a mythical Chinese emperor and culture hero who was credited with being the inventor of the plough]. He was an immortal lord of heavenly guidance. He was therefore capable of being emperor to one region [Vietnam] while the Northern Court was to another [China]."[24]

The whole myth-explanation of Vietnamese history is prolix, but it is not ambiguous. One united Vietnamese kingdom had existed from the dawn of history. It incorporated much of southern China as well as modern northern Vietnam. Its antecedents were as venerable as China's. (Medieval Vietnamese historians "appear to have become greedy and selfish," one modern Vietnamese historian has commented.)[25] Therefore China had no right to sovereignty over this southern kingdom. The "Việt" component of its name, it was claimed, descended from the period of the Chinese Chou dynasty, when the enterprising kingdom took the name Việt-thường.[26]

At the same time, Vietnamese historians like Lê Văn Hưu and Ngô Sĩ Liên founded their faith in Vietnamese equality with China fundamentally upon much later history—upon the results of China's invasions of Vietnam, all ultimately unsuccessful, in 981, 1075–1077, the 1250's and the 1280's, 1406–1427, and 1788. After each one of these valuable episodes, vacancies in the pantheon of the historians' heroes became progressively fewer. It is possible that men like Liên and his successors gradually and artfully transformed the Vietnamese memories of these victories over China into more than recorded history, into a historical force in their own right.[27] Certainly such historiography served important needs. Otherwise it could never have survived its own limitations in the rational Sino-Vietnamese world.

Among other things, by its picturesque tales of conflicts with the Chinese, such history writing reinforced the political search for harmony under one ruler in Vietnam. It created a psychological equilibrium of forces between inner order and outer (Chinese-caused) strife, thus ironically confirming Chinese forms of power holding in Vietnam. Nationalism or proto-nationalism did not stimulate Vietnamese historians so much as a gravely treasured sense of cultural discrepancies between China and Vietnam. This sense was not dispelled by the procrustean policies of Chinese invaders in the fifteenth century, which ranged from book burning to the imposition of Chinese clothing. Of the consequences of the final defeat of these invaders, one fifteenth-century Vietnamese text remarks, "The soil is again the soil of the Southern kingdom. The people are again the people of the Việt race. Coats and skirts and customs are in agreement with those of the past. The moral and political order is reestablished as of old."[28] But when the triumphant Lê Lợi asked his ministers in the 1430's why the Chinese "bandits" had been defeated, the reasons they gave (in Liên's account) were not that the Chinese colonialists were foreigners. Rather, their "excessive punishments and harsh government had long lost the hearts of the people."[29]

Confucian rather than nationalist, imperial Vietnam was influenced by Chinese institutions without being unshakably partial to the "Northern Courts." It was capable of absorbing Chinese learning so completely that its Chinese origins became irrelevant.[30] In fact most Vietnamese scholars were disposed to show great equanimity in recognizing the alien sources of court and village culture in Vietnam—had all the alien sources been Chinese. Despite its surface content of Chinese socio-political terminology, the Vietnamese language was different from the Chinese. Some of the communal houses in Vietnamese villages which housed the local tutelary deities were built on stilts, an architectural custom of the Malay and Indonesian peoples which was profoundly un-Chinese. Historically, Vietnamese women had more freedom than Chinese women and even looked back to a dim matriarchal political tradition. Vietnamese clothing was different from Chinese, favoring skirts for women and narrow-sleeved rather than wide-sleeved tunics for both sexes. Pervasive in rural Vietnam, to the discomfiture of officials, were peasant customs like betel chewing, tattooing, and teeth blackening.[31]

Some of these cultural divergences were deeply cherished, but others were feared as fatal blemishes which could distort the performance of Sino-Vietnamese institutions and cast a "barbarian" pall over Vietnamese society. One thing above all was patent. The environment, with its monsoon climate and its rainy seasons, was undeniably Southeast Asian. The north China plain could not be re-created here. The greatest classical scholar that Sino-Vietnamese civilization ever produced recognized the uniformity of the economic factors that worked in mainland Southeast Asia, when he wrote in the 1770's: "The borders of Nghệ An are several hundred li from Champa, and from Champa to Cambodia is again a half month's journey. I have read accounts of Cambodia's climate and customs, so I know they do not essentially differ fron Nghệ An's. Half the year this country has rain, half the year it is absolutely without."[32]

But Lê Quý Đôn touched only the safest part of the subject. If Vietnam was a Southeast Asian society whose sinicization was less than perfect, what hidden things really lay beneath the surface, in wait for the imperial bureaucrat, the classical bookworm from Huế?

Southeast Asian Features in Vietnamese Society and Culture

Non-Chinese Elements in Vietnamese Courtly Culture. It is, of course, as easy to exaggerate Vietnamese divergences from China as it is to exaggerate similarities. The more obvious Chinese, or at least Sino-Vietnamese, patterns in Vietnamese culture and institutions were not merely surface patterns, even if their predominance was not as total as appearances indicated. Furthermore, it is dangerous to be deterministic in ascribing all differences between Vietnam and China to the Southeast Asian environment. Historical truth is endangered by the formation of extravagant polarizations of data which leave no middle ground between "the Chinese model" and the "Southeast Asian infrastructure."

Yet nineteenth-century Vietnam cannot be understood if it is not clearly remembered that the Vietnamese people had only recently expanded south, from present-day northern Vietnam. Gia-

long (or perhaps more accurately, Minh-mạng) was the first Vietnamese emperor in history to rule the Mekong delta as well as the
Red River delta. This irresistible Vietnamese expansion had meant
the absorption of vast tracts of territory previously controlled and
still inhabited by "Indianized" Southeast Asian peoples—the
Cambodians and the Malayo-Polynesian Chams. The inevitable
intermarriages that took place were figurative and cultural, as well
as literal and social. Trương Quốc Dụng, a degree holder and
official of the Minh-mạng period, pointed out in his writings that
after the state of Champa had been conquered by the Vietnamese
and converted into the province of Quảng Nam at the end of the
fifteenth century, there had been 178 districts (*huyện*) in the Lê
empire. In the nineteenth-century Nguyễn empire, which now
reached all the way south, Dụng counted as many as 283 *huyện*.[33]
By Vietnamese criteria the inflation of administration and territory
in the period 1490–1847 had been immense. Dụng himself was
hardly accustomed to the idea of present-day southern Vietnam
being Vietnamese rather than Cambodian. He occasionally employs
the term *Nam-kỳ* in his writings—the conventional Vietnamese
expression for southern Vietnam—to refer to Cambodia, rather
than to the provinces grouped around Saigon.[34] (Such confusion
also reflected Vietnamese designs upon Cambodia.)

What Vietnamese historians like to call Vietnamese-Cham culture
(*văn-hóa Việt-Chiêm*) faded after the fourteenth century. But it left
ambiguous residues. It was not for nothing that one of the Tây-sơn
brothers had himself declared king (*vương*) of Vietnam in 1776
among the stone elephants, lions, and stupas of the old Cham capital
of Vijaya. After all, from the eleventh century to the fifteenth, Vietnamese elites had been influenced culturally almost as much by the
Chams as by the Chinese. Their capital of Thăng-long (the site of
modern Hanoi) had been, by its situation on the bank of the Red
River, significantly equidistant from China and Champa.[35] Similarities existed in Vietnamese and Cham legends.[36] Lý emperors had
translated Cham music into Vietnamese. Musical instruments for
Vietnamese court music, like the famous rice drums (a kind of
elephant's foot drum, with small surfaces and a long body, which
produces its best sounds only when thin rice cakes have been smeared
across its two ends), had probably originated in Champa.[37] All

this would not be of much importance to historians of nineteenth-century Vietnam if it were not for the fact that Nguyễn literati savored and carefully preserved these memories. A Lý emperor "ordered his musicians to play Cham compositions, which were called the tunes of Champa," wrote Võ Văn Lập, the author of a nineteenth-century "wild history" (*dã sử*). "Its sadness made melancholy sounds, and those who heard it wept."[38]

The influence of Cham music in Vietnamese courtly culture was undeniable. But it was probably insignificant. The theory and practice of warfare provided a much more important dividing point at the Vietnamese court between Chinese civilization and Southeast Asian custom. Elephants were the key to military mobility on land in Southeast Asia, as they were not in China. The search for a reliable "elephant market" obsessed Vietnamese military planners. It probably constituted one of the motives behind Minh-mạng's incursions into Laos and Cambodia in the 1820's and 1830's. In methods of warfare Vietnamese rulers took pride in departing from the Chinese tradition. Indeed, they believed that the more culturally alien their tactics and weapons seemed to Chinese generals, the more difficult it would be for Chinese armies to conquer Vietnam. In the late 1830's, Minh-mạng commented that the Ch'ing Ch'ien-lung emperor's forces had been defeated in Vietnam fifty years earlier essentially by the Tây-sơn army's elephant brigades: "Cam-lộ [in Quảng Trị] elephants are very docile and quick-witted, and are superior to Cambodian and Siamese elephants. However, in the task of arresting bandits we should use small elephants ... From now on we shall divide our elephants. When we send them out to the provinces we ought to use small elephants, but large elephants we should retain for service in the imperial retinue in Huế ... The Tây-sơn impostors used elephants lavishly in their battles with the Northern [Chinese] soldiers. The Northern horses are afraid of elephants. When they saw them, they fell prostrate. For that reason they were defeated."[39]

In warfare, therefore, Vietnamese rulers borrowed culturally from other Southeast Asian societies as much as from China. This was deliberate. It meant, in turn, that tensions between the Nguyễn civil and military bureaucracies were aggravated by different cultural orientations, as well as by routine competition for greater professional and political influence. But the Vietnamese court's veneration of elephants, which had no parallel in China, was not confined to the question of their military utility. As symbols of Vietnam's anti-Chinese military tradition, elephants soon assumed roles in the official corporate religion. The spirits of the Nguyễn elephant army were worshiped four times a year, in the second, fifth, eighth, and eleventh lunar months, at a special temple in the vicinity of Huế. Imperial funds were provided for the purpose.[40]

It would be hazardous to argue that Vietnamese courtly culture was variable enough, within its Sino-Vietnamese framework, to imitate the famous elephant cults of other Southeast Asian courts. To Mon, Burman, Siamese, and Lao peoples, Brahmanical lore made white elephants omens of power and prosperity, and Buddhist traditions suggested that they represented Emergent Buddhas. Yet it would be almost equally hazardous to deny the muted influence of these cults in the ostensibly very different atmosphere of the Nguyễn court. Similarities between Nguyễn military traditions and those of other Southeast Asian societies were patent. The shadow line between military mythology and court ceremonial religion was easily crossed. And it is a fact, small but significant, that when Nghệ An highlanders presented Minh-mạng with a rare "white-flower elephant" in 1835, historical compilers at Huế carefully recorded for posterity both the deed itself and the official name of the elephant.[41] The importance of the elephant in military technology and political ceremonial seems to have amounted to a kind of cultural consensus everywhere in mainland Southeast Asia.

Undercurrents in Vietnamese Village Culture. Sinicization had spread to the lower levels of the Vietnamese socio-cultural system as well as to the higher levels. The Vietnamese peasantry's wholehearted adoption of the ideals, not always realized, and forms, of Chinese familial organization furnished the most remarkable proof of this fact. These forms were so unquestioned in Vietnam that land-hungry peasant rebel armies were constituted, as in China, on a generalized familial basis. The poem of a rebel army leader of the 1740's in Hải Dương province proclaimed, "Rising into the sky stand our blue and yellow standards; an army of fathers and sons [that is, officers and men] will join battle to appropriate land."[42] Vietnamese peasant rebellions were rarely equaled elsewhere in Southeast Asia. This may well have been evidence that Vietnam's inheritance of institutions from China worked two ways. It gave Vietnamese governments greater cohesiveness than governments of neighboring peoples, but it also supplied the means—the pervasiveness of familial organizational concepts—for more formidable opposition to develop.

Nonetheless, sinicization was not as intense or as conspicuous in the villages as it was at the court. A native infrastructure of customs, of modes of communal thought and action whose defenses could not easily be forced by outsiders or by Vietnamese sinicizers, did exist. Furthermore, its ramifications were extensively canvassed and discussed by Vietnamese rulers and officials themselves. For example, in 1825 Minh-mạng proposed that such a situation offered special justifications and opportunities for strong imperial rule in Vietnam: "Petty-minded people of the Ch'ing country all know its laws. Hence it is easy for them to cheat those laws. Our people still do not completely understand the laws. So by being punished they will learn fear. Consequently our people would appear to be (more) easily civilized . . . I do not dare to be idle for an instant."[43]

Unfortunately, the modern analyst must largely approach nineteenth-century village culture through the medium of Vietnamese dynastic records. To the compilers of these records, non-Sinic elements in village culture were noteworthy only when they spelled subversion. Which village institutions did they watch the most cautiously?

Vietnamese village plays and rural operas owed a probable debt to Champa as well as to China. Among these plays were the famous musical performances known as *hát-chèo* and *hát-tuồng*. (These terms are mainly non-Sinic Vietnamese, although *chèo* is a corruption of the Sino-Vietnamese word *trào*, "satire.") Their ritualized acting, with disguises and masks, often mocked court ritual; their dances appear to have had a strong Cham content. (A site exists in northern Vietnam today which has a tableau carved into the side of a stone platform at the foot of an abandoned column. The scene depicts two groups of performers dancing a *hát* beside a pagoda fig tree meant to symbolize the Buddha. The dancers bend their bodies in a manner reminiscent of dances of Champa and India.)[44] Ironically, after Lê Lợi's victory over the Chinese in 1427, sinicization, as practiced by themselves, became more seductive to the Vietnamese. The Nguyễn emperors of the 1800's probably tried to approach the Chinese model more closely than emperors of any other Vietnamese dynasty. In doing so they feared the village operas because of their marginal disloyalties and cultural heterodoxies. Minh-mạng even attempted to ban performance of the omnipresent village dramas in the neighborhood of Huế in the spring of 1840. He remarked, "I hear that a stupendous number of males and females, old people and young people, watch these plays. This must definitely be an evil custom."[45]

Such an outburst was more than a conventional expression of disdain similar to utterances made by Chinese emperors about the Chinese "little tradition." In Nguyễn Vietnam, unmistakable cultural apprehension combined with politics to produce Gia-long's set of regulations, promulgated in 1803–1804, for controlling village communities. These regulations were known as the *hương đẳng điều lệ*. One theme behind the regulations was undoubtedly Confucian frugality and fear of the political instabilities that class warfare caused. For example, villagers were forbidden to consume wine and meat at communal discussions of village business. Only areca nuts and betel were allowed.

Especially, the laws attempted to limit the costs of village marriages and funerals. In marriages, villagers were ordered to follow Chinese customs and conform to the "six rites." (The six rites—*lục lễ*—included the sending of presents to the prospective bride's home, the asking of names as a preliminary to betrothal, the sending of presents after happy auguries had been received about the matching of the two names, the requesting of a time for the wedding, the sending of betrothal presents to complete arrangements, and the groom's going in person to fetch his bride.) Villagers were also ordered not to write contracts mortgaging land as part of the marriage settlement. Traditionally, Vietnamese grooms also had to pay engagement fees to the villages where their brides lived. Until this marriage tax was paid, villagers of the receiving village would "obstruct the street" (*lan nhai*) or the passage of the groom to his bride's parents' house. Although this custom had originated in China, it eventually became far more elaborate and more important socially in Vietnam than in the society of its origin. The laws of

1803–04 attempted to prevent the inflation of this informal intra-village or inter-village transaction by stipulating that rich house-holds should pay one fixed sum, middle households only two fifths as much, and poor households only one half the sum of middle households. In funerals, too, mourning families were constrained not to "quote precedents and squeeze" their neighbors and relatives. They were also cautioned to avoid mountain tops, military drill grounds, temples, and towns in selecting sites for tombs.[46]

However, the laws of 1803–04 attacked other types of activity besides undue transfers of rural economic resources. They forbade the construction of new village Buddhist temples. The kinds of sacrifices that could be used at village feasts in honor of Buddhist deities were strictly specified: one water buffalo, or one ox and one pig, and betel wine. The amount of village singing or musical dem-onstration (*ca xướng*) at such festivals was limited to one day and one night. Indulgence in the "hundred amusements" (*bách hí*) was made illegal.[47] The hundred amusements was a battle-hardened Sino-Vietnamese phrase which referred to such specific pastimes (popular in Southeast Asia) as cock-fighting.

The Vietnamese court feared that Vietnamese village communi-ties embraced a host of Southeast Asian folk customs which, if allow-ed to flourish, would undermine the village pedagogue's attempts to uphold sinicization and the behavior recommended in Chinese books. If that happened, education would go under, and so would bureaucratic recruitment. But why were the local pagodas or tem-ples, and possible misdemeanors in their name, made the focus of so many of these laws?

In the early nineteenth century, the higher Buddhist clergy in Vietnam depended heavily upon the Nguyễn court. From it they received their ordination licenses, as well as temple lands, sutras, candles, clothing, Chinese medicines, and other items of patronage.[48] The world they lived in was culturally almost as Sino-Vietnamese as the world of the Huế civil bureaucrat. Because it was, moreover, more isolated from politics than the world of the civil bureaucrat, higher priests were even more culturally conservative. Typically, a surviving book of instructions on mortuary rites for Buddhist and Taoist priests of the Gia-long era, printed in Vietnam in 1817, informs us that these priests still used the word Annam, the ancient

Chinese word for Vietnam, in documents and seals in the early 1800's.[49] This occurred despite the fact that the name of the country had been officially changed. Annam was both an anachronism and ultra-Chinese in usage.

Nonetheless, Vietnamese records of the early 1800's also suggest that this historical and cultural conservatism of the Buddhist clergy was slowly cracking under the strain of Vietnamese social expansion. In northern Vietnam, the church might remain stable and orthodox. Its temples were filled with dependable, if occasionally time-serving, crowds of monks and attendants. A byword for general evasion of responsibility was the saying in a poem by Nguyễn Công Trứ, "With so many pagoda watchmen, no one closes the pagoda's doors."[50] In recently settled southern Vietnam, however, Sino-Vietnamese Mahayana orthodoxy was endangered. The pressures of Cambodian Theravada Buddhism were strong in most provinces around Saigon. Also, as Vietnamese civilization had expanded south to the Mekong delta, its pioneers had fallen heir to abandoned Cham and Cambodian temples. Vietnamese immigrants took over these non-Vietnamese temples and simply superimposed Vietnamese names upon them. The province of Bình Định, in particular, was full of so-called "Viet-Cham" temples. In one instance, that of the Nhạn-sơn temple in Tuy Viễn district south of the old Cham capital of Vijaya, Vietnamese monks draped Vietnamese clothing over two Cham-made stone idols they had found in the temple precincts. The monks absorbed these idols into Vietnamese worship although they were quite unclear which deities the two Cham idols had originally represented.[51]

In the wake of religious confusion came other confusions that were more disquieting. Southern tolerance of Cham and Cambodian influences eventually reached the point where Sino-Vietnamese forms of official corporate religion were threatened. In 1838 the financial commissioner of Gia Định reported that wooden religious idols had driven Confucian-style tablets, representing the city's tutelary deity (*thành hoàng*) out of the Saigon city temple. This report of a tense struggle in southern towns between the Chinese-style tablets of the official religion and popular Buddhist idols alarmed Minh-mạng.[52] Here was evidence that the official Sino-Vietnamese religious conflation of Confucianism, Taoism, and Buddhism was breaking down. As Vietnamese society spread south, Vietnamese Buddhism seemed to become more "Indianized." For these reasons, Huế emperors sought to envelop Buddhist temples in a maze of restrictions and prohibitions, hoping to prevent their religious and cultural deviations from becoming too great.

Aspects of Commerce and Industry in Vietnam. In the eyes of early nineteenth-century European visitors to Vietnam, the most interesting difference between the Nguyễn kingdom and other Southeast Asian societies was the high degree of bureaucratization prevailing in Vietnam. John Crawfurd wrote of the Vietnamese court in 1821–22, "There is nothing of the slightest moment done here, in public matters, without writing—whereas at Siam, on the other hand, it was found impossible to get the officers of government to commit a single sentence to paper upon almost any subject."[53] But when Europeans compared the Vietnamese with the Chinese, the chief difference they noted was the inferiority of Vietnamese commerce. George Finlayson, a Scottish surgeon and naturalist who accompanied Crawfurd to Saigon and Huế at the beginning of Minh-mạng's reign, was a grudging admirer of Vietnamese civilization. Regarding Saigon, he testified that "the plan of the streets is superior to that of many European capitals."[54] The barracks of Minh-mạng's palace guard at Huế "would lose little in comparison with the best we have in England."[55] In Huế itself, "Everything was in a style of neatness, magnitude, and perfection, compared to which, similar undertakings by other Asiatics were like the works of children."[56] But Finlayson also wrote, "It is difficult to conceive that a population so extensive can exist . . . with trade on so small a scale."[57]

Traditional Vietnamese theories of class structure were derived from the Chinese classics. Treating social and occupational classes as if they were coessential, such theories ranked classes hierarchically in order of importance, four in all. Scholars came first. Peasants came second, artisans third, and merchants fourth. But these theories matched realities even more poorly in Vietnam than they did in China. An indigenous merchant class as important as the one in China failed to develop in Vietnam. Its failure was in turn related to the weak development of Vietnamese crafts and industries. A more realistic profile of occupational classes in nineteenth-century

Vietnam would have emphasized the existence of a landed, literate, leisured elite, a mass of peasants, a Buddhist clergy, and a powerful, alien Chinese merchant class. Such a pattern approximated the situation of other Southeast Asian societies far more than it did that of China. Traditional Sino-Vietnamese descriptions of Vietnamese class structure were alien and misleading, although they were ideologically necessary.

Family crafts epitomized nineteenth-century Vietnamese industry. There were also itinerant handicraft workers, like carpenters and bricklayers, who combined into family-like organizations. One foreman (*thợ cả*) represented them, negotiating their work and their wages. In towns and cities, Vietnamese artisans organized themselves into wards (*phường*) or companies (*ty*). These guild-like associations met once or twice a year to elect heads and perform rites to the founders of their professions. They possessed common funds, and helped their members with wedding and funeral expenses. All this seems similar to Chinese practices.

But there were at least four reasons why Vietnamese crafts never succeeded in matching the growth of crafts and industries in China, even proportionately to the smaller scope of Vietnamese society. Vietnamese crafts were totally subordinate to agriculture. Rich peasants did not work at crafts at all; they abandoned them to poor peasants who needed to supplement their income. A map of the traditional Vietnamese economy would reveal that it was the villages with poor agricultural potential—villages with meagre or infertile land—that specialized in crafts like pottery, copperware, weaving, and hat making.[58] As supplements to agriculture, these crafts required little capital, few imported materials, and few tools. Second, the spread of stimuli to economic development in traditional Vietnam ran counter to the values of village solidarity. Because of their tenacious parochialism, one group of villagers would attempt to prevent other Vietnamese villages from adopting their crafts. Some villages even forbade their marriageable girls to go to neighboring villages to marry or disseminated traditional craft formulas only among their male population. Third, industry and commerce found it difficult to coexist in such a small country with a centralized, pervasive, Chinese-style bureaucracy. Because of Vietnam's smallness, the Vietnamese court, far more than the Chinese court, had the means to control Vietnamese guilds and tax their artisans out of business. The fate of clever artisans in nineteenth-century Vietnam was a kind of labor slavery rather than an opportunity to accumulate profits and capital. Fourth, Vietnamese artisans and merchants had to compete with Chinese artisans and merchants. The latter had longer traditions of expertise, social development, and foreign contact behind them. Also they could evade the Vietnamese court's depredations more easily, by virtue of having two geographical bases, one in south China and one in Vietnam.

Nineteenth-century Hanoi was divided into blocks or wards, each of whose inhabitants followed the same trade—hemp stores, tin shops, sail shops, bamboo basket shops, sugar retailers—and often came originally from the same native place or village. But from the standpoint of comparative social history, these wards suggested a super-aggregation of rural economic units rather than more significant urbanization. In Tokugawa Japan in the early 1800's, for example, distribution of goods seemed to follow a pattern of producers–wholesalers–small merchants–consumers, whereas in Nguyễn Vietnam the pattern was producers–periodic markets–consumers. In cities like Hanoi markets might be permanent rather than periodic. But urban consumer demand remained far weaker than it was in Japan of the same period and much more concerned purely with the purchase of daily necessities. There were no Vietnamese equivalents of those large, specializing dry-goods stores of pre-modern Tokyo like Matsuzakaya (from 1707) and Daimaru (1726), for instance, which accumulated capital, developed large-scale operations, and then evolved into modern department stores in the twentieth century.

Most Southeast Asian of all, socio-economic stratification in Vietnamese cities reflected the dominance of the alien Chinese merchant class. Two-storey, tile-roofed houses were usually seen only in the streets occupied by Chinese merchants. The existence of an ethnic factor in urban stratification and residential styles was a characteristic of Southeast Asian cities, not usually of Chinese ones before 1840. As an historical theme it was obvious to every Vietnamese from the emperor down. Southeast Asian awe of the Chinese plutocracy and its love of conspicuous consumption even enters Minh-mạng's comparison in 1839 of the Chinese and Vietnamese tax systems:

Ch'ing land taxes and those of our country are no different. But every item of the remaining tax legislation [of the two countries] is dissimilar. Take our uniform poll and labor taxes for rich and poor, with each man paying one *mân* and five *mạch*; since their collection is difficult and the amounts that are gained are small, the Chinese are caused to disregard such taxes. But the Chinese stress the customs tax . . . When it comes to establishing a cloth tax [in China], the largeness or smallness or breadth or narrowness of a family does not matter. They only consider how many gates the one household has and make that their criterion for collecting taxes . . . Rich and powerful households [in China], wishing to show off their fine appearances, build many gates. Their taxes are so great that they resist computation . . . The customs taxes that we have created have not been numerous. But the cargoes that our merchant junks carry are only adequate for their means of livelihood. If you compare them with the cargoes carried by Ch'ing merchants, the difference is I don't know how many times greater.[59]

Vietnamese emperors, aware of the important discrepancies in economic development existing between China and Vietnam, as Minh-mạng's disquisition on Chinese taxes shows, were nonetheless not deterred by this awareness from borrowing Chinese fiscal and economic institutions. But their reasons for doing so were often the reverse of the reasons that had justified such institutions in Chinese history. The names might be the same, but the actual rationales, not always made explicit by the court, were different. Here new problems arise for specialists in comparative history, who need all the acumen at their command to detect the unexpected realities prevailing behind the deceptively smooth transpositions of terminology. One nineteenth-century example is illuminating. *Chiao-tzu* were paper vouchers whose creation marked the beginning of paper money in medieval China. They were developed in Szechwan by the early eleventh century. They were used to replace heavy metal coins in large inter-provincial transactions, when such coins would have been cumbersome. Eight centuries later the Nguyễn court introduced these Chinese-style vouchers to Vietnam, where they were known in Sino-Vietnamese as *giao-tử*. Agencies for issuing paper vouchers which could be cashed in a number of provinces were created in northern Vietnamese border areas like Lạng Sơn in 1837. But their emergence here was essentially artificial, not having been inspired by expanding commerce, as it had been in Sung China. In nineteenth-century Vietnam, *giao-tử* represented a purely defensive expedient to preserve the dwindling silver supplies of certain northern provinces. The province of Cao Bằng imported most of its food, clothing, and tools from "distant merchants," Vietnamese and Chinese. These merchants habitually took away with them local silver in payment. Their depletion of Cao Bằng's silver resources caused a province-wide inflation in the value of silver. By introducing the paper vouchers, borrowed in name from an earlier China, as replacements for local silver in such exchanges, the dynasty hoped to reduce Cao Bằng's vulnerability to its adverse trade balance by diffusing its liabilities.[60] Hence, the paper vouchers, which had been the symbols of thriving trade in China, became the means of bureaucratic equalization of a regional economic burden in Vietnam.

Finally, the evidence suggests that within the same large Confucian framework of theoretical contempt for merchants, the Vietnamese official view of merchants in the 1800's diverged slightly from the Chinese. Chinese court ideology scorned merchants (overtly but not covertly) because it considered them parasitic and unproductive, compared to scholars and farmers. Vietnamese rulers and bureaucrats tended to discriminate against merchants more because successful merchants commanded immoderately large resources in a poor society. Their acquisitiveness seemed grotesque and immoral. In Nguyễn Vietnam, it was as much the visible results as the functions of entrepreneurship that were invidious. Originally this attitude may have been more a consequence than a cause of the general weakness of Vietnamese commerce, but it did reinforce economic stagnation.

For example, Vietnamese literature in the early 1800's often concerned itself with the ideological problem of what might succinctly be called fool ascription. Which social types in the ideal society should be recognized as fools? Fool ascription was, of course, a device of status reduction and social control. Assigning the role of fool to a certain social type was a collective process of status adjustment, re-

lated to conceptions of propriety in conduct, because the fool represented a collective notion of a person or type of conduct believed to
be inferior. Not by accident, Nguyễn Công Trứ (1778–1858), the
great mandarin poet, satirized the early nineteenth-century Vietnamese merchant "upstart" who managed to accumulate a little
wealth:

> He puts on a mandarin's bonnet, and borrows the
>   colors of [Confucian] morality.
> But he usually eats his meat in a big lump, very
>   greedily.
> The upper storey of his house is stuffed with lutes,
>   chess games, wine, and poetry.
> He is so over-adorned that he no longer knows if
>   his body is beautiful inside his clothes.
> O Heaven and Earth, what [a hideous] kind of man
>   is that.[61]

Here the rich man became a fool because he acquired too many
clothes and ate too much. Conspicuous consumption was his social
downfall. As a historical document, Trứ's poem probably illustrates
how much greater the gulf between the bureaucratic elite and the
small, underdeveloped merchant class was in Vietnam than it was
between the two corresponding but more equal classes in Ch'ing
China.

Echoes of South China: A Qualification. In addition to its classical
Chinese political institutions, and the Southeast Asian cultural elements which competed with them, nineteenth-century Vietnamese
society had another aspect. The actual racial and geographical
origins of the Vietnamese people are controversial and unresolved.
But it seems certain that the history of south China, before and after
the irruption of the original Chinese Yellow River civilization into
its area, is related to the history of the population of mainland Southeast Asia. Some anthropologists have linked the culture of the ancient
state of Ch'u (in modern Hupei and Hunan) to the culture of various
peoples of mainland Southeast Asia.[62] What is historically demon-
strable, at least, is that customs that were popular in southern China

also tended to have an exaggerated vogue in traditional Vietnam. The compilers of an important cultural and ethnological dictionary of Kwangtung, published in China in 1700, wrote of the Cantonese people that from the time of the Ch'in and the Han they had "not lost the pure, virtuous spirit of the Central Plain" of north China.[63] But other traditional Chinese ethnographers, like Li Tiao-yüan in the 1700's, noted that the Cantonese indulged in Southeast Asian habits like betel chewing.[64] At the other end, south Chinese peasant festivals sometimes loomed larger in Nguyễn Vietnam than they did in much of Ch'ing China.

One such festival was the summer Dragonboat Day, *Tuan-wu* or *Tuan-yang* (Đoan-ngọ and Đoan-dương in Sino-Vietnamese). It was celebrated on the fifth day of the fifth lunar month. The boat races which were a part of this festival were originally considered to be ritual ceremonies to offer to save the Ch'u poet and minister Ch'ü Yüan from drowning. The dumplings eaten on the festival day were originally sacrifices. In pre-modern China, however, the holiday also came to represent the promotion of summer hygiene. The boat races exercised and washed their participants, the sprinkling of sulphur powder throughout houses served as a disinfectant, the hanging of artemisia and garlic heads above doorways warded off diseases.In China this festival was universal. But its roots were especially deep south of the Yangtze, for good reason. A sixth-century Chinese text informs us: "On the fifth day of the fifth month the people of . . . Ch'u all went gathering the hundred herbs and grasses . . . and suspended them above the doors of their houses, in order to avert by sacrifice poisonous spirits."[65]

This ancient Chou period festival was second only to the lunar New Year as a public holiday in nineteenth-century Vietnam. While peasants in provinces like Nghệ An, Hà Tĩnh and Thanh Hóa hung herbs above their doors to drive away pestilences and malaria,[66] peasants in provinces like Bình Định offered major sacrifices to their ancestors only on the New Year and on the fifth day of the fifth month.[67] Pressures from the peasantry reached the Nguyễn court. The court declared that the New Year, Dragonboat Day, and the emperor's birthday would be its "three great holidays" (*tam đại tiết*). This decision marked a deviation, momentous in

Vietnamese eyes, from the Ch'ing Chinese observation of the New Year, the emperor's birthday, and the winter solstice. Government business and corvee were suspended, yellow banners were flown, cannons were fired, and Nguyễn emperors gave formal Dragonboat Day banquets at the Hall of Supreme Harmony, in Huế.[68]

Officials at the Vietnamese Board of Rites were disturbed by the cleavage between Peking court rituals and this Huế exaltation of Dragonboat Day. They besieged Nguyễn emperors with advice to "shorten" the celebrations of the fifth day of the fifth month and "lengthen" those of the winter solstice. But Vietnamese emperors were less willing to follow idealized examples set by Peking at the cost of ignoring their own cultural environment. Minh-mạng argued uneasily that the cold winter climate in China justified the winter solstice holiday in Peking, but that in tropical Vietnam tradition and climate favored the fifth day of the fifth month instead.[69] Perhaps a holiday that revolved about the prevention of sickness was understandably popular in the Southeast Asian tropics. In the great plague epidemic of 1820 alone, 206,835 people disappeared from the Vietnamese court's population registers.[70] Perhaps also the strange fate of Dragonboat Day in nineteenth-century Vietnam illustrates how environmental needs could combine, not impossibly, with folk instincts from a very distant past somewhere in south China. The result of the combination, if this was what it was, was Vietnamese alteration of imported Chinese court styles.

Familial Institutions and the Sino-Vietnamese Social Order

The relationship between the traditional bureaucracy and the traditional family was strong in Nguyễn Vietnam. Officially it was as strong as it was in Ch'ing China. Here imitation of China reached at least moral perfection. In both societies, if the father of the great world was the ruler, the ruler of the small world was the father.[71] As has been stated, filial piety was admired as being the forerunner of a more professional obedience to the emperor. (It also tended to make obedience to the emperor secondary, however.) And ceremonial care of the ancestral altar (*bàn thờ*) in the northern shrine-alcove of the ideal southward-facing Vietnamese house was thought to be a preparation for all the rituals surrounding the imperial presence at court.

Then, too, the Sung neo-Confucian Vietnamese father, following Chu Hsi's fondness for the doctrines of *The Great Learning* (*Đại Học;* *Ta-hsüeh* in Chinese, one of the Four Books) was supposed to teach his son that self-cultivation at home prefigured and presignified service to others. A man should cultivate himself (*tu thân*) and regulate his family (*tề gia*) before he thought about the government of the country (*trị quốc*) and the peace of the world (*bình thiên hạ*). What these priorities really meant, reshuffled in practice, was that the individual man's desire for a bureaucratic career sprang from a more basic desire for the enhancement of the reputation and the power of his family. "If one man becomes an official, his whole lineage can depend upon him" is a Vietnamese proverb that might have originated in China, but did not.[72] Behind all the panoply of Confucian moralization the traditional familial and bureaucratic systems were inseparably intertwined. This was one reason why twentieth-century Vietnamese social novelists like the brilliant, astringent Khái Hưng have felt themselves compelled to attack the former in order to ridicule and expose the latter.

Characteristically Chinese dilemmas therefore came to be faithfully reflected in Vietnamese imperial politics. "Cliques inevitably issue primarily from the father-son and elder brother–younger brother relationship and later spread to other men," Minh-mạng noted in 1839.[73] But if family ties united official cliques, which then conspired to diminish the influence of the emperor (whose peace of mind depended upon a politically atomistic bureaucracy), they were also the rudimentary sources of the bureaucracy's self-discipline. "Filial piety can be transferred to matters of state, so the prince who is searching for loyal ministers must visit households with filial sons," Gia-long remarked sententiously in 1814.[74] The traditional Sino-Vietnamese view of socio-political integration was that of a society held together by the three bonds (*tam cương*). The three bonds were the bureaucrat's loyalty to his emperor, the son's obedience to his father, and the wife's submission to her husband. As in China the family ethic usually was allowed to stand supreme over considerations of bureaucratic efficiency, as a result.

All officials, including local ones, were forced and encouraged to leave their posts whenever they were confronted with mourning obligations to their parents. The Vietnamese bureaucracy itself was meant symbolically to suggest a gigantic family, with the emperor and his relatives standing at its summit. Its political-familial mourning degrees were scrupulously graded, not this time by blood ties and by relative genealogical distance but by rank and by proximity of given officials to the palace. When the octogenarian empress dowager died in 1811, all officials of the first three ranks in Huế had to wear mourning clothes for three months and, if possible, attend the mourning ceremonies. Officials from the fourth rank down had only to wear white cotton turbans. Provincial officials escaped more completely. As mourners their classification was "beyond the threshold"(*ngoại khổn*). Those of third rank or above needed to wear white turbans but not full mourning dress. Such regulations spread to many spheres. In 1811 high officials could not wear red or purple costumes or hold marriages in their families for three years, but lower officials had to observe such prohibitions for only one year.[75] Here the link between imperial power and familial institutions was obvious. The latter provided an easily comprehensible scheme—the notion of a mourning hierarchy—by which the former could array all the members of its bureaucracy on one vertical scale of status and simultaneously emphasize the status schism between its upper and its lower officials.

Rigorous maintenance of the Chinese family system and its attendant behavioral peculiarities meant more kinds of stability than this. To bureaucratic discipline and self-discipline was added another dividend, a well-ordered countryside. What made the large family unsurpassed as a unit of social control and responsibility was not merely its own hierarchical self-regulation but also its typical localization in a particular village. This made it a dependably permanent fact in most government registers. If soldiers defected from Gia-long's armies their parents, brothers, and "lineage relatives" were immediately found and canvassed for replacements. And if the canvass was a failure, responsibility was then spread outward to the village, which in turn had to supply men.[76] Concessions to the importance of having families attach themselves irrevocably to a specific native place were vital to the dynasty. Even in the midst of climactic military operations against the Tây-sơns in central Viet-nam, Gia-long had paused to spare ships to carry dead soldiers back to graves in the soldiers' southern homeland.[77] Revenue expectations as well as political theories and military recruitment rested upon the immutability of the localized *gia-đình*. Here both peasant families and families of property proved elusive. Officials of Phú Yên province reported in 1839 that fathers and sons (of the latter especially) were pretending to live apart, in order to fragment their family registration and avoid corvee. The court responded with a law that "all men must be registered according to the formal surname-residences of their grandfathers and fathers."[78] But the ideal squared with the real in rural Nguyễn Vietnam about as often as it did in China.

Dynastic patronage of selected exemplary pillars of the Confucian family system closely resembled such patronage in China. Filial sons (*hiếu tử*), obedient grandsons (*thuận tôn*), and chaste widows (*tiết phụ*) all received honors, at the court's instigation, in their local communities. The definitions were broad; one "virtuous wife" of 1843 was rewarded for stabbing a tiger that had attacked her hus-band in the mountains of Khánh Hòa.[79] The countryside, as in China, was dotted with monuments to these heroes of society with impeccable Sino-Vietnamese inscriptions (*hiếu hành khả phong*, "filial devotion which should be made a custom") engraved upon them. For the wives of dead bureaucrats, motives for chaste widowhood were materially reinforced by the institution of *khuyên tiết điền* (lands to encourage virtue). These lands were estates awarded such widows (half the size of what had been their husbands' official lands, if the husbands had been 1A–5B in bureaucratic grade) on condition that they not remarry.[80] More obviously a Vietnamese domestica-tion of Chinese procedure was the custom of rewarding households with five generations together in the same family hall (*ngũ đại đồng đường*). The most simple form of this type of family was father, son, grandson, great-grandson, and great-great-grandson. Any patriarch still breathing who had been omnicompetent enough to hold so many of his male descendants under his own roof was rewarded with money. He was also rewarded with the construction of an honorary arch (*phường*) over nine feet high with imperial dragon patterns flaunted upon it and with a tablet with his name, province, prefecture, village, age, and achievements engraved upon it.[81] Such patriarchs were of course to be found more in the north than in the raw, newly settled, culturally crypto-Cambodian (in the bureaucracy's eyes) south.

What was really intended to be honored by such pomp was not the philoprogenitive father but the discipline-dispensing family head, not a larger population but rather visible social control obtained through familial methods. Despite its deviations in culture and social structure from China, traditional Vietnam, like China but unlike Japan, failed to develop alternative forms of control in the absence of family controls. Vietnam had become independent from China at the end of the T'ang dynasty. But Vietnamese family rules tended to imitate later rather than earlier Chinese formulations, like the *Chu tzu chia li* (The family rites of Chu Hsi) of the Sung rather than more remote texts like the *Yen-shih chia hsün* (The family exhortations of Mr. Yen). Consequently, family rules stressed not the external relations of the family so much as its internal regulation and the special duties of the family head.

But a large family of the stereotyped "five generations" was probably more extraordinary in Nguyễn Vietnam than it was in China, where a bureaucratic search for such families in 1785 yielded a list of 192 households among all China's millions.[82] It is difficult to say why the Vietnamese family, which had just as great a sense of itself as an historic organism, failed to equal the elaborate structural splendor of the celebrated Chinese "big house." Because there was less wealth in traditional Vietnam, which lacked the large cities and indigenous merchant class of China, proportionately fewer rich families in Vietnam may have been capable of advertising their rising status by sustaining genealogies beyond the third ascending generation. Another possible explanation is that higher mortality rates in tropical Vietnam caused many nominal kinship positions in the Vietnamese family and lineage to go unfilled, making an elaborate Chinese-style kinship system even more ideal than actual there than it was in China. Certainly warfare and its attendant disruptions were more common in medieval Vietnam than they were in south China, which went relatively untouched even by the Mongols. A third not completely impossible explanation is that in borrowing the forms of this cornerstone of the Chinese social order, the Vietnamese reduced some of their original elements in the very act of reproducing them. This is not unknown in cultural borrowing.

Still, analysts can arrive at a comparative evaluation of the two family systems by an important side door: matching the outlooks on their respective family systems of Chinese and Vietnamese ideologues in this century. For example, the traditional Chinese family that Pa Chin attacked in his novel, *Chia* (The family), published in 1933, differed unmistakably in the structural locations of its tensions from the traditional Vietnamese family that Khái Hưng attacked in his novel, *Gia-đình* (The family), published in Vietnam in 1938. Family elders are the social villains in Pa Chin's family, and an amazing range of relatives play influential roles. In Khái Hưng's novel, however, it is not the hero's grandfather who is the destructive incarnation of an unregenerate past. Rather, it is the hero's unenlightened, politically ambitious wife. Although the comparison is arbitrary, conservatism in the changing Vietnamese family has been more intensely associated with the demands of a tradition-bound marriage partner, less intensely associated with the unbearable proximity of male members of earlier generations.

On the whole, in nineteenth-century Vietnam there were fewer specific local institutions, fewer examples of apparatus that might ensure a life cycle for everyone that would be managed on Confucian terms, than there were in China. The Nguyễn court could not match local Ch'ing institutions of welfare and moral persuasion (Chinese, *feng-chiao*). It could not match the state-supported foundling halls (*yü-ying-t'ang*) which had begun to appear in Peking in the 1660's and which had spread into the wealthier Chinese provinces by the 1720's, where they were financed by gentry subscriptions solicited in "places where men and smoke are concentrated."[83] There were fewer free cemeteries in Vietnam, fewer state doles, fewer charitable granaries, fewer members of a local elite (gentry) who could draw upon commercial income as well as upon political-academic reputations. Hence there was less interaction between the court and such an elite to produce family-supporting or family-supplementing institutions. This, of course, was merely one aspect of a general situation. China was worth imitating. But China, because of its cities, its wealth, its professional differentiation, and its accumulation of skills, was, at the same time, prodigious. In the eyes of poorer

Southeast Asians, the very size of Chinese society had exerted effects upon Chinese culture which raised it above the level of that of any Southeast Asian society.

This generalization may be used, perhaps, to introduce another specific feature of Vietnamese cultural borrowing from China related to the social maintenance of the Vietnamese family or *gia-đình*. Idealized institutions of the Chinese tradition that were within Vietnamese reach could sometimes be overdeveloped in Vietnam, relatively speaking, possibly in compensation for the recognized underdevelopment of other borrowed elements. For example, the concept of "lands for incense and fires"—the subtraction of a certain fraction of land or income from the estate of a dead person for the purpose of supporting temple rites to the deceased—does not make a strong appearance in the T'ang law code, from which medieval Vietnamese laws were nominally derived. (It does appear in the *Chu-tzu chia li.*) But in Vietnam the institution of "lands for incense and fires" (*hương hỏa điền*) bulked large in law codes and assumed a social importance that it lacked in China. Indeed, the term *hương hỏa* soon evolved as the only phrase the Vietnamese ever used to describe ancestral cult funds. Of course, as in China, it also served as the covering expression for state patronage of Buddhist temples, for which government lands in Quảng Trị and other provinces were converted into tax-free property.[84] State recognition of the need for ostentatious "incense and fire" for dead officials and soldiers also required the exemption of thousands of villagers from corvee to serve as "tomb attendants" (*mộ phu*). Pigneau de Behaine, who had been buried in Vietnam, received court-supported "incense and fire" until 1836, when Minh-mạng took special measures to terminate it.[85] It is difficult to explain why *hương hỏa* should have become a minor Vietnamese example of what is sometimes called "pattern saturation"—the indigenous elaboration and specialization of a borrowed idea or term. Yet its Vietnamese inflation should suggest the organic—and untidy—nature of Sino-Vietnamese acculturation. It should also add another category to the catalogue of types of changes that occurred when Chinese institutions came to Vietnam: the cultural parallelisms (the dual theory of monarchy), environmental-institutional tensions, and divergences in social structure and resources that have already been mentioned.

In role performances, intra-familial relationships, and domestic religious observances like ancestor worship, at least as important in Vietnam as in China,[86] the Vietnamese family conformed closely to its heritage of Chinese beliefs and customs. Family registers were assiduously kept even by commoners and sometimes by younger rather than by older sons. "I criticized this," wrote Nguyễn Văn Siêu, a celebrated scholar of the Minh-mạng and Thiệu-trị periods, when a younger son tried to atone for the neglect of his elder brother by putting together a seven-generation register and asking Siêu to write the introduction.[87] Many lineages maintained ancestral halls (*từ đường*), whose purpose, Siêu wrote, was "to differentiate the branches and sub-branches and to clarify genealogy."[88] The lineage itself (*tộc* in Sino-Vietnamese; *họ* in non-Sinic Vietnamese) was of patrilineal descent from a common male ancestor. It consisted only of direct and collateral male branches, possessed communal property, and had a lineage head (*trưởng tộc*). The latter was in principle (but not always in fact) the head of the oldest branch within the lineage. Behind these confidently Sino-Vietnamese features there seemed to lurk only one immediate mystery, the curious Vietnamese poverty of lineage names. "The governors-general [of Vietnamese provinces] all have the Nguyễn surname and belong to the king's lineage," wrote the irrepressible Chinese geographer Hsü Chi-yü,[89] affecting to see in this a lack of Chinese-type universalistic standards in the Vietnamese bureaucracy.

His assertion was wholly false. But here Chinese confusion only reflected a Vietnamese divergence which has never been satisfactorily explained historically. (A census of 1931 in Bắc Ninh province revealed that 85 percent of the province's families shared just twelve lineage names.)[90] One of its effects was a further divergence from Chinese custom. Marriages between men and women of the same surname were not uncommon. This was a tendency which orthodox Nguyễn officials deplored and at times—especially in the 1820's—asked the court to prohibit, particularly in the north.[91] But in the end they were incapable of resisting it.

The Vietnamese were not always able to follow the Chinese ideal of lineage surname exogamy because of the paucity of surnames. Other tensions which Sino-Vietnamese familial institutions harbored were even more significant. Respect for the rights and the powers of women had always been more the mark of Vietnamese social conventions than of Chinese. The disparities between Vietnamese customs and Chinese principles of social organization, it is true, never reached the dimensions of those between Indian civilization and "Indianized" Southeast Asian kingdoms, where Indian-style caste systems, for example, were usually absent. But diffusion of Chinese patriarchal ideas in Vietnam, although thorough, was uneven.

Medieval Vietnamese law—specifically the Hồng Đức law code of the late 1400's—often altered the sense and even the substance of the Chinese T'ang legal codes which Vietnam had inherited. Daughters as well as sons could inherit the land of deceased parents. If there were no sons to serve as the trustees of ancestral cult funds, daughters could serve in their place. And although the T'ang code showed a strong tendency toward the recognition of communal property rights in the family, with fathers and sons managing the land jointly, the Vietnamese code was more inclined to stress parental property rights—of the wife as well as of the husband. Children could not claim their inheritance unless both father and mother were dead; the word "both," as Makino puts it, was hardly ornamental.[92] Even second wives who had borne their husbands no children could claim lands from their husbands' estates when they died, as necessary concessions to penurious widowhood. Such concessions were called "nourishment for one generation" (*cấp dưỡng nhất thể*). Husbands who deserted their wives for five months (or a year, if there were children) lost all conjugal rights.

This Vietnamese toleration, even support of female property rights and rights of inheritance, was unique in the history of East Asian classical civilization. There were few consonances of any kind in the traditional laws of Japan, Korea, or China. Vietnamese historians have advanced diverse explanations for the liberality of the Hồng Đức code. Some have argued that it palely reflected ancient matriarchal biases in Vietnamese culture from before the Chinese conquest. Others have argued that it was influenced by newer matriarchal trends in the Cham society that was being defeated by the Vietnamese in the late 1400's. And some have even suggested that it sought to reward Vietnamese women for their role in agriculture and handicraft enterprises, in support of Vietnamese soldiers, during the exhausting war with China in 1406–1427. The controversy over the code, and its obstruction of Chinese patriarchal forms in Vietnam, is not likely to end soon. The Nguyễn law code of 1812, which made a greater attempt to match Chinese laws, reduced the legal status which women had won in the 1400's. But all it really seems to have succeeded in doing was create an everlasting discrepancy between the code and certain areas of popular custom.

Laws were kinder to women in Vietnam, but so were folk traditions. Around the Trưng sisters, who had led Vietnamese armies into a desperate last stand against Chinese invaders in the first century, were woven artful mythologies by scholars and by rural storytellers. By the twelfth century the Trưngs had become goddesses with temple cults. Orthodox court historiography naturally attempted to "masculinize" their legend. It attempted to accentuate the roles of their husbands against the enemy, in order to give their tradition a greater patriarchal intelligibility—in line with the demands of Chinese culture. But because the legend belonged to all Vietnamese, Confucian scholars were notoriously unsuccessful in changing it. When a rebel dynasty less infected by Chinese learning and closer to the folk moralities of the peasants arose to seize power, notably in the late 1700's, the early rudiments of the legend were almost effortlessly rediscovered. The unsinicized women rebels were freely allowed to dominate court mystique again as well as village pantheons. Tây-sơn documents dating from 1792 and 1802 reveal that Tây-sơn emperors even conferred posthumous nobility upon two lesser female generals of the Trưng queens (Nguyệt Thai and Nguyệt Độ) as a deliberate commemoration of the Vietnamese tradition of xenophobic, matriarchical rebellion against China.[93] All this set the stage for the Nguyễn reaction after 1802, the stringent imposition of every aspect of Confucian hierarchical thought which formally denied women an equal place in Vietnamese society. It also set the stage for the rise of one of the most famous and formidable women in Vietnamese history.

Hồ Xuân Hương is an improbable figure in Vietnamese literature. Vietnamese historians are virtually unanimous in acclaiming her as the "most special" poetry writer who ever lived in Vietnam. But if she was an improbable figure in nineteenth-century Vietnam, she would have been an impossible figure in nineteenth-century China. There lies one of the important if elusive differences between the two societies.

Hồ Xuân Hương was born to the concubine of an official serving in northern Vietnam sometime in the late 1700's. Because she was a woman, her dates have not been preserved, but because of her literary jousts and exchanges with the scholar Phạm Đình Hổ, who lived from 1768 to 1839, she is assumed to have been his contemporary. She herself became a concubine (of a prefect) when she was about thirty years old. Her marriage chances were poor partly because she was an extraordinarily talented woman. She was, by the Nguyễn court's standards, overeducated. Later in her life, when her first husband was dead and her notoriety as a writer was well-established, younger male scholars became intrigued by her, but would not think of marrying an ex-concubine. This only increased her distemper, for she wrote of them: "Careful, careful, where are you going? You group of know-nothings! Come here and let your older sister teach you to write poems. Young bees whose stingers itch rub them in wilted flowers. Young goats who have nothing to do with their horns butt them against sparse shrubbery."[94]

Hồ Xuân Hương was forced to reflect with horror upon the low formal status of women within Vietnam's Chinese-style family, as manifested in the existence of a double moral standard. She was also embittered by the fact that women of literary merit like herself could not find socially sanctioned public careers. But where most educated Vietnamese women only had outraged feelings, Hồ Xuân Hương had whimsical and learned powers of satire. She wrote poetry which, for all its playfulness, may have been the darkest assault upon Confucian ethics ever delivered by a literate scholar of a classical East Asian society. Most modern Vietnamese writers agree that she often went too far, to the point where her contemporaries regarded her as a "monster," whose influence should be obliterated. One socially subversive feature of her poems was their use of the traditional Vietnamese equivalent of "pig Latin," namely the reversing of the proper vowels of two juxtaposed words, often in the interests of profanity. Women were not supposed to understand such techniques. Hồ Xuân Hương's poems in content ridiculed the eunuchs of the Nguyễn court—and, in this way, the court itself.

Or they talked lightly about the sexual orgies that the poetess believed occurred in Buddhist temples. Or they speculated how the writer herself would have behaved if she had been born an army general.

More seriously, Hồ Xuân Hương attacked the institution of polygamy. In a patrilineal system of the Chinese kind, polygamy was, of course, furthered by Confucian filial piety and a man's need to please his ancestors by having many sons. In both China and Vietnam husbands had the right to take concubines if their wives failed to bear them the male successors they needed. The Nguyễn law code of 1812, based as it was upon the Ch'ing Chinese law code, stipulated that the wife was noble and that the concubine was vile and that elevating the latter to the status of the former upset morality. Perhaps few articles in Gia-long's whole artificial legal system—a copy of China's system—frustrated the expectations of certain sectors of Vietnamese opinion more than this one. Hồ Xuân Hương wrote of the institution of polygamy:

> One wife is covered by a quilted blanket, while one wife
>   is left in the cold.
> Cursed be this fate of sharing a common husband.
> Seldom do you have an occasion to possess your husband,
> Not even twice in one month.
> You toil and endure hardships in order to earn your steamed
>   rice, and then the rice is cold and tasteless.
> It is like renting your services for hire, and then receiving no
>   wages.
> How is it that I have turned out this way,
> I would rather suffer the fate of remaining unmarried
>   and living alone by myself.[95]

This sensualistic woman rhetorician, who wrote in *nôm* rather than in classical Chinese, is considered to have escaped Chinese cultural influences more completely than most other Vietnamese writers and ideologues of this early modern period. Certainly her frank comparison of the roles of two marriage partners to an exchange of labor for wages, in which the woman was deceived by receiving no payment, was a revolutionary strategy in her attempt to reinterpret the Vietnamese social system outside the walls of the court. It made a convincing mockery of the court's borrowed legal perspectives. In fact, in other criticisms of polygamy, Hồ Xuân Hương even jokingly praised pregnancies outside marriage, in a poem full of word plays:

> The eternal guilt is borne completely by you, young man.
> The results of our love I, the concubine, ask to carry
> And I do not care if the mouths of public opinion disagree
>   with me.
> Only people who become pregnant while lacking husbands
>   are good.[96]

Poems like this one were written in a social milieu in which Confucian moral standards and actual practices did not always comfortably harmonize. Anonymous folksongs in Nguyễn Vietnam also attacked polygamy. They sympathetically portrayed the concubine with the "solitary sleeping mat," who slaved in obedience to the orders of the first wife but had few of her pleasures. Other folksongs more generally attacked Confucian principles of hierarchy.

In the remainder of this study, which is concerned primarily with the Nguyễn bureaucracy, the emphasis will be on the institutional sinicization that took place in Huế under Minh-mạng's aegis. But it is vital to remember that Hồ Xuân Hương, unusual as she was, was an upper-class woman who possessed a surprisingly keen ear for the language of the peasant world. Her writings were significant repositories of Vietnamese social history. They—and folksongs—suggest that in the early 1800's, practical norms in rural Vietnam came closer than they had in the past to Confucian ideals only unwillingly and tentatively if at all, despite the impressive growth of a Chinese-style bureaucracy. The very existence of Hồ Xuân Hương's poetry in the nineteenth century should convey cautionary suggestions to the modern historian that although within Vietnamese Confucian culture all the overt statements of the cardinal, orthodox concepts of politics and ethics were probably made just as often as they were in China, in Vietnam they may not have been quite so completely reinforced by, or synthesized with, sympathetic covert apperceptive habits—that is, by outlooks which are so taken for granted in a culture that they are rarely put into words. The distinction, admittedly, is a difficult one.

Linguistic and Literary Bridge-building between China and Vietnam

The office-holding Vietnamese scholar, intellectually polished and philosophically mature, entered the world of Chinese books with the greatest of ease. He read Confucius and the Ch'ing dynasty statutes in their original language, classical Chinese, whose pronunciation he "Vietnamized" by following Vietnamese phonetic laws and also by distantly obeying Chinese pronunciation conventions of the late T'ang period. (Cultural historians should not ignore the occasional similarities in the pronunciation of modern Cantonese and modern Sino-Vietnamese.) But this did not mean that the leverage of classical Chinese in Vietnam, even in Huế palaces, was endless. It was the written language of government documents but it was not always much else. The actual spoken Vietnamese language, whose words are a challenge to any etymologist, was the product of a complicated mixture of many languages. It had patently known the influence of a number of language families, Mon-Khmer, Thai, and Chinese.[97] Its variety was and is confusing. One word for "rice" is Sino-Vietnamese (*mễ*), another is Mon-Khmer in origin (*lúa*), and still another is from Thai (*gạo*). Varied linguistic predispositions meant varied cultural predispositions. Indeed the language only reflected Vietnam's own extraordinary career as a cultural crossroads, a sinicized society in mainland Southeast Asia. No automatic linguistic transitions ever facilitated the passage of institutions from Ch'ing China to Nguyễn Vietnam. Spoken Chinese was alien, so alien that when Minh-mạng heard Michel Chaigneau speak French for the first time he remarked that it resembled "a continual whistling—a little like Chinese."[98] The Vietnamese were such good Southeast Asians that they learned Thai and Laotian vocabularies much more easily than those of other peoples—despite their Indianized scripts. Curricula for the study of foreign scripts (*ngoại quốc văn tự*), initiated in Huế in 1836, were candidly based upon the assumption that "the sounds and the words of the Western countries are more difficult than those of Siam and Laos."[99] Students at the

Nguyễn Interpreters' Office (*Tứ dịch quán*) were ordered to learn seven or eight Thai and Laotian words a day to only two or three "Western" words during their first three months of study in 1836, after which the rates were increased to twelve and six words a day respectively.[100]

The Chinese written language naturally remained a much smaller part of Vietnamese culture than it was of its homeland's. It reached its limits of usefulness much earlier, even at the Huế court, not because the inherited Sino-Vietnamese vocabulary was inadequate, in terms of richness of range, but because it had never been deeply rooted enough in Vietnam either historically or socially. Much of it, when spoken, was beyond the comprehension of the Vietnamese peasant. Even to the elite it was often a stumbling block. In writing poetry, for example, Vietnamese scholars found that their own reactions, aesthetic and literary, and those of their readers were likely to be more substantial and more emotionally conditionable if everyday words were used—mainly non-Sinic Vietnamese. But they were still under the Chinese cultural spell. When they created their own writing system they often merely fashioned more complicated characters out of the existing Chinese ones. The curiously hybrid Vietnamese characters which resulted were called *chữ nôm*, "southern characters."

The composition of these "southern characters" had definite rules but was not always strictly logical. This only reveals their dynamic rather than static nature as a written emergent symbolism. Sometimes two Chinese characters would be combined. One of the two would represent the meaning of a given Vietnamese word while the other would approximate, in its Sino-Vietnamese pronunciation, the sound of the Vietnamese word. At other times *nôm* characters might consist of one Chinese character and one already created *nôm* character. The Vietnamese were also inclined to adopt existing Chinese characters and merely use them differently, thus setting traps for unwary readers of Vietnamese historical documents. Examples of all these principles appear in the glossary.

This motley system represented one more attempt by an Asian people living on the edge of Chinese society to find Chinese-style characters for words in their own language which had nothing to do with Chinese. The Vietnamese may have succeeded in matching the original Chinese writing system more closely than the Japanese and the Koreans did because their language was not inflected or agglutinative. Their attempt invites tentative comparisons with that of Tangut scholars of the medieval Hsi Hsia kingdom in northwest China to create their own mysterious but Chinese-like modes of writing.[101]

Successful as they were, the Vietnamese almost walked on the edge of chaos. For the Vietnamese language consisted of words which had originated in China and sounded like Chinese when the Vietnamese pronounced them (*dân,* "people"). It consisted of words which had originated in China but whose sounds diverged when the Vietnamese pronounced them (*côi,* "to be orphaned"). It consisted of words which probably originated in China but whose sounds were so different that only traces of meaning remained (*nhà,* "house," which may have been derived from the Sino-Vietnamese word *gia*). It consisted of words which did not come from China at all but whose sounds resembled those of Chinese characters, which were then used for them (*một,* "one," which used the Chinese character *mei,* pronounced *một* by Sino-Vietnamese convention). And it consisted of words which did not come from China and lacked sounds analogous to those of Chinese words.[102]

Nôm sprang primarily from the need to find written forms for this fifth category. Although one modern linguist has argued that *nôm* was ultimately inadequate as a writing system[103] its history indicates that it was socially and intellectually more liberating than inhibiting. Even synonyms in non-Sinic Vietnamese for Sino-Vietnamese words usually reveal functional variations. But what was the significance of *nôm* for Vietnamese borrowing from China and for Vietnamese political society?

Some students have argued, more from faith than from evidence, that the Vietnamese people and the Mường people (a minority now living in Thanh-hóa province) were originally one people, whom uneven responses to acculturation with China drove asunder. Supposedly, *nôm* was derived from the primordial writing script of this one race in remote antiquity.[104] Probably not all the real evidence is in, but the earliest *nôm* characters known to have existed are those which appear in a list of the names of twenty villages on a stone monument in Ninh Bình province, erected in the fourteenth century. *Nôm* was surely a consequence of Vietnam's Sinicization—rather than a relic of the period which preceded it.

Between the fourteenth and the nineteenth centuries it was favored as a written language parallel to classical Chinese. Sixteenth-century Vietnam scholars, even those who won doctoral degrees in the Lê examination system, delighted in playing verbal games with it.[105] But it was more often employed to express ideas and forms which lost something of their Vietnamese flavor if they underwent forced conversions into classical Chinese. In 1625, for example, the Trịnh ruler of northern Vietnam and the Nguyễn ruler of central Vietnam exchanged a famous pair of letters whose purpose was to win propaganda victories for both sides before the fatal outbreak of hostilities between the two regions in 1626. The art of the Trịnh letter especially was centered in its astute manipulation of informal kinship terminology, its public suggestion that the Nguyễns were guilty of violating family bonds by creating an independent kingdom in the south, its tendentious reminder that the Trịnh ruler was a "nephew" (*cháu* in non-Sinic Vietnamese) of his Nguyễn adversary. Had Chinese rather than Vietnamese characters been used, the stinging intimacy of the document might have been lost in Vietnamese eyes.[106]

Although traditional Vietnamese scholars called Sino-Vietnamese literature "serious literature" and *nôm* literature "the literature of pleasure," this dichotomy is obviously misleading. It is true that *nôm* vocabulary tended to be more concrete than abstract. But *nôm* allowed Vietnamese writers to escape more successfully from the cliches of the Chinese classics than Chinese writers could, and it also enabled them to draw upon the folk literature of the common people. By the 1700's, facility in both classical Chinese and *nôm* was expected of the truly versatile Vietnamese scholar. Lê Quý Đôn wrote learned commentaries on the *Classic of Documents* (*Thư kinh*) in the former. Supposedly he also wrote moralistic tracts for family guidance, like *Dạy con về nhà chồng* (Instructions for a young girl who is going to her husband's home), in the latter.[107] *Nôm* was not itself a separatist trend within the Chinese cultural world. It nonetheless testified to an important degree of cultural separation between China and Vietnam. It served as a bridge by which Chinese meanings might enter Vietnamese verbal contexts. Coexistence of the

two scripts encouraged coexistence of the two peoples. One famous
eighteenth-century school of poets in southern Vietnam (Hà Tiên)
where Chinese settlement was strong had thirty Chinese members
who wrote Chinese poems and six Vietnamese members who converted them into *nôm*.[108]

Coexistence of the two scripts might be possible in the 1800's in
the raw frontier lands of Hà Tiên. It was not always possible within
the confined world of the emperor and his court at Huế after 1802—
or rather, after 1820. Purists protested. *Nôm* was not orthodox. If
its ungainly characters appeared in communications to the throne
(memorials) or in bureaucratic commissions, it would undermine
Sino-Vietnamese style. Running battles were fought. With the
explosion of the Tây-sơn Rebellion in the 1770's and the subsequent
collapse of the two long-established regional courts in northern and
central Vietnam, the Vietnamese examination system had moldered
and briefly died. As a consequence, in the period 1802–1820 Gia-long
was compelled to recruit his officials mainly from settler families
in the south who had served in his armies. Qualifications for recruitment were more usually pre-1802 loyalty than scholarship. Old Lê
period scholars were unearthed occasionally to serve as educational
officials in the north, but on the whole militarists with homespun
learning ruled Vietnam. Such a situation was not unfamiliar to
Chinese society during and immediately after a dynastic interregnum.
But the Vietnamese accent within this Chinese pattern was that
without the impetus of the examination system, many Vietnamese
officials and their underlings had found it almost easier to remember
Vietnamese characters than Chinese ones. In fact *nôm* was at the
height of its popularity in the very early nineteenth century. Gia-long
encouraged it, out of necessity if not out of desire. A law of 1814
stipulated that when a secretariat (*thư tả ty*) was created for the
regional government of the north its fifty members must be drawn
from underlings who were particularly "skilled at writing Southern
and Northern character styles."[109] It was a sign of the times that
"Southern" (*nôm*) preceded "Northern" (Chinese).

Minh-mạng wasted little time in reacting. In the first year of his
reign, 1820, he attempted to deal a death blow to *nôm* at the Huế
court by ordering that from then on all memorials, and all compositions written at Vietnamese examination sites, be written in charac-

ters identical to those in the imported K'ang-hsi dictionary (*K'ang-hsi tzu-tien*; Sino-Vietnamese, *Khang Hy tự điển*) rather than in "confused rough scripts."[110] Secretarial underlings after 1820 had to know four styles of characters: old characters, seal characters, rough "grass" characters, and ordinary characters. But all of them were Chinese, none of them were "Southern." In 1832 students writing poetry in the second stage of the regional and metropolitan examinations were prohibited the use of "rustic books" and "privately assorted characters."[111] This was proof that *nôm* was still very much alive.

This revolution was very superficial because even Minh-mạng had to accept the services of *nôm* when it came to teaching Confucian ideas to Vietnamese schoolchildren. Chinese characters alone—and their strange Chinese word order—were not sufficient to reach them. In provinces and villages the classical tradition was usually expounded in educational primers like the *Sơ học vấn tân* (Asking the way in elementary studies), in use from the beginning of the nineteenth century. Such primers typically had one row of purely Chinese characters followed by a complementary row of characters which mixed Chinese with *nôm*. For example, when Vietnamese children first happened upon the myth-truths that

> The Fire Emperor, the Heavenly Farmer
> Taught the people to sow and to reap
> And used drugs to cure their sickness

it required six lines rather than three in the primer to expound them. The term "Fire Emperor" was written in the first line in Chinese (*Yen-ti*; *Viêm Đế* in Sino-Vietnamese) and in the second line in a mixture of Chinese and *nôm* as "indigenous-style ruler Fire Emperor" (*vua Viêm Đế*). The word "taught" in the second line (in the third and fourth lines in the actual primer) was written first as *chiao* (Sino-Vietnamese, *giáo*) and then in the Vietnamese way as *dạy*.[112]

The *Sơ học vấn tân* itself was a summary of Chinese and Vietnamese history down to the nineteenth century. It also contained a collection of moral maxims for children, for example, "only the Confucian creed is orthodox." The second row of mixed Chinese and Vietnamese characters not only preserved the idiomatic Vietnamese word order but also gave fuller explanations of the meaning. If the Chinese row stated merely that Chinese Ming dynasty had fallen to "abrupt bandits," the mixed row identified the bandits as including Li Tzu-ch'eng. Vietnamese who wrote purely classical Chinese considered it unsophisticated to make too many allowances for their readers' ignorance of things Chinese. By employing both scripts, they could maintain their high standards with the first one and enlighten a Southeast Asian audience with the second one.

Furthermore, *nôm* had other purposes besides improving classical indoctrination techniques. Vietnamese poetry differed from Chinese poetry, unless it was consciously imitating Chinese forms, in a number of ways. For one thing, the Chinese were fonder than the Vietnamese of verses with odd numbers of words in their lines (like five-word and seven-word verse). Vietnamese poets preferred even numbers of words per line. This preference reached the apogee of its expression in the most popular verse form of traditional Vietnam, "six-eight" (*lục-bát*) poetry. This style shows structural affinities with Thai and Cham poetry, although conservative-minded Vietnamese scholars are more willing to find evidence of its origins in certain passages in the Chinese *Classic of Changes*.[113] Both *nôm* and "six-eight" poetry, however, ironically played vital roles in helping to bring the diverse heirlooms of Chinese literary culture more within the reach of literate Vietnamese. Before the twentieth century, Chinese novels and dramas could be read in Vietnam in their original form—an idiosyncratic chrysalis of classical Chinese intermingled with Chinese vernacular—only by a very few. To gain more Vietnamese readers, they had to be translated into "six-eight" poetry, written partly in Chinese characters and partly in *nôm*. Having become literary exemplifications, in their new forms, of the very intricate demands of the transposition process whenever Vietnam borrowed from China, these curious "six-eight" novels and plays were then expected to harmonize, when read, with the songs Vietnamese peasants sang as they poled their boats or transplanted rice seedlings.

The Yüan drama *Hsi-hsiang chi* (Tales of the western sector) made its debut in Southeast Asia as 1,744 lines of Vietnamese "six-eight" poetry. Chinese princes inevitably metamorphosed into Vietnamese-style *vua* in the Vietnamese versification entitled *Tống chí truyền* (Chronicles of the Sung), which related colorful episodes of medieval Chinese history. The Vietnamese text, which dates perhaps from the 1600's, still exists.[114] Famous Chinese poems could also be freely translated into colloquial Vietnamese. In the Vietnamese translation of Po Chü-i's "Ballad of the Guitar" ("P'i-p'a hsing"), done by a Vietnamese court official about 1820, a Chinese sentence like "The autumn wind murmurs through the maple leaves and the reed flowers" could become (roughly) "Softly the breath of autumn whispers through the reeds and leaves a lonely peace." Many Vietnamese writers considered their own versions to be refinements of the Chinese originals. In public, their attitudes were not inordinately deferential.

All these uses of *nôm* were the uses of the Vietnamese elite. But *nôm* literature had another side to it. It also functioned as the written medium of propaganda of Vietnamese peasant rebels. The most important rebel in northern Vietnam in the early nineteenth century (and the competition was severe) was a charismatic peasant named Phan Bá Vành. Vành actually managed to launch a multi-class uprising which included peasants, Lê loyalist scholars, village notables, landlords, canton heads, and even Mường tribesmen.[115] As he swept through Nam Định in the middle 1820's, he proved so successful at first that Nguyễn commanders sent to fight him did not dare to march to drumbeats, their usual custom, because villagers would hear them and give Vành warning. Floods which devastated Nam Định on the eve of Vành's uprising may not have underwritten his appeal very much more powerfully than a portentous comet which appeared in the sky. It provided the excuse for the ballad sung by his followers:

> Above us in the sky we have the revered comet,
> Below on the ground we have the ruler Bá Vành.[116]

When this ballad was committed to writing, of the fourteen words in the ballad in the Vietnamese original, only five were represented by characters that a Chinese could recognize. This was a long way, a very long way, from the literature or the documents of the Sino-Vietnamese court. And Vành's name constituted two of the five words which appeared in the version of this ballad written in Chinese characters rather than in *nôm*. The cultural gulf between a rebel and the court was considerably greater in Vietnam than in China. The sealing off of the elite language from the language of the people was more exaggerated. Had Vành employed Sino-Vietnamese poetry the reactions from his peasant soldiers would have been puzzled or weak. Had he styled himself as a *hoàng-đế* or as a *vương*, rather than as a *vua*, these two Sino-Vietnamese titles would have had much less stimulus value in the villages of Nam Định and his movement might have suffered. Sino-Vietnamese titles were obviously not strong "iconic" signs recalling some easily understandable corresponding form or person in the villagers' past experience.

Nôm, in brief, had the capacity to become the literary medium of a universe of discourse that was only weakly related to that of the official social order. It could become the instrument of social sub-systems where cultural change occurred at a different rate than it did in the classical Sino-Vietnamese world. Evidence that this was actually happening in Minh-mạng's Vietnam on a small scale emerged ten years after Vành's rebellion ended. Christian missionaries and their Vietnamese acolytes began to distribute in the country-side a printed text entitled *Thánh-giáo yếu lý quốc ngữ* (Essential principles of Christianity in the national language). This tract was openly subversive; it even ignored the Vietnamese dynastic date—Minh-mạng 18—for the Western one, 1837. It inculcated the ten commandments, the doctrine of the trinity, and nature of Christ (both God and man) in colloquial Vietnamese. And it identified the Christian God by a partly *nôm* phrase as the *đức chủ trời*.[117] *Trời*, the non-Sinic word for heaven in this phrase "lord of heaven," was far more potent—and thus more subversive—among peasant believers than the Sino-Vietnamese word *thiên* could ever be. Both the Christian God and the rebel Vành clothed themselves in seditious *nôm* formulas.

Thus the use of *nôm* in traditional Vietnam both furthered the domestication of classical Chinese culture and symbolized the tense complexities of the less than complete integration of the peasant and bureaucratic worlds.

The Hazards of the Vietnamese Throne

Beyond its paradoxes, which bore heavily upon its emperors, Nguyễn Vietnam was unique: a sinicized kingdom in Southeast Asia, a bridge of many layers between Southeast and East Asia. Vietnamese emperors were fertile in inventiveness because they had to be. Court hymns were customarily sung to them during the annual New Year celebrations at Huế. "All peoples look up to the Son of Heaven; how illustrious is his nature; like a jade tablet . . . he displays virtue . . . May Heaven grant him the purest happiness, and may he receive good fortune forever and ever."[118] But none of them ever set records for personal longevity, or ruled, like the occasional Chinese emperor, for fifty or sixty years. If mainland Southeast Asia was a crossroad of civilizations, the "Europe of Asia" in its juxtaposition of competing cultures and societies, traditional Vietnam was a crossroad within this crossroad, especially after it had seized the Mekong delta. The sum of all the political difficulties and the cultural tensions was tremendous. What kind of administrative structure could possibly have ventured to govern?

Two
Nguyễn and Ch'ing Central Civil Administration: Power Structures and Communications Processes

Minh-mạng was the first Vietnamese ruler ever to govern a unified kingdom from the China border to the Gulf of Siam through sophisticated, zealously domesticated Chinese administrative laws. This chapter can give only the most superficial sketch of the growth and diversification of his administration, and of the ways in which stimuli from that colossus in the East Asian world, the mammoth Ch'ing bureaucracy, reached and affected Vietnamese life in the 1800's.

Imperial Power in Bureaucratic Confucian Society

One of the cardinal self-appointed tasks of the Vietnamese historiographical tradition was the cultivation of concepts of self-definition of "our kingdom" (*ngã quốc*) and the erection of boundaries, real or mythological, between China and Vietnam. These boundaries were erected primarily to prevent the Chinese from ever resurrecting any legitimate claims to participation in Vietnamese political society. But Vietnamese historians, from Lê Văn Hưu in the thirteenth century to Ngô Sĩ Liên in the fifteenth century to Phan Huy Chú in the 1800's, also saw themselves as bicultural scholars who linked their country in an idiomatically Vietnamese way to the Chinese institutional tradition, if not to the Chinese. In turn they depended upon the precepts of social stratification advanced by that tradition to maintain their own preeminence in Vietnam. This intense group interest of the pre-modern Vietnamese elite in the Chinese tradition was not unfaithfully saluted by Nguyễn Công Trứ, one of Minh-mạng's leading officials, in his famous early nineteenth-century poem "Scholars": "From the time of the Chou and the Han, our own scholars have had high value."[1]

In Vietnamese eyes the Chinese institutional tradition was not a haphazard accumulation of innovations by individual courts. Instead it was believed to represent a complex of parts which were all specifically interrelated, which had proven their utility as a system in China, and which could be fundamentally modified by a people who had not created them only at great peril. Indeed, the Vietnamese tended to endow the written Chinese statutes of government with a greater premeditated coherence than they actually possessed, perhaps because Huế and Hanoi bureaucrats read the formal Chinese *hui-tien* (compendia of institutions) avidly but were less familiar with day-to-day Chinese records which exposed informal vagaries. The twentieth-century Western historian of China who has read the memoirs of Liang Chang-chü and Chao I, and the modern essays of Chinese political scientists like Teng Chih-ch'eng almost certainly knows more about the workings of the Ch'ing Grand Council than Minh-mạng did. Yet Minh-mạng governed all Vietnam in the late 1830's through his personally contrived facsimile of the Peking Grand Council, the Cơ Mật Viện. In the apparatuses of decision making, of coercion and punishment, of resource determination and allocation, and of political recruitment and role assignment, Vietnamese rulers struggled to ensure that their governments attained a correspondence to the governments of China. The closer their approximation, they believed, the greater would be their effectiveness—and the greater their ability to maintain Vietnamese independence from China.

In both Peking and Huế the emperor or Son of Heaven stood at the top of three basic hierarchies, civil, military, and censorial or censorial-judicial. The hierarchy of civil bureaucrats in both China and Vietnam was divided into eighteen grades, 1A to 9B. The grades were marked off from each other by different styles of clothing, different perquisites, different salaries, and different degrees of access to the imperial court. The links between bureaucratic posts and hierarchical grades were largely but not completely similar in Ch'ing China and Nguyễn Vietnam. Nguyễn board presidents, for example, were called "great ministers" (*đại thân*), a unique usage of Ch'ing China. But they held the more lowly hierarchical grade of 2A, as did their earlier counterparts in Ming China. In Ch'ing China the governor-general at the summit of the formal provincial administration occupied the grade of 1B and the district magistrate at the bottom of the same administration found himself in the seventh grade. But in Vietnam the equivalent posts were 2A and 6A–6B respectively, an arrangement which may have reflected the less extensive gradation of difficulty and scope of jurisdiction between the two commissions in a smaller country.[2] In fact the major divergences of the Nguyễn bureaucratic rank system came at the sub-provincial level of the territorial administration. Here hierarchical positions descended as intricately as they did in China, on paper, but differentiations of function lost their sharpness, comparatively speaking, and faded out.

Neither in China nor in Vietnam did these ranks or grades guarantee power. Power was derived from commissions in the bureaucracy, not from statuses—and commissions were personally conferred by the emperor. In this way Chinese and Vietnamese governments, as wholes, represent peculiar mixtures of bureaucratic and non-bureaucratic elements. If the obedience the official offered to the emperor was an obligation of his status rather than of personal individual life-long loyalty, the emperor's control of the official was distinctly personal. Success as a ruler in the Sino-Vietnamese political scheme depended upon this direct control of the bureaucracy through personal manipulation, rather than upon direct proprietary custody of resources, which in fact was decentralized in China and Vietnam. Some of the more obvious techniques of imperial control which Chinese courts invented and Vietnamese courts inherited included the periodic circulation of bureaucrats in office (to prevent them from developing local power bases), the manipulation of social mobility channels (by setting regional quotas in the examination systems), the adroit balancing of one group of bureaucrats against another (by means of an internal intelligence network of censors, and periodic ratings of inferiors by superiors) as well as the personal authorization of all appointments.

Such an emphasis on personal relationships between the emperor and his bureaucrats was an integral part of Confucian idealism. Yet in nineteenth-century China and Vietnam it served the personal power needs of the emperor far more than it served the bureaucrats. In the vast Ch'ing empire the emperor rarely was able to conduct "personal interviews" (*yin-chien*) with all the officials whom he promoted or transferred. For the most part he confined his attention to higher officials. In smaller Vietnam it was possible to make personal audiences (*dẫn kiến* in Sino-Vietnamese) a far more widespread procedure. Minh-mạng's revival of this institution in 1820 was one of the early landmarks of his centralization of power. "I have read that [Han and T'ang emperors] generally checked names with realities," he commented in 1823.[3] After the early 1820's it was impossible for Vietnamese officials to win routine promotions merely on the strength of their bureaucratically documented career records. They had to see and be seen by the ruler. Lists had been compiled in 1820 of provincial officials serving under Gia-long who had not recently appeared at the Huế court. They were now compelled to come forward and participate in court discussions in order to show that "the central and provincial governments constitute one body."[4]

By the 1830's Vietnamese civil officials were required to write their own versions of their record of conduct in office as a preliminary part of the *dẫn kiến* process. These literary self-investigations were written upon red paper purchased from China and were called *thủ bản*, "personal handbooks" or summaries. They were supposed to describe family backgrounds, official records of conduct, and honors and punishments received. They had to be accurate, could not be written by anyone else but the official concerned, and could not be written in an "antithetical, elegant" writing style.[5] Unsuccessful attempts were made to limit them to 300 words, so that the "intimacy" of the emperor's relationship with the official would not be lost in a superabundance of jargon.[6] These "personal handbooks" and the "personal interview" institution to which they belonged were explicitly Chinese bureaucratic devices[7] imported by Vietnamese rulers to counteract the decentralization and regional segmentation of their governments. (The modern East Asian passion for name cards comes from the same tradition as this old bureaucratic custom of lower officials presenting their own written self-introductions to higher officials and rulers.)

As in China, Vietnamese emperors sought to preserve their freedom of action outside the constraining model framework of their administration. Their administrators in turn struggled to build a-round them an unshakably predictable, consistent world of general, learnable rules of procedure. Paradoxically, as Minh-mạng discovered in the 1820's, the price of imperial centralization was bureaucratization and increasing concessions to the bureaucrats. When officials were degraded and punished, modifications of their punishments depended upon the types of honors they had previously received. But under Gia-long no rules stipulated whether "previous military achievement" or "previous imperial favor and rewards" should be given more weight. The emperor's discretionary whims benefited from the lack of uniformity in the precedents. In 1825 Minh-mạng was forced to allow the bureaucracy to establish a formal hierarchy of three modifying considerations in which "military achievement" was significantly placed last.[8]

A more fundamental tension arose—significantly enough in the Minh-mạng period but not in the Gia-long period—between senior officials' desires to increase the numbers of the bureaucracy in order to differentiate clerical functions, and the emperor's determination to keep his government superficial and, as a consequence, personally manageable. In 1830, for example, the Board of Appointments requested more underlings to draft the honorary commissions of parents of officials. Minh-mạng refused.[9] Only a year before he had had to reject a collective memorial from all Six Boards suggesting an expansion in numbers of their middle officials and sub-bureaucrats. His reply had defined the conflict with unmistakable clarity: "In the first years of my reign I created minor official posts which, compared to the [numbers of the] Gia-long period, represented increases but no decreases. Recently I further considered the complexity of the business of the Boards of Finance and War and increased officials there, doubling the numbers of the previous years. If I now accede to what you request, at what point will it come to an end? . . . You want the quotas [of officials] daily to increase, but . . . it will be like 'corpses in office idly taking the pay.'"[10]

In addition to stressing the importance of personal relationships between sovereign and officials and maintaining an officialdom of small, artificially fixed numbers, Vietnamese emperors, like their Chinese counterparts, dreaded the appearance of specialized skills and talents among their higher officials. They exalted the ideal of the "generalist." Specializing administrators were dangerous because they could more easily become indispensable and because they could checkmate rulers by developing funds of expert knowledge, or knowledge of regional affairs, which rulers could not themselves understand or learn. The higher the official was in status and commission, the more he was expected to share the emperor's own uncomfortable remoteness from specific administrative concerns. This remoteness was called "style" (*thể*). In 1835 Minh-mạng told Nguyễn Khoa Minh, the president of the Board of Finance, "Recently I have heard that you personally attend excessively to minutely detailed business. Since loss of the style of a great minister, and cursory treatment of important things because of careful attention to the unimportant, are unavoidable consequences, you ought to abstain from this."[11]

It is evident that the famous "generalism" of Chinese and Vietnamese scholar-officials was the historical outcome of more than just classical Confucianism, which defined officials as being moral and cultural paragons, "gentlemen" rather than "tools." It was, like so many other of the group characteristics and patterns of behavior within the bureaucratic hierarchy, the product of a centuries-old balancing process in power-dependence relations between the court and the bureaucracy. If it cannot be wholly ascribed to the expositions of Confucius and his disciples, whose paternity of historical forces and ideas was really not as impossibly fertile as is sometimes thought, the admission must nonetheless be made that narrowly specializing administrators would have become aloof and inaccessible as a social elite. That is, they would have become less imitable by other people. Thus they would have been less able to communicate the generally relevant values of their culture to the rest of their society by personally enacting them. The resulting social-cultural disintegration and reorganization would have undermined them as much as the ruler. Their very imitability came from the time-tested generalness of their superiority, which allowed them to make their own standards all-pervasive. "Generalism" served both the official inside the bureaucracy and the emperor outside it.

It was, however, the behavioral reflection of only a weak convergence of interests. Vietnamese emperors, like Chinese emperors, recognized that the family involvements of the officials below them, together with the rational standards of the bureaucracy itself and its autonomous sense of mission as a historical organization, all combined to prevent their regular civil administration from ever becoming a completely dedicated instrument of their personal rule. As the Vietnamese bureaucracy grew in the 1820's and 1830's, Minh-mạng encouraged this growth to a point. But he simultaneously borrowed more and more of the defensive strategies of the Chinese emperors. For example, after 1838 local officials were compelled to forward annual reports to their superiors concerning the existence of eunuchs in their bailiwicks.[12] Eunuchs served the emperor from the age of 13 to 65 (by statute). They became wardens of the seals which were the emblems of his authority and supplied him with the concentrated personal devotion, in return for his protection, that he could not expect from his bureaucrats. Perhaps their roles were generally not too dissimilar from those of the celibate clergy, also without family preoccupations, whom medieval European kings employed. Even today this tendency of the solitary ruler to create auxiliary non-bureaucratic forces to buttress his personal power is extinct neither in China nor in Vietnam. Because the Nguyễn bureaucracy was never as large or as difficult to control as its Chinese model, eunuchs, the emperor's antidote, are far less conspicuous in Vietnamese political history than they are in Chinese. The "eunuch evil" never attained its conventionally demoralizing Chinese proportions in Huế. Intrigues within the palace were not uncommon, however. When Thiệu-trị died unexpectedly in the autumn of 1847 without having publicly named a crown prince, the suspicious regular bureaucracy had to be openly coerced by soldiers to accept Tự-đức as his successor.[13]

An Overview of Sino-Vietnamese Central Civil Administration

Vietnamese emperors governed through a number of secretariats and councils the degrees of whose similarity to secretariats and councils in Peking varied. In order of importance the most prominent were the Cơ Mật Viện, which will be called the "Privy Council" for convenience and which was created in 1834–35; the Nội Các, which will be called the "Grand Secretariat" and which evolved from the forms of several predecessor offices in 1829; and the Hàn-lâm-viện or "Literature Secretariat," one of the few Nguyễn civil institutions erected by Gia-long which survived intact. The Privy Council and the Grand Secretariat were so important in Nguyễn government, and their adoption reveals so much about Vietnamese institutional borrowing from China, that they require separate attention.

The Literature Secretariat looked back to a similarly named parent institution in T'ang China (*Han-lin* in Chinese), which had controlled bureaucratic commissions. It had been so powerful during the T'ang dynasty that it had been known to Chinese then as the "inner prime minister." In Peking in the nineteenth century, examination system winners who passed with the most illustrious honors were still assigned to it as the place in which to begin their bureaucratic careers, even though it had lost some of its T'ang dynasty functions. On a smaller scale the same process occurred in Vietnam. The medieval Trần dynasty had zealously imitated many T'ang institutions, and its Hàn-lâm office had served as the place where imperial edicts and decrees had been drafted.[14] At later Vietnamese courts it retained its prestige but no longer played a central role in the legislative process. Although it was created (or rather recreated) by Gia-long in 1802, it lacked a building of its own in Huế until 1830.[15] As in Ch'ing China superior degree holders were first assigned to it, where they addressed themselves to miscellaneous secretarial functions.

Of the basic plan of central institutions which persists in Chinese history from the T'ang dynasty onward, the Six Boards (*liu-pu, lục bộ* in Sino-Vietnamese) of appointments, finance, rites, war, justice, and public works are, collectively, an outstanding feature. The Six Boards were not secretarial organs. Rather, they crowned the administrative hierarchy. The Vietnamese practice was carefully to duplicate all of them and to maintain them in their Chinese order.

The Huế Board of Appointments (*Lại Bộ*) was, like its Peking model, the agency that suggested and supervised the specific appointments, transfers, promotions, and dismissals of individual civil officials in the bureaucracy. It presided over the triennial ratings of officials. It also drafted their commissions.

The Huế Board of Finance (*Hộ Bộ*) was responsible for assessing and collecting taxes. It also was a clearing house of socio-economic data, because famines or floods in distant provinces required immediate relief action, often initiated by the board itself with imperial approval. Like the Chinese Board of Finance, it was responsible for syntheses of the information of local land and population registers. It was also responsible for regional price adjustments, currency circulation, the disbursement of officials' salaries, and the proper maintenance of the imperial treasuries.

The Nguyễn Board of Rites (*Lễ Bộ*), following the Chinese pattern, attended to the educational system and the initial recruitment of new officials through examinations. It was the leading administrative organ of court rites and imperial temple rituals. Its officials studied both the Chinese classics and Ming-Ch'ing records for information related to Chinese court procedures in such matters as spring agricultural sacrifices by the emperor. It advised Vietnamese emperors on the length of their mourning for their parents. Because diplomacy and court rituals were indivisible elements in the expression of a proper imperial style, the Board of Rites was also responsible for diplomatic relations with China and the rest of Southeast Asia.

The Board of War (*Binh Bộ*) presided over the military bureaucracy. It proposed the promotions, demotions, and assignments of military officers, and the deployment of troops. It also managed the imperial military corvee records.

The Board of Justice (*Hình Bộ*) stood, with the Grand Tribunal (*Đại Lý Tự*) and the Censorate (*Đô Sát Viện*), at the top of the judicial hierarchy. It was responsible for supervising the efficiency of provincial judicial offices in dealing with local lawsuits. At the end of each year it reported to the emperor the numbers of people in jails throughout the empire and the numbers of cases remaining to be solved on the "judicial cases names' list" (*hình danh sách*). Neither was supposed to be high. Assignments to the Board of Justice were far from popular in the Nguyễn bureaucracy.

The Board of Public Works (*Công Bộ*) was, as its name suggests, in charge of artisans and of the building of imperial palaces and roads and bridges. In the 1830's it was the office that organized abortive Vietnamese attempts to construct Western-style steamships. Normally it supervised the building of a variety of types of junks.

But this differentiation of administrative concerns is even more ✓ misleading for Vietnam than it is for China. For one thing, the Boards operated jointly in many matters. Both the Board of Rites and Board of Works were responsible, for example, for the preservation of imperial temples and graves.[16] Moreover, the Chinese classical system of government, by cohering symbolically about a single emperor, avoided becoming a "household government" because the ineluctable pressures of business of a vast empire forced upon its officials a comprehensive array of duties. Because Vietnamese officials had less business to transact, the absence of enough institutional precautions against a "household focus" in politics was occasionally more serious. The distinction between central government and local territorial duties was also blurred. Until 1835 high Board officials, rather than a local power holder like the capital city prefect, were responsible in turn for monthly tours of inspection of the crop lands adjoining Huế.[17] "Functional specificity" was even less in evidence in the Vietnamese bureaucracy than it was in the Chinese. At the same time it was probably more in evidence in Vietnam than it was in contemporary Thai and Burmese governments.

The internal structures of the Vietnamese boards reflected both a desire to conform to current Chinese models and an inveterate unwillingness to jettison influences and terms of the past. Each board had a president or *thượng-thư* to match the *shang-shu* of Ming–Ch'ing boards. But the two vice-presidents of each Vietnamese board were called *tham-tri*, a title which had existed in China (*ts'an-chih cheng-shih*) from the T'ang through the Yüan but which the Chinese had abandoned from the Ming period on. The third highest board officials were the two *thị-lang* (*shih-lang* in Chinese, the vice-presidents of the Ming–Ch'ing boards), who were added in a faintly conformist afterthought by Minh-mạng in 1826.[18] Like the Ming–Ch'ing boards, the Vietnamese boards at this point subdivided themselves into panels or *thanh-lại-ty* (*ch'ing-li-ssu* in Chinese). The panels were staffed, Ming–Ch'ing fashion, by directors (*lang-trung*), vice-directors (*viên ngoại lang*), and secretaries (*chủ sự*).

Despite the fact that Nguyễn Vietnam was not very much more than the size of a Ch'ing province, the Huế Six Boards as a whole had almost 100 directors, vice-directors, and secretaries serving on their panels in the mid-1840's, as compared to an equivalent figure of more than 400 in Peking.[19] This comparison reveals the very real importance of the hundreds of documentary clerks or *pi-t'ieh-shih* at the Peking boards; the Vietnamese boards were largely without them. Dominated by the exigencies of the business of a vast empire, the Chinese board panels were often monuments to regional diversification. The Ch'ing Board of Finance possessed 14 *ch'ing-li-ssu* devoted to the affairs of 14 provincial groupings. The Ch'ing Board of Justice had 17 such panels. The Nguyễn Board of Finance, on the other hand, was subdivided (after 1844) into 6 *thanh-lại-ty*, only 4 of which looked after regional interests. The four regions were, of course, the northern provinces (*Bắc-kỳ*), the southern provinces (*Nam-kỳ*), the four inner "metropolitan" provinces about Huế, and the provinces immediately north and south of the metropolitan ones.

A dissection of the internal structures of the Six Boards hardly tells the true story of their significance in the Huế world. It must not be forgotten that when the Vietnamese borrowed institutions from China the borrowing process itself was bureaucratically managed— by regular Nguyễn officials. Bureaucratic discipline naturally produced a formalistic approach to administration. After all, promotions were won by adhering scrupulously to a body of written rules. Because institutional borrowing was a constituent feature of administration in Vietnam, in the minds of Vietnamese officials disciplined conformance to the Chinese model often became an immediate value in itself, thanks perhaps to this inherent professional exaltation of written rules. The patterns of Chinese institutions received as much stress as their original purposes. In 1838 Minh-Mạng, claiming that the business of the Board of Appointments was less difficult than that of the Board of Works, subtracted ten unranked clerical officials from the former and added them to the staff of the latter. A censor, Lê Đăng Doanh, protested vehemently: "The business of the Board of Appointments may not be comparable in complexity to that of this other board, but the matters that devolve upon it are not excessively simple. Moreover, the Board of Appointments is senior among the six offices. Consequently it ranks first among civil official bodies. For the sake of political decorum its old quota of officials should be maintained."[20] Ten clerks without bureaucratic rank could not change places without causing an uproar. The Six Boards had become symbols of formal Chinese-style hierarchy. These symbolic attributes, which had become so closely attached to them, threatened the ruler's ability to make even minor innovations. Such battles between symbolic primacy and functional primacy possessed a chronic sharpness in Huế which historians will find less readily in Peking.

In borrowing institutions and techniques from the greatest bureaucratic tradition in history, Vietnamese courts, including the Nguyễn, inevitably brought the Chinese Censorate to their country. Although senior censors were highly ranked bureaucrats, the burden of making the Chinese censorial system work usually fell upon more lowly ranked censorial officials. These men traveled throughout the provinces of China passing judgment upon provincial officials more highly ranked than they, in confidential memorials to the throne. The twin premises of this system were, of course, that "insiders" in an organization are likely to evaluate its achievements more favorably than "outsiders" and that members with higher status in an organization are likely to evaluate its achievements more favorably than members with lower status. The emperor was outside the bureaucracy, and he valued the information of its lower status censors. These two premises have not yet hardened into cliches in Western political and sociological theory. But for centuries, along with other insights still undiscovered by formal organizations in the West, they were commonplaces in Chinese bureaucratic formulas.

For the most part, the Nguyễn Censorate (*Đô Sát Viện*) was a scrupulous copy of its Ch'ing model. Its senior officials were called Censor-in-chief of the Left (*tả đô ngự sử*) and Censor-in-chief of the Right (*hữu đô ngự sử*). The Censor-in-chief of the Left was the conventional head of the institution.[21] The Vietnamese Censorate, like the Chinese one, sheltered six "offices of scrutiny" (*lục khoa; liu-k'o* in Chinese) with six "senior supervising secretaries" (*chưởng ấn cấp sự trung*) attached to them. This organization compared with the twelve senior supervising secretaries and twelve supervising secretaries (*chi-shih-chung*) attached to the six offices of scrutiny of the Peking Censorate. However, in 1837 Minh-mạng increased the numbers of Vietnamese supervising secretaries slightly. His reason was that "I hear that at the Northern Court . . . each censorial office and circuit has five or six censors apiece."[22] Each office of scrutiny kept its critical eye on several specific government bodies. For example, the office of scrutiny of finance (*hộ khoa*) watched the Board of Finance, the imperial household department, and the transport administration (*taò chính*) for evidence of misdeeds.

The Vietnamese Censorate differed from the Ch'ing one in at least two ways. The Ch'ing Censorate had twice as many chief censors, just as the Ch'ing Six Boards had twice as many presidents and assistants as each of their Vietnamese counterparts. The purpose was to give Manchus a number of high positions in the Ch'ing bureaucracy equal to the number of high positions held by Chinese. These strangely expanded numbers of the bicultural Ch'ing dyarchy had no relevance in Huế and were not imitated.

The second difference was more important. The six "offices of scrutiny" within the Vietnamese Censorate played shrunken roles in comparison to the duties of their Ch'ing counterparts. The Nguyễn bureaucracy was smaller and less complex than its model. As a result, Vietnamese emperors did not borrow and apply extensively all the devices for bureaucratic control which Chinese courts had developed. For one thing, the almost interminable Ch'ing "laws of avoidance" were poorly developed in Vietnam, as will be shown. Vietnamese censors were not so frequently required to inspect the kinship ties of provincial officials, in order to ensure that they had no relatives serving under them or near them. Furthermore, Vietnamese officials traveling to and from provincial offices were not governed by travel regulations as systematically as Ch'ing officials. Time limits in the Nguyễn bureaucracy were less comprehensive. Thus the Vietnamese office of scrutiny of appointments (*lại khoa*) was not compelled, like its Chinese counterpart, to ascertain whether individual officials had traveled from the capital to their provincial posts within the time limits granted them (30 days to K'ai-feng prefecture in Honan, 158 days to Ili),[23] or whether "expectant" officials living in their home provinces had observed the time limits in going to posts in other provinces.

Censors most active in exercising the power to impeach fellow officials were "investigating censors" (*giám sát ngự sử*). These men were assigned to 16 circuits (*đạo*), which included all Vietnam. They matched the Ch'ing *chien-ch'a-shih*, who belonged to 15 Chinese circuits. In addition to surveying the provincial administrations comprehended by their circuits, the investigating censors collaborated with the censors at the six offices of scrutiny in watching specific Huế offices. They also carried out miscellaneous tasks like serving as inspectors at examination sites. More important, the censors of the 16 circuits and the six offices of scrutiny supplied a pool of officials from whom were drawn the "officials who note the emperor's risings and reclinings" (*khởi cư chú viên*). These officials were two censors who wrote down every word the emperor spoke while he was transacting business. They followed him (after 1834) into every pavilion in Huế unless he took formal precautions to grant a secret audience[24] and in general made it possible for posterity to have a full account of his idiosyncrasies. Again, this was a faithful domestication of Chinese practices.

Vietnamese censors never really significantly enlarged in Huế the sphere of influence which their Chinese exemplars enjoyed within the Chinese bureaucracy in Peking. In this respect they were unlike traditional Korean censors. In matters of policy in the 1830's more than one Huế censor exhibited the philosophically conservative, anti-Western attitude that Chinese censors were soon to demonstrate so remarkably. Vietnamese censors were just as courageous as their Chinese counterparts in rebuking individual emperors. An unforgettable example is Giang Văn Hiển's attack on the poetry-loving Thiệu-trị in 1842.[25] Although no very tangible evidence exists to support his pretensions, it is still significant that Minh-mạng should have prided himself upon preserving greater freedom of speech at his own court than he thought prevailed at Peking. He said in the early 1830's: "A Ch'ing Tao-kuang edict once said that because in the Chia-ch'ing period [1796–1821] there had been a court lecturer who, in expounding classical writings, had intended to mock the court . . . that from this point court classical lectures were to be abandoned . . . Surely one should not instantly cause the lectures to languish just because of this one thing? I would not behave that way. Between myself and all my officials equally there is nothing that we know that we do not say, nothing that we say

that we do not say to the utmost . . . [An example like that of the
Ch'ing lecturer] is something shameful and despicable!''[26]

*Nguyễn Variations within the Basic Administrative Plan Borrowed from
China*

The names of Vietnamese central civil institutions, the titles of
their officials, and even their descriptions in the Vietnamese court
statutes, all displayed a deliberate correspondence to the institutions
and titles of the Chinese central civil government. But because
Vietnamese society itself did not correspond nearly so neatly to
Chinese society and because the real institutions of a people are
often actually systematized in a manner different from and perhaps
in a manner more simple than the one explicitly formulated, such a
correspondence is treacherous and misleading. This generalization
applies not only to Vietnamese borrowing from China but also to
the borrowing of Chinese institutions by other East Asian peoples
like the Koreans and the Japanese.

In fact an outstanding cautionary example is that of the early
eighth-century Japanese adoption of T'ang administrative laws
which governed bureaucratic grades. The original T'ang code
emphasized the distinction between graded bureaucrats and those
too lowly to be graded. In practice its Nara imitation sought instead
to draw a line between the ranks of the Japanese imperial princes
and the positions of more remote nobles outside the imperial family.
T'ang and Nara social structures were completely different. Yet on
paper the Japanese changed only one character in the three-charac-
ter classical Chinese title of the T'ang institutional code they were
borrowing. The Chinese version, *kuan-p'in-ling*, became *kan-i-ryō* in
Japan; the character "grade" became the character "position" or
"status."[27]

A mere change of a single character in the transposition of an
institution from Peking to Huế was almost equally likely to provide
a deceptively modest surface index to starkly divergent sub-surface
patterns. As has been shown, many factors worked to produce close
copies of Chinese institutions in Vietnam: the group interest of the

scholar class, bureaucratic professional conservatism, a determination to preserve political independence from China through Chinese-style centralization. Yet historians must still view Nguyễn Vietnam's China-like statutes with intelligent skepticism.

For one thing, the Vietnamese elite of the early 1800's believed that their society was far from stable. They felt that they were witnessing profound institutional change. But this was change of a different kind from that of the revolutionary twentieth century. It did not involve a revolution of social structure or rural-urban acculturation or a rejection of traditional ideology. Early nineteenth-century Vietnamese intellectuals conceived of change as taking place in an "arena" or on a moving "theatrical stage" (*cuộc hí-trường*)—a restricted, socially homogeneous environment. They assumed that such change circulated at the top of Nguyễn society and did not rapidly penetrate downward into non-political rural society. But the corollary of this assumption was that change was all the more rapid and concentrated within the purlieu of the court and the bureaucracy. The esoteric court view of Vietnamese institutional borrowing from China in the 1800's was confident and optimistic. The more exoteric reaction to this process, of intelligent Vietnamese outside the court but still within the educated oligarchy, was less enthusiastic. The bitter pages of the poetry of the northern poetess Bà Huyện Thanh Quan, who lived at this time, provide illustrations of this attitude:

> Why does the Creator have to set up such an arena?
> So many years have flown by [from the beginning]
>   until now.
> The ancient paths of the horse carriages are completely
>   enveloped by weeds,
> The old foundations of the once great homesteads
>   are lit by the setting sun.
> But the stones still remain unmoved and steadfast
>   from season to season,
> And the waters still ripple with frowns at the
>   rapid changes.
> This thousand year old mirror reflects the present
>   and the past.

There is the scene, and here we are, cut to pieces
by sadness.[28]

The city of Hanoi, only barely described, was supposedly the subject of this poem, "In Remembrance of Thăng Long" ("Thăng Long thành hoài cổ"). But more than dynastic and regional loyalism echoed here. The "arena"—a word that appears in many other Vietnamese writings of the early 1800's— was really a state of mind. The uncertainties of institutional acculturation, which existed in Vietnam but not in China, were profound. Because Vietnamese scholars could not predict in advance which Chinese institutions would be renewed or introduced in Vietnam after 1802 and which would not, many of them lacked deep role commitments or self-conceptions as officials in the period immediately after 1802, so that rules and guidelines which governed their actions at particular times and places in the "arena" or "stage" were indispensable. Procedural specificity, and conservatism of terminology, provided antidotes to the tensions of acculturation. Some of the terminology of the Nguyễn bureaucracy, by lagging behind that of the Chinese bureaucracy several centuries in time, minimized the psychological impact on the Vietnamese elite of the "thousand year old mirror's" changing cross-cultural reflections.

Thus the Vietnamese written bureaucratic language tended to remain more frozen and unchanging than its Chinese equivalent. Terms which had become archaic or semi-archaic in Peking appeared quite regularly as echoes from an older Chinese past in nineteenth-century Vietnamese documents. Nguyễn bureaucratic credentials were often called *cáo-thân*.[29] This was a phrase which would have been more familiar to T'ang Chinese officials than to Ch'ing ones, who called credentials *kao-ch'ih*. Vietnamese degree winners at regional examinations from 1807 to the mid-1820's were known as *hương-cống* (*hsiang-kung* in Chinese), which again was a term in use in T'ang China rather than in the China of the 1800's. A category which appeared on the officially issued vouchers for merchants in the northern Vietnamese provinces after 1836 was the expression *sắc-mục*.[30] It may have referred to the racial origins of the merchants. But it probably descended from the famous term conventionally designating "racial miscellany" (*se-mu* in Chinese), which was in official vogue in China only briefly under the alien Yüan dynasty.

If anything, this conservatism, a source of stability within the acculturation process, only heightens the impression that Vietnam offered a strikingly rigid institutional loyalty to China. But if the denotations of the Sino-Vietnamese words which Vietnamese officials spoke or wrote were the same as the denotations of these words in China, often imperceptibly their connotations changed. For example, a greater gulf separated the bureaucratic written language from the ordinary spoken language in Huế than it did in Peking. Thus classical Chinese words of respect often sounded more unnaturally formal to Vietnamese ears than they did to Chinese. Only this peculiarity explains why Minh-mạng went to such great lengths to persuade his Board of Appointments, in 1835, that when he issued written credentials to his provincial governors-general, the Sino-Vietnamese written term of address which he should personally use to refer to them should be *nhĩ* rather than *khanh*. Both words meant "you." But the latter, *khanh*, was far more respectful. In Vietnam use of it would obviously confer too much prestige upon those whom it designated.[31] Hence it never became politically functional, although it did appear in the historical records from time to time as part of a lifeless classical Chinese representation, never actually spoken, of the emperor's non-classical Chinese conversation with his ministers.

More important, Vietnamese rulers would use politically sacramental Chinese historical terms to classify realities in Vietnam that were not, in substance, truly susceptible to such classification. The most vivid demonstration of this tendency is probably found in the system of "allotment lands" (*khẩu phân điền chế*), which Gia-long introduced in 1804. This system was intended both to endow his chief supporters with estates and, at the same time, to halt the regional economic depredations of landlords who had flourished during the Tây-sơn rebellion. These landlords had taken advantage of the decay of the public land registers but had not necessarily rallied to the Nguyễns.

The name of Gia-long's system (ultimately derived from the *Kung-yang chuan*, *Tradition of Kung-yang*, a Chinese classic of the third century B.C.) was intended to evoke memories of T'ang China's

"equal-field system." In this system each adult male was awarded
100 *mou* of land, 20 of which were permanently his and 80 of which
were returned to the state when he left its tax registers in his old age.
But in early nineteenth-century Vietnam lands were allotted hierarchically, not equally. A bureaucrat who ranked 1A received 15
parts (*phân*) of land, a 2A official received 14 parts, a 9B official, who
was lowest ranked, received 8 parts, and the most land a vigorous,
taxpaying adult male peasant could expect to receive was 6½
parts. According to this 1804 law, ranked officials who resigned
from their posts were still allowed to retain the "land allotments"
and "seating order" (presumably in village groups and lineage
meetings) which their original rank had brought them. But unranked
lesser officials who withdrew from "current service" had their
"seating order" modified so that they occupied a position ahead of
taxpaying peasants but behind scholars who had won tax and
corvee exemption through local tests.[32] The system's first purpose,
that of buttressing Gia-long's newly created official hierarchy, was
patent. Its second purpose, that of making the distribution of lands
among all non-bureaucratic classes more equitable, achieved negli-
gible results. Although great aristocratic Chinese families continued
to hold vast parcels of land under the T'ang equal-field system, the
T'ang system had not created their estates for them the way the
Nguyễn system did; the discrepancy between the T'ang memory
and the Nguyễn law was considerable.

The salvation of the peasantry in each cluster of villages was
supposed to lie in the "public lands" (*công điền*), which theoretically
belonged to the local village as a whole. A law of 1803 forbade the
villages to sell these lands. They could be rented to private cultiva-
tors, but only for a maximum of three years. The rent money had to
be devoted to village business. Landlords who bought village public
lands in defiance of this ban forfeited their investment. In 1844 the
law was reissued with added refinements. Village leaders (*xã trưởng*)
lost the power to decide whether such lands could even be rented
for three years. Now, the written rental documents had to be signed
as well by ten members of the village. These documents had to
explain the villagers' emergency which necessitated the renting of
the lands. They also had to specify which lands were being rented
and what their values were.[33]

Unhappily, however, village public lands were virtually non-existent in recently settled southern Vietnam before the 1830's.[34] Bureaucratic and non-bureaucratic landlords do not appear to have been fettered very successfully by the court anywhere in Vietnam. It is difficult to deny the verisimilitude of Hồ Biểu Chánh's twentieth-century historical novel, whose setting is the early Nguyễn period, *Ngọn cỏ gió đùa* (The stalk of grass the wind plays with; published in the early 1930's). In this novel his famous peasant hero, Lê Văn Đỏ, is imprisoned for stealing a cooking pot. It would have been difficult for him to have stolen much land.

In a sense this early Nguyễn distribution of land ownership and control upon the basis of a hierarchy of official ranks was more the characteristic of a so-called feudal society than of a so-called bureaucratic one. It was reminiscent of contemporary early nineteenth-century Southeast Asian societies like Burma, where high officials received the revenues of whole districts and lower officials were assigned lands on the royal domain. But as the Vietnamese civil power structure became more Chinese in form, the Chinese bureaucratic tradition of fixed monetary salaries for officials, rather than simple apportionments of land, was introduced piece by piece. Contemporaries viewed the rise of a bureaucratic salary system in Vietnam as an important political landmark.

Yet the precise historical beginning of fixed salaries in Nguyễn Vietnam is difficult to locate. Trương Quốc Dụng, who wrote in the middle of the 1800's, was both a bureaucrat himself and a dedicated private historian of the bureaucracy. He stated that graded salaries in cash and rice for the entire civil hierarchy were initiated in 1816. This scheme of 1816, he claimed, had continued unaltered until 1839–40, when it had been reorganized.[35] In 1813, at least, if the contents of a state granary in the provinces were destroyed, the negligent local official involved was required to indemnify the court not with money but with oxen. This law explicitly belonged to a pre-salary age.[36]

But in 1813 an important court debate took place between Gia-long and his ministers over the question of creating a salary system. The debate concluded with Gia-long saying, "My intention is to consult and institute the stipends for officials of the imperial Ch'ing."[37] In 1814 Gia-long granted all district magistrates serving in provinces from Quảng Bình south a monthly salary of money and rice and a yearly sum of money for "spring clothes."[38] In 1825 Minh-mạng began to award exiguous stipends to sub-officials.[39] The real turning point probably did not come until 1839, when a graduated salary system was devised which paid fixed salaries in money and rice to officials from 1A to 3B in bureaucratic rank twice a year, to those from 4A to 7B four times a year, and to those from 8A to 9B once a month. The yearly sum of money a 1A official received (400 *quan*) was more than 21 times the yearly salary of a ninth grade official (18 *quan*). It was only in 1839–40, significantly, that the court attempted to deny participation in the communal profits of the "public lands" in their neighborhoods to salaried bureaucrats and to reserve these profits exclusively for peasants and unsalaried sub-bureaucrats.[40]

But what really distinguished the Vietnamese court's payment of its officials from that of other Southeast Asian societies, and ultimately brought it into belated conformity with its Ch'ing model, was its dispensing of special salaries to provincial officials. These were known as salaries "to nourish incorruptibility" (*dưỡng liêm*). The name (*yang-lien* in Chinese) and the practice were borrowed directly from Ch'ing China, which had been paying these special stipends since the first half of the eighteenth century. The rationale of this practice was, of course, to give local officials with expensive assignments a better chance of remaining solvent—and thus honest—and yet avoid having to pay them the status-conferring large primary salaries of high ministers. In Vietnam *dưỡng liêm* money was paid to prefects and district magistrates on a sliding scale commencing one month after they went to their posts (according to a law of 1831).[41] District magistrates often received only two thirds as much as prefects. Until the late 1830's the money was paid on a graduated scale of bureaucratic rank. In 1838–39 the law changed, functional considerations now transcending hierarchical ones. Prefects and district magistrates in "the most demanding jurisdictions" received 100 percent of the original sums, those in "demanding jurisdictions" received 80 percent, those in "median jurisdictions" received 60 percent, and those in "easy jurisdictions" received only 50 percent.[42] In this way dynastic expenditures were stabilized.

If the Nguyễn salary system eventually became, on paper at least, a fairly literal adoption of a Chinese institution, with other Ch'ing institutions the Vietnamese court was less successful. In fact, Vietnamese borrowing from China exhibited the usual variegated patterns of acculturation in which some institutions and objects spread rapidly from one society to another, some spread more slowly, and some do not spread at all or are rejected. Almost from the beginning of the nineteenth century a Vietnamese postal service existed, under dynastic auspices. It consisted of one chain of post stations extending north from Huế to the China border and another chain running south from Huế to Cambodia and to the Gulf of Siam. It was under the management of the Huế Board of War. In 1805, significantly, there appear to have been 36 stations between Huế and Hanoi. But there were only 7 between Hanoi and the Chinese border, which was considered then to be at least one quarter of the Huế-Hanoi distance.[43] The stations served also as inns. Travelers in the early nineteenth century countryside had to choose between them, the reluctantly offered amenities of the local canton chief's home, and the homespun hospitality of the real inn, whose "roof of rugged wild grass thatch" was vividly described in a contemporary poem by Hồ Xuân Hương.[44]

In 1804 the statutory deadline for the transmission of a public document by this system from the Saigon area to Huế was 13 days. That for a document from the area around Hanoi to Huế was 5 days. Couriers were flogged if they were more than 2 days behind the deadline.[45] By 1820 the service had apparently improved to the extent where a "most urgent" communication from Saigon could be delivered in Huế ideally within 9 days.[46] The organizational rules of the service were continuously being elaborated in the 1820's and 1830's. After 1833, for example, "most urgent" communications and memorials from the south to Huế were sent instantly. Those of "secondary urgence" were sent twice a day in the early morning and at dusk. And "ordinary" ones were sent in periodic batches once every three days.[47]

Underneath these superficial triumphs, the service never managed to function as smoothly in Nguyễn Vietnam as it did in Ch'ing China. Minor abuses and flaws in the service in China became major abuses and flaws in Southeast Asia. The inner life of the Vietnamese institution differed.

Close relatives of local officials rode the horses and exploited them on private, non-urgent business. Horses, rare in an environment where normal official travel was by boat, foot, and even by elephant, were expensive and therefore became preeminent focuses of corruption. In provinces remote from Huế, men who lacked bureaucratic credentials nonetheless found it easy to usurp the service and use it for their own purposes. Unofficial, locally appointed couriers and agents emerged to whom the regular, centrally designated members of the postal hierarchy became subservient, as Minh-mạng admitted in 1820.[48] It was one thing to construct bureaucratic institutions, imported from China, in Huế and its immediate environs. It was another thing to make Chinese bureaucratic machinery work at all levels, in all the provinces. Here the facade of bureaucratization sometimes wore thin.

This problem of the extent to which Chinese bureaucratic characteristics really dominated Vietnamese provincial administration in the 1800's is a crucial one, not easily resolved. In Huế it was remarkable how carefully the Vietnamese imitated the complex Chinese organization and formalizations of official appointments—initial commissions (*trừ*), supplementary appointments (*bổ*), changes from one post to an equivalent one within the same hierarchy (*chuyển*), changes from one hierarchy to another (*cải*), promotions (*thăng*), and transfers (*điều*)—and the complex Chinese subdivisions of rewards and punishments. But the Chinese bureaucracy was also famous, particularly outside Peking, for its "laws of avoidance." These laws gave the Chinese emperor an important means of controlling his officials. They also spread a spirit of impersonality and universalism throughout an administration that governed a society in which the moral qualities of particularistic attachments were venerated. The bureaucrat became a bureaucrat for the sake of family interests. If these family interests grew too strong they could destroy the bureaucracy. Yet paradoxically these interests also constituted the source of the motivations which made it work. The "laws of avoidance" controlled these interests. The laws contributed to that formalization of relationships without which uniformity and coordination, in a civil service where the distance between decision making and administrative operation was vast, would have been impossible.

Basically, Ch'ing laws stipulated that active officials should avoid (1) their home provinces and native places, (2) their relatives, (3) officials who had examined them or whom they themselves had examined. Officials in the Chinese Boards of Finance and Justice could not deal with any fiscal or judicial matters which concerned their home provinces. Provincial officials in China could not serve in their home provinces or in posts within 500 li of their native place; and (after 1742) if they had resided long in Peking they could not serve in Chihli either. In addition to having to "avoid" members of his lineage, a Chinese provincial official also was specifically prohibited from having his maternal grandfather and uncles, his wife's father and brothers, his brothers-in-law, or his cousins on the maternal as well as paternal sides of his family, serve in bureaucratic positions near him.[49] Far from tallying only with the formal patterns of patrilineal association of the Chinese family structure, Ch'ing laws of avoidance candidly took account as well of the informal patterns behind them.

These laws of avoidance were never duplicated in their entirety by the smaller Vietnamese bureaucracy. A law of 1831 forbade the recruiting of the registrars in district yamens from the localities in which they served. But it was not until 1844 that "avoidance" (*hồi ty*) was inaugurated, in provincial yamens, of all relatives within the patrilineal five mourning degrees. In contrast to China, with the exception of brothers-in-law, relatives by marriage did not fall within the ambit of the prohibitions. On the whole, Nguyễn "avoidance" policies were passive rather than active. Particularistic proximities among provincial officials were tolerated, unless flagrant misgovernment occurred as a result.[50] More "universalistic" than those of other Southeast Asian societies, perhaps, Vietnamese administration was less so in terms of promulgated rules than Chinese administration. Once again, in this three-dimensional perspective, Vietnamese political society followed the middle way.

The Imperial Secretariats and the Flow of Information from Village to Throne

Because in both Ch'ing China and Nguyễn Vietnam the emperor, in theory, made all the important decisions, the administrative hierarchy under him possessed two purposes. One was to produce a reliable upward flow of information upon which his decisions could be based. The other, of course, was to carry out his decisions and, by the use of the hierarchical status system within the bureaucracy itself, to give the imperial laws and statutes that passed downward through it immediate as well as ultimate authoritativeness.

Of all the features of the Ch'ing bureaucracy which it borrowed, perhaps the nineteenth-century Vietnamese court valued most the techniques of the Chinese hierarchical status system. Ideally, these techniques were designed to induce a desire for imitative harmony among the lower levels of the civil service as well as respect for authority, which by itself was not enough. The Ch'ing and Nguyễn bureaucracies were not the formidable instruments of oriental despotism that they seemed. Individual emperors had to consider many policies at once. They lacked both the time and the information to formulate policies specifically and in detail. Consequently, they delegated this power to underlings. Underlings in turn reshaped policies, in giving them greater practical specificity at lower levels. The self-interest, perceptions of reality, supplies of information, and goals of these underlings might diverge dramatically from those of the throne, especially in times of social unrest. Thus many of the activities that occurred in the traditional Chinese and Vietnamese bureaucracies were completely unrelated to the goals of the throne or even of the highest officials. Vietnamese emperors, beginning with Minh-mạng, relied upon a tightly status-bound bureaucratic communications system, borrowed from China, to maintain their control in the face of three weaknesses in their position: inadequate time to consider business, inadequate information, and inadequate contact with the villages. In doing so, they created a fourth weakness: administrative inflexibility.

The Ch'ing hierarchy of statuses played a vital part in giving authoritativeness to the passage of communications and orders in China. Despite the inappropriateness of its huge scale, the Vietnamese were assiduous in copying it. Management of administrative communications in the Chinese manner demanded it. First of all, after 1831 Vietnam's provinces were ruled by a Chinese-style hierarchy of officials. From the top down, it included governors-general or *tổng đốc*, whose responsibilities spanned two or three provinces each; provincial governors or *tuần phủ*; provincial financial and judicial commissioners or *bố-chính-sứ* and *án-sát-sứ* respectively; and, below the provincial level, prefects (*tri phủ*) and district magistrates (*tri huyện*). Second, it was the duty of these officials to transmit information, and recommendations for action, upward. Following the Chinese fashion, the documents which the governors-general, governors, and commissioners sent to Huế were called memorials (*tấu*). Third, except in extraordinary circumstances, memorials were received and processed by a variety of secretarial agencies before the emperor actually saw them.

Under Gia-long there were three small secretariats at Huế, the Thị Thư Viện, the Thị Hàn Viện, and the Nội Hàn Viện. Lack of sufficient documentation makes their historical roles obscure. But it is probable that the first two secretariats drafted and stored decrees and other official papers while the third one applied itself to the emperor's personal writings and papers. Above them supervened a loosely defined council of ministers, commonly called the Công Đồng (its full title was Hội Đồng Đình Thần Công Đồng). It met for joint discussions four days a month (the second, the ninth, the sixteenth, and the twenty-fourth days) in the headquarters of the military rather than the civil bureaucracy at Huế. It was charged with solving, in the words of an 1805 statute, "all important matters which the middle rank officials of all yamens have been unable to decide; all provincial litigation and judicial cases which have not yet been redressed; and all grievances of soldiers and civilians whose circumstances cry out."[51] Both the leading military commanders and high civil officials were members of it. Its passive, tribunal-like posture was representative of the decentralized, military simplicity of Gia-long's reign. Before 1816, even at the most formal court audiences in Huế, clothing which indicated rank was not always worn. Military and civil officials did not always form distinct ranks on opposite sides of the court. And bowing to the emperor was far from automatic.[52] But after 1820 Gia-long's three secretariats and Công Đồng began to disappear, and from 1820 to 1829 the most important secretariat in Huế was the Văn-thư-phòng.

The creation of the Văn-thư-phòng in 1820 marked an important step forward toward a Vietnamese approximation of the Chinese conception of an imperial secretariat. Its personnel ranged from high officials to "apprentices" (*hành tẩu*), who were often, as in 1826, regional examination degree holders actually recruited by officials at the examination sites.[53] Its officials worked in shifts, and it exhibited the increasing discretion which is usually a behavioral hallmark of bureaucratic consolidation; in 1820 Minh-mạng forbade 20 clerks of Gia-long's old, less secret secretariats to enter it.[54] It was especially charged with signing and certifying every five days the records of the seven sub-treasuries of the imperial household (*Nội vụ phủ*). It stored the secondary copies of the expenditures records of the Board of Finance, the primary copies being kept at the Board itself.[55] Minh-mạng continued Gia-long's custom of holding ordinary audiences four times a month, which were attended by Huế civil officials from the fifth grade up, as well as two more ceremonial "great audiences" a month. But the Văn-thư-phòng did not function consistently as a policy-making or policy-suggesting organ. In the 1820's it was the Board of Appointments, not the Văn-thư-phòng, which processed memorials from the provinces and presented them to the emperor.[56]

More than a quarter of a century after the dynasty was founded, in 1829–1830, the Vietnamese court finally established a court secretariat which linked itself in name and operation to a Peking institution. The Văn-thư-phòng was suddenly subsumed under a new and larger body, the Nội Các or Grand Secretariat. This Vietnamese Grand Secretariat consisted of four senior officials; 28 underlings or *thuộc-viên*, who served as readers, copyists, and recorders (by 1844 the number of *thuộc-viên* had risen to 34); and 8 more apprentices.[57] It was, of course, far smaller than its unwieldy, multi-racial Ch'ing model, which comprehended roughly 250 specific positions, more than half of which were filled by Manchus.[58] The bureaucratic ranks of the Huế Grand Secretariat's recorders and copyists were low. Its higher officials, who naturally took the importance of bureaucratic rank more seriously than the ruler outside the bureaucracy, tended to appoint underlings and clerks of corresponding rank at the Six Boards to these posts, rather than scholars from the examination system. Because the Secretariat's copyists were nonetheless responsible for initiating some of the most sensitive administrative work in the bureaucracy, by 1847 the Nguyễn court was becoming increasingly alarmed at their "clerical backgrounds and superficial learning."[59]

The Grand Secretariat was as internally differentiated as its predecessor, the Văn-thư-phòng, had been. It possessed four subordinate offices which changed their names several times in the period 1829–1845 but retained the same basic division of responsibilities. As it was known in 1845, the Thượng Bửu Sở (Imperial Seals Office) preserved vermilion copies of all proclamations dispensing the imperial favor, the rough copies of all patents conferring titles of honor on high officials, the secondary copies of edicts and decrees, and of course the seals of various government agencies. The Ty Luân Sở (Imperial Legislation Office; literally, "Silk Threads Office") studied, and drafted comments upon, memorials. It also preserved such documents as the daily "lecture and study" diaries of the various imperial princes and secondary copies of the annual judicial records. The Bí Thư Sở (Imperial Books Office) stored collections of imperial poetry and all documents, maps, and communications relating to diplomatic relations. Here the classical style was mirrored even in secretarial substructures: because nothing was ever considered fundamentally to change in foreign relations, literature concerning them was kept apart from court business. Finally, the Bản Chương Sở (Imperial Records Office) received memorials, records, and their supplements from the first two offices at the end of every month, categorized them, catalogued them, and bound them into archives (*đang án*).[60] Such a functional subdivision was impeccably secretarial in appearance. Where then lies the administrative (and "administrative" means "political" in an agrarian-bureaucratic political society) significance of the Grand Secretariat?

The fact of the matter was that in Ch'ing China the Grand Secretariat (*Nei-ko* in Chinese) had slowly subsided into a position of secondary importance in Ch'ing government. It performed its duties under the shadow of the more powerful Grand Council (*Chűn-chi-ch'u*). It was allowed to deal with routine memorials (*t'i-pen*), but it did not usually deal with the more important—and more secret—incoming memorials known as *tsou-che*, which were processed by the Council.[61] Each day imperial edicts were received by the Ch'ing Grand Council; "Those that ought to be sent out to be copied are all to be sent down to the Secretariat."[62]

Eighteenth- and early nineteenth-century Chinese statutes, however, failed formally to express all the real ramifications of the

Grand Council's influence and the Grand Secretariat's decline. To curious but distant Southeast Asian eyes, the power of the Chinese Grand Secretariat, like the power of the light from a dying star, ironically still seemed to be more formidable than it actually was. Classical rigorists in Huế, of whom the emperor was one, commanded most of the available *historical* literature on Ming-Ch'ing institutions but lacked much experience with the institutions themselves. By the 1820's the available literature on Ch'ing secretarial institutions was out of date.

The result was that Minh-mạng was obsessed with the fear, not of creating a weak Grand Secretariat, but of establishing one that might become too strong. He became determined to rewrite Ming history in Vietnam, and give it a different ending, two centuries after the Ming court had collapsed. In his decree creating the Nội Các in 1829 he declared that no official higher than third grade (3A) in his bureaucracy could ever become a member of his Secretariat. Furthermore, he explicitly required ministers of his Secretariat to stand behind all the board presidents at court audiences. He forbade his heirs ever to increase the rank of Secretariat ministers. He also personally made certain that copies of his edict were distributed to all government agencies.[63] The prestigious title of "scholar of great learning" (*đại học sĩ*; *ta-hsüeh-shih* in Chinese), which usually indicated senior officials of the Grand Secretariat in Peking, most certainly did not refer to them in Huế. Because this title was synonymous with high rank, in Vietnam it indicated scholars who had no political role at all. The dead hand of late Ming history, when Grand Secretariats were dominant in China, exercised a lively influence in Huế in 1829.

Chinese and Vietnamese Grand Secretariats essentially affected history by their role of editing and pre-digesting bureaucratic communications for emperors. In Vietnam secret memorials (*mật chiếp*) from the provinces and, after 1839, all memorials concerning the sailing of government junks from Đà Nẵng to foreign countries,[64] were sent directly to an inner office at Huế called the Thị Vệ Sở. More ordinary incoming memorials were received at Huế by the Transmission Office or Thông Chính Ty. This office had been created in 1834 merely to relieve the strain upon the postal service of deciding which memorial should first be seen by which government yamen.[65] Originally, in Chinese theory, a memorial was presented to the emperor, he gave his reaction to it orally, his secretaries embodied his reaction in writing, and he endorsed what they had written. In practice, however, both in China and in Nguyễn Vietnam, laws were made differently. The Grand Secretariats read the types of memorials that they were allowed to see long before the ruler did. They summarized these memorials for him, and then drafted their own proposals of what they thought his imperial response should be.

These proposals were first drafted on "rough slips" (*thảo kiểm*; *ts'ao-ch'ien* in Chinese), by underlings at the Secretariats, and then studied by senior officials. The proposals were next converted, if the senior officials approved, to "primary slips" (*chính kiểm*; *cheng-ch'ien* in Chinese), which, in Ch'ing China, were written in both Chinese and Manchu. The whole process of writing these proposals was called "tally suggestion" (*phiếu nghĩ*; *p'iao-i* in Chinese). When the emperor received the suggestions he could reject them outright and send down a separate decree; he could modify them with his vermilion brush; or he could simply sign them in acceptance.

But it is a measure of how irregularly the emperor really governed, even in small Vietnam, that in 1837 Minh-mạng threatened to punish his Secretariat officials if he were forced personally to change more than "three or four characters" upon the tally suggestions he received from them.[66] In making appointments and promotions within the bureaucracy, of course, the emperor still had to have some knowledge of the men involved. He would receive a tally suggestion list of proposed names and place a vermilion dot beside, or a circle around, the names on the list which he chose, as in 1820, when Minh-mạng approved only three names upon a presented list of more than thirty.[67] After 1842 Vietnamese Secretariat officials were required to record upon slips the date when they had received a memorial and the length of time it had taken them to deal with it and draft a proposal. The normal deadline was a maximum of ten days. If this were exceeded, an extension had to be formally requested.[68] Day and night shifts processed memorials at the Nội Các. Absence from scheduled shift duty without sick leave for five successive days or more than six scattered days in a month brought impeachment.[69]

Restriction of the individual emperor's participation in drawing up orders actually improved their likelihood of being carried out.

When examination-system-trained officials gave orders to fellow officials they tended to be more understandable and, perhaps, more realistic. The whole train of procedures remained in bureaucratic hands. At the same time the tally suggestion process certainly represented a devolution of imperial power, and Vietnamese preoccupation with the mechanics of *phiêu nghĩ* ran high. In Ch'ing China the Grand Secretariat, although without access to vital memorials, nonetheless monopolized the drafting of tally suggestions for the routine ones. The Vietnamese Grand Secretariat, on the other hand, was far more likely to see confidential memorials, but it had to share the power of preparing tally suggestions in response to them with the Huế Six Boards. This divagation from the Chinese example was consciously planned. Minh-mạng said in 1837: "At the Northern Court under the Ming and Ch'ing statutes the high officials of the Grand Secretariat receive memorials from all over and monopolize the drafting and the sending out of decrees, so that the power of the Secretariat has gradually become immense . . . I have personally established that those who are selected to manage the affairs of our Grand Secretariat will be only third and fourth grade officials, and that memorials from the provinces shall be distributed among senior officials of the Six Boards, who will draft the tally suggestions and carry them out. We will avoid the Grand Secretariat's stealing the power of the Six Boards."[70]

In the true bureaucratic fashion, the orders which these drafted tallies suggested were merely applications of general rules. Emperors could change such rules only at the cost of endangering administrative stability. Thus a Vietnamese edict of 1841 stipulated that drafters and memorialists must "draw upon precedents" for all business they proposed. Only for those "items which have not yet been regulated" could there be "no harm in each man using his opinions."[71] Furthermore, officials imposed custom-heavy categories upon all memorials as they came into Huế. Emperors were at the mercy of these categories. When in 1842 Thiệu-trị wanted to aid the people of Nghệ An province after a natural disaster, his own response was energetic. But his Board of Finance perversely classified his demand for an edict proposal on the subject as "routine" (*tầm thường*). In the words of the aggrieved emperor, the board "lightly sent it down to underlings for them to suggest an edict, as a result of which what they have written is full of errors and neglects and abbreviates many items.''[72]

The bureaucracy's increasing professionalization, its resistance to outside stimuli and the dulling of its reflexes by routine, was most threatening of all to the emperor's peace of mind. By 1839 the Nguyễn Board of War had become so absorbed in its own administrative world that it even ignored the absence of an imperial "vermilion dot" on a proposal it had drafted. It proceeded to have the proposal copied and sealed as law, despite the fact that the emperor had not yet actually signed it. "This is not to be compared with an ordinary error," Minh-mạng commented violently.[73]

Bureaucratic jargon crept inexorably into the tally slips, disconcerting emperors who were not bureaucrats. In eighteenth-century China, Ch'ien-lung complained bitterly about his Secretariat's confusing habit of shorthanding place names. Points like Tolun Nor in Inner Mongolia (To-lun-no-erh in Chinese) were becoming simply *no* on its tallies.[74] As might be expected, the tally-drafting process became a far more formidable monument to the immutability of bureaucratic conduct in Peking than it did in Huế. Chinese emperors who wanted to promote officials of whom their Board of Appointments had a low opinion customarily ordered their Secretariat to prepare two or more tally suggestions, one of which "followed the board's argument" while the other proposed special circumstances which the emperor could cite to get his way.[75] This common Chinese variation of drafting two or three tallies was never institutionalized in Vietnam.

Obviously the Chinese and Vietnamese imperial secretariats were in a position to shape their rulers' awareness of the societies which they ruled. Even more important, however, was the nature of the imperial communications systems below the secretariats. In the East Asian classical world the term "silk threads" was a conventional euphemism for the ruler's issued orders.[76] To the pessimistic, at least, it implied the descriptive hypothesis that most imperial words of decision were the socially expensive products of a complicated political organism and were likely to prove fragile under stress. Communications were freer at the bottom of the social pyramid than at the top. A prominent Vietnamese proverb celebrates the generous availability of information in the villages: "One can fill up a river or plug

up a well, but who can stop up the mouth of the world at large?"
(*Lấp sông, lấp giếng, ai lấp được miệng thiên hạ?*). As official messages
traveled upward through the bureaucracy, however, this proverb
became less germane, and a new expression, this time Sino-Vietnamese, replaced it: "The purpose of literature is to carry doctrine"
(*Văn dĩ tái đạo*).

Formal memorials and other bureaucratic communications were
literature. And because ideology went hand in hand with literature
in Ch'ing China and Nguyễn Vietnam, transmitters of such messages
from the provinces to the palaces where the emperors read them
believed that it was more important to salvage ideological rectitude
than to offer their imperial readers endless streams of undisciplined
data. Symbols of the orthodox and the already known took precedence over raw information. Minh-mạng had to forbid his Grand
Secretariat to remove characters which were ceremonially taboo in
Vietnam from books which had been purchased in China.[77] In a
more technical sphere, memorialists could be punished for sending
memorials which did not have their writing respectfully elevated in the
proper places, which were even slightly stained or torn, or which did
not have the senders' names and ranks written properly upon them.

The point is that punctilios related to the preservation of existing
statuses within the hierarchy were more sacred than techniques
related to the spread of news. The apotheosis of ideological purity
and official status conventions in the political communications systems of the Chinese and Vietnamese bureaucracies made it more
difficult than it should have been for elites in Peking and Huế to
acquire the detailed knowledge about particular activities that
officials near the bottoms of their hierarchies possessed. The rigors of
these technical procedures certainly circumvented inefficiency and
lack of coordination. But the Vietnamese inheritance of the Chinese
bureaucratic characteristic of overvaluing the apparatus of bureaucratic communication itself, and of the need for ideological refinement within it, had consequences. It helped to inhibit the development of unconventionally creative leadership when political-military
conditions began to change in Asia after 1840.

If information, then, was not culturally legitimate at its source it
had usually become so by the time it reached the ruler's eyes. There
was little a ruler could do about this. Thiệu-trị made a lonely figure

as he pleaded in 1846 with his incorrigibly incurious local officials in Saigon to give him more than just purified cryptic token data about the activities of the British: "Recently Trần Văn Trung and other officials of Gia Định province memorialized saying that according to the accounts of Chinese merchants, the English barbarians have prepared 20 ships and have fixed a date to attack Siam . . . Surely they would not plot an attack against another people's country and yet clearly fix a distinct date for it in order to show those people? This talk would appear to be illogical. However, in matters that concern the circumstances of another country, there is no harm in asking a question or two! You must notify these provincial officials to keep asking the Chinese merchants, asking them until it is clear, where does this tale come from? Where did they hear it? Also, what are conditions in Siam like? What are Siamese travel routes like? They should clarify all this."[78]

The emperor was more curious than his officials. But he was at the wrong end of the information-processing system.

Vietnamese memorials were generally more informal and less time-conscious than Chinese ones. Their evolution toward Chinese standards of precision was slow. Before 1815 Nguyễn memorialists wrote in *nôm* as often as in classical Chinese and signed their memorials only with their official ranks, not with their names. The business of Vietnamese society not being as complex as that of China, Vietnamese administration perhaps possessed less need for rigid time scheduling. In 1820 the tendency to date government documents incxactly by writing devious expressions of time like "post-fourth month" (*kế tứ nguyệt*) instead of "fifth month" on them was formally suppressed only when the character "post" (*kế*) was specifically prohibited.[79] Before 1825 the development of an extended chronology of official documentation was frustrated by the fact that years were indicated on government documents only by the Chinese system of "stems and branches." Recording the succession of years by use of dynastic reign titles (*niên hiệu*) was only gradually introduced.[80] As late as 1826 Minh-mạng was receiving memorials from territorial divisions unsigned by any individual bureaucrats. When he asked his court advisers who had actually written these memorials they did not know.[81] On some occasions villages even memorialized the throne, although they were quite outside the bureaucracy.[82] Provincial officials were expected to write their own memorials personally. But illiterate military officers were allowed to request the provincial financial and judicial commissioners, or relatives, to write theirs.[83]

The basic fact of life which underlay imperial power, in Vietnam as in China, was that while the authority to define values or at least to set administrative goals was concentrated as much as possible at the capital, the authority to determine empirically what the existing circumstances were that would influence the formulation and achievement of those goals resided far down the hierarchy—in the provinces, prefectures, and districts. The factual premises of decision making depended upon the discretion of numerous subordinates. Starved for information, and determined to control that discretion as systematically as they could, Nguyễn emperors cultivated two special types of memorial.

After 1832, every provincial governor-general and governor was required to write, four times a year (the first month of each of the four seasons) a "respects-paying memorial" (*thỉnh an tấu*). In it the officials gave synoptic descriptions of all the political, military, and economic conditions existing in their jurisdictions, as well as impressions of the talent and "ability to handle popular aspirations and feelings" of all the local officials under them. Twice a year, in the fifth and eleventh lunar months, the provincial commissioners had to write the same kind of memorial, this time appraising their superiors in the province as well as their inferiors.[84] By Chinese standards these memorials were physically small and intimate, having only five columns of thirteen characters each, including elevated characters. (The average memorial from a Chinese province had six columns of twenty characters each.) Minh-mạng made it clear that scholastic jargon was the bane of the communications system. Officials who made memorial writing a parasitic form of poetry writing or philosophy would not be tolerated: "You must not employ adornments, or elegant phrases, or lose yourselves in overextended writing about the seasons, in language like 'the pines blow, the grass is dry, and the cassia-moon shines brightly' . . . Excessive words must not be used, in order for you to show your trustworthiness."[85]

Perhaps an even more important form of communication in Nguyễn Vietnam between provincial officials and Huế was the second memorial type, which also had a statutory periodicity to it as early as 1808. This was the "rice prices report" (*tấu báo mễ giá*), in some ways the quintessential documentary genre in an agrarian-bureaucratic society. In the Gia-long period provincial officials in the five inner protectorates around Hanoi were required to send such reports to Huế once a month. Officials in the outer six northern protectorates were required to do so every three months. "Rice prices reports" were complicated documents consisting of records stating (1) whether "heat" and rain in their areas had "agreed with the norms" (*thuận thường*) or whether there had been drought or floods, and how many days they had lasted; (2) how favorable the rains had been to agriculture; (3) what the market prices of rice were. In 1823 the reports were expanded to include the harvest percentages of individual districts. After 1825 each administrative capital was compelled to send both monthly and emergency "daily chronicles of wind and rain" (*phong vũ nhật ký*) as part of the reports. If the "respects-paying memorials" were designed to tighten political controls, the "rice prices reports" were designed to test the bureaucracy's interaction with its socio-economic surroundings.

However, the sensitivity of the court to economic trends among the peasantry depended upon the competence of its Chinese-style bureaucratized postal service, which has already been described. Emergency reports of rice prices were sent according to a sliding scale of price changes. But because the number of centers sending reports increased and the postal service subsequently became overburdened, this sliding scale became progressively more crude as the century wore on. In 1825 if the price of one *phương* of rice changed upward or downward by one *mạch* and thirty *văn* an emergency report was sent to Huế. But by 1832 an emergency report was occasioned only by a change of two *mạch*, and after 1833 its need was determined only by a change of three *mạch*. This was double what the scale had been in 1825.[86]

By the 1840's the organization of rice prices reports had become so sophisticated that massive collections of reports from one province for a three-month period were now presented to emperors four times a year. Prices in the markets of the provincial capitals themselves were selected as the standards. But reports had to compare current provincial prices with those of previous months. If the price of rice in a provincial district varied by more than one *mạch* from that prevailing in the capital of the same province, a special statement had to be inserted. As of 1847 cantons and villages sent harvest reports to district magistrates, who certified them and dispatched them to provincial officials for further ratification. If the cantons fabricated data the entire hierarchy suffered the consequences.[87]

Whatever the shortcomings of the system, the "rice price report" was perhaps Vietnam's most triumphant domestication of Chinese literary administrative methods of processing information. Many of these reports survive to the present in the dynasty's *Vermilion Books*. The existence of troublesome areas like the Mekong delta made this triumph particularly necessary for the dynasty. Nguyễn Văn Nhân's description of the delta in 1821 to an impatient Minh-mạng is almost as relevant today as it was a century and a half ago: "This land abounds in swamps, and it is easy for bandits to 'assemble at the sound of a whistle'; moreover, its people do not ordinarily understand techniques of storage [of food], and they do not grow anything other than 'the five cereals.' When they suddenly encounter a year of deficient harvests, it easily produces heterodox creeds."[88]

The Nguyễn Privy Council and Minh-mạng's Work of Centralization

In general, Vietnamese institutional borrowing from China was conditioned by the sequence of evolution of institutions in China itself. The older a Chinese institution was, the more important it was considered to be. Gia-long created the Nguyễn Six Boards, but a Nguyễn Grand Secretariat was not completely constructed until 1830. Several years later, Minh-mạng felt free to attempt to match another institution in Peking, even newer than the Grand Secretariat. From reading Chinese texts, more than from listening to returning Vietnamese envoys, he learned that the Ch'ing "Office of Military Plans" (*Chün-chi-ch'u*) or Grand Council bulked large in Chinese administration. By late 1832 he had determined to borrow it. In a long speech he told his court: "I have recently been reading the Ch'ing statutes. What they refer to as 'the great ministers of military plans' I would like to imitate and effect here. Its name is called 'Military Plans,' so it looks as if it is limited to the deliberation of military matters, like the Sung dynasty's so-called 'State Confidences Council' (*Shu-mi-yüan*). Now we should compare and consider the old and the new, and by following our own convenience establish an organ to be called the 'Plans and Confidences Council' (*Cơ Mật Viện*) which will concern itself with the secret strategies of a military country and confidential business."[89] For convenience, Cơ Mật Viện will be henceforth translated as "Privy Council." But it should be recognized that its actual Vietnamese title was an heroic amalgam, evidently contrived by Minh-mạng himself, of the titles of the Sung and Ch'ing councils from which it was so artificially descended. It did not really begin to function in Huế until 1834–35. What is important is that Minh-mạng was imitating a Chinese institution which he himself had never seen in operation. His imitation could only be as faithful as the fullness of the description of the original institution in official Chinese texts permitted it to be. How faithful, indeed, was it?

The great eighteenth-century Chinese historian Chao I, who served on the Ch'ing Grand Council under Ch'ien-lung, recorded the conventional explanation of its creation in the late 1720's in his memoirs: "Armies were being employed in the northern and western regions, and because the Grand Secretariat was outside the T'ai-ho Gate those on duty were greatly anxious about the leaking of business. It was then that a 'military essentials headquarters' was first set up inside the Lung-tsung Gate."[90]

From this beginning close to the throne the Peking Grand Council soon supplanted the Grand Secretariat as the administrative power-house of Ch'ing government. It became so august that the Ch'ing Board of Finance once even incorrectly elevated its name in a memorial.[91] At the same time, unlike the Sung dynasty's Shu-mi-yüan, which Minh-mạng so closely associated with it, it was a completely informal agency, with no fixed number of high officials. Its ministers were drawn from board presidents and Grand Secretaries as well as from imperial princes and military commanders. These men were responsible for advising their emperors, during military campaigns, about the quantity of men, horses, salaries, and provisions that would be needed, and about the heights of mountains, the depths of valleys, and the lengths of roads that would be encountered. They had to be bibliophiles with military interests, because all this information was to come from "ancient books" and from "the various maps and histories."[92] The Grand Council also involved itself with nearly every aspect of civil government, from bureaucratic appointments to diplomatic relations to judicial review, because of its exemplification, greater than that of any other Peking body, of the three characteristics of industriousness, rapidity of executive transition from one subject to another, and secrecy.[93]

Nonetheless, throughout Ch'ing history, side by side with this other business it always retained its original concern with the special military problems of the Ch'ing empire outside China proper. It was the organ, for example, which regularly checked the rotation of service of the fifteen or more major military commanders in "northern and western regions" like Chahar, Ili, and Tibet. It presented an annual list to the emperor of the names of those who had fulfilled their three-year terms and prevented any one of them, by such surveillance, from becoming a permanent, independent frontier ruler.[94] In addition, the Ch'ing Grand Council harbored such offices as the Fan-shu-fang, which translated Manchu writings into Chinese and Chinese writings into Manchu.[95] On the whole it served two purposes—the supervision of an unprecedentedly vast central Asian empire, and the facilitation of bilingual government—which did not exist in Nguyễn Vietnam.

Moreover, from the standpoint of long-distance imitators, its structure was peculiarly elusive. Below its ministers there lurked a crucial group of so-called "little Grand Councillors." The "little Grand Councillors" were actually thirty-two secretaries, known as *chang-ching*. These secretaries consisted of sixteen Manchus and sixteen Chinese, who were divided into two shifts of eight Manchus and eight Chinese each. Despite the fact that high Council officials were ordered not to divulge business unnecessarily to the *chang-ching*, inevitably the secretaries soon came to dominate the Council informally, even to the point of occasionally feeling free to remove its secret maps and take them to their private homes in Peking.[96] The secretaries followed the emperor on all his travels. Chao I, perhaps the most famous Council *chang-ching*, wrote with unforgettable vividness of the times when he lay prostrate on the ground in a military tent in Mongolia, writing confidential documents upon the yellow memorials' box which served him as a table, while wax gutterings from a crude candle "completely stained my body."[97] It was the secretaries who often drafted military orders. Emperors like Ch'ien-lung merely contented themselves by adding obscure, hortatory four-character phrases from works like the *Later Han History*.[98] After 1820 these secretaries had to be nominated by the Grand Secretariat and the Six Boards and tested by Council officials before they could gain their positions.[99] Official Ch'ing statutes which described the Grand Council mentioned the *chang-ching*. But the statutes hardly did justice to their true role. As a recently created institution which was both informal and shrouded in deliberate mysteries, the Ch'ing Grand Council was an object of Vietnamese institutional borrowing that was unusually challenging.

In view of these difficulties the Vietnamese did amazingly well. The Nguyễn Privy Council consisted of four great ministers, whose rank could be no lower than third grade (just as that of the officials of the Nội Các could be no higher) and who usually held other commissions concurrently, like Chinese Grand Councillors. Below them labored eight "apprentices" (*hành tẩu*) of the fifth, sixth, and seventh bureaucratic grades, who were chosen by court officials from among the personnel of offices like the Six Boards. Ministers and subordinates alike were forbidden to disseminate information to outsiders. All military maps originally stored at the Grand Secretariat were transferred to the possession of the Council. On the other hand, while it is true that the Privy Council was situated in the "Forbidden City" of Huế while the Grand Secretariat was outside the Forbidden City in the Imperial City (*hoàng thành*) the distance between the two was so much less than in Peking that, in terms of the maintenance of secrecy, it was again almost more symbolic than functional. And while the Ch'ing Grand Council had begun its career in the inner precincts at Peking, significantly enough the Vietnamese Privy Council first met in 1834 in the headquarters of the Grand Secretariat itself, only subsequently moving nearer to the emperor.[100] In fact the real distinction between Grand Council and Grand Secretariat which prevailed in China—the former being a secretive, highly important, informal body almost within the emperor's household, the latter being a distant, extremely large, routine group of administrators—was never really successfully transferred in practice to Vietnam, although the effort was made. In 1842 Thiệu-trị referred to the Grand Secretariat, not the Privy Council, as a "close, forbidden place" which dealt with fundamental strategies of war and peace.[101]

The Ch'ing statutes talked about the Chinese Grand Council's *chang-ching*. But the Vietnamese did not know what to make of this term. Because it seemed to be an essential part of the Ch'ing Grand Council, it was borrowed anyway. In 1836 Minh-mạng ordered the underlings of his Privy Council to be assigned to two subordinate offices within it, the "southern and northern *chang-ching*" (*nam chương kinh, bắc chương kinh*). It was only in 1837 that the Vietnamese learned that the term *chang-ching* really meant "secretary" in Peking. The following entry for 1837 appears in the Vietnamese court statutes: "The names 'southern and northern *chang-ching*' in the Ch'ing statutes are really the names of individual Chinese and Manchu officials, who are differentiated in order to concern themselves with Chinese and Manchu linguistic duties. They are not the names of government bureaus. Our previous discussion and investigation of this was not careful and as a result this discrepancy was produced."[102]

In effect, the pessimistic consensus among critically minded Vietnamese classical scholars in Huế in the late 1830's was that the Ch'ing Grand Council had been the most intractably difficult Chinese institution for them to borrow. Humiliation over this initial failure to understand the sense of one of the basic components of a major Ch'ing institution, a failure which required a painful written confession in their own statutes, occurred at a significant time in Vietnamese history. After 1837 enthusiasm for imitating Chinese institutions distinctly began to wane at the Nguyễn court. One source of the Vietnamese confusion over the inner structure of the Ch'ing Grand Council had stemmed from its very newness in China itself. Classical historical perspectives could not be brought to bear upon it. In Minh-mạng's eyes, even the Ch'ing Grand Secretariat was the very image of certain trends in Ming history, trends undesirable but clearly comprehensible to any classicist, which he was determined to correct when he created his own Grand Secretariat.

A second cause of what the Vietnamese regarded as the fiasco of 1836–37 was the gradual appearance in Ch'ing civil administration of recondite fragments of bicultural Sino-Manchu terminology. The term *chang-ching* was not orthodox classical Chinese at all. It was originally a Chinese approximation (*mei-le chang-ching*) of a Manchu military title in the Ch'ing Eight Banners. Such Sino-Manchu terminology placed an added burden upon the reflexes of cultural transmission from China to Vietnam.

Obviously Minh-mạng did not create his Privy Council in 1834 merely to make his Southeast Asian replica of Ch'ing government more perfect. The Council was created during a time of serious regional rebellions, especially in the south, where the militarist Lê Văn Khôi managed by a program of strategic murder, political dissimulation, and surprise control of the local junk fleets to seize all six southern provinces for a brief time in the early 1830's. Designed to increase the number of high officials dealing with crucial regional matters at Huế, the Privy Council retained its essential subdivision of a "southern" office which surveyed Vietnam from Quảng Bình province south and a "northern" office which received secret memorials and watched developments from Hà Tĩnh province to the China border. These two offices (which were called *chương kinh* or *chang-ching* only in the period of confusion of 1836–37 described above) were particularly charged also with problems which arose from contact with foreign countries. The southern office became increasingly concerned with Western traders and the northern office stressed relations with "northern foreign countries," of which China was the most prominent. The vulnerability of the long Vietnamese coastline with its numerous ports, as well as domestic regional subversion, supplied the motives for such a structure. The most important accounting operations in Huế, those linked not only to control of the domestic circulation of luxury goods but also to the control of foreign trade, had to be certified by the Privy Council as well as by the Censorate, the Board of Finance (which supervised the imperial treasuries), and the Board of Works (which managed the junks).[103] During the Vietnamese subjugation of Cambodia (1834–1841) army commanders received their orders through the Privy Council. But Minh-mạng was quick to suppress a dangerous tendency that developed when some of them, instead of memorializing the emperor, began to send reports to the Privy Council itself.[104]

Even if regional rebellions and Western ships had not darkened Vietnamese horizons in the 1830's, however, the Privy Council would probably have been created, if only because it was part of the long process of bureaucratic centralization begun by Minh-mạng in 1820. Under Gia-long two regional overlords had, as mentioned, ruled most of the northern and southern provinces of Vietnam from Hanoi and Saigon respectively. These overlords were not completely independent of Huế; two of the men who filled the positions, Nguyễn Văn Thành and Lê Văn Duyệt, were personal rivals whom Gia-long was able to play off against each other. But this game ended astonishingly and bloodily in 1816 in an episode which revealed the emperor's sense of insecurity. Thành's son, a degree holder with many acquaintances in the newly emerging Nguyễn scholar class, wrote an eccentric poem to two other scholars in Thanh-hóa in which he spoke of new leadership from the countryside changing the circumstances of the age. Whether or not incipient treason was intended in this compliment to his friends, intrigue by Duyệt ensured that Gia-long saw the poem, with the consequence that the son was executed and Thành was driven to suicide. This was perhaps the most unsettling *cause célèbre* in Nguyễn politics before the stormy Tự-đức period (1848–1883). Gia-long's destruction of Thành, the hero of the battle of Qui-nhơn in the Tây-sơn wars and the compiler of the dynasty's law code, revealed that no one else was as powerful as the emperor but also that the emperor feared for his position. Why had he nursed such fears about men like Thành and why did Minh-mạng seek antidotes in the Chinese statutes?

The overlords, before the erosion of their authority in the 1820's, dealt with both the civil and military affairs of their regions. They commanded personal armies in areas with little tradition (especially in the north) of loyalty to the Nguyễn rulers. There was little differentiation of administrative function or of the business of the various areas under them. If the problems of their jurisdictions were to come to the attention of the emperor in Huế, the overlords themselves had to present them.[105] Provincial officials did not circulate from office to office but enjoyed almost unlimited tenures in the same posts. In 1825 the Board of Appointments reported that more than twenty district magistrates had been in the same districts between six and nineteen years. In 1828 Minh-mạng was forced to demand a special report on the actual tenures of all fifth and sixth grade officials (that is, district officials) holding offices.[106] Trần Công Hiến, a famous example, served as protector (*trấn thủ*, the chief civil official of a province or protectorate under one of the regional overlordships in the Gia-long era) of Hải Dương from 1802 to 1817. Nguyễn Văn Hiếu, another famous example, was protector of Sơn-nam-hạ (later known as Nam Định) from 1810 to 1823.[107]

As a further sign that the levers of command were not really in Huế, the overlords in Hanoi and Saigon monopolized all regional seals of office. It was only in 1829 that centrally managed seals offices were created in these two citadels for their remaining two years of semi-autonomous existence before a Chinese-style provincial system was introduced in 1831.[108] Controlling the seals, the regional over-lords were able as well to appoint their personal secretaries to the prefectural and district commissions under them.[109] Credentials for the readers at regional examination sites in the Gia-long period were issued if not actually written by the regional power holders.[110] Minh-mạng knew so little about the conduct of the administration in Hanoi in 1821 that he was compelled to ask one of its officials whether power holders from outside Hanoi, from the ring of "protec-torates" around it, were allowed to participate in discussions of judicial cases or whether this was confined to one or two key men in Hanoi itself.[111] Lack of codified procedures meant imperial igno-rance. As a concomitant of lack of centralization, Gia-long's inchoate bureaucracy lacked any sense of a symbolic or practical need for discretion at its core. Most significantly the name "Forbidden City" (*tử cấm thành*) was not borrowed from Peking to describe the em-peror's palaces at Huế before 1822.[112] The consequences of all this decentralization kept rising relentlessly to the surface in the first decade after Gia-long's death, as in 1825, when it was discovered that the local corvee registers for the area around Saigon had been written in rough, abbreviated form and were illegible.[113]

What is crucial, therefore, is that Minh-mạng believed that the comprehensive application of long-descended Chinese bureaucratic techniques and formulas was the historic key to the restoration of a unified, centrally ruled political society, after centuries of disunity. Consultation of the encyclopedic Chinese statutes stood for more than just classical pantomime. The Chinese statutes, Minh-mạng believed, contained the knowledge that would allow him to develop a growing number of specific administrative tasks within an ex-panding, centrally focused bureaucratic hierarchy. Provided that he did not go too far in this direction, this would allow him to erode the authority of a number of individual regional political grandees without putting him too completely at the mercy of the new bureaucrats he was creating. Imperial safety lay in more bureaucratization than the grandees desired and less than the bureaucrats sought.

Some of the external evidence of the successfully increasing complexity of Minh-mạng's bureaucracy along Chinese lines is interesting. In 1834, thirty-two years after the military unification of Vietnam, communications among officials themselves within the civil administration received a formal hierarchical stylization for the first time. When any of the Six Boards sent a communication to the Grand Secretariat after 1834 it had to follow a form that was classified as a *chiểu-hội*; the Secretariat itself could send only communications known as *tư-trình* to the boards.[114] (These types of communications were borrowed directly from China. The first, *chao-hui* in Chinese, was addressed to officials slightly inferior in rank and the second, *tzu-ch'eng*, was conventionally addressed to officials slightly higher in rank than the sender.[115] But because the Nguyễn Grand Secretariat possessed less status, and more power, in Vietnam than its Chinese model did in China, Ch'ing communications procedures were reversed in Vietnam. In China, one of the boards would have sent a *tzu-ch'eng* to the Secretariat.) When the Six Boards communicated with provincial officials they had to send *tư-di* to the governors-general and the governors and *chiểu-hội* to the commissioners; they received in return *tư-trình*. After 1834 hierarchical distinctions also had to be expressed in official signatures on these communications. High officials could sign themselves directly as "this official" (*bản chức*). But underlings could only refer to themselves as "lowly official" (*ty chức*), and had to write this expression on the margin of the message.

As the external forms of hierarchy, Chinese-style, became more consistent and more emphasized, the informal existence the court had led in Gia-long's reign receded into the past and became nothing but an unreal memory by the 1840's. The letters patent and credentials of office holding which officials received from the emperor also became diversified hierarchically in the 1830's, as the Nguyễn bureaucracy continued to grow ceremonially from the top down.

High officials like privy councillors and governors-general received *sắc-thư*. Important intermediate officials like district magistrates received *cáo-sắc*. Lowly officials like board underlings, provincial registrars, and dynastically patronized leaders among the highland peoples were granted *sắc-văn*. Again these were imported Chinese terms, although Vietnamese courts occasionally altered their patterns. The increasing differentiation of these credentials magnified the official's awareness of the possibilities of centrally conferred promotion. This in turn heightened imperial prestige.

But even here problems could arise to confront Vietnamese cultural borrowers. This chapter has sought to suggest a number of the causes and consequences of the Nguyễn bureaucracy's deviations from its Ch'ing model, even when such deviations were not fully intended. The Vietnamese court followed an historicist methodology in its program of institutional borrowing. It used its interpretations of the historical outcomes of given Chinese institutions as instruments for their classification. However, by 1830 Ming-Ch'ing institutions had not yet worked out all the implications of their development. Thus one type of deviation could be caused by the Vietnamese court's lack of enough classificatory touchstones. This led to Ming–Ch'ing institutions being borrowed with their Ming rather than with their Ch'ing reputations. Minh-mạng's anachronistic horror of the power of Ming Grand Secretaries eventually produced a Vietnamese Grand Secretariat which was not identical to either of its Ming or Ch'ing counterparts. A second type of deviation could be caused by the Vietnamese court's acceptance of the face value of Chinese institutional terminology in Chinese statutes running ahead of its ability or willingness to investigate the substance behind such terminology. This tendency produced a Vietnamese Privy Council whose sub-offices in 1836–37 possessed the inappropriate personal titles of the Chinese Grand Council's junior secretaries. But a third type of deviation could stem from Vietnam's lack of enough resources to reproduce Chinese bureaucratic institutions in the full glory of all their appurtenances and details.

The physical cost of defining their bureaucratic stratification system as rigidly as China's was too much for the Vietnamese. The Vietnamese court statutes quoted a long passage from the Ch'ing statutes (under the Board of Works section) which explained that the proper material for commissions for officials of the fourth grade and higher was five-colored embroidered silks. Then the Vietnamese statutes commented upon this Chinese passage: "Up until now our country has lacked artisans who could weave embroidered silk. If we use silk borders [for the credentials] and send them to embroiderers, we will not avoid vast costs . . . We should respectfully follow the art of making commissions as in the previous [Vietnamese] statutes . . . However, if the commissions given for promotions and the commissions officials hold before being promoted both resume using [the traditional unembroidered silk border type] we fear there will be no way of telling them apart. We propose that we should follow the regulations of the Ch'ing people regarding stationery for commissions. The commissions that have been decided upon will acquaint everyone with the celebrated glory of [their holders'] backgrounds, and the [Chinese] stationery being firm and good, it can also be preserved for a long time."[116] The Chinese stationery came in different sizes and colors and background patterns. These variations distinguished rank.

As if the diversification of types of credentials were not enough, their contents also underwent methodical transformations. Before 1830 the *chiểu-văn* (a common name for the *sắc-văn* before 1838) of a transferred official might simply have the identity of his new post written upon it. After 1830 it also described his old post and his personal origins. After 1822, dates upon the credentials had to be written in complicated rather than simple characters. Thus tampering with documents was made more difficult. (A requirement like this, applying to provincial memorials dealing with revenue statistics, became universal in Ch'ing administration in China only about 1808.)[117] These elaborations of office holders' credentials, unimportant as they seem, were perhaps more meaningful in Nguyễn Vietnam than they would have been in China. For they actually represented in their quiet way a hierarchical socialization process, in which local officials were made increasingly aware not only of the standards but also of the priorities and scale of statuses of a large, formal, Chinese-style professional bureaucracy. From the time of their origin, therefore, they cast a long shadow over the "patron-client" officialdom of personal attachments which was so pervasive

in the rest of Southeast Asia and which was dominant enough in
Nguyễn Vietnam in the very early 1800's.

Ratings in the Vietnamese and Chinese Bureaucracies

But none of these measures compared with Vietnamese domestication of the Chinese bureaucracy's famous "rating" procedures, in
which higher officials reported periodically to the throne upon the
behavior in office of lower officials under them, and higher officials
themselves were expected to write self-criticisms known as "self-pres-
entations" (*tzu-ch'en*). In Ch'ing China ratings of certain Peking
officials (for example, of readers at the Grand Secretariat by the Board
of Appointments) were called "capital investigations" (*ching-ch'a*)
and took place every three years. The rating books of all offices were
sent to the Board of Appointments before the fifteenth day of the
third lunar month of the ratings year. Ratings of provincial officials
(for example, of the commissioners by the governors-general) were
called "great accountings" (*ta-chi*). They also took place every three
years (but on different years from the "capital investigations") and
had to be completed in the provinces in the last month of the year
before the ratings year.[118]

In Vietnam, ratings were extremely sporadic in the Gia-long period. In 1804 more than twenty district magistrates from the central
provinces—those immediately under the emperor's rule—came to
Huế to be tested by three of the Six Boards.[119] In 1811 regulations
were announced that would have caused the rating of every prefectural and district official every three years and terminated their
tenures in their posts every six years.[120] In fact, however, it was admitted as late as 1826 that appointments to office before that year had
not been based upon ratings at all but merely upon the "recommendations of great ministers."[121] Ratings for the first twenty-five years
of Nguyễn rule were really subsumed by the regional overlords under
the apparatus of their personal rule. As Minh-mạng pointed out in
1829, the criteria of evaluation that these overlords cited in their
reports to Huế centered upon technical matters like the calligraphy
of their underlings. The criteria did not involve the underlings' past
records of promotion, demotion, and geographical variety of places of

service, which, had they been cited, would have exposed them as non-bureaucratic, personal dependents of their superiors.[122]

Tenure of official posts in the Gia-long period was, quite simply, indefinite. A limitation of tenures to six years was not made the formal, if not always observed, law until 1820. To encourage compliance with the law, however, high provincial officials were ordered to present each spring a list of the names of the competent officials serving under them, a "list of those awaiting promotion" (*hậu thăng sách*). They were ordered simultaneously to present another list setting forth the names of incompetent underlings, a "list of those awaiting transfer" (*hậu điều sách*).[123] Needless to say, these names and procedures all came from China. In the Nguyễn court's struggle with regional vested interests to bring about a genuine circulation of centrally appointed officials throughout Vietnamese society, one of the truly important themes of early nineteenth-century Vietnamese history, they loomed large.

When the Vietnamese ratings system (*khảo tích*) was fully developed it resembled the general Chinese procedure of superior officials rating inferior officials triennially. The criteria (*khảo ngữ*, "ratings language") for evaluating officials were similar. They included, for local officials, judgments upon their ability to collect taxes, raise soldiers, "gather in" pirates and bandits, cause the cultivated fields and population in their jurisdictions to increase as the result of benevolent rule, and arrange legal disputes "without a popular outcry in reaction." An elaborate framework of time limits and percentages was erected to gauge how satisfactorily local officials fulfilled these criteria. Judicial cases involving bandits had to be solved within three months. Those involving marriage and property disputes (which were often interrelated) had to be solved by the local official within two months. A case solved within the deadline was called a "superlative" performance. One that was not was called "inferior."

The records of all the local officials within one province were combined into a "list of superlative and inferior legal actions" (*hình danh tối điện sách*), of which there were three copies. One copy remained at the Board of Appointments, one copy remained at the Board of Justice, and one copy was kept by the province.[124] An official who was linked to an equal number of "superlative" and "inferior" cases was ultimately rated "ordinary" (*bình*). One who had up to four more "inferior" cases on his record than "superlative" cases was rated "sub-standard" (*thứ*). And one who had five or more surplus "inferior" cases was rated "poor" (*liệt*).[125]

Such a sliding scale was also applied to the measurement of the local official's prowess at recruiting soldiers and collecting taxes. If he collected all his taxes he was "excellent" (*ưu*). But at the other end of the scale if he failed to collect at least 80 percent he was "poor." And if the amount of taxes he collected dropped to as low as 60 percent of the original quota he was likely to be impeached immediately, and underlings who did not normally fall within the ratings system, like canton chiefs, were also likely to be punished.[126] Although the Boards of Justice, Finance, and War received separately this "ratings" information, which concerned legal action, tax collection, and military recruitment in the provinces respectively, it was, in the end, the Board of Appointments that digested it and prepared the final synoptic ratings report. The wide initial circulation and dissemination of ratings criteria and information within the bureaucracy were deliberate. The object was to generalize an ideal level of predictability of performance.

But of course the ratings process was just another bureaucratic information-gathering system. The officials themselves molded, one way or another, the information the ruler was to receive. To prevent collusion, both in China and in Vietnam, emperors compelled board officials to submit separately and individually the lists of the names that they recommended for official posts, after the ratings had been completed. But this did not really hinder officials from combining upon candidates beforehand. In 1762 in China, Ch'ien-lung became suspicious when an obscure Manchu clansman whose talent he considered commonplace received a unanimous endorsement from his board officials.[127] The same Chinese emperor had abolished the custom of written self-criticisms by high capital and provincial officials in 1752 because he considered their formulas inflexible, cliche-ridden, and insincere. Consequently, this celebrated bureaucratic literary type (*tự trần* in Sino-Vietnamese) flourished in the 1800's in Vietnam but not in China.[128]

In fact the whole scope of the ratings process retained its pristine importance in Nguyễn Vietnam long after it had lost it in Ch'ing China. For in 1785 in China a system of quotas for provincial promotions emerged which diminished the function of ratings. That is, regardless of how many of them possessed true merit as revealed in the ratings, only four lesser educational officials, for example, in populous Kwangtung or Szechwan could be promoted in a given ratings year while two of them could be promoted in unpopulous Kweichow or Kansu.[129] (On the other hand, before the quotas were established it was, perhaps, harder to win merit in a densely settled province, where the problems of government were greater, than it was in less populous ones.) Because promotions did not depend upon provincial quotas in Vietnam, these Chinese-style ratings were often distinct turning-points in the careers of Vietnamese officials.

In general the ratings process offered a fascinating reflection of the autonomous aspects of both the Chinese and Vietnamese traditional Confucian bureaucracies. Centralized ratings only made a negative contribution to the power of the emperor, by limiting the ability of regional overlords to appoint unqualified henchmen to offices under them. The civil official was supposed to offer "loyalty" (*trung*; *chung* in Chinese) to his emperor. But the meaning of this word in China and Vietnam was extremely broad and diffuse. It was completely unlike the Western (or Japanese) concept of a legally binding personal allegiance to an active superior. Thus, in practice, it was useless to Chinese and Vietnamese rulers in assessing the behavior of their officials. It was the most important one-word definition in the Chinese classics of what the minister owed his sovereign. Yet it suffered the bizarre fate of not appearing at all in the more realistic criteria of the ratings process. "Loyalty" is almost a mistranslation of *trung*, a fallacy of misplaced concreteness. The word embraced too many other vague meanings: sincerity, attentiveness, unselfishness, straightness, right conduct.[130] And because the bureaucratic ratings never measured loyalty to a specific emperor or to a specific dynastic house, they exemplify the way in which China and Vietnam were controlled, managerially as much as by any other way. The two societies were governed by a written body of formal, codified techniques that any ambitious ruler could inherit and manipulate—but never monopolize.

The ratings process with its lack of stress on personal allegiance was a symptom of heavy bureaucratization. But it also betrayed the persistence of a cyclical political perspective within the ranks of officialdom. Such a perspective tended to minimize the significance of dynastic collapse. It assumed that disorder would be evanescent and would not undermine the traditional administrative system. Vietnam's most famous nineteenth-century monument to this cyclical perspective is the poem "A Song in the National Language of a Troubled Escape to Shu." The poetess-consort of Tự-đức, Nguyễn Thị Bích, wrote this poem in the 1880's after the French seizure of Huế. She described the flight of the Nguyễn court to Quảng Trị in 1885, which she compared to T'ang Ming-huang's exile in Szechwan during the An Lu-shan rebellion in eighth-century China. But the significance of the demolition of the Nguyễn empire escaped her. She wrote of Vietnam's loss of independence, "Under the protectorate there will again be high mandarins. Surely they will recover and govern as in the past."[131] This was the verdict of a brilliantly talented middle-aged woman who had spent more than thirty-five years of her life in the Huế palaces, cut off from life outside them. Two thousand years of history buttressed her poem; and all of them had become irrelevant.

But Nguyễn Thị Bích belonged to the second half of the nineteenth century. For the Vietnamese peasant the earlier part of the century was hardly a golden age economically and socially. But in traditional Vietnamese political history, in some respects there was no period more significant than this one. Vietnamese civil government experienced institutional consolidation at the capital, in the form of the Grand Secretariat and the Privy Council. It experienced a near revolution in communications, in the forms of the respects-paying memorials and rice price reports. And it experienced an ambitious attempted renewal of its professional standards, in the form of the "nourishment of incorruptibility" salaries and the expansion of its ratings system. Life in Bà Huyện Thanh Quan's "arena" might have been far from placid, but in the 1830's it lacked even an obvious foretaste of the decadence that was to overtake the Nguyễn court two or three decades later. In the dark legend which disappointed French missionaries furiously wove around him, Minh-mạng was an inconvenient, petty "Confucian revivalist." In fact he was probably as great a bureaucratic centralizer as Vietnam has ever known, as great as Lê Thánh-tông of the late fifteenth century, who laid many of the foundations of Vietnamese unity and bureaucratic government.

Three
The Borrowing Ideals
of Court Bureaucrats
and the Practical Problems
of Provincial Administrators

In nineteenth-century Vietnam, as in China, a gulf existed between the relatively homogeneous cultural world of the scholarly elite in Huế and Hanoi and the multifarious, heterogeneous cultural traditions and milieus of the thousands of peasant villages. Conventionally, the elite culture is usually identified as the "Great Tradition" of its society. The cultures behind the "bamboo walls of the villages" (*lũy tre làng*) are recognized in turn as forming a myriad of "Little Traditions."

But in Nguyễn Vietnam a second gulf existed between the capital and the provinces. This was the gulf between institutional inspirations on the one hand and social realities on the other. The elucidation of the nature of this gulf, which did not perhaps exist to so extreme a degree in Ch'ing China, is vital to an understanding of Vietnam's relationship to the Chinese institutional model.

Methods and Factors in the Diffusion of Chinese Books and Ideas

In Huế in the 1800's, the latest blueprints of sophisticated institutions from China circulated with intoxicating facility. Among civil bureaucrats serving in Huế, the euphoric expectation sometimes sprang up that the next shipment of Chinese statutes would solve all exigencies. But when these civil bureaucrats went to the provinces, to serve as governors, prefects, or district magistrates, they encountered frustrating situations. It was in the provinces that local configurations and predispositions, geographic, ecological, cultural, and social, came into play, configurations which did not exist in China, which had naturally not been considered by Chinese institutional innovators, and which sometimes obstinately resisted the uninterrupted application of all the Chinese blueprints. The infallible in China became the fallible in Vietnam.

First of all, urbanization was not as significant in Vietnam as it was in China. There was not, in practice, the same graded descent of settlement sizes in the Vietnamese countryside, although a greater hierarchy of settlement sizes may have existed in Vietnam than in most other Southeast Asian societies, thanks to the importation of the Chinese territorial administrative system. The era of the one or two "primate cities," which had many times the population of the next largest centers to them, had not arrived. But it was perhaps partly foreshadowed.

Second, in certain important areas of Nguyễn Vietnam—the Sino-Vietnamese border, the Laotian-Vietnamese border, the Cambodian-Vietnamese border, and the plains and delta regions of southern Vietnam, so recently conquered—a racial preponderance of sinicized Vietnamese did not exist, or else it existed only precariously. Unlike most of the ethnic minorities of China, Vietnam's minorities occupied a disproportionately large amount of territory for their numbers.[1] Especially against the Cambodians of the south, as a consequence, the Vietnamese application of Chinese institutional blueprints became a weapon in a thinly disguised land war between the two Southeast Asian cultures and races.

Third, Vietnamese bureaucrats were compelled to search constantly for compromises between the operational limitations imposed upon them by Vietnam's smallness and the seductions inherent in importing to Southeast Asia the total governmental edifice of the Chinese empire. As will be shown, this question particularly concerned Vietnamese emperors. Ruling in the manner of a Chinese Son of Heaven, how could they preserve the mystique of Chinese institutions in Vietnam and yet keep those institutions structurally proportionable to the far more modest society which so immodestly coveted them? At times the life of the whole people, peasants as well as scholars, revolved around this dilemma of scale, consciously or unconsciously. Between the bureaucracy's ambitions, which books from

China whetted and encouraged, and provincial needs, which the environment molded, there was not always as strong an interdependence as there usually was in China.

The court's ambitions—or at least the literary and architectural surroundings which kept them alive—will be considered first. Books from China not only suggested new institutions but also, occasionally, even bred the illusion that a complete mastery of all the possible formulas of administration, no matter what the environment, was within reach. Thiệu-trị said in 1842 of one Chinese text that he greatly admired: "These 'Pictures and Descriptions for the Emperor's Scrutiny' [*Ti-chien t'u-shuo;* preface dated 1573] were compiled by the Ming ministers Chang Chü-cheng and Lǔ T'iao-yang. From the time of high antiquity of Yao and Shun, down through successive ages, what they have brought together are the good things that one ought to make into law: 81 things classified as wisdom of the sages, as virtuous patterns; and the evil things that one ought to avoid [making into law]: 36 things classified as being mad and stupid, as warning portents. The good things are auspicious and of the *yang* principle; hence one follows the numbers [multipliers] of *yang*, 9, 9. The bad things are disastrous and of the *yin* principle; hence one follows the numbers of *yin*, 6, 6."[2]

Most Chinese books naturally arrived at the Vietnamese court by way of the tributary system. Under this system, controlled international trade was facilitated in East Asia at the same time that supposed vassal rulers of China sent missions periodically to the Chinese capital and received seals from the Chinese emperors to mark their own ceremonial investitures at home. Most of the system's principles have been described and analyzed in other studies and will not be summarized again here. But the Vietnamese, for purposes of institution building, valued the opportunity to send envoys to Peking. Such envoys took with them Vietnamese goods that could be traded in China for the three Chinese products described in 1840–41 by Minh-mạng as most "fulfilling our country's needs"—ginseng, drugs, and books.[3] Other Chinese products also found important markets in Vietnam—notably tea and paper—but were more likely to come in the cargoes of Chinese merchant junks.

Because the book traffic was so integral a part of the Sino-Vietnamese diplomatic relationship, Vietnam's most accomplished scholars were customarily sent as envoys to Peking. Once there, their two principal tasks were to recognize and purchase the latest works of Chinese scholarship and to challenge Chinese and Korean scholars to poetry-writing competitions. When a Vietnamese envoy like Lê Quý Đôn triumphed in such a "letters trap" (as the Vietnamese called these competitions) his success was considered a national success. The story of his competition became imperishable. It even filtered downward into Vietnamese folklore. Every student in the Nguyễn examination system knew of the fourteenth-century envoy whose brilliant reception in China had justified his Vietnamese nickname, "the highest graduate of both countries simultaneously" (*lưỡng quốc trạng nguyên*).[4] Cultural pride energized diplomatic relations on both sides. In 1840–41 Minh-mạng only told his bureaucrats what they already knew: "All envoys who are sent to the Ch'ing country must have literary and linguistic accomplishments before they can be selected. If such people are avaricious and vulgar, upon their return they are despised by the other country."[5]

Vietnamese court records indicate that in the first two Nguyễn reigns (1802–1840) diplomatic missions visited China in 1802, 1803, 1804, 1809, 1813, 1817, 1819, 1825, 1829, 1831, 1833, and 1837.[6] The pretexts ranged from normal tribute purposes to requests for investiture (1802–1804) to special homage to Chinese emperors on their birthdays (1819 and 1831). Thus senior Vietnamese bureaucrats, of whom at least three went on every mission, visited Peking almost every three years, although the rules usually specified every four years. Higher official circles in Huế were well populated with men who had seen the Chinese court at first hand. One exception was significant. The most important figure of all at the Vietnamese court had never seen China—the emperor himself.

Among the crowds of bibliophilic envoys who brought books back from China, some were even of recent Chinese ancestry. These men belonged to an important, racially mixed Sino-Vietnamese social class which had originated in Vietnam in the seventeenth century, when loyalists of the crumbling Ming dynasty in China had fled to central and southern Vietnam and had there been allowed to create their own villages, apart from the general Vietnamese population. Such immigrants had then usually married Vietnamese women. But they had adhered to Ming Chinese clothing styles and other customs.

They and their sons remained a separate group, at least as long as they adhered to trade as a profession.[7] Distinct both from the Vietnamese and from later overseas Chinese merchant communities, which of course retained strong links with south China, they were and are known to the Vietnamese as the Minh-hương people, "Ming loyalists," or, more literally, men who maintained the "incense" and altar fires to the memory of the defunct Ming. They lived in villages like Hội-an (Faifo) in Quảng Nam and Thanh-hà-xã in Biên Hòa. They lost their minority-people mentality only when their sons became members of the Vietnamese bureaucracy. This was possible for the racially mixed Minh-hương class but impossible for overseas Chinese merchant families in Vietnam.

The latter, like the Arabs in T'ang and Sung Canton, lived in communities with their own headmen distinguished by the Vietnamese as *bang* (congregations). Upward movement from the Chinese congregations, which were characteristically composed along provincial lines (the Kwangtung *bang* or the Fukien *bang*), into the more esteemed Minh-hương social category, with its greater privileges and lower taxation, was possible for a Chinese male in nineteenth-century Vietnam only if he were a second or a third generation resident of Vietnam who was conspicuous in his refusal to shave his hair and wear a queue.[8]

Minh-hương families did not remain merely the sterile devotees of an historically fossilized way of life. Instead, they supplied the Vietnamese court with an important group of cultural middlemen who were almost indispensable in relations with China. Vietnamese enough to be loyal to Huế rather than to Peking, Minh-hương men were also Chinese enough to understand the ways of the Chinese court better than most Vietnamese.

The outstanding Minh-hương official in early Nguyễn Vietnam, Trịnh Hoài Đức (1765–1825), is a good example. Đức's shopkeeper grandfather had emigrated to Biên Hòa from Fukien. Đức himself was a member of the future Gia-long emperor's entourage as early as 1788 and became president of the Board of Finance in 1802. In 1803 he was entrusted with a vital diplomatic mission, an uncertain visit to China to seek Ch'ing ratification of the new Nguyễn dynasty. He was accompanied by Ngô Nhân Tịnh, another Minh-hương of

Kwangtung antecedents with whom he had once founded a southern Vietnamese Minh-hương poetry association. Đức traveled by ship and then overland from central Vietnam to Jehol beyond the Great Wall. This was the longest journey a Vietnamese envoy to China had ever made.[9] But when he and his party eventually reached the Ch'ing summer court, the Ch'ing emperor, according to Đức's autobiography, informed these Nguyễn Minh-hương emissaries that because they were conversant with the "northern speech" and the "language of officials" all Chinese court interpreters could be dismissed. Ch'ing recognition of the Nguyễn court soon followed.

Typically for a Minh-hương, Đức faced both ways culturally. He wrote in his autobiography that his "original native place" was Fukien. Nonetheless, he seems to have given vent to homesickness for Vietnam in a bitter poem that he wrote while he was traveling in China.[10] Like other Minh-hương, Đức was an important bicultural architect of Sino-Vietnamese institutions at Huế. He was especially responsible for the formulas for the distribution of merit and demerit in the Nguyễn bureaucracy. He was not a solitary example. At lower levels Minh-hương men, hovering constantly in the background of Vietnamese cultural borrowing from China, performed more informal services as middlemen for the Nguyễn court. In 1840–41 Minh-mạng derived most of his knowledge about the Sino-British opium crisis in Kwangtung by sending a Minh-hương spy, Lý U'ng Lợi, to Canton to make a secret investigation.[11]

Scholarly envoys to China justified their selection because their knowledge of the classics gave them leverage in international classics-dominated court politics. Lý Văn Phức, for example, the Hanoi scholar of recent Chinese ancestry, arrived in Peking as a Vietnamese envoy in 1841. He discovered that the Manchu court had assigned him official lodgings bearing the offensive title "Vietnamese Barbarians' Hostel" (*Yüeh-i hui-kuan*). Immediately ordering his attendants to destroy the sign, Phức composed a querulous impromptu essay, "On Distinguishing Barbarians" ("Biện di luận") which he then presented to the startled—and himself racially barbarian—Tao-kuang emperor. In his essay Phức pointed out the Confucian nature of Vietnamese elite culture in impeccable scholarly language. He demanded, "if mankind did not dare to regard Shun and King Wen as barbarians, can it then dare to regard us as barbarians?'' The Chinese response, according to Vietnamese accounts, was "most ashamed and grateful.''[12]

It is more important to remember that the scholarly nature of these Vietnamese envoys influenced the cultural inventory of Chinese institutions and governmental methods which they transmitted back to Vietnam. It was one more factor which ensured that the civil bureaucracy in Vietnam would approach its corresponding Chinese model more closely than would the Vietnamese military hierarchy. Civil institutions in Vietnam were more thoroughly "Sino-Vietnamese" than military ones partly because Vietnamese military officers more rarely visited China.

The community of classical scholarship which Vietnamese envoys to China took pride in sharing with the Chinese inspired them with the ideal of creating a corresponding Sino-Vietnamese community of administrative practices. The occasional resistance of the Vietnamese emperors, who had not traveled to Peking, and of the dissimilar Vietnamese environment, were the obstacles to this ideal. But the sightseeing of bookworm envoys in China nonetheless gave the ideal a certain impetus, for few of them were unlike Nguyễn Siêu, a Vietnamese envoy of 1848, who spent days on his travels to and from Peking lovingly searching for such sites as the places where the two Ch'eng brothers of the Sung neo-Confucian revival had lectured.[13]

Vietnamese emperors were less interested in indulging in such bookish daydreaming than in gaining concrete information about China. All Nguyễn envoys who visited China were compelled to send back rigorously defined reports of what they saw there. These reports were officially known as the "Daily Chronicles of the Progress of the Embassy" ("Sứ Trình Nhật Ký"). The data supplied by the "Daily Chronicles" were considered at Huế in conjunction with the envoys' more grandiose accounts of the latest Chinese institutional innovations. If the former revealed a disaffected countryside in China, Vietnamese rulers' enthusiasm for institutional borrowing slackened noticeably. The "Daily Chronicles" were, in other words, a practical touchstone by which Huế-confined emperors could assess the validity of their scholar-envoys' zealous promotion of new Chinese political devices. The envoys themselves, less interested in this deflationary function of the "Daily Chronicles," occasionally failed to meet the emperors' standards for them, as in 1832, when Minh-mạng's edict, referring to three returning envoys, declared: "With regard to the making of comprehensive inquiries [in China], namely the "Daily Chronicles," their investigations of the conditions of the Ch'ing country are generally all roughly written sketches. There is not one that is fit to be read at court . . . Because their "Daily Chronicles of the Progress of the Embassy" only contain the names of geographical places and the distances between them in li, but do not once relate the circumstances of the people or the affairs of the country . . . from now on on every occasion of an embassy [the Board of Rites] must transmit a decree to the envoys to make full inquiries as to whether the situation of the people is prospering or ailing, whether within the country calamity or good fortune prevails. They must understand [these things] and enter them in the "Chronicles." As far as the names of places and the distances between them in li are concerned, we already have documents that we can consult. We have no need of tautological descriptions."[14]

Emperors found it difficult to anticipate what new ideas or projects of institutional imitation their envoys to China would bring back with them. This is a constant theme in Vietnamese history. In 1158, for example, the Lý envoy had returned from China and had told the Lý ruler of a marvelous copper casket for receiving memorials which he had spied at the Sung court and which he hoped his sovereign would also want to have.[15] In the Nguyễn period, when Nguyễn Hữu Thận returned from Peking in 1810, he brought with him a Ch'ing work on calendrical astronomy. The work summarized that body of Western astronomical knowledge which had formally been accepted by the Chinese from Jesuit missionaries in the K'ang-hsi reign in the late seventeenth century. In a memorial, Thận informed Gia-long that late Ming astronomical notions were now out of date. The longer they were consulted, "the greater will be the errors . . . Please give this book to the Imperial Observatory and command its astronomers to study and seek its rules."[16]

In 1820, ten years later, Phan Huy Thực came back from Peking full of enthusiasm about the Ch'ing system of selecting "tribute scholars" and making them apprentices at the Six Boards, so that they could get accustomed early in their careers to bureaucratic regulations and methods of administration. Encouraged by Thực, and upon the basis of his originally unsolicited report, Minh-mạng summoned a group of examination system students in Huế, gave them a supplementary examination, and posted them to his own Six Boards as *hành tẩu* (apprentices).[17] The transfer of institutions within the Sino-Vietnamese world was often as casual and as unpremeditated as this. Brought back in the baggage of returning envoys from China in the spring of 1820 as well were two live long-tailed goats, male and female; nothing in China was considered to be too uninteresting or inappropriate to be carted back to Huế for closer inspection. This collecting of Chinese animals and birds also suited the taste of Vietnamese neo-Confucian scholars for the "investigation of things" (*cách vật*) and the classification of natural objects.[18]

Perhaps the strangest trophy Vietnamese envoys ever brought back from China in this period was the name "Vietnam" itself. It dates from 1803 and is perhaps the most obvious tangible legacy of the old Chinese tributary system still surviving in East Asia. Gia-long had originally wanted to call his kingdom *Nam Việt* (*Nan-yüeh* in Chinese). He had sent his envoys to Peking to seek Ch'ing approval not only of himself but also of this new name. To Chinese ears, however, *Nam Việt* or *Nan-yüeh* suggested an overweening, patrimonial invocation of the name of an ancient state, conquered by the Han dynasty, which had once included the territory of Kwangtung and Kwangsi as well as northern Vietnam. The Ch'ing emperor therefore carefully rearranged the order of the two elements in Gia-long's proposed name to form the word *Yüeh-nan*—or Vietnam. In trepidation Gia-long's envoys had to return to Huế with this Chinese diplomatic concoction, an outrageous *fait accompli*, resting upon their consciences.[19]

The word *Việt* stood for the older part of the country, the northern and central areas, which had borne the name *Đại Việt* under the Lê. The word *Nam*, "south," referred to the newer areas, the colonized south, which had never previously been involved in the traditional Vietnamese kingdom. But the name "Vietnam" as a whole was hardly so well esteemed by Vietnamese rulers a century ago, emanating as it had from Peking, as it is in this century. An artificial appellation then, it was used extensively neither by the Chinese nor by the Vietnamese. The Chinese clung to the offensive T'ang word "Annam," although communications they addressed to the Vietnamese bearing this name were promptly returned on the direct orders of the emperor, as in 1847.[20] The Vietnamese court, on the other hand, privately invented another official name for its kingdom in 1838–39 and did not bother to inform the Chinese.[21] Its new official name, *Đại Nam*, the "Great South" or "Imperial South," appeared with regularity on court documents and official historical compilations. But it has not survived to the present.

Upon this flow of books and ideas from Peking to Huế depended the development of the centralization techniques of the Vietnamese ruler, the power of his bureaucrats, literary stimulation for Vietnamese poets, and even prestige for provincial schoolmasters. But because Chinese institutions were more often imported to serve such various general purposes than more narrow specific functions, emperors cherished the constant fear that the process could go too far. Skepticism about Chinese behavior thus remained almost as strong as the desire to borrow Chinese institutions. "Decadent China and orthodox Vietnam" was a favorite theme of Minh-mạng's.

This theme was reinforced by the Confucian perspective that positions and power do not have a residual grandeur which they confer upon men. Rather, men who are moral paragons confer grandeur upon their positions. Respect for a Chinese emperor might be tendered formally through tribute. But behind the scenes his very soul was questioned—often through analyzing at a distance the poetry he had written. How respectable was his *tình-cảnh*—the way in which his feelings or his moral personality (*tình*) had interacted with his environment (*cảnh*)? Even these trifles exercised a subtle influence upon the decision to borrow or not to borrow. Of the Ch'ien-lung emperor's poems, of which there were more than 24,000, long and short,[22] Minh-mạng said in 1835: "Of the ones I have read, all are plainly written, and their subjective reactions to the external world are not artificially elaborate or full of frivolous words. However, they abound in vulgar usages. For example, in singing about ginseng, he says, 'Its five leaves and three branches cluster auspiciously, embracing its phallus-like stem. The emissions of its vermilion fruits are sweet and universal.' In my various writings I merely please my senses and describe what I see, but in use of words I never attain such coarseness and vulgarity."[23]

Thus Chinese emperors' poems were read at Huế along with the envoys' "Daily Chronicles." Discussing contemporary China in 1840, after having consulted the latter, Minh-mạng predicted that the opium blight and the Sino-British war might dissolve the tributary system in fact if not in name: "I hear that at the Northern Court imperial princes, princes near the throne, and high civil and military officials all smoke opium . . . If their own country is in such a state, how can they give laws to foreign countries?"[24]

Vietnamese officials who had served in China as envoys were required to suggest new Chinese institutions that might be profitably domesticated in Vietnam. But they were also compelled to write essays exposing Chinese institutional deficiencies, perhaps as a kind of psychological or cultural cure, after they had returned to Huế. One of these envoys, Phan Huy Thực, recounted one of the major findings about China set forth in these literary self-purifications for Minh-mạng in 1840: "Our country's envoys [to China] have written that each time the Ch'ing emperor holds court and discusses affairs with all his assembled officials, when he talks to the Chinese he speaks Chinese and when he converses with Manchus he speaks Manchu. Ministers at his court who do not have a comprehensive understanding of languages are completely incapable of carefully understanding court business." Minh-mạng immediately reminded him of the moral of this discovery: "If it is a situation like this, with such discrepancies of attitude and viewpoint the passage of feeling from high to low is obstructed and does not circulate. Those who are ministers cannot avoid privately harboring suspicions and fears. Who is willing to dedicate himself totally?"[25]

In 1824 Minh-mạng had drawn this lesson for another of his officials, Hoàng Kim Hoán, who presided over the national college in Huế, by telling him that the Manchus were barbarians, that they had taken precedence over the Chinese, and that in any case Vietnam, a southern country, should never rely solely upon the "northern people."[26] Ten years later he stressed another Ch'ing vulnerability, by commenting that he had heard that evidence was elicited by flogging in Chinese judicial yamens. In his opinion this would make innocent men confess but not intimidate hardened criminals.[27] On the whole, China regarded Vietnam's smallness as a tell-tale revelation that the Vietnamese had hardly risen to China's own standards of sophistication in political organization, but the Vietnamese believed that the smallness of their imperial court and of the society it ruled was the most profoundly convincing proof that it represented classical purity, that it recaptured, far more successfully than any dynasty in Peking ever could, memories of the intimate feudal city-state political environs of the golden Chinese Chou period, when the Confucian classics had been written but before China had been unified. This belief was a convenient one for the relatively small Nguyễn kingdom. Strangely enough it was also perfectly sincere, for the Vietnamese, as the borrowers of the sanctioned patterns of the overt culture of another people, did not always borrow the unconscious, implicit systems of meanings and qualifications which lay behind these patterns. They were often, in other words, more literal-minded about Chinese political ideals—which celebrated the small Chou states—than the Chinese themselves.

Outside the tributary system, Chinese books were brought to Vietnam as a matter of profitable private enterprise by south Chinese merchants. The court had advertised its willingness to pay lavish rewards for foreign books of all kinds, Western as well as Chinese. In 1820 Minh-mạng bestowed Western eyeglasses and bottles of perfume upon his assembled officials, and urged them to borrow and read the "strange books from the four corners of the world" that he kept in his library.[28] It is difficult to reconstruct from fragmentary evidence the lags in time between the publications of books in China and their arrivals in Vietnam. But it seems certain that, after Chinese dynastic statutes, which were imported by tributary envoys, the books which came the most quickly were scholarly compilations printed in south China. In 1831, for example, the Chinese merchant Ch'en Ying unloaded from his junk in Quảng Nam the *Huang Ch'ing ching-chieh* (Exegeses of the classics of the imperial Ch'ing). This was, of course, a vast, 1,478-*chüan* collection of exegetical texts of the Thirteen Classics put together by Juan Yüan, the famous Ch'ing official, at his "Sea of Scholarship Studio" (*Hsüeh-hai t'ang*) in Kwangtung. The date of the preface to this work was 1829, so it had not taken the Nguyễn court long to receive it.[29] On the other hand, records show that in 1809 a Chinese merchant came to Hanoi to offer the Vietnamese some books that he had studied in China as a child, including the Sung work *Ta Hsüeh yen-i* (An expanded popular text of the Great learning) and its Ming supplement. These, when they were presented to Gia-long by the Hanoi overlord, were equally well received.[30] The court could also purchase Chinese books in the thriving southern marketplace of Chợ-lớn. In the words of Trịnh Hoài Đức, who had, of course, traveled all across China, "from the south to the north, from the rivers to the seas, there do not exist goods which they [the Chợ-lớn merchants] do not have."³¹ Needless to say, the demand for Chinese books existed all over classical East Asia. Minh-mạng's Japanese counterpart may well have been the Tokugawa shogun Yoshimune (ruled 1716–1745). Yoshimune once, in a fury, returned a shipment of Chinese books from Edo to Nagasaki merely because the shipment was incomplete. He caused the six edicts of the first Ming emperor of China to be read in eighteenth-century Japanese elementary schools with their Japanese exposition by Muro Kyūsō. And he gained his awareness of Western learning through reading the latest Chinese translations.³²

But the similarities are not overpowering. In a previous chapter it was suggested that one reason why Vietnamese institutional borrowing from China was so wholehearted was that it was governed by Vietnamese bureaucrats' ingrained formalistic respect for written rules of all kinds. Japanese borrowers were less professionally bureaucratic. But another factor in the sinicization of Nguyễn administration after 1820 was the gross imbalance that existed between the sheer bulk of Chinese literature dealing with Chinese government and the comparative paucity of similar Vietnamese literature dealing with past Vietnamese institutions.

Possibly this imbalance was greater in the nineteenth century than in any previous period. Eighteenth-century China in the Ch'ien-lung period had been marked by a stupendous output of gazetteers, statutes, military campaign records, linguistic handbooks, and poetry. The flood of books had been greater than that of the almost equally long K'ang-hsi reign earlier. This was a fact of great political importance in Huế. Furthermore, the imbalance was unlikely to disappear. Each member of the army of Chinese copyists at the Peking Historical Institute (*Kuo-shih-kuan*) was regularly required, under the Ch'ing, to produce 1,500 characters a day. Their collective production added up to a large standard of achievement in Vietnamese eyes.³³

In Vietnam a comparable Historical Institute (*Quốc sử quán* in

Sino-Vietnamese) did not exist before 1821.[34] Civil war in the 1700's, when China was peaceful, and an essentially military, regionalized government in the Gia-long period had led to little scholarly production at Huế before 1815, apart from the dynasty's law code. Minh-mạng was compelled to ransack private libraries after 1820 for pre-1820 Vietnamese records. Old books, after all, could confute new institutions. Even old poetry had a prophetic power in the villages and the court knew how to fear it. Phan Huy Chú (1782–1840), an official who presented an extremely valuable work on past Vietnamese institutions, the *Lịch triều hiến chương loại chí* (A reference book to the institutions of successive dynasties), to Minh-mạng in 1821, in order to bridge the gap, wrote in his book that it was difficult to reconstruct the nature of Vietnamese institutions before 1400.[35]

One reason for this has never been forgotten in Vietnam. The Ming Chinese colonial regime in Vietnam in 1407–1427 had systematically tried to destroy Vietnamese dynastic records. It had seen these records as symbolizing Vietnamese independence. Among the many works that apparently perished were the Lý dynasty's *Hình thư* (Book of justice), the Trần dynasty's *Quốc triều thông lễ* (Comprehensive rites of the national court), and *Trần triều đại điển* (Statutes of the Trần court) and others.

Still another reason why the Nguyễn court consulted Chinese statutes more often than the records of previous Vietnamese dynasties was that it was of central and southern origin. Lê historical documents had been written under the aegis of northern politicians, who had followed the Trịnh versions of historical events. The Trịnh family having been the rival of the Nguyễns, Minh-mạng complained in 1839 that Lê histories possessed "many inaccuracies."[36]

Thus Chinese texts were more abundant, went back farther in time, did not arouse Vietnamese factional partisanship, and seemed more free of the regional language variations and battles over the use of *nôm* which bedevilled Vietnamese compilers. As a sample of the technical controversies and disagreements over the latter, which sprang up among the literati in Huế, in 1840 one of their newest compilations, the *Tập vận trích yếu* (Epitomies of harmony and rhyme) was judged to have "errors"—unacceptable words—in more than six hundred places.[37] A multiplicity of factors like these lurked behind the influence of Chinese books—and the diffusion of their ideas—in Vietnam.

The Borrowing of an Imperial Milieu: The Rise of Huế

Of all the monuments existing in Vietnam which expressed dynastic ambitions to bring the forms and images of the Chinese imperial tradition to Southeast Asia, none were more imposing than the Nguyễn palaces themselves in Huế, the imperial capital. Huế pavilions and audience halls were more than just objects of borrowed architecture from China. More important, they were the architectural foundation of the borrowing process itself, one of its influences, an encouragement to its continuation as well as one of its ends. The reason for this was that their names, their interrelated locations, and their appearances all reinforced the classical modes of perception of such things as court politics, the ruler's relationship to the universe, his relationship to his society, and the purposes of government.

The traditional Sino-Vietnamese name for the area in which nineteenth-century Huế was to grow, Thuận Hóa, succinctly captured its early history, for the territory first entered Vietnamese hands in 1301–1306, when the Cham king Jaya Sinhavarman III gave it to the Trần court in return for the hand of a Trần princess. By "agreement" (*thuận*) the area "changed" (*hóa*) civilizations, foretasting the eventual fate of the remainder of the Cham kingdom.[38] Although the power of the Nguyễn family, which ruled central Vietnam from the sixteenth century on, had radiated from Thuận Hóa in theory and in fact for two hundred years and more, Huế itself, as a Southeast Asian facsimile of the Chinese capital at Peking, only emerged in the early nineteenth century. It consisted of three cities in one, with the "Forbidden City" at its core, the "Imperial City" (*Hoàng thành;* known to the French as the *enceinte jaune*) surrounding the "Forbidden City," and the "Capital City" (*Kinh thành;* known to the French as the "citadel") encompassing both. (Many Vietnamese referred to the emperor's residences collectively as the "imperial inner place" or Đại Nội, an old-fashioned Sino-Vietnamese term more in vogue in T'ang Ch'ang-an or in Sung Hangchow than in Ch'ing Peking.) Huế's three cities in one were the symbols both of the old Nguyễn family and of the new Nguyễn dynasty, which had successfully reunified the country. They also symbolized a major political transition, the transition of power from Hanoi to them. Thăng-long, the historic capital of Vietnam, had been abandoned by a ruling dynasty for the first time in centuries.

The debate in Vietnam over the merits and disadvantages of this shift of capitals in 1802 has never ended. Some Vietnamese historians have argued that the change was disastrous, that the mountains of central Vietnam isolated Huế from the rest of the country. This effect was exacerbated by Huế's lack of a position on a crucial river system. In Vietnamese history the mountainous central area had specialized in harboring successful rebel movements but only short-lived dynasties.[39] Other historians have argued with some ingenuity that the change was culturally beneficial. Vietnamese literati, instead of concentrating themselves in one northern city, lived after 1802 in all parts of Vietnam. Central and southern Vietnamese writers like Nguyễn Du (Vietnam's greatest poet, who however came from the north central area and was regarded by Minh-mạng as a northerner) and Nguyễn Đình Chiểu thrived under the Huế-based dynasty, while northern writers—like Cao Bá Quát and Hồ Xuân Hương— wrote with a greater, more iconoclastic freedom.[40] Possibly there is truth in both opinions.

The Huế area had been the historic homeland of the Nguyễn family. Yet this appears to have been a secondary factor in its selection in 1802. According to Minh-mạng, Gia-long had wanted to make the protectorate capital of Nghệ An his imperial capital. He had been dissuaded from doing so by Nguyễn Văn Nhân. Huế was the center of the kingdom, and its geographical centrality had earned it its role.[41] Although its imitations of Chinese-style grandeur are its principal concern to this study, it must be remembered that these imitations were never enjoyed or greatly understood by its non-bureaucratic population. Nguyễn court records document episodes in which the people of Huế interfered with imperial processions through the streets, offered little respect to officials in sedan chairs,[42] and indulged in hooliganism. Huế in the early 1800's was renowned for its discordantly noisy food peddlers, whom a desperate Minh-mạng tried to license.[43] The Sino-Vietnamese imperial dream coexisted uneasily with the Southeast Asian market town.

The Huế imperial city was located in the southernmost part of the capital city or citadel. It was itself oriented toward the south, in line with the Chinese classical tradition that the sages had faced south in order to listen to, and understand, the world. It was about 614 *trượng* in diameter. (The *trượng* is a unit of ten Vietnamese feet.) It possessed four gates. It was surrounded by the undulating, fortresslike wall of the capital city, which was more French than Chinese in style. This wall was more than 2,487 *trượng* around, with eleven gates, seven of which faced the south and the east.[44]

The name of the south front gate of the imperial city, the Zenith Gate (*Ngọ Môn*), suggested the time when the sun reached its highest point above the earth. It was intended as a complimentary salute to the emperor, the most exalted human being. Outside the Zenith Gate most capital city bureaucrats performed their work. Such buildings as the Six Boards, in the southeast of the capital city, and the Censorate, in the west of the capital city, remained excluded from the imperial city. Once a man had passed through the Zenith Gate, he was in the emperor's precincts. He proceeded north from the gate itself to the courtyard of the Hall of Supreme Harmony (*Thái Hòa Điện*), where the emperor held audiences on great occasions like the New Year and the fifth day of the fifth month. Beyond the Hall of Supreme Harmony he came to the wall of the Forbidden City, which was more than 306 *trượng* in diameter and which possessed seven gates. Inside the Forbidden City he encountered the Hall of Diligence in Government (*Cần Chính Điện*) where the emperor held ordinary audiences, and behind it the imperial palaces (the *Kiến Thành Cung* and the *Khôn Thái Cung*).

As in Peking, all these buildings were located in succession on a south-north axis. As in Peking a Zenith Gate (*Wu-men* in Chinese) marked the threshhold of the Son of Heaven's sanctuary, although in larger Peking, the Zenith Gate was the south gate of the Forbidden City, not of the Imperial City. As in Peking a Hall of Supreme Harmony was the major throne hall. Huế, of course, was much smaller. Its cosy dimensions were converted into objects of homespun poetry by a local folksong, which, in celebrating the pine tar lamps that burned at night in the Forbidden City, claimed that "when they are lit in the Hall of Diligence in Government, they shine beyond the Zenith Gate."[45]

Names like "Supreme Harmony," which the Vietnamese had borrowed from China, were commonplaces of cosmological suggestiveness which were understood by everyone from scholars to marketplace fortune tellers. The terms *kiền* and *khôn*, for example, parts of the names of the two Nguyễn palaces, conveyed a cluster of polar ideas like heaven and earth, the sun and the moon, male and female, northwest and southwest. They were cliches so deeply entrenched in the Chinese classical world that Matteo Ricci, appreciating the persuasive familiarity they would have for Peking court scholars in the late Ming period, had unhesitatingly chosen them for the title of the book in which he had tried to smuggle Western mathematics and astronomy into China—his *Ch'ien-k'un t'i-i* (roughly, A fundamental interpretation of heaven and earth).

Ten thousand soldiers, an enormous number for early nineteenth-century Vietnam, labored on the construction of the Hall of Supreme Harmony in 1833, on a site further south than that of Gia-long's similar smaller and earlier Hall.[46] Minh-mạng pretended to be personally skeptical about such traditions as the southward orientations of all buildings: "This adhering to a rule of not violating what is taboo, these are the theories of geomancers. I do not believe in them deeply. But planning and building city walls and moats is strategy for the country's long survival. There is certainly no harm in following the auspicious and avoiding the calamitous."[47]

The Chinese influence in the building of Huế was direct as well as indirect. In 1810 Gia-long had ordered the leader of the Kwangtung congregation in Vietnam to recruit Chinese tile artisans in Canton. A group of such artisans apparently came to Huế to demonstrate the firing of blue, yellow, and green glazed roof tiles for Vietnamese workers to imitate.[48] In 1837 this Chinese influence was balanced perhaps by the insertion of Western window glass in some of the palace windows.[49] Elaborations were, in fact, added endlessly to Huế architecture, like balustrades of a florid style above the Zenith Gate in 1833. Consequently, Vietnamese imperial buildings as a whole were not only smaller but also were less austere and more heavily ornamented than their Peking counterparts. It is just possible, although not very likely, that these elaborations were a defensive, competitive response to cultural pressures from the West, which were felt in this young coastal capital in a way that they were not in north

China. It is certainly true that the Vietnamese were aware of the growing wealth of such settlements as Singapore. With the new Christian heterodoxy spreading slowly in the provinces, in 1838 Minh-mạng changed and expanded the architecture of provincial Confucian temples, which now became larger and more ornate.[50]

Huế imitations of Peking landmarks were mainly representational rather than structural or proportional. A small pool inside a court-yard of the Imperial City was even named after the *T'ai-yeh-ch'ih* (Great Clear Pool), a large lake outside and west of the west gate of the imperial city in Peking. In 1835, not content with imitating the Ch'ing Chinese imperial milieu alone, Minh-mạng ordered the cast-ing of nine large bronze urns (*cửu đỉnh*) further to symbolize Nguyễn power. This resurrected on Vietnamese soil a precedent of the Hsia, Shang, and Chou dynasties in which urns formed of the gold tribute donated by local rulers were cast by Chinese rulers and important writings and drawings were engraved upon their sides, making them in effect cultural and political dictionaries of their reigns.[51] Upon Minh-Mạng's nine urns of 1835 were carved a host of Vietnamese flora and fauna, properly labeled, and also exotic items like "a flower which comes from the Great Western Ocean and whose Western pronunciation is *đô-da*"—the European rose.[52]

Huế palaces possessed at different times two sets of names, "auspi-cious names" (*gia danh*), which were designed to obtain the favor of fate, and more historical "palace names" (*cung danh*), which were intended to evoke an affinity with all the ancient political purposes of the classical world. In other words, Huế buildings were supposed to embody and organize a specific system of metaphorical identifica-tion as well as represent the physical site of government. This was illustrated by the names controversy of 1833, in which Minh-mạng declared that Chinese-style buildings must be accompanied by the requisite titles: "In the early Gia-long period the Đại Nội [the emperor's household area] was built, and up into the Minh-mạng period there have been further additions. All the palaces and halls and towers and pavilions were given 'auspicious names,' but do not yet have 'palace names.' This year construction has been consum-mated according to the model and they ought to have names in order to establish the importance of the imperial residence . . . The palace name Kiên Thành takes 'making things perfect' as its meaning. What comes under that term is broad, like the duties of perfecting men, perfecting living things, and perfecting the universe."[53]

Most of the names were drawn from Chinese statutes by Hà Quyên, a doctoral degree holder of 1822. He informed the emperor that there was a surplus to choose from, although "terms such as 'Permanent Happiness Without End' [actually, the names of two Han dynasty palaces] were universally used by recent generations. Then at the beginning of the Ch'ing they used different names like 'Equable Harmony.'"[54] Because the Vietnamese ruler was more an imitator than a successor of Chinese dynasties of the past, he feared the mockery of his officials—who were Confucians as orthodox as their Chinese counterparts—if he employed "false names" (*ngụy hiệu*) or misread texts. Perhaps this excessively fundamentalist christening of Huế palaces by Minh-mạng in 1833 answered the need for methodological dramatizations which such an imitator often felt.

Huế also had to conform architecturally to Peking because the ritualistic movements of the Vietnamese emperor and his court had to conform to the Chinese codes. Many of the rituals in the life of the Chinese emperor were associated with sites or specific buildings in Peking. In 1835, for example, after a rebellion had been suppressed in southern Vietnam, Minh-mạng ordered his officials to consult the Chinese statutes in order to discover their rituals for presenting prisoners of war to the throne (*phú lễ*). The answer came that, according to the Ming statutes, if the emperor personally commanded a military expedition, when he returned he presented his prisoners at his ancestral shrine. If he had remained in Peking, prisoners were presented to him at the Zenith Gate. Minh-mạng followed this example and went to his own Zenith Gate to survey the captured rebels from Saigon.[55] In Vietnam imperial proclamations were first read from the Huế Zenith Gate, accompanied by music and meticulous gestures. A proclamation reader faced south and began the ritual by chanting "there is a proclamation" (*hữu chiếu*) in Sino-Vietnamese.[56]

Finally, it must be remembered that when the Chinese political and social stratification systems were imported into Vietnam, the basic architecture of Chinese imperial politics had to be imported too. This architecture, consisting as it did of walls, gates, moats, pools, bridges, and numerous audience halls, amounted to a collection of physical barriers which matched the figurative boundaries of etiquette and styles of dress that separated higher members of the bureaucracy from lower members and all members of the bureaucracy from the emperor. The architecture reflected the hierarchical principles of the society.

Imitation of Peking's walls and moats, which were associated with these hierarchical principles, seemed far more important to the Vietnamese than imitation of Peking's spatial grandeur, which seemed less associated with them. It was characteristic of this attitude that Nguyễn Siêu, a Vietnamese envoy to Peking of 1848, commented in his travel diary not that Peking was much larger than Huế but rather that he was surprised by the lack of enough soldiers at its important gates.[57] And just as Huế imitated Peking's architectural barriers without imitating their dimensions, so the Vietnamese bureaucracy itself imitated all the levels of status within the Chinese bureaucracy but nonetheless remained much smaller in size and numbers.

Regionalism and the Breakdown of Administrative Homogeneity

Surrounded by Chinese-style architecture in Huế and conditioned to expect an unceasing flow of enlightening books from the Ch'ing empire to his own capital, the Vietnamese bureaucrat might acquire an optimistic faith in the conquest of all administrative problems that official life in the provinces would shatter. As a first step toward a description of the discrepancies that emerged between Huế ideals and the solution of local problems, it should be pointed out that even above the village level there was great regional diversity in nineteenth-century Vietnam. The cultural heterogeneity of the society as a whole challenged the relative cultural homogeneity of its governing Confucian elite, as it did in China. But in Vietnam the costs of challenge and response may have been greater. The Vietnamese official who was appointed to a post in Bình Định, for example, or Khánh Hòa remained culturally unimpeachable by doggedly studying the Cham ruins there with the aid of ancient Chinese texts like the *Shui ching chu* (Commentary on the Water classic; with a section on Champa) and by learning two names for every bridge and provincial market, a Sino-Vietnamese name (Vĩnh-điêm thị) as well as a less artificial non-Sinic Vietnamese name (Chợ Doanh).

Four factors were at work behind nineteenth-century Vietnamese regional differentiation. First of all, the variety of climates and environments that existed between the China border and the Gulf of Siam naturally necessitated different forms of agriculture and different styles of settlement and housing. Second, as in China, there was little cultural standardization at the village level but rather a lavishly variegated spectrum of village traditions and beliefs. Third, from the sixteenth century to 1802 north Vietnam on the one hand and central and southern Vietnam on the other had evolved into two separate political units, each with its own institutions and schemes of taxation. Fourth, the slow movement south of the Vietnamese people had left each region with a different historical background of absorption into Vietnam. The province of Bình Thuận, for example, had been part of the Cham state until the fifteenth century and had not emerged as a prefecture bearing the name Bình Thuận until the 1700's, while the province of Thanh Hóa had been "sinicized" during the Han conquest, its own name emerging during the eleventh century. The Vietnamese language was spoken with a profusion of accents. In Huế in the 1800's the Quảng Nam accent (of south of Huế) was considered the correct one.[58]

It is worth looking at this regional diversity for a moment from the point of view of the dynasty. In the court's eyes the basic regional problem was how to win support in the north. Many northerners regarded the Nguyễns as southern usurpers who had deprived Hanoi (Thăng-long) of its long-descended function as capital. Concessions were made to the city of Hanoi, which had been damaged by Gia-long's campaign against the Tây-sơns. It was rebuilt in 1803–04 by corvee labor as an "auxiliary capital," with an inner and an outer city. The first three Nguyễn emperors received their seals of investiture from China there rather than in Huế. In the Gia-long period imperial currency was minted in Hanoi rather than in Huế. This was a practical measure as well, because the north was the home of traditional Vietnamese industry, especially of mines. The official seal of the Hanoi regional examination site from 1807 to 1827 was larger than those of the other regional sites. Because there were no higher metropolitan examinations in Vietnam before 1822, this privilege gave Hanoi a capital-like preeminence.[59] Economic motives as well as political ones dictated Nguyễn patronage of Hanoi and its environs. As Minh-mạng said in 1840, "Hanoi is the major province of the north, and no other jurisdiction can be compared to it in terms of the importance of its lands and settlements."[60]

Regionalism affected the degree and the nature of Vietnamese conformity to Minh-mạng's sinicization policies. The cultural frontier between northern Vietnam and central and southern Vietnam was the Spirit River (*Linh giang*) in Quảng Bình province. (Today it is known as the Gianh River.) The Trịnh family had formerly ruled the lands north of the Spirit River and the Nguyễns had ruled those south of it. After 1802, Vietnamese conformity to the new Sino-Vietnamese socialization process sponsored by Huế was occasionally more constrained than conscientious "north of the river." For example, "south of the river" Vietnamese women commonly wore buttoned-up tunics and trousers, following the Chinese custom favored by the Nguyễn house. Northern Vietnamese women, however, continued to wear skirts in the 1800's. Because Minh-mạng's objective was large-scale cultural reform, in which the inculcation of correct clothing styles was almost as important as the borrowing of the proper bureaucratic institutions, in 1828 and 1837 he issued long edicts commanding northern women to change from skirts to trousers.

Minh-mạng's clothing laws were effective only in the cities and towns of the north, among the wives of merchants but not among peasant women. Cultural borrowing from China was more rapid at the top of Nguyễn society than at the bottom. One reason was that the educated elite's predispositions to borrow were greater than those of the peasants. But another reason was that acculturation was expensive. The peasants could not afford cultural change. In this instance, peasant women were too poor to buy trousers. Compliance with Huế's edicts in public would have simply forced them to wear their husbands' clothing, while their husbands remained at home. A satirical nineteenth-century folksong said:

> The edict issued by Minh-mạng
> Forbidding skirts, terrifies the people.
> If you do not go to the market, it will not
>   be crowded.

> But to go to the market, how can you have the
> heart to undress your husband?[61]

Regional fiscal discontinuities also undermined the effective growth of Minh-mạng's bureaucracy in northern Vietnam. As of 1820, the Nguyễn dynasty's newly cast lead coins were circulating well only "south of the river." From Nghệ An north, the people still remained addicted to the old copper coins of the Lê dynasty.[62] In the very far north, along the Chinese border, in provinces like Cao Bằng, at least up until 1830 the dynasty even reluctantly accepted the payment of its tax quotas in Chinese small coins of the Tao-kuang era. This practice threatened to undermine the whole economy of the borderlands. The coins were actually cast privately by Chinese merchants, who did not use copper substances in their manufacture, the inevitable consequence of which was a flood of such quasi-official Chinese coins and a progressive inflation of prices.[63] Nonetheless, despite the persistence of this cultural and economic patchwork, Minh-mạng spoke optimistically in 1832 of the "ungrateful, demoralized" minds of the people of the north returning rapidly to the ways of purity and excellence.[64]

Indeed it would be foolish to underestimate the achievements the dynasty undoubtedly made in integrating north, center, and south into one polity. Political and cultural disunity was far less formidable in 1847 than it had been in 1802. Regional rebellions occurred on numerous occasions. One authority has counted 105 separate uprisings in the Gia-long period alone.[65] Another Vietnamese writer has suggested that there were close to 200 rebellions in the Minh-mạng period.[66] But these eruptions were well distributed regionally, rather than being confined to one area, and few of them were really serious. More and more, regional feelings found an outlet not in the separate regions themselves so much as at Huế. Here factions inspired by geographical associations appeared in the imperial bureaucracy. A censor, Nguyễn Bá Nghi, gives us something of their flavor with his declaration in 1835–36 that increasingly among officials there was "discrimination between south and north. Through good fortune the southerners are flatterers and braggarts, and everything they say and do occupies the position of advantage. Consequently, the northerners are ashamed within themselves."[67] Many of these "southerners" actually came from families resident in central Vietnam whose previous generations had fought with Gia-long in the south before 1802. Opposed to them were the northern scholar families who remembered the old Lê court and whose sentiments, oddly enough, were captured in a poem by Nguyễn Công Trứ, the degree holder from Hà Tĩnh of 1819 who had become one of Minh-mạng's most loyal officials. Although he had offered his loyalty to the Nguyễn rulers as early as 1804, the faithful Trứ wrote a rather unfaithful description of Hanoi under the Nguyễns, poetically brilliant but false in most circumstances, in which he portrayed the city as a sad, museum-like former capital overrun by the wilderness and betrayed by its abandonment:

> In reflections on the water's surface the sails of
>   the fishermen droop mournfully,
> A profusion of flowers and ferns in the capital's
>   vicinity greets the spring season.
> The homeland is immersed in nostalgia over the
>   past's vicissitudes.
> The wild things of nature claim the place by envelop-
>   ing it in sad, convulsive changes.
> Wandering visitors sightsee and ask [sarcastic]
>   questions:
> "How many times in the past the stars have moved and
>   the living world has changed—
> "Which particular king's palaces and imperial temples
>   are in which particular place?"
> Ridiculingly the monkeys answer them with lonely calls,
>   and the mango-birds say, "Good day!"[68]

After 1802 dependable southern officials were placed in control of most of northern Vietnam, although lesser officials in the north, like provincial, prefectural, and district educational officials, were almost always northerners. Nguyễn Văn Thành (1757–1817), for example, the overlord of the north in the first decade of the Gia-long period, came from a family which had been resident in the Gia Định area (around modern Saigon). From Hanoi he surveyed a political and economic landscape which, being different from that of the south, was also perhaps more susceptible to the application of classical Chinese methods of local rule. In 1835 Minh-mạng described public works—a leading concern of local officials—in southern Vietnam as consisting of "city walls, moats, junks, granaries, offices, and roads."[69] In north Vietnam, however, a bureaucrat from the south discovered another exigency relatively new to him—the building and repair of dikes.

Artificial water control along the rivers was essential to public administration in Hanoi, Bắc Ninh, Sơn Tây, Hưng Yên, Nam Định, Hải Dương, Ninh Bình, Hưng Hóa, and other northern provinces. This meant that dikes that had already been built must be constantly strengthened. Money to recruit laborers to build the dikes must reach the hands of the canton chiefs without being plundered by other officials on its way down the hierarchy, and peasants must be prevented from knocking holes in the dikes to obtain greater fishing profits. Vietnamese provincial officials, having inherited smaller administrative bailiwicks than their Chinese counterparts, could afford the luxury of watching the individual dike sections of villages under them for signs of decay.

Although private dike-building certainly occurred, the dynasty exercised much greater direct control of it through its local officials than Chinese courts could ever do in China. There was no real corresponding group of local "reservoir heads" (*p'i-shou*), directly or indirectly representing the local gentry and managing key irrigation projects, in Vietnam as there was in a Chinese province like Fukien.[70] There was less need for them. Vietnamese water control was miniature but probably more highly developed. It is significant that Nguyễn Siêu, the Vietnamese envoy to Peking of 1848 who has already been quoted, wrote that he had read Chinese documents dealing with river administration. Inexplicably to him, they concerned themselves merely with new dike construction and with the digging of new channels for the lower reaches of rivers only. In his eyes the Chinese paid little attention to the digging of new channels in the upper reaches of their rivers, and were poor at defending and consolidating already existing dikes.[71]

His critical perspective, of course, ignored the much greater size of Chinese provinces and districts and the continuing informal activities of the Chinese gentry, which were not likely to be described in full in court memorials. But the skilful way in which Vietnamese provincial officials were required to protect and preserve old dikes in northern Vietnam is revealed in the fund of data contained in the 1829 report to Minh-mạng, *Bắc-thành công tư đê tổng sách* (Comprehensive records of public and private dikes in the north), which was prepared by his dikes commissioner, Lê Đại Cương. In the four provinces of Sơn Tây, Sơn Nam, Bắc Ninh, and Nam Định, spanning forty-seven districts, this 1829 report disclosed that of the 237,439 *trượng* of publicly built dikes then existing in these areas more than 200,000 *trượng* had been built in the Lê period before 1802.[72] The age of these dikes is proof of the administrative control which kept them intact despite rebellion and unrest.

Vietnamese dike-building techniques mixed Chinese and Southeast Asian elements. Bamboo rafts were employed to transport rocks to the dike sites. Elephants, few of which were privately owned, were used to pound down the earthen bases of the dikes.[73] River sizes and the heights of dikes were bureaucratically categorized in Huế. "River poles" (*hà can*) were placed along the dikes to measure the normal and abnormal levels of the water and suggest the points that needed strengthening (these poles tallied with records kept in officials' offices of past disaster levels), and disaster could ensue if the poles blew down or if sub-bureaucrats moved them.[74] Officials serving in the north had to master this tangle of needs.

The southern bureaucrat who proceeded by appointment to the north in the early 1800's discovered another regional factor of importance. The area governed by an overlord from Hanoi possessed, as Phạm Như Đăng, a southern adviser of Gia-long's (who however had originally come from Thanh Hóa), was to say in 1808, half the wealth of the whole country.[75] All the industrial and commercial bases of the traditional Vietnamese economy—mines of gold, silver, copper, iron, zinc, lead, salt, and sulphur—were in the north. One writer has suggested that a total of 124 mines were worked in northern Vietnam in the period 1802–1858, thirty-eight of which were in Thái Nguyên province.[76] Administratively, a comparison of the customs tax lists for all Vietnam in the two years 1817 and 1838 reveals that their tax quotas for the north and center were roughly identical in both lists but that quotas for most of the southern provinces appeared only on the 1838 list.[77] Economically the south was weaker than the north in 1802 and remained so in 1847, although the gap between them had begun to narrow, as the slow spread southward of this commercial taxation shows.

More important, despite the southern and central origins of the dynasty, in fiscal administration its bureaucracy developed an inevitable northern bias, thanks to the north's economic preponderance. Five types of agricultural fields were recognized by Nguyễn officials for taxation purposes: summer fields (*hạ điền*), which were sown in the winter and harvested in the summer; autumn fields (*thu điền*), which were sown in the summer and harvested in the winter; summer-autumn fields (*hạ thu điền*), which were harvested in both the summer and the autumn; and two varieties of dry field (*hán điền*). North of Nghệ An summer fields and autumn fields both existed. There were two harvests—and two tax collections—a year. South of Quảng Bình on the other hand summer fields alone predominated. There was only one rice harvest. Ruling the far south as well as the north was a new situation for a countrywide Vietnamese bureaucracy. After 1802 Huế officials found it difficult to adjust to the different number of annual harvests in each region. Until 1825 southern officials were actually required to prepare crop damage reports for the annual crops of their virtually non-existent autumn and dry fields.[78] Uniformity in this sphere was reluctantly discarded after 1825. Each region demanded separate consideration.

A less formidable population density then as now gave the southern provinces a rice surplus. As of 1839, however, in the yearly regional rice tribute to Huế, northern Vietnam was expected to send 212 junkloads—106 junks making two trips a year—to the capital with a total cargo of 500,000 *phương* of rice. (One *phương* of rice in this period has been estimated as having been equal to 33.54 kilograms. A soldier lived on about two *phương* of rice a month officially.)[79] Ten southern provinces, on the other hand, from Quảng Nam to Gia Định, were expected to send only 135 junkloads in a year, amounting to a tribute of 100,000 *phương* of rice and 100,000 *hộc* (one *hộc* of grain was worth slightly more than two *phương*) of grain, as well as other natural products.[80] Commutation of taxes in kind to money payments had meant that there was a greater accumulation of cash in the dynasty's treasuries in 1835 than there was in 1815 but a relatively smaller accumulation of grain, a trend that alarmed Minh-mạng.[81] Competition in the south from private dealers in rice who wished to export Vietnamese rice to south China and to the rest of Southeast Asia threatened this fragile bureaucratically managed rice traffic. Chinese merchants in Saigon were often more efficient in controlling south Vietnamese rice crops than the court itself up in Huế. In the 1830's their junks would often carry southern rice to Southeast Asian ports and return with opium, a two-way illicit trade that was indeed "licentious commerce" (*gian thương*).

The official rice junks themselves, known as "public duty ships" (*dịch thuyền*), sailed once a month from the third month of the lunar calendar to the sixth. A bureaucratic calendar, the result of centuries of research by Chinese astronomers, linked the junks' departures and returns to the twenty-four categories of solar conditions (*tiết khí*) occurring in the year. That is, a junk might leave port about the time of the summer solstice (*hạ chí*) in the middle of the fifth lunar month and be expected to return about the time of the "great heat" (*đại thử*) in the middle of the sixth lunar month.[82] The coastal rice traffic, official and unofficial, really signalized the inveterate economic inequality of the three regions, north, center, and south. It was an inequality that might see desperate official purchasing of rice in Gia Định in order to raise the dangerously low market price of rice in the south, but the commutation to money payments of 60 percent of the rice taxes of northern provinces like Hải Dương and Thái Nguyên because of crop blight there at the same time and in the same year—1815.[83]

It was, however, central Vietnam that faced the worst predicament. Its depressed seaboard economy could not survive without the annual palliative of "southern rice" (*nam mễ*) from Gia Định. The court often had to buy rice wholesale in Saigon for the needs of the center. But southern rice brokers customarily used the pretext of poor sailing weather between the south and central Vietnam to inflate their prices. Rice prices in the vicinity of Huế rose or fell with suspenseful instability depending upon the volume of southern rice imports. A local official explained high prices in central Vietnam to Thiệu-trị in the autumn of 1842 by declaring that in previous years his region had usually received more than two hundred junkloads of southern rice but that in 1842 the center had received little more than seventy junkloads.[84]

Apart from their rice surpluses, the southern provinces possessed their own distinct regional administrative problems. Intersected by streams and lagoons that were difficult to control, they were heavily populated by families whom Huế bureaucrats disdainfully called "river route people" (*giang lộ nhân*), who lived afloat and found it easy, because they were mobile rather than living in landed communities, to avoid corvee and taxation. Some desperate officials proposed engraving "registration licenses" (*bài chỉ*), with the names of villages, upon the bows of their boats and then establishing military transit posts (*xích hậu*, a term that descends from the Chinese Chou period, appears in the *Shu-ching*, and was usually employed in China to describe posts which guarded against another kind of nomad— those of the steppes) at intervals on the rivers to check the licenses of this floating population. Another procedure favored by officials in Saigon and elsewhere was to paint the bows of all river craft in south Vietnam with different colors for different provinces, that is, red for Gia Định, black for Vĩnh Long, green for An Giang, and green also for Cambodian shipping in the 1830's. In this way order might be imposed upon the chaos of sampans, pirogues, and larger vessels that cluttered inland waterways.[85]

In sum, the Huế administrator who left the cloistered peace of the citadel in order to journey to the provinces faced uncertain prospects. In applying his bureaucratic expertise at first hand among the Vietnamese people, he was likely to encounter a new mixture of dilemmas in each region. In a long, narrow country which depended extensively upon maritime communications, the Nguyễn bureaucracy's brilliant adaptation of the intricate system of Chinese provincial administration may well have stood between the dynasty and regional political disintegration.

The Chinese Provincial System's Transposition to Vietnam

This system did not reach its apogee in Nguyễn Vietnam until after 1831. As has been mentioned, in the period of regional, quasi-military government under Gia-long, Vietnam was divided territorially into twenty-three protectorates (*trấn*) and four military departments (*doanh*). Eleven protectorates of the twenty-three were in northern Vietnam. They were Sơn-nam-thượng (later to be known as Hà Nội province), Sơn-nam-hạ (later changed to Nam Định province), Sơn Tây, Kinh Bắc (later known as Bắc Ninh), Hải Dương, Tuyên Quang, Hưng Hóa, Cao Bằng, Lạng Sơn, Thái Nguyên, and Quảng Yên. Five of the protectorates, on the other hand, were in the south: Phiên An or Gia Định, Biên Hòa, Vĩnh Thanh (later Vĩnh Long and An Giang), Định Tường, and Hà Tiên. The remaining seven protectorates ranged from north central Vietnam to south central Vietnam and included Thanh Hóa, Nghệ An, Quảng Nghĩa, Bình Định, Phú Yên, Bình Hòa, and Bình Thuận. The four departments, whose names in 1802 were Quảng Đức, Quảng Trị, Quảng Bình, and Quảng Nam, surrounded the imperial capital of Huế and were ruled much more directly by Gia-long.

The eleven northern protectorates, however, besides having their own separate protectorate governments, were also combined into one great unit, which was ruled from Hanoi by a powerful "overlord of the citadel of the north" (*Bắc-thành tổng trấn*). A similar "overlord of the citadel of Gia Định" (*Gia Định thành tổng trấn*) ruled a unit of the five southern protectorates from Saigon.

In Chapter 2 it was shown how Minh-mạng fought the personal rule of these two regional overlords with help from the Chinese statutes. By the 1830's, according to the evidence, centralized bureaucracy was temporarily victorious and the overlords' regional cause was lost. Yet when Minh-mạng imposed the Chinese provincial system upon his kingdom in 1831, for the most part he merely converted the old administrative areas, Gia-long's protectorates and departments, into *tỉnh* (provinces). He added four new administrative bailiwicks (Hưng Yên, Ninh Bình, Hà Tĩnh, and An Giang) to the twenty-seven already existing ones in order to reach a total of thirty-one provinces. At different times in the nineteenth century the individual names of these provinces suffered slight mutations. The names might change, but the thirty-one different jurisdictions remained relatively constant in number. Vietnam, which was itself the size of one Chinese province, thus had thirty-one provincial units to China proper's eighteen.

But this division was not necessarily owing to the grandiose desires of its emperors. Rather, it was because modern Vietnam's long stretch of territory had been occupied historically so slowly and so untidily by the Vietnamese people themselves. The different provinces on the map represented different stages in time of the people's military and cultural drive southward, stages which national histories commemorated and which emperors could not reshape. Chinese-style territorial divisions dignified a Southeast Asian-style ethnic and cultural mosaic. Adding their own special determinism to the making of this administrative patchwork were of course the ineluctable geographical forces—mountains and rivers—that created such natural self-contained environments as the one shared by the three north central provinces of Hà Tĩnh, Thanh Hóa, and Nghệ An. But Vietnam's abundance of Chinese-style provinces in the 1800's was to have far-reaching consequences.

Below the twenty-seven protectorates and departments of 1802–1831 and the thirty-one provinces that emerged in the early 1830's, Nguyễn territorial government organized itself in a descending series of increasingly smaller jurisdictions, the prefecture (*phủ*), the sub-prefecture (*châu;* this usually indicated the presence of minority peoples), the district (*huyện*), the canton (*tổng*), and the cluster of hamlets around one common religious and social focal point, namely the village or the "commune," the *xã*. One mid-nineteenth-century source suggested that in 1803 there had been 57 prefectures, 41 sub-prefectures, 201 districts, 4,163 cantons, and 16,452 villages or village-type settlements of one kind or another in Gia-long's Vietnam.[86] But it is reasonable to assume that there may have been fewer than 200 districts in Vietnam in the first few years of the dynasty. New districts were created regularly after 1802, however, often merely by elevating cantons to a higher status, as in 1813.[87] By the 1840's it seems certain that Vietnam possessed a number of prefectures between 70 and 90, and a total number of districts between 250 and 270,[88] although a scholarly private source of the early Tự Đức period has claimed that there were 72 prefectures, 39 sub-prefectures, and as many as 283 districts.[89]

Assuming that there were at least 250 districts in Nguyễn Vietnam as of 1847, superimposed upon a population that could not have been in excess of eight million people, Vietnamese districts almost certainly had the smallest individual populations of any in the Chinese classical world. Even Yi Korea, whose total population size was possibly about the same as Vietnam's, possessed only about 175 districts, in a territorial administration that was, like Vietnam's, derived at least in part from the Chinese model. In Ch'ing China itself approximately 1,500 districts shared the burdensome responsibilities for collecting taxes and maintaining order among perhaps three hundred and fifty million people or more in the 1840's. This was a ratio of one district to about 235,000 people. In Vietnam of the same period a district organized outwardly along the identical administrative lines as a Chinese district would need to concern itself with only 30,000 people or fewer. Unhappily, population statistics cannot be cited precisely. But the extent of the actual deviation of administrative realities at the local level in Vietnam from those prevailing in China—a deviation which was paradoxically caused by Vietnam's very imitation of the Chinese system together with its plethora of provinces—is very obvious indeed.

Before 1838 there were no "head prefectures" (*thủ phủ*) or "head districts" (*thủ huyện*) in Vietnamese provinces, that is, prefectures and districts distinguished by their proximity to provincial capitals. But impeccable fidelity to the time-honored Chinese ways of bringing order out of the multiplicity of district administrative idiosyncrasies was still more often the rule than the exception. As in China, all Nguyễn districts were classified according to the "four [types of] posts" (*tứ khuyết*). These classifications specified in relative terms how difficult given districts were for magistrates to rule. There were districts that were "very important" (*tối yếu*), those that were "important" (*yếu*), those that were "medium" (*trúng*) in difficulty, and those that were merely "simple" (*giản*). A Huế survey in 1831 of some 183 districts found 12 very important ones, 37 important ones, 62 medium ones, and 72 simple ones. But these four categories were shuffled constantly in their applications.[90] Some of the things that officially made a district "very important"—in other words, troublesome—included proximity to a provincial capital, because this meant construction of buildings and thus the necessity of conscripting much corvee labor; the presence of market towns, for this meant thefts and commercial quarrels; proximity to the mountains or the coast, where bandits and pirates usually lurked; being located near the border of another province, a situation allowing malefactors to escape easily from the district's jurisdiction; the presence of roads and bridges and postal stations, which required additional defensive measures; great dependence for agricultural welfare upon the performance of dikes in storms; a high population density, which meant a relative increase in lawsuits; and the presence of many rich families, who could evade tax burdens. In these respects the bureaucracy's ideal unit of administration—almost like Lao-tzu's—was a district of farmers, neither very rich nor very poor, inland and away from major population centers, whose inhabitants did not participate very much in commerce.

It is doubtful whether any other contemporary Southeast Asian court had such a close-textured empirical awareness of the nature of the landscape of villages which it ruled. The Sino-Vietnamese *tứ-khuyết* classifications of districts and prefectures were based upon meticulously gathered data. Clues which indicate that the borrowing of the Chinese system of provincial administration allowed the Vietnamese government to control the lives of its peasants, to devolve both solicitude and sorrows upon them, with greater effectiveness and regularity than any other traditional Southeast Asian government, are supplied by court debates at Huế in 1834–1841 over the future of Cambodia. Much of Cambodia had been absorbed into Vietnam in the mid-1830's by Vietnamese armies and converted into the short-lived Vietnamese province of Trấn Tây. This brought Vietnamese colonial administrators in Cambodia, notably the controversial general Trương Minh Giảng, face to face with the fact that Cambodians were unaccustomed to the Sino-Vietnamese bureaucratic heritage. They were unfamiliar with the glories of an officialdom based upon merit—or with systematic military corvee and land and population registers. "The Cambodian territory is broad . . . but up until now its soldiers and adult males have wandered about and have not been registered and controlled," complained one Huế memorial in 1834, which also declared that the ordinary principle of storage of rice and grain (*sừ tích*) was historically strangely absent in Cambodia.[91] (Vietnamese occupying armies in Cambodia had to receive their provisions—20,000 *hộc* of rice in one requisition—from An Giang, Định Tường, and Vĩnh Long. This drain in turn reduced the amount of rice south Vietnam could send to Huế.)

Newly appointed Vietnamese prefectural pacification officers in Cambodia were ordered to draw up corvee registers. They were instructed to select one man out of every ten for corvee duty and to send these newly created Cambodian registers to the governor-general of An Giang and Hà Tiên provinces in southern Vietnam for certification. Before Vietnamese armies withdrew from their Cambodian cultural laboratory in the 1840's that country was the scene of a political-cultural battle between the Chinese-Vietnamese formula of direct, permeative bureaucratic management and the formula more common elsewhere in Southeast Asia of indirect rule through deputies. This battle revolved around the question of local administration. But it was merely one facet of the more general continuing cultural confrontation between "sinicized" and "Indianized" Southeast Asian societies.

Under Gia-long, each of the twenty-seven protectorates possessed both a military and a civil bureaucracy. The military administration of a protectorate was headed by a protector or *trấn-thủ* (3A in the military bureaucracy). This term, famous in Vietnamese history, recalled the protectors Lê Lợi had deployed in important areas in the fifteenth century.[92] The civil administration, which included prefects, district magistrates, and educational officials, was led by a *hiệp trấn* (3A in the civil bureaucracy), whose name—"associate defender" would be a rough translation—significantly also had a military ring to it. For the most part the military protectors held most real local powers, subject to the approval of their Hanoi and Saigon overlords and the Huế emperor. The *hiệp trấn*, if they were paragons, were nonetheless confined to reinforcing the efforts of local schools. They did this not always in the manner of the unchastened Nguyễn Hoài Quỳnh, "associate defender" of Thanh Hóa from 1808, who earned fame by asking students how many men traveled on a nearby road in the course of one day. (The answer of course was only two: the upright man and the profit-seeking man.)[93] Yet on rare occasions the associate defenders could engineer protectors' impeachments, as Quỳnh also did.

After 1831–32 the thirty-one provinces were ruled by Chinese-style governors-general and governors (*tổng đốc* and *tuần phủ; tsung-tu* and *hsün-fu* in Chinese). Nomenclature now became identical. But unlike Ch'ing China there was no really regular pattern of one governor-general for every two (or three) provinces and one governor for every province. The Nguyễn bureaucracy had borrowed all the titles, ranks, and levels of status of the Chinese territorial administration. In discreet but compulsive recognition of Vietnam's smallness, however, it did not award them to as many people. Provinces were associated in pairs (Bình Định and Phú Yên were known together as Bình-Phú) in the Chinese fashion. But if the governor-general of the pairing resided in one of the two provinces, the province where he resided would have no governor below him. In all, there were usually about twelve governors-general in Nguyễn Vietnam and eleven governors.[94] (See Table 2.) Of course it should be mentioned that although they were the highest provincial officials, occasionally the emperor would appoint a "commissioner in charge of patrolled border lands" (*kinh lược sứ*) above them to superintend the entire regions of north or south Vietnam. This title was a Vietnamese version of a term which referred to border military officials in seventh-century T'ang China but which was no longer really used in the China of the 1800's. In Vietnam it became more important as the century wore on. French confiscation of the powers of the *kinh lược sứ* in north Vietnam in 1897 was to be a milestone in the growth of the colonial administration.

If this regional distribution of high power holders is considered closely, it is plain that Nguyễn Vietnam's formal subdivision into thirty-one provinces suggested a more top-heavy provincial administration than actually existed. The authority of a governor-general was spread over the two or three provinces that belonged to his title only in matters touching military strategy, frontier affairs, the apprehension of bandits and rebels, the transfer of troops and the distribution of provisions. In other words, he was a governor with super-provincial military authority. If he encountered a governor while he was traveling, protocol required him to dismount from his sedan chair and bow, but the governor had to perform these acts first. Although governors-general exercised supreme military authority provincially, they were not necessarily professional soldiers. Interchangeability of civil and military functions among the upper provincial hierarchy was a rather prophetic desideratum which the threat of Western naval attacks in the 1830's and 1840's only strengthened. Minh-mạng said in 1839: "All civil officials ideally should be forced to learn the military arts and all military officials should be forced to learn civil business. That is why in the various

Table 2. Governors-General and Governors in Nguyễn Vietnam.

Provincial pairing	Provinces included	Residence of governor-general	Residence of governors
Nam Nghĩa	Quảng Nam, Quảng Nghĩa	Điện Bàn prefecture, Quảng Nam	None
Bình Phú	Bình Định, Phú Yên	Hoài Nhơn pref., Bình Định	Tuy An pref., Phú Yên
Thuận Khánh	Bình Thuận, Khánh Hòa	None	Hàm Thuận pref., Bình Thuận
Định Biên	Gia Định, Biên Hòa	Tân Bình pref., Gia Định	Phước Long pref., Biên Hòa
Long Tường	Vĩnh Long, Định Tường	Định Viễn pref., Vĩnh Long	Kiến An pref., Định Tường
An Hà	An Giang, Hà Tiên	Tuy Biên pref., An Giang	An Biên pref., Hà Tiên
Trị Bình	Quảng Trị, Quảng Bình	None	Triệu Phong pref., Quảng Trị
Thanh Hóa	Thanh Hóa	Thiệu Hóa pref., Thanh Hóa	None
Hà Ninh	Hà Nội, Ninh Bình	Hoài Đức pref., Hà Nội	An Khánh pref., Ninh Bình
An Tĩnh	Nghệ An, Hà Tĩnh	Anh Sơn pref., Nghệ An	Hà Thanh pref., Hà Tĩnh
Định An	Nam Định, Hưng Yên	Thiên Trường pref., Nam Định	Khoái Châu pref., Hưng Yên
Hải An	Hải Dương, Quảng Yên	Bình Giang pref., Hải Dương	Residence not listed
Sơn Hưng Tuyên	Sơn Tây, Hưng Hóa, Tuyên Quang	Quảng Oai pref., Sơn Tây	Gia Hưng pref., Hưng Hóa
Ninh Thái	Bắc Ninh, Thái Nguyên	Từ Sơn pref., Bắc Ninh	None
Lạng Bình	Lạng Sơn, Cao Bằng	None	Trưởng Khánh pref., Lạng Sơn

provinces the governors-general alternate between being civil and military officials. Civil officials must not consider guns and cannon to be the sphere of responsibility of military bureaucrats."[95]

In the same way, although the provincial judicial and fiscal hierarchies below the governor were led by judicial commissioners (*án sát sứ*) and financial commissioners (*bố chính sứ*) not every one of the thirty-one provinces had two commissioners as in China. The governor himself often served also as provincial financial commissioner. As of 1832, Vietnamese bureaucratic records show a total of thirty judicial commissioners and twenty-one financial commissioners.[96] Each financial commissioner was served by a staff of subordinates whose names often corresponded to those of underlings in prefectures and districts in China, rather than provinces. Thus each Vietnamese province's financial commissioner's office had on its staff one or two *kinh lịch*—the title of a prefectural records keeper in Ch'ing China. The importance of these parallels and non-parallels is that the formal status systems of the Chinese provincial administration—the various levels, province, prefecture, district, of its hierarchy of command—were completely reproduced in Vietnam without their concomitant density of bureaucrats. This meant that communications and orders within Nguyễn Vietnam's officialdom could enjoy the same stylized authoritativeness that they did in China, bureaucratic obedience being an obligation of statuses. But the mobilization capacities and administration costs of the Chinese provincial bureaucracy, which Vietnam had no need for and obviously could not support, were not imported.

Nevertheless, even with all these disguised qualifications, one effect of introducing the forms of such a vast territorial administration into such a small country was that business transacted by district magistrates in China often stopped at prefects' yamens in Vietnam. Prefectures and districts, at the bottom of this oversized hierarchy in Vietnam, were relatively so similar in size that it was impossible sometimes to maintain Chinese-type distinctions between them. This was especially true in the southern provinces, where the new forms were unfamiliar. An edict of 1822 declared: "Up until now, from Quảng Bình south, the sub-prefecture and district offices have merely confined their attention to managing criminal matters and litigation.

But tax collections, provisions and all corvee programs have been separately attached to the various officials of the original prefecture . . . How can we discriminate higher from lower?"[97]

Data from the *Vermilion Books* (*châu bản*), the unedited public documents of the Nguyễn court which survive, suggest that as of 1820 protectorate officials as much as district ones might regulate the litigation and tax collections of a difficult district like Hoằng Hóa in Thanh Hóa.[98] At provincial tax collection stations after 1838 the transportation of tax produce and the recording of collections were supervised by an official known as a *cai lại* (a superintendent sub-bureaucrat). But the ratio of the numbers of these tax superintendents to local administrative units was revealing: one to a "large" district or one to two small districts.[99] Most district capitals were merely villages. One way in which the dynasty could distinguish prefects from district magistrates was to pay the latter (as of 1816) only two thirds of the former's "postal station and highway expenses" when they set out from Huế for their posts.

Hence the Vietnamese borrowed the whole Ch'ing provincial system of formal differential responsibility but not the whole Ch'ing system of mobilizing power, especially at the local level. Interlocking hierarchies in China which remained outside the descent of the ordinary Chinese territorial administration—the grain transportation hierarchy, the salt administration, the river conservancy administration—made no real appearance in their own separate right in Nguyễn Vietnam. Despite all this, Vietnam's adoption of the continent-spanning forms of Ch'ing territorial administration still meant that government, in effect, came one notch further down the scale from capital city to village in traditional Vietnam than it did in traditional China. The Vietnamese district magistrate became a virtual neighbor to his peasants, rather than ruling them, as his more aloof Chinese counterpart did, from a distant market town. The division of the responsibility for linking the peasant community to the larger political world, between a formal elite in office and an informal localized elite, thus became less crucial to Vietnam's agrarian society than it was to China's.

If both the Chinese and Vietnamese bureaucracies were composed of small elites who sought to govern a sea of rural villages, the mandarin who was appointed to a provincial post in Vietnam was less disarmed by the size of his administrative bailiwick than he would have been in China. Consequently he needed the informal services of locally resident members of his own class far less in spreading his power throughout his jurisdiction. A local "gentry" of retired officials, literate landlords, and ambitious schoolteachers certainly did exist in nineteenth-century Vietnamese villages. But it did not serve the dynamic, indispensable functions of repairing temples, financing schools, building bridges, and maintaining ideological orthodoxy among the peasants to nearly as celebrated or as conspicuous an extent as the Chinese "gentry" did in China.

In 1841 Thiệu-trị piously affected to believe that public works in Vietnam did not oppress the peasantry as much as they did in China: "For the sake of [building] its imperial graves, the Ch'ing court exploits the financial strength and resources of its people . . . I do not follow this example. These episodes of public corvee never trouble the people [in Vietnam]. I only employ soldiers of the guard to serve on them."[100] Although the example of imperial grave building, not a common event, is not entirely appropriate, an echo of a difference between China and Vietnam does sound in this curious passage. Peasants who built dikes and temples and graves in Vietnam more often did so under the formal command of members of the civil and military bureaucracies, both of which could reach the villagers more effectively than either hierarchy could in China. They became "soldiers of the guard" first. In China, peasants who were engaged in such work more often toiled under the informal manipulation of "gentry" worthies.

It is also entirely possible that such a superabundance of regional administrative centers in traditional Vietnam—31 provincial capitals, 250 or more district capitals—weakened as much as it seemed to strengthen the substantive growth of urbanization as a whole before the colonial era. Cities, of course, fulfilled a variety of functions, administrative, economic, and religious. But in classical Chinese civilization it was usually their original administrative function which overshadowed and attracted the other activities to them, so that all activities then became concentrated in the one site. The thirty-one Vietnamese provincial capitals, however, were the foci of a greatly depreciated administrative system. There were so many of them distributed throughout the one small society that each individual provincial capital represented far less concentrated administrative power, even proportionately to its society, than a corresponding Chinese provincial capital. Individually each center attracted far less trade and other supplementary enterprises. At least Minh-mạng said in 1835: "I have heard that in the Ch'ing country the height of the walls of provincial capitals just exceeds the top of one's shoulder, and that there are no deep moats. Hence there are bandits who can come right up under the city walls. In our country the provincial capital walls are high and the moats are deep. Surely it is impossible to come right up under them. If there is a revolt then the small cannon on the tops of the city walls are sufficient."[101]

Notwithstanding the malicious inaccuracy of the emperor's description of contemporary Chinese cities, it is clear that the sterile concept of provincial capitals as walled administrative "citadels" was carried farther by the Vietnamese than by the Chinese, perhaps because it was easier to do so in Vietnam. There was not quite so great a daily inflow and outflow of merchants and traders to profane these bureaucrats' enclaves in the countryside. On the other hand, the danger that walled provincial citadels could be converted into strongholds of the dissident was patent. In theory a court statute forbade Vietnamese provincial capitals to have walls that were more than one *trượng* high or moats that were more than five *trượng* across.[102] Prefectural capitals were, of course, no more than walled villages. These villages contained a small prefectural hall (*phủ đường*) and a granary for the storage of tax rice, managed by one sub-bureaucrat who guarded the *hộc* and *phương* wooden measuring buckets and ladles by which tax payments were assessed. They ranged from 266 *trượng* or more in circumference (an example in Sơn Nam province in the north in 1829) to 72 *trượng* in circumference or less (an example in Bình Thuận province in the south in 1838), the latter being less than one quarter the circumference of the Forbidden City in Huế.[103]

"The Laws of the Emperor are Less than the Customs of the Village"

A description of the entire manifold of political behavior of traditional Vietnamese villages would of course require a completely separate study. Yet one must attempt to appreciate certain features of the villages' relationship to the bureaucracy. How great was the weight of a universal empire's (China's) institutional system upon a smaller Southeast Asian kingdom at the village level?

The basic unit of settlement in the Vietnamese countryside was the *xã*. The *xã* was usually an aggregate of two to five multi-family settlements or hamlets. The latter were often known in turn as *thôn*. The name *xã*, which was Sino-Vietnamese, originally referred to the god of the earth and to his altar and still preserved with a faded dogmatism this sense of a religious focal point. But in Vietnam it had come to designate, beyond this, a cluster of multi-family settlements, linked by paths or small waterways, which owned some property in common and which shared a common place of worship and of social consultation, the *đình*. Because of the structural peculiarities of the *xã*, the English word "village" is not totally adequate as a translation. In fact the traditional French translation of *xã* was "commune," although this choice led to the different error of suggesting radical patterns of social organization and ideology which were completely alien to Nguyễn Vietnam. Of necessity I will use the inadequate English word "village" for *xã* and will render *thôn* as "hamlet." It is worth noting that whereas *xã* means one thing and one thing only to the Vietnamese, to a Chinese the word *she* (the Chinese pronunciation of the character for *xã*) presents so many suggestions of meaning that it must be further defined to be specific. In China it can refer to a literary association, to a business firm, to a unit of militia, or to an informal, non-administrative cooperative farming unit of about ten families, like the familiar *ch'u-she* of traditional north China.

Some Vietnamese believe that their villages and hamlets were, in traditional times, semi-autonomous settlements which were at least as free of Huế as Chinese villages were of the Ch'ing dynasty in Peking. Certainly the Southeast Asian jungle made individual villages more difficult of access than, say, communities on the north China plain. Many Vietnamese villages were more isolated and their hamlets were, perhaps, more closely integrated socially than equivalent rural settlements in China. It is impossible to decide upon a "typical" rural community in either society. To the historian, however, the weakness of inter-village relationships seems even more obvious in nineteenth-century Vietnam than the weakness of the relationship of the *xã* with the provinces and the court. Economic cooperation among different villages, although not impossible, was very rare. When famine struck one village, its inhabitants were as likely to "fold their arms and suffer losses to heaven" (*khoanh tay chịu thua trời*) as to go to other villages and "beg for food in a foreign place" (*tha phương cầu thực*).

Nonetheless, Vietnamese villages did attempt to cultivate a recognizable attitude of independence or indifference toward the bureaucratic hierarchy. One rural proverb, "It is better to be the head of a chicken than the tail of an elephant" (*thà làm đầu gà hơn là đuôi voi*), emphasized the preference for anonymous insignificance of Vietnamese villagers. (It may have been inspired by a Chinese proverb, "It is better to be the beak of a chicken than the buttocks of an ox," the Vietnamese elephant replacing the Chinese ox.) Another, "The laws of the emperor are less than the customs of the village" (*phép vua thua lệ làng*), exalted the supposed inability of centralized political power to dominate the villagers' lives. The other side of the coin was that the villagers traditionally ascribed to their own village elders both real political power and high social status, as yet another proverb commemorates: "The village association is a small court" (*hương đẳng, tiểu triều đình*).

Xã originated as recognized local units at least as early as the tenth century in Vietnam. Although the history of their evolution is too complicated to be summarized here, one of its watersheds was important. Before the late fifteenth century the village chiefs or *xã trưởng* were local officials (actually known as *xã-quan*), appointed by the central government, who then became resident in the villages. After the 1460's they were more commonly ordinary villagers whom the villagers themselves chose, subject to the approval of the courts, which sporadically specified that they be minor degree holders, or sub-bureaucrats who had had some administrative experience, or retired soldiers.[104]

In the early nineteenth century village life was managed not so much by the village chiefs (who were known, with greater fidelity to Chinese usages, as *lý trưởng* in the Minh-mạng period) as by the village elders or council of notables, known collectively as the *hội đồng hào mục*. The village chiefs, the intermediaries between the bureaucracy and the villagers, collected taxes and carried out court orders. The elders (*hào mục*) dealt with village business that was of less interest to Huế, a wide spectrum of affairs ranging from inchoate lawsuits to night patrols designed to guard the interests of village property owners. They were a heterogeneous group of men—true elders, retired officials, lesser degree holders, and former village chiefs. They constituted a permanent village elite and were led by a *tiên-chỉ*, the man who possessed the highest status among them. Status went first to the scholars (in theory) and next to retired canton and village chiefs who were the oldest in age. Unlike the village chiefs, the elders did not serve specific three year or five year terms. Time did not limit their power. (In 1921 the French resident superior in north Vietnam improvidently tampered with this system by demo-cratizing these village councils of elders and encouraging young men without recognized status to join them. The result was that the natural leaders of the village lost "face" (*thể diện*) and "prestige" (*uy tín*) if they remained members of the councils. It was no longer re-spectable for them to act as links with Hanoi. In 1927 the French were forced to abandon many of the changes.)

It cannot be denied that the village chiefs and the village elders exercised power. Despite the fact that Vietnamese provincial admin-istration penetrated the Vietnamese countryside more extensively than territorial administration did in China, the main modes of the legitimately expected behavior of these administrators themselves were defined in the Chinese manner, institutional patterns being of course cultural patterns. In other words, servitude to the written traditions of Chinese political science often prevented Vietnamese local officials from realizing the greater functional capabilities which their smaller bailiwicks conferred upon them. Thus a Vietnamese district magistrate, so much closer to his villagers than his counter-part in China, nonetheless was inclined to indulge in judicial arbitra-tion of their quarrels only as a last resort. Pitched battles could break out between villages before the local administrator intervened.

A definitive episode occurred in Thừa Thiên in central Vietnam in 1830. Its circumstances have been preserved in the dynasty's *Vermilion Books*, which are a mine of transcribed socio-economic data of value. Local officials reported: "In our jurisdiction there is Cổ Lão village in Đông Lâm canton in Quảng Điền district. Three of its retired village chiefs, Hoàng Tăng Đạo, Phạm Hữu Đoan, and Phan

Văn Chất, have laid the accusation that the boundary of their village's public lands squeezes the boundary of the fields of Dương Sơn village. On the fourteenth day of the seventh month of this year the village chief of Dương Sơn village, Trần Văn Tài, who has Christian habits and in sum does not respect the law, on his own authority led his village's soldiers and people to that spot, where they built up with earth a new path which violates [Cổ Lão] village's old graves. Moreover they took the stone tablet markers [of the fields] and moved them to another place . . . [A retired village chief of Cổ Lão village] led his village men en masse to a brawl, his village soldiers and people were wounded . . . they protested to the district, which decided that their village was the one that should be curbed. They renewed their outcry [at this] and it reached the prefecture."[105]

The use of Christianity as a defamatory political weapon with which to blacken the reputations of opponents revealed the inroads Christian heterodoxy had made in central Vietnam by 1830. But from the standpoint of administration what this incident showed, of course, was the almost untrammelled discretionary power of village leaders to shape the relations of their village with nearby communities. What it also showed was the residual prestige of former village chiefs, whose influence probably was only heightened when they retired and joined the ranks of the *hào mục*. And even actively serving village chiefs were not effectively denied by the Huế court the capacity to behave despotically toward the peasants within the bamboo stockades of their villages. They could privately sell exemptions from corvee to rich peasants, who then became known as *ông nhiêu* (roughly, "Mister exempt"; the character *nhiêu* was used more extensively in Vietnam than in China) to their fellow villagers.[106] Although regional practices varied, it seems clear that the *lý trưởng* were indeed more the agents of their village elders than tools of the provincial governments. A memorial to Huế from Nghệ An in 1828–29 complained that the chiefs' activities were never reported to provincial officials and that the chiefs were "privately established" in their positions by the people.[107] On the other hand, this conflicted with a policy introduced in 1809, at least for northern Vietnam, which required that all village and canton chiefs receive wooden seals from the bureaucracy before they engage in public business.[108] In the Gia-long period (but not so much later on) the village leaders themselves had to take the initiative in communicating to the prefectural and district officials the fact that their fields had been damaged by drought or by pests. Otherwise their taxes would not be reduced.[109] Last but not least, village chiefs were the ones who reported to district officials, four months before official regional examinations began, the names of the scholars in their villages who were morally eligible, as loyal and filial men, to participate in them.[110] However, this was another power which declined in relative importance as the century wore on.

Yet it would be fair to generalize that the Nguyễn provincial administration occupied a much greater position of strength, where controlling Vietnamese villages was concerned, than Ch'ing provincial administration could enjoy with respect to villages in China. It did not always exploit this position. Ist penetration of village life was, Chinese fashion, usually highly selective. It did so mainly to collect taxes or to preserve order. But it is significant that fewer dynasties were overwhelmed in Vietnam than in China by great regional rebellions which gained a fatal momentum among hundreds of villages before the court and its officials could intervene. Such intervention, despite the intractable environment, was easier in Vietnam. Vietnamese villages were rarely armed, although in 1833 the court did issue fowling pieces to coastal villages in Bình Định, Phú Yên, and Khánh Hòa as a means of protecting them against the forays of Malay pirates.[111]

The potent "small court" of elders in each village could not prevent its villagers from being conscripted for corvee. Nor could it prevent its entire village from being converted into an exemplary "artisans' village" of shipbuilders or carpenters or weavers, which then performed manufacturing tasks for the court in return for "labor money" (*công tiền*). Village chiefs were allowed to make "oral decisions" (*khẩu xử*) in miscellaneous village legal disputes only as a convenience to the bureaucracy. Those who did not perform specific duties—like reporting, accurately, the number of taxable adult males in their village or apprehending taxpaying peasants who had fled from their village—as well as they should might be flogged or made "elephant slaves" (*tượng nô*) in the army.[112] Perhaps most significantly of all, the Vietnamese court felt, very slightly, more able than the Chinese court to address itself to the suppression of minor day-to-day activities in the villages that might, in time, become socially pathogenic accumulations of abuses. This was reflected in such legislation, more possible in Vietnam than in China, as the laws of 1839 which controlled village land transactions. These laws ordered that all absolute sales be recorded as such in the deeds of purchase and forbade village land mortgages to extend beyond a maximum of thirty years.[113]

In fact, the greater potentialities of power that local officials enjoyed in Nguyễn Vietnam were a matter of concern to the emperors in Huế. Many of these officials failed to develop permanent local power bases in their areas only because they did not want to be "permanent" in them, because the Chinese idea of a progressive bureaucratic career, of professional upward mobility, had taken very deep root. But opportunities for them to develop such bases did exist. The orthodox application of Chinese devices of rural control in a smaller country often ironically furthered them. This provided an interesting source of tensions between the court and its provincial officials.

Chinese Methods of Rural Control: The Court Confronts Provincial Officialdom

It is useful to remember, again, that despite the similarity of their institutions, questions of political power and control in the Ch'ing empire, with its three hundred and fifty or four hundred million people, were different in scale, if not in kind, from those of a country like Vietnam. The only extant population figures for nineteenth-century Vietnam are those contained in the tax registers, namely the numbers of adult males (*đinh*) between 18 and 59 years of age who were unfortunate enough to be known to the tax collectors. Table 3 shows population growth for the years between 1803 and 1847 as it was recorded in the official Nguyễn registers.[114]

As of 1840, the 970,516 adult males in the registers worked 4,063,892 *mou* of land, which also represented an increase in acreage of substantial proportions from 1820. But much of this growth was unreal. The statistics of 1803, for one thing, are abnormally low, for Gia-long was just barely consolidating his rule. The records of the

Table 3. Population Growth as Seen in Official Records.

Year	Number of adult tax-paying males
1803	465,058
1819	612,912
1820	620,240
1829	719,510
1840	970,516[a]
1847	1,024,388

a. Including the Cambodian province.

Board of Finance were not reviewed and rated before 1825,[115] and landholdings in southern Vietnam were not exhaustively surveyed until the mid-1830's. Seven or eight million people would seem to be a reasonable estimate of the total population in the 1840's, although some contemporary Western estimates were more generous.[116] Of the 900,000 or more officially recorded male taxpayers in Vietnam in the late 1830's, at least one out of every seven lived in the three northern provinces of Hanoi, Sơn Tây, and Bắc Ninh, where a regional census of 1837 disclosed about 134,000 adult males on the registers.[117] The population figures of central Vietnam, on the other hand—those of the provinces grouped about Huế—were far less impressive.

This demographic weakness of the geographically constricted center had important historical consequences for Vietnamese cultural borrowing. The emperors lived in the central region, and their views of the need or lack of need for rigorous techniques of rural control in Vietnam were largely colored by their visions of a landscape—the Huế landscape—which had more officials than its population required. Minh-mạng said in 1837: "I have studied land maps of the Northern Country [China]. One district there may amount to 20,000 people [presumably, tax-paying males, although he uses the word *dân*], although in our country the entire jurisdiction of Thừa Thiên [in which Huế was situated] cannot match [the situation of] the land of one district of the Northern Country."[118]

It has been suggested that the emperors, who never visited China, were sometimes more empirically (or skeptically) minded than their officials when it came to borrowing Chinese institutions. Whereas some of their officials wished to copy the Chinese model without qualification, emperors were more likely to consider the consequences of domesticating inappropriate aspects of it. Nowhere in Vietnamese government was this theme dramatized more remarkably than in the realm of rural control.

In China, the most famous institution of rural (and urban) social control was the *pao-chia* system. Its organizational principle was security through mutual guarantee. In Ch'ing China, every ten households were combined into a unit led by a *p'ai-t'ou*, every hundred households became a unit led by a *chia-t'ou*, and every thousand households formed a unit led by a *pao-chang*. Each household carried a sign above its door with the name and the number of its household residents written upon it. Each group of households was responsible for the behavior of the members of its group. Thus it was difficult for one household to shelter a criminal without other households reporting it. In nineteenth-century Vietnam, the *pao-chia* system (*bảo-giáp* in Sino-Vietnamese) played little part at all in Minh-mạng's institutional development. This was a significant omission in Vietnamese borrowing from China.

In fact, the question of whether or not to borrow the Chinese *pao-chia* system was highly controversial in Huế. In 1840, the judicial commissioner of Phú Yên province, Lê Khiêm Quang, made an eloquent plea for its introduction into Vietnam. This was not the first time that such a proposal had been made. Minh-mạng rejected it. Possibly he had read accounts of the decay of the *pao-chia* groupings in China in Vietnamese envoys' "Daily Chronicles." But an understanding of this 1840 debate between the emperor and his bureaucracy over the instrumental value of such a fundamental Chinese control institution for Vietnam is vital. The dialectic typically produced a compromise between the Chinese tradition and Vietnamese society in which the potential Vietnamese *bảo-giáp* system remained stillborn. Minh-mạng said: "The *pao-chia* law of the ancients in its pristine period showed no blemishes. Then it deteriorated, becoming an empty name and nothing else . . . Within each of our provinces we have high officials like the financial and judicial commissioners. We further have prefectural and district officials. Coming to the cantons, we have canton chiefs, to the villages we have village chiefs. Side by side [with these officials] also every pass and military outpost has

special investigative responsibilities ... consequently, how can illegitimate and petty activities be spawned? ... [The provincial
hierarchy must order] the cantons and villages wholeheartedly to
make searching investigations. They must investigate, arrest, and
take to court all loose criminals and deserting soldiers, for which they
will receive rewards ... Since there will be no profit to the villages
[in not obeying] ... order each one to investigate according to its
territorial delimitations. Then of illegitimate persons and criminals
there will be none who can freely hide, and there will be no need to
set up the *pao-chia*."[119]

Minh-mạng's Vietnamese view of the *pao-chia* system's lack of
utility deserves to be compared with nineteenth-century Chinese
views of its irretrievable decay in China. Feng Kuei-fen, one of the
most brilliant political theorists and polemicists of the late Ch'ing
period, put forth as his panaceas for post-1840 China the study of
Western culture and weapons but also the retrenchment and reorganization of Chinese local government. (His inspiration came, in
part, from the famous, provocative essay on feudalism of the late
T'ang philosopher, Liu Tsung-yüan, which had declared that local
officials should come first and the Son of Heaven last in the ideal
polity.) Regarding the *pao-chia*, Feng declared that it was ineffective,
and went on: "Since the military revival [of the T'ai-p'ing period]
every province has organized and trained militias, which have
militia leaders ... which are, in comparison with the *pao-chia*, effective ... The *ti-pao* [the local constable] is a menial duty, and being
head of the *chia* is similarly a menial task. Neither of these men belong
to officialdom. But the [new] militia leaders are gentry. They are not
officials, but they are close to officials. Only officials are able to rule
the people."[120]

When specific institutions were involved, the same political tradition could be made the parent of two different outlooks. Here the
Chinese and Vietnamese approaches to the same institution in the
same century diverged. The Chinese version of the shortcomings of
the *pao-chia* system was that its leaders were too lowly in status to
gain the villagers' respect. They were too remote from the bureaucracy. Other "brokers" with better upward connections—the
gentry—were required to salvage the situation. The Vietnamsee
interpretation was almost the opposite. The regular bureaucracy

came so close to the villages, Minh-mạng argued, that a *pao-chia* system was superfluous.

In fact, of course, divergence was not complete. *Bảo-giáp* groupings were very occasionally created in Nguyễn Vietnam. But this was done more exceptionally than regularly and in the cities rather than in rural areas. To control the floating population which gathered in the suburbs of Hanoi, the largest city in the early nineteenth century, a mutual guarantee household organization, as well as day and night military patrols, appeared in Hoài Đức prefecture in 1821.[121]

The Vietnamese debate over the Chinese *pao-chia* system is an important part of the historical background of any typology of classical East Asian institutions. In the pattern which persisted, Vietnamese provincial officials sought the realization of intensive Chinese forms of local control, while Vietnamese emperors resisted.

Apart from the controversy over the *pao-chia* system, there was a recurrent controversy in nineteenth-century Vietnam over the building of relief granaries in the provinces. Provincial officials proposed in 1821 that granaries be built at the prefectural level. By 1834 they were suggesting the installation of granaries in the villages themselves. To the 1821 proposal Minh-mạng retorted that "'Ever Normal' granaries belonged to an excellent law of the past. But to practise it now would be most difficult."[122] In the early 1830's, however, Nguyễn Đăng Giai, the financial commissioner of Thanh Hóa, became a leading bureaucratic crusader for the creation of Chinese-style institutions of social engineering and social control in the provinces.

In 1834 Giai wrote in a "respects-paying" memorial, "My request is that we should imitate the communal granary law of the Sung Confucian scholar Chu Hsi." In Giai's nineteenth-century Vietnamese formulation, this meant levying an additional summer tax of ten dry pints of rice from each *mou* of taxable land cultivated by the villagers and an additional winter tax of five pints per *mou*, and storing the rice so collected in granaries (*xã thương*) under the management of "men of substance," who would lend the rice out at interest for five years. At the end of that time the granaries would presumably be stocked richly enough to be able to rescue any village caught in a period of famine.[123] In a brusque reply Minh-mạng commented that "ages are different and customs are dissimilar." Despite Giai's allusion to local men of substance, his memorial makes it clear that his granaries would have represented an extension of the influence of local officials. The emperor's response—founded as it was upon the conviction that provincial officials were already powerful enough—was unsurprising.

Historians may disentangle another definitive episode from this complicated skein of provincial proposals and imperial responses of the early nineteenth century. In 1841 the governor-general of Bình Định and Phú Yên memorialized that wine merchants in local market towns were cornering all available supplies of rice and that their actions were driving rice prices up. He proposed as a consequence that private rice wine distilleries be outlawed and that only one public distillery be allowed in each district, under the surveillance of prefectural and district officials, where peasants could go to obtain their necessary wines for sacrifices and for the making of medicinal cakes. The emperor rejected the scheme. He explained that he feared that it would open the door to sub-bureaucrats' manipulations of the provincial wine markets.[124] Wine brewers (who also sold the wine) squandered rice supplies in China as well as in Vietnam. But few Chinese officials could ever have seriously suggested that each Chinese district have only one licensed wine distributor. The difference in scale made greater local control feasible in Vietnam, and this affected the ambitions of Vietnamese mandarins.

In sum, the Vietnamese provincial bureaucracy's recurrent predilection for Chinese-style neighborhood mutual guarantee security systems, communal granaries, and public wine distilleries, and the Vietnamese court's suspicion of the uses to which these same institutions might be put in a smaller country, are only too plainly demonstrated in Nguyễn public records. But this was only one aspect of the continuing dialogue between the court and the provinces over formulas of local government. Strange results occurred when the most commonplace Chinese devices were used in the Vietnamese countryside. Chinese-type land and population registers were employed in both the north and the south. In terms of the criteria of assessment they employed, they were essentially unchanging literary and bureaucratic types. Little was to be left to the anarchic imaginations of the district magistrate's underlings. The land registers, the *địa bộ*, were compiled every year from 1805. The population registers, the *đinh bộ*, were compiled every year from 1807.

Every five years the central bureaucracy in Huế, which possessed copies of all the annual registers, collated them. It measured the growth or decline of the numbers of tax-paying peasants and the rise and fall in the value and portions of their land. It also matched the names in the register of one district for one year with the names in the register of the same district for another year. This was to make sure that individual landholders had not had bogus transformations of status (that is, from corvee-eligible middle age to corvee-ineligible old age) performed in the records on their behalf. The land registers charted, in the Chinese way, the boundaries of all parcels of land in their jurisdictions. These boundaries were marked by Chinese-style acreage poles (*mộc biểu*) or stone tablets (*thạch kiệt*). Hence at the lowest level in the territorial administration the flow of administrative conventions from China to Vietnam was supposedly preserved unbroken.

But the Vietnamese official, orthodox as he was, struggled with unseen sources of discord. One Vietnamese hamlet or *thôn* might differ incorrigibly from another in resources and in human economic conditions. To obtain the complicated census data that these Chinese-style registers required—the name of every adult male peasant, his age, his health, the amount of land he cultivated, his involvement or lack of involvement in lawsuits over land—local officials and their deputies were compelled to collect it on a hamlet-to-hamlet (*thôn-to-thôn*) basis. Only in this way could they penetrate the disguising diversities of village social habits and informal manipulations of landholding.

At the same time, Vietnamese *thôn* were much smaller than their Chinese namesakes, the *ts'un*, much smaller than the local settlement units upon which Chinese taxation was based. In terms of expenditure of bureaucratic effort it did not pay the central government in Huế to assess taxes or to conscript soldiers at the level of the hamlets. In fact, because of the Vietnamese hamlets' smallness and the absence of a neighborhood *pao-chia* system, the *xã* or village—which spanned several hamlets or *thôn*—became the local pivot of tax assessments and of the distribution of corvee duties. As the Huế Boards of War and Finance pointed out in 1842, the percentage conscription formulas of China depended upon the institutional preservation and viability of the super-hamlet unit, as opposed to the hamlet, in smaller Vietnam: "In northern Vietnam soldiers are conscripted from every jurisdiction on the principle of one conscript from every seven male taxpayers. Among these jurisdictions, suppose there is one village of two hamlets with a total of seven men registered as taxpayers. Only one conscript may be selected [from the village]. Now if you split it [the village] and consider it as two [hamlets], then each hamlet will say that it does not have the necessary number, and as for the soldier that was originally to be taken, upon which hamlet will you place the responsibility?"[125]

At this point the Chinese census registers, with their smooth schematizations and their demands for highly specific data, collided with the administrative exigencies of the small Vietnamese environment. The nature of the registers required that the territorial unit of reference for the census be no higher than the hamlet. But the smaller environment and population required that the unit of reference for the application of local tax quotas and conscription be above the hamlet. Otherwise, most peasants would have slipped under the net of the central quotas, not into it.

To the Vietnamese provincial official who was trapped in the collision, the solution was to go below the village. Nguyễn Đăng Giai, who had risen to become the acting governor-general of Bắc Ninh and Thái Nguyên provinces in the north in the early 1840's, suggested as much. Of the many Vietnamese documents of the 1840's which can be sifted for data bearing on the problem of the adjustment of Sino-Vietnamese institutions to Vietnamese provincial needs, his memorial is as concise as any. It is a good specimen of the provincial bureaucrat's view of the social microdynamics involved in the relationship of several *thôn* to their one *xã*. Giai wrote in part:

> Under my jurisdiction, in many instances the people of the hamlets within each village have the title of being "of the same village." Yet the dwellings of these people, their ancestral halls, their Buddhist temples, and their landholdings are all separate and distinct [for each hamlet]. Moreover there are no blood connections associated with descent from the same lineages between them. In every instance where you have one village divided into two or

three or four or five hamlets, up until now the categorized demands of the government registers, the abundance or scarcity of their landholdings, the density or thinness of their taxpayers, the heaviness or lightness of the distribution of military corvee, the increases or decreases of their tax regulations, their mutual lawsuits . . . have all been subsumed under the rubric of "the same village." When you meet an instance where Hamlet One is populous and rich but Hamlets Two and Three are declining, or where Hamlets Two and Three are populous and rich but Hamlet One is scattered, you take the mean among them [as a standard for requisitions]. When taxpayers and soldiers scatter and are lost to the registers, or when tax payments are deficient, if you place the blame upon "the same village," since the landholding taxpayers [of the individual hamlet] originally held themselves separate, consequently they are completely unwilling to move over and shoulder responsibilities in the place of someone else . . . With the exception of same villages but separate hamlets whose inhabitants' dwellings and cultivations mix with each other and whose ancestral halls and Buddhist temples are not distinct and separate—these do not require discussion—please in every instance . . . allow the headings "the landholdings of such-and-such hamlet" and "the soldiers and the taxpayers of such-and-such hamlet" to be clearly set forth within the registers.[126]

Part of the completely negative response by the Boards of Finance and War to this provincial request has already been quoted. The proposal was too "complicated" (*phân trương*). What were at stake, in the court's eyes, were the institutional tolerabilities of a Southeast Asian society which was hardly a universal empire like its neighbor.

The Chinese registers could not be discarded. Upon the credibility of the registers depended the practicability of agrarian taxation, and upon the practicability of agrarian taxation depended the plausibility of the classical bureaucracy itself. Yet they could not be allowed to lead, as their formulas combined with the technical possibilities of the smaller environment suggested they do, to a socially insupportable hamlet-by-hamlet diffusion of tax quotas. One reason, then, why the *xã* retained its administrative prominence was that the court—as opposed to local officials—protected and defended it, as a compromise unit of settlement which would not completely undermine the use of Chinese registers yet which would permit the bureaucratic organization of tax collections in ways more suitable to the differences in scale and economic strength between Chinese and Vietnamese societies. The *xã* quotas, rather than inflicting unfair liabilities upon the more dutiful hamlets, more often artificially forced an adjustment of unevenly distributed rural wealth and poverty. The common dictum was that "fertile and infertile hamlets reinforce each other" within the village. Needless to say, this was the Huế viewpoint—not the viewpoint of the local official actually charged with drawing up the Chinese-style registers and fulfilling the tax quotas.

Chinese-style land and population registers served many purposes in Nguyễn Vietnam, one factor in their ascendancy. In the southern provinces, newly conquered from the Cambodians, they were employed with great finesse to facilitate the spread of Sino-Vietnamese civilization in a racial no-man's-land. Ancestral temples (*từ tự*), Confucian shrines (*miếu vũ*), and graveyards, all expressive of Vietnamese but not of Cambodian culture, paid no land taxes. The lands of landlords who died and left no descendants, a not uncommon occurrence among pioneers in the tropical jungles, were redistributed as "public lands" among southern Vietnamese villagers. The details of the redistribution were quickly and legally enshrined in the registers. Benevolent landlords who held titles to lands in the south but who allowed Vietnamese peasants to have the increments from them saw these lands also classified, for taxation purposes, as "public lands" in the registers. Lastly, the registers were used to fortify newly devised provincial and village boundaries, which were often artificial to non-Vietnamese peasants.[127] Minh-mạng left no doubt about his determination to "Vietnamize" the highlanders and Cambodian settlers of the southern provinces: "We must hope that their barbarian habits will be subconsciously dissipated, and that they will daily become more infected by Han [that is, Sino-Vietnamese] customs. The surveying of land and the erecting of settlements, the promulgation and completion of the quotas and the registers, these things are essential demonstrations of 'using Hsia to change barbarians.'"[128]

The paraphernalia of a hazardous cultural morality play in which Cambodian culture was the predestined victim, Chinese-style registers were introduced into the south only slowly. An important document in the *Vermilion Books* reveals that the Board of Finance in Huế sent model registers to districts in Bình Hòa province in the summer of 1818 to teach local officials and villagers how to read them and compile them.[129] The official climax of the morality play came in 1836, when central, Huế-appointed officials systematically surveyed landholdings in the southern provinces for the first time. It was hardly any accident that less than six years later, such a climax was followed by violence. In 1841–42 most of the minority groups in southern Vietnam, ranging from the Cambodians to the highland peoples, were in open rebellion against the Nguyễn court. It was at this point that the Vietnamese province in Cambodia itself had to be abandoned.

Hence a typical Chinese local institution—the omnipresent land or population register—could affect the nineteenth-century Vietnamese peasant and his immediate official overlords in a variety of ways qualitatively remote from the Chinese experience. Ordinary as these registers appeared, the fate of the bureaucracy—and of political organization in Vietnam as sophisticated as China's—was firmly riveted to their durability and impermeability in the face of regional and environmental colloquialisms. The process of the political (and cultural) sinicization of Vietnam, which was in full force as recently as a century ago, hardly left anyone or anything untouched. A simple literary-bureaucratic form like a census book could shape the future of a Huế emperor and a Phú Yên salt peddler, a Hanoi scholar and a Saigon peasant.

Four
Education and Examinations in Nguyễn Vietnam

Like the Ch'ing civil bureaucracy, the Nguyễn bureaucracy was composed predominantly although not exclusively of degree-holding scholars, who had been selected at periodic public examinations. In fact, Chinese-style civil service examinations, based on the Chinese classics, appeared in Vietnam as early as the eleventh century. In the first few centuries after their inception they were held irregularly, focusing upon Buddhist doctrine almost as much as upon Confucian texts.[1] But by the late fifteenth century they had attained a definitive maturity under the Lê dynasty, and it was the Lê system that Huế rulers inherited in the 1800's.

The examinations dramatically inaugurated, renewed, and consolidated the entire Sino-Vietnamese bureaucratic process. The generality of the bureaucracy's rules demanded, if the behavior of the bureaucracy's members was to be reliable, the constant use of categorization, the classification and treatment of a miscellany of disconcertingly specific problems on the basis of previously designated cultural and administrative criteria. Many of these criteria—the relative unimportance of commercial expansion, the precedence of the family hierarchy, the undesirability of administrative activism except in crises, and many others—were supplied in Vietnam by the Chinese classical texts. But it was the examination system itself which first made rigid devotion to the texts and their creeds a necessity of vocational self-advancement. In Vietnam as in China the graduate of the system who entered the bureaucracy after passing these examinations was unlikely, in later official life, to offer unique or eccentric interpretations of organizational policies. The transfer of authority and the succession of new officials within the organization was, as a result, stable. New officials, molded by the same examinations as their predecessors, rarely symbolized undesired changes to the underlings they inherited or to the colleagues they encountered.

The influence of this molding by the examinations even affects students of Vietnamese traditional society today. The bureaucratic chroniclers who were the original authors of Vietnamese historical documents often refused or were unable to recognize socio-economic change when they saw it. Consequently, such change was abnormally minimized in traditional records. The description of historical events had to conform to the civil service's own long-descended framework of explanations. This framework in turn suggested an almost equally long-descended framework of bureaucratic procedures as palliatives or antidotes. The perspective was efficient but unnatural. Bureaucratized historiography was relatively changeless. On the whole, the continuity or stability of expectations within the Nguyễn bureaucracy began with the examination system. Stability or continuity became an absolute goal in itself. The examination system in Vietnam, like the examination system in China, played an important role in limiting the court's capacity to adapt itself to changing conditions after 1850.

An Overview of the Vietnamese Examination System in the 1800's

Nguyễn Vietnam's first regional examinations (*hương thi*) were held in 1807, at six provincial sites. Higher metropolitan examinations (*hội thi*) were not offered at Huế until 1822. The topmost part of the structure, the palace examination (*đình thi*), also held at Huế, was not added until 1829.

In the Gia-long period, in other words, when bureaucratic centralization had barely begun and military rule overshadowed civil administration, only the regional examinations took place, at six-year rather than at three-year intervals, in 1807, 1813, and 1819. This strangely long six-year gap between examinations was originally an accident. Initially the 1810 examinations had merely been postponed, setting a precedent, when drought and famine in northern

Vietnam preoccupied officials.[2] But the infrequency of examinations before 1821 suited a court which relied more upon government by soldiers than by scholars. From the early 1820's, regional examinations began to be held every three years, as in Ch'ing China.

In the Gia-long period winners of degrees at the regional examinations were called *hương cống* (literally "local tribute"). This was a title favored in the later years of the Lê dynasty and descended from the usages of the T'ang dynasty in China. Under Minh-mạng, however, they received the title of *cử-nhân* ("recommended man"), the Sino-Vietnamese equivalent of the term *chü-jen*, by which regional graduates were known in Ch'ing China. Scholars who then went on to further triumphs at the triennial metropolitan and palace examinations in Huế from the 1820's onward were saluted, as in China, as "presented scholars" (*tiến-sĩ*, the Sino-Vietnamese equivalent of the Chinese word *chin-shih*). These titles carried great prestige in Vietnamese traditional society. But it was prestige that was quite unmistakably the property of the degree holder's family almost as much as of the degree holder.

The wife of a regional graduate shared his title by being called *cô cử*. (*Cô* is a respectful term of address for women in Vietnamese, specifically meaning "father's sister" or "aunt" but generally being applied politely to young women; *cử* is the first part of *cử nhân*, the husband's degree.) If he became a doctoral degree holder, her own title changed to that of *cô nghè*, and she participated in the triumphal procession, which his village neighbors were required to tender him after he had won his degree, from the provincial capital back to his native village. Vietnamese novelists have enjoyed satirizing the social-climbing pretensions of doctoral degree holders' wives who, never having seen such processions before, ostentatiously fretted about what the correct posture of a "presented scholar's" wife should be. The procession itself was called a "glorious return" (*vinh qui*). Expensive to the villagers as a social burden they could not avoid, it gave rise to the cynical saying, "The student who has not yet passed his doctoral examinations is already a threat to his canton neighbors" (*chưa đỗ ông Nghè đã đe hàng tổng*).[3] It was actually less formidable in the 1800's than it had been in the late fifteenth century when, Vietnamese tradition has it, as part of these festivities a doctoral degree holder could select any rice field which he desired near his native place and take possession of it merely by standing his sword in its soil.

Regional graduates and doctoral degree holders were the most important degree holders in nineteenth-century Vietnam. But they were not the only ones. A third group were the licentiates or *tú-tài* (literally "flowering talent," the Sino-Vietnamese version of the Chinese term *hsiu-ts'ai*). In Ch'ing China licentiates were students who had not yet entered the regional or provincial examinations but who had passed a series of three local qualifying "school examinations" in their districts and prefectures. In Vietnam, on the other hand, licentiates were actual winners of a sort in the regional examinations. They had passed all but one of three or four successive stages of these examinations when they received their degree. Just one stage in the regional examinations thus defined the difference between a *tú-tài* and a *cử-nhân*. In the smaller society, the distances between examination system statuses were not so extreme. They were further blurred by the fact that the Vietnamese bureaucracy was proportionately larger to the size of the population of Vietnam than the Ch'ing bureaucracy was to the swelling nineteenth-century population of China. This meant that there was a greater need for talent but a smaller reservoir of talent to exploit. Despite the fact that they had not completed all the stages of the regional examination, Vietnamese licentiates were often allowed to enter the metropolitan examinations at Huế, sometimes by a cluster of special imperial indulgences, like one of 1846 which permitted all prefectural and district educational officers of either regional graduate or licentiate background to compete.[4]

Apart from the doctoral degree holders, regional graduates and licentiates, the Vietnamese educational world knew a variety of types of students whose titles were borrowed directly from those of similar students in China. At the National College or Quốc-tử-giám at Huế, itself a sub-model of the Kuo-tzu-chien at Peking, there were assembled regular students (*giám-sinh*); "tribute students" (*cống-sinh*) chosen upon a yearly basis by the prefectures; "shade students" (*ấm sinh*), who were sons enjoying the protective "shade" or sponsorship of preeminent bureaucratic or military fathers; and students from the imperial house, or various branches of it (*tôn-sinh*).

After 1829 a further distinction was made between scholars who performed ably at all stages of the metropolitan examination and who were then eligible to take the palace examination and become *tiến-sĩ* and scholars who did not fail the metropolitan examination but who did not complete it as satisfactorily as the others. Before the Tự-đức period the latter were not allowed to enter the palace examinations. Instead, their names were inscribed upon a "subordinate list" (*phó bảng*) of winners. The men themselves were referred to as "subordinate list" degree holders.[5] One Vietnamese historian has described the "subordinate list" as a "cruel invention" of the Nguyễn court, because its members were not doctoral degree holders, were not entitled to a "glorious return" to their native villages, yet were prevented from continuing in the examination system in quest of *tiến-sĩ* status.[6] In fact the "subordinate list" (*fu-pang* in Chinese) had been invented in China. But in Ch'ing China it made its most significant appearance at regional examinations. There it was a device which allowed examiners at sites in populous provinces—sites with a superabundance of well-educated candidates—to transcend the quotas of winning candidates which had been set bureaucratically for their sites. These examiners were now enabled to confer at least the lesser status of the "subordinate list" upon some of the overflow of scholars.

For each five regional graduates who were chosen at regional sites in Ch'ing China, one name was allowed to be entered upon the site's "subordinate list." This was not always a professional dead end. "Subordinate list" scholars of Chinese regional examinations commonly went to Peking to resume their studies. On one occasion in 1726, by special dispensation, men who had earned "subordinate list" status twice were suddenly made regional graduates. As such they were allowed to enter the metropolitan examinations.[7]

In Vietnam the use of the "subordinate list" at metropolitan examinations may well have been intended to permit the preservation of high academic standards (and the prestige of the *tiến-sĩ* degree) on the one hand and the salvaging of poorer scholars for some form of bureaucratic employment on the other. "Subordinate list" members were commonly sent to the provinces to wait for vacancies in the provincial administration for associate prefects. Far from being outnumbered five to one by regular degree holders, "subordinate list" members were numerous in Vietnam. In the 1844 metropolitan examination there were 15 *phó-bảng* graduates to 10 *tiến-sĩ*, a total of 25 men in all out of 281 candidates.[8]

From the first, the Chinese examination system's two principles of

(1) organizing a political and social stratification system based upon graded degrees of academic achievement and (2) creating a ruling elite drawn from any social class upon the basis of literary skill were accepted in Nguyễn Vietnam to a large extent. But some of the intricate patterns of the Chinese system evolved more slowly in Vietnam.

Before 1840, for example, the Huế court was only notified by regional examiners of the numbers of successful candidates who had passed at regional sites. It was not informed of their individual names or backgrounds or of the percentages of the triumphant who were *cử-nhân* rather than *tú-tài*.[9] Before 1843, the best three scholars at the Huế palace examinations were not exceptionally honored as they were in China, because of a sensitive Vietnamese illusion, entertained at some distance from Peking, that the Chinese court's honoring of its three highest graduates was more academically portentous than indeed it was. Only at the 1843 examinations did Thiệu-trị banish this suspicion: "I have observed that at palace examinations at the Ch'ing court those who are chosen the three most eminent winners are not very much above the average. It is merely a matter of that man being better than this one. Since the time that this court has inaugurated examinations, for a long time the selection of the three highest graduates at the palace examinations has received only empty stress . . . The writings [of Mai Anh Tuấn] are rather versed in systems of government and are comparatively better than those of previous examinations. We ought to make him the 'first-ranked' in order to encourage numerous scholars."[10]

In the Chinese scheme the rank of the successful candidates at the palace examinations determined their bureaucratic assignments, after the examinations were concluded. First-class doctoral degree holders commonly received academically influential posts at the Hanlin Academy. Lesser degree holders might become more lowly secretaries at the Six Boards, or district magistrates in the provinces. (Their provinces were chosen for them by lottery at the Board of Appointments.) Vietnamese doctoral degree holders of the early Nguyễn period—when the need for new civil officials was great—usually received higher, more important initial posts than their Chinese counterparts. Yet before the 1840's the order in which they finished in the palace examinations merely governed the nature of their first appointments, and then was forgotten, in contrast to the customs of the Chinese bureaucratic environment, where "highest graduates" enjoyed immeasurable prestige during most or all of their official lives. In 1844 Thiệu-trị attempted to introduce a more methodical differentiation of appointments and of subsequent series of promotions for degree holders, dependent upon the results of their last examinations.[11] But appointments strategy in Huế appears to have had less of an unswerving sense of academic hierarchy.

According to a blunt formulation of the late 1830's, the Vietnamese political elite (defined for purposes of corvee exemption as men of the "governmental background category" or *chức sắc hạng*) comprised all bureaucrats from first to ninth grade, doctoral degree holders, regional graduates, "shade" student sons of illustrious fathers, and licentiates.[12]

The licentiate class of degree holders played a more important role in the Vietnamese bureaucracy than it did in the Chinese. In China, licentiates (*sheng-yüan*) received appointments—usually unimportant clerkships—more in spite of their titles than because of them. In Vietnam, however, *tú-tài* regularly appeared in influential administrative offices. In 1834, twenty-two "below average" and "inferior" licentiates were made salaried apprentices at the Huế Six Boards. Later they were sent to selected provinces as "expectant" officials. There they waited for more substantive appointments and performed such tasks as coordinating inter-provincial administrative activities.[13] Furthermore, their more substantive appointments normally insinuated them into positions as district educational officers.

The development of the whole Nguyễn examination system depended upon the district educational officers. Because the appointment of humble licentiates to these formal positions in the provincial educational hierarchy marked a radical departure from Chinese practices, it was vigorously criticized by clairvoyant officials like Nguyễn Công Trứ. While serving as the governor-general of Hải Dương and Quảng Yên, Trứ wrote in a memorial of 1836: "Up until now many prefectural and district educational officials have not received the confidence or the obedience of local scholars. Licentiates have been used to fill educational offices. Since their scholarship is unable to surpass that of other men they do not command the scholars' admiration. Please increase the use of . . . regional graduates, and remove the original licentiate prefectural and district officials and return them to their studying to wait for future examination periods."[14] Minh-mạng answered that not all *cử-nhân* were necessarily superior to *tú-tài* in learning. There were not enough *cử-nhân* to fill the provincial educational commissions.

This answer revealed the absence of sufficiently meaningful hierarchical distinctions among the various types of Vietnamese degree holders. It also revealed the lack in general of enough scholars thoroughly trained in the Chinese classics who could maintain the standards of the educational system. Most of the great Vietnamese scholar-producing families, as will be shown, had clustered about the environs of Huế or at Hanoi and in the Red River basin. There were not enough of their sons to go around. The Nguyễn bureaucracy, spread over thirty-one provinces, was extended too far. Ordinarily, where *tú-tài* were concerned, only superior— if over-age—ones were appointed to provincial educational posts. Thirty-seven out of a group of one hundred and seventy licentiates of forty years of age or more qualified for such appointments at tests in Huế in 1839.[15] Later, in the colonial period, the *tú-tài* degree was to loom even larger as the Vietnamese equivalent of the French baccalaureate. Today many Vietnamese revolutionaries will speak disparagingly of the whole fusion of Confucian and colonial education merely by referring to the old-style *tú-tài* degree holder as a useless "bag of words" (*một túi chữ*).

There was a more important difference between China and Vietnam than just the greater bureaucratic prominence of the Vietnamese licentiate. Vietnam failed to duplicate the famous Chinese school examinations (*t'ung-shih*) at the base of the examination system. In China an ambitious student had to pass three sets of school examinations in his district and prefecture before he was allowed to enter the higher examination system which promised political and social preferment. These were the district examination (*hsien-shih*), the prefectural examination (*fu-shih*) and the "academy" examination (*yüan-shih*). Actually, these school examinations had originally been designed, as their name in Chinese implies, for youths (*t'ung*) who were under fifteen years of age. They were purposive academic versions of the ancient capping ceremony which publicly signalized maturity. As such, these examinations were marked indulgently in the Ming–Ch'ing period unless inappropriately elderly students attempted to take them. Many districts in China consequently became familiar with forty- or fifty-year old students who lied about their age and shaved their heads to look like children for these examinations, only to return home later and go unrecognized by their equally elderly wives.[16] It has also been suggested that these examinations were loosely supervised and that many candidates used substitutes to write their examinations for them.[17]

Nonetheless, aspirants to scholar-official status were reduced to a more manageable number at these local examinations. Such students were socially, morally, and politically screened by local officials before they rose farther in the system. To enter the school examinations a Chinese student required five guarantors who would vouch for the nature of his ancestry. (The guarantors had to confirm that his father, grandfather, and great grandfather had not been rebels or practitioners of mean professions, like brothel keeping.) In addition, he had to submit information upon his age, health, mourning obligations, and physical characteristics, all of which was entered in a dossier (*ko-yen ts'e*).[18] But in Vietnam this elaborate three-tiered structure of preparatory qualifying examinations did not exist. By Chinese standards (if not by the standards of a smaller society) the hierarchical levels of the Vietnamese examination system were underdeveloped. There was no inseparable relationship between entering the higher examinations and participating first in official and educational activities at local schools.[19]

It was true that yearly tests were held in Vietnam. Success in them brought exemption from corvee and recognition as a member of the pool of local scholars. At the same time, scholars' backgrounds were bureaucratically certified as being suitable for competition in civil service examinations just before the actual regional examinations. A law of 1807 required village chiefs to prepare a list of names (and professions) of any potential candidates whom they knew and forward it to district officials, four months before the first Nguyễn regional examinations occurred. Men who were unfilial, unharmonious, or rebellious were not to be included, but subjective evaluations meant punishment. The next month the district officials compiled four lists of names of candidates. One of them was sent to Huế, one of them went to the regional overlord, one of them was kept by the province or protectorate, and one of them belonged to the provincial educational commissioner.[20] A law of 1821 stipulated that scholars who were mourning their parents or patrilineal grandparents could not compete. And "wandering scholars" (*du học sĩ nhân*) who went to other provinces in search of less competitive examination sites were called to account and forced to return to their home sites.

Finally, from 1825, prefectural and district educational officials were ordered to give preliminary four-stage tests (*khảo hạch*) to all candidates who wished to enter the regional examinations. The results of these tests, and the test books themselves, would be reviewed by the provincial educational commissioners. If candidates of shallow learning had not been completely removed from the golden paths of the "examination hell" as a result of these local tests, the officials who had given them would be punished.[21] These local tests were the closest that Vietnamese practice ever came to approximating the series of local examinations, with their attendant quotas, that prevailed in China. Even in the "registers of scholars' names" (*sĩ nhân danh sách*) which were sent by the provinces to the Board of Rites in Huế, no later than one month before the regional examinations, in order to allow the board to estimate how many candidates there would be at each site and how many examiners it should send to each one, the most elementary details about the candidates' careers had to be supplied, like the geographical and official or private sources of their education. They had not been truly screened before. Standardization only began at the regional sites in Vietnam.

This was a luxury which the Vietnamese examination system could afford, because of its relatively small scale. The total number of Chinese doctoral degree holders or *chin-shih* who received their degrees at fifteen examinations held in Peking from 1821 to 1850 was 3,269, an average of 218 per examination.[22] In Nguyễn Vietnam in the same period, the total number of doctoral degree holders or *tiến-sĩ* who received their degrees at thirteen metropolitan examinations held in Huế was 124, an average of just under 10 per examination. This was a ratio of about 26 to 1. (Seven of the thirteen metropolitan examinations mentioned took place in the space of less than a decade, 1841–1849. It was in this period that a majority of the cited degree holders—68 out of the 124—won their degrees.)

In the seven decades from 1822 to 1892, 30 metropolitan examinations were held at Huế. Five hundred and six men are recorded as having won laurels in these examinations, 229 as *tiến-sĩ* and 277 as members of the "subordinate list." But of these 229 doctoral degree holders who were recorded by 1892, only 56 had emerged by 1840.[23] In China, about 8,000 regional graduates might converge upon Peking to compete in the metropolitan examinations every three years they were given. The total numbers of candidates who competed at the Vietnamese metropolitan examinations in Huế from 1822 to 1847 were much smaller (see Table 4).[24]

One feature of these statistics is the sudden flood of scholars at the metropolitan examinations in the 1840's. It had taken twenty years for Minh-mạng's policies of bureaucratic centralization and circumscription of the authority of regional militarists to stimulate a sustaining interest in administrative recruitment through civil service examinations.

Overall, an average of 170 candidates came to Huế in quest of doctoral degrees every three years. Sometimes, of course, additional "imperial favor" examinations were also given, as in China, interrupting this three-year cycle—examples being the Huế examinations of 1842, 1843, and 1848. But this small group formed the nucleus of the Nguyễn civil service. Obviously the chances of individual candidates in Huế were undeniably better than they were in Peking. The reason for this was that the Nguyễn bureaucracy was larger in proportion to the size of the population of Vietnam than the Ch'ing bureaucracy was to the population of China. In domesticating the Chinese bureaucracy in Vietnam, the Vietnamese court was faced with the problem of how to find enough competent men to fill that bureaucracy's thousands of posts, not all of which could be abolished in the transition of institutional blueprints from China to Southeast Asia. From the Vietnamese viewpoint, Chinese institutions loomed

Table 4. Number of Candidates at Huế Examinations.

Year	Number	Year	Number
1822	164	1841	119
1826	206	1842	164
1829	167	1843	171
1832	173	1844	281
1835	123	1847	175
1838	136		

larger than life or at least larger than the numbers of native scholars who could fill their many prescribed statuses.

This crisis of supply and demand which the Chinese model generated in Vietnam could of course be compared in a way to the situation new dynasties faced in China in their early years. In Vietnam, however, the crisis was more serious and lasted longer. In 1825 Minh-mạng ordered an investigation of all district educational officials, blaming them for the lack of new scholars.[25] Because of their difficulty in finding enough scholars for their civil service, Vietnamese courts largely failed to imitate the elaborate Chinese scholarly quotas systems. In eighteenth- and nineteenth-century China each district and prefecture was assigned a fixed quota of students who were allowed to work for, and pass, the preliminary school examinations. Quotas were employed in some instances (not all) as a device to prevent students from becoming so numerous that the system could not accommodate them. The pressure of population growth, especially in areas like the Yangtze delta, kept driving the quotas up and inflating even the categories, so that in 1724, for example, 25 districts in Chekiang were given the student quotas of prefectures.[26] In Nguyễn Vietnam there was no system of quotas in the districts and prefectures, and no quotas at the metropolitan examinations. Quotas were introduced for individual provinces only in the regional examinations, from 1807. Disturbed by the paucity of Vietnamese degree holders, Thiệu-trị learned about the swarms of candidates in China and concluded that the Chinese quotas were designed to increase the numbers of scholars (by compelling examiners to pass a maximum number of aspirants) rather than curb them: "I have read in the Ch'ing statutes that both their regional and metropolitan examinations have established quotas. If the elderly pass examinations but are unable to serve as officials, they too obtain an increase in rank and return home to retirement. Their examinations' searching for talent is as broad as this."[27]

Minh-mạng believed that the Ch'ing examination system was more successful than his own because the average provincial Chinese scholar had access to many more libraries and books than his Vietnamese counterpart. In Vietnam, most of the major collections of classical works were confined to Hanoi, the old capital, or Huế, the new one. These cities were the twin geographical foci of Vietnamese borrowing and buying of scholarship and books from China. Minh-mạng, competing with the Chinese as always, looked on the bright side of things: "Although the things that our country's scholars study are not very extensive, at least their phraseology is elegant and there is indeed enough to read. At present and in the future the trend of events will be to make human literary knowledge daily more abundant, and the Ch'ing court will not necessarily be able to excel us."[28]

By the Tự-đức era, which began in 1848, the crisis had eased slightly, enough to allow mid-century officials to indulge in sharp criticism of the excessively generous breadth of qualifications for appointment in Minh-mạng's bureaucracy. For example, from 1827 to 1848, every three years, callow imperial household students (*tôn sinh*) and "shade" students studying at the National Academy had been given superficial tests on the Chinese classics and their commentaries and on Vietnamese legal texts. Then they had been awarded bureaucratic commissions. After 1848 the situation changed. Such students had to be thirty years of age, or more, and were now required to pass stiff, three-stage eligibility examinations, before they could be employed.[29]

Yet the supply and demand crisis never wholly disappeared. Confucian Vietnam paid a price for its sophisticated duplication of the institutions of the Chinese empire. At times the Nguyễn bureaucracy was physically and socially overextended.

Students, Teachers, and Texts

The influence of the Confucian pedagogue ran from the top to the bottom of nineteenth-century Vietnamese society. "Growing up deep within the palace," Minh-mạng's sons at Huế in 1820 had their own tutor, Ngô Đình Giai. He was an aged scholar who was addressed as *tiên-sinh*, a conspicuously Chinese form of greeting. (Normally, teachers were and are called *thầy*, a non-Sinic Vietnamese word, like *thầy đồ*, the title of a Confucian teacher at a private school. *Thầy* was a respectful term of address that was also applied to players of socially didactic roles like soothsayers, priests, and middle level officials, for example, the district magistrate—*thầy huyện*.) Giai was renowned, too, for the correctness of his deportment, which

Minh-mạng hoped he could transfer to his imperial pupils.[30] Apart from studying with their venerable tutor, imperial princes were enrolled in a palace school known as the Tập Thiện Đường (School of the Concentration of Excellence). This had been created, with a staff of lecturers, in 1817.

The most important school in Huế was, of course, the National College or Quốc tử giám. It was filled with the sons of imperial relatives—as many as sixty in 1821—and the privileged sons of high civil officials. But it also harbored regional graduates who were studying for the metropolitan examinations and tribute students nominated annually by districts and prefectures. After 1844, when the son of a middle-ranked soldier from Cao Bằng successfully appealed to be admitted and was made one of the "shade" students, the descendants of lesser military officers could also join the school.[31] Membership as one of the blue-gowned, black-turbaned students led either to bureaucratic employment or to a better competitive opportunity in the examinations.

Only one National College was allowed to exist. With the change of dynasties in 1802–03 the gold gate tablet of the old National College in Hanoi had been removed, and its buildings had been converted into those of a prefectural city school.[32] The makeshift Huế National College of the Gia-long period was in turn replaced by a more permanent complex of buildings in 1821. These were situated in the village of An-ninh, west of the Huế citadel.[33] The head of the National College carried the title of *tế-tửu*, an extremely ancient designation, which was originally applied in the Chinese feudal period to the visiting elder at a formal banquet who made a ritual sacrifice with wine. As chancellor of the school and administrative custodian of its talent, he was required to memorialize the throne once a month upon the academic (and bureaucratic) prospects in the college.

In order to encourage the students at the college to improve their fortunes, the court paid them stipends and rations (*lẫm hý*) on a sliding scale. The scale was determined by the results of tests, given at regular periods within the school. The "excellent" student received double the money and also more rice and "lamp oil" than the "sub-average" student did in a month.[34] The lowest (fourth) ranked students in the school's recurring tests were dismissed from its registers. However, from 1844, tribute students from the far northern, multiethnic provinces of Tuyên Quang, Cao Bằng, and Lạng Sơn, where educational standards were low, were given separate tests at the school and were graded far more leniently. This was done to preserve the breadth of the geographical base of the student body's composition.[35]

Not all the students of the school were overwhelmingly devoted to its sense of bureaucratic discipline. Minh-mạng grumbled in 1824 about some of their more notorious extracurricular intoxications: wine, sex, fawning upon high officials in Huế society who had power and influence, gambling, stealing, and living scattered outside the school's jurisdiction.[36] "Presumptuous" absence from lectures was not unknown. In 1825 one enterprising student of the college was caught selling away the monthly rice rations of several others, at a time when Huế was haunted by threats of famine.[37] When a three-stage examination was administered to some of the students in this year for purposes of bureaucratic selection, only three out of thirty or more students were deemed capable.[38]

In the provinces, the Nguyễn educational structure seemed just as compulsively imitative of the Chinese as it was in the capital. The provincial educational commissioner was known as the *đốc-học*. Below him, in the prefectures, there were prefectural educational officers (*giáo-thụ*), and in the districts, district educational officers (*huấn-đạo*). (In Ch'ing China, however, the latter title—*hsün-tao* in Chinese —stood for the subordinate district educational officer, the primary district educational officer being known as the *chiao-yü*). Not every Vietnamese province possessed its own educational commissioner or every prefecture and district its own officers. One source suggests that in the 1840's in Vietnam there were 21 provincial educational commissioners, 63 prefectural educational officers, and 94 district educational officers.[39] Sixty-two of the 94 district officers listed were found in provinces from Nghệ An north. Although these numbers were likely to fluctuate, they may be compared with the more than 3,000 prefectural, sub-prefectural and district educational officials who served in such posts in Ch'ing China.[40]

As in China, the provincial educational commissioner was supposed to be qualified to lecture on the Confucian classics. By attracting to him vast throngs of bright students, he was supposed at the same time to be attracting them into the bureaucratic environment. To a lesser extent than in China, his rivals were independent-minded teachers in private schools. These men, European observers noted, could woo his students away from him.[41] Although his own quality as a teacher was supposed to be high, a sharp line was drawn in traditional Vietnam (and sometimes continues to be drawn) between "great learning" (*đại học*) and "small learning" (*tiểu học*). This meant, in effect, that prefectural and district educational officials would always be lesser men. High educational officials could not serve in the villages. Thiệu-trị rejected appeals from provincial governors and censors in 1843 and 1844 that he increase the bureaucratic grades of prefectural and district educational officers.[42] Aged Lê dynasty degree holders, licentiates, supernumerary apprentices at the Six Boards, or degraded or previously punished regional graduates customarily staffed these posts. Youth stayed in Huế; old age went to the provinces. Northern licentiates were perhaps the most typical lower educational officials.[43] But there were always many vacancies. And sometimes prefectural educational officers who were commissioned to serve in specific prefectures preferred to offer their pedantries at more prestigious schools in provincial capitals, remaining at a comfortable distance from the eager villagers who required their services.[44]

In the lives of local scholars, the provincial school was the place where Sino-Vietnamese culture received its most authoritative early crystallization. Lectures were supposedly given at every official school in Vietnam, from the National College in Huế to the district "palm leaf" school, if one existed. According to the curriculum inaugurated in 1826, on odd days of the month the lectures treated the Chinese classics and their commentaries. On even days of the month it was the turn of "orthodox histories"—Chinese histories. Students living near the school who had received corvee exemption were required to attend and "sit meditatively" (*tịnh tọa*). Tests were supposedly held at the schools on the third, ninth, seventeenth, and twenty-fifth days of each month, at which examination topics were issued approximating topics of the regular civil service examinations. In the middle ten days of the eleventh lunar month of every year, one province-wide test or "joint examination" (*hội khảo*) would be given at the provincial capital, to which district educational officers were required to lead the students of their bailiwicks to participate.[45]

Methods of initially qualifying for the coveted status of "local scholar" varied. In the Gia-long period a student who could pass one stage of the four-stage regional examinations received exemption from corvee and military duties for two years. One who could pass even two stages became exempt for three years.[46] In 1825 this arrangement was superseded by new, twice-a-year local tests, which took place on the fifteenth day of the first and the tenth lunar months. A year's exemption from corvee was the reward of students who obtained an "excellent" rating in these tests. But the more mediocre could look forward to scholarly freedom for only six months. The test books were scrutinized by both the prefectural and district educational officials and later by higher provincial officials. Students could no longer win exemption by struggling to pass just one of the stages of the regional examinations. But in an effort to prevent marginal scholars among them from becoming politically discontented, students who completely failed the regional examinations were allowed to take "continuation tests" (*kê khóa*) the following summer—a second chance for potential derelicts to try to stay out of the army.[47]

Here was an educational system whose purpose was to conserve certain kinds of knowledge rather than to change them. It was a system which tried to make social differentiation, rather than variegated occupational selection, more efficient. Needless to say, as such, it was the antitype of the educational system of any modern industrial society. Before they gravitated to the schools and became subject to the schools' curricula and way of life, young Vietnamese students only absorbed Sino-Vietnamese culture piecemeal. The content of Sino-Vietnamese culture—its ideas, its symbols, its orientations—had surrounded them from childhood, at least if they were raised in scholar-teacher families. Now, in the local tests and at the schools, they were introduced for the first time to its established patterns of bureaucratic form. But it is important to realize that local Confucian schools in Vietnam—of the court-sponsored kind—were relatively poorly developed, except in the area of Hanoi. Private schools were another matter.

In Ch'ing China state schools were supplemented by ubiquitous provincial academies or *shu-yüan*. Both the imperial government and local gentry endowed the *shu-yüan*, whose heads or *shan-chang*—literally "mountain leaders," a name which was a relic of Sung times when academies had been private mountain retreats—came from the Hanlin Academy in Peking.[48] These academies gave local examinations. Their existence generally improved the opportunities for scholarships and social mobility of students in the areas where they were situated. The tradition of the Chinese *shu-yüan* was comprehensively duplicated in Yi Korea. There, *sŏwŏn* became the chief educational institutions.

In nineteenth-century Vietnam, on the other hand, Chinese-style *shu-yüan* did not dot the countryside. State educational institutions did not inevitably appear in every district or prefecture. The significance of all this was that Vietnamese scholars could rise more easily to the top of their examination system without ever having set foot in a government school than Chinese scholars could. There were fewer educational half-way houses between the village and the palace examinations in Vietnam than there were in China. This meant that the education which aspiring Vietnamese scholars received was perhaps less standardized and repetitive.

Still another factor prevented the Vietnamese educational world from ever completely paralleling China's. Compared to Chinese printing enterprises, the Vietnamese printing industry, impressive by Southeast Asian standards, was relatively primitive. Perhaps it would be more accurate to say that its social exploitation was both narrow and controlled. In the eighteenth century, stories were told of books being copied by hand and then being passed informally from family to family, from Hanoi to Hà Tiên, becoming completely worn out in the journey. Vietnamese dynasties, more than those of any other East Asian classical society, attempted to centralize and control their printing facilities and keep them from being socially and geographically diffused.

Lê dynasty regulations of the seventeenth and eighteenth centuries forbade villagers to "cut printing blocks and to engrave and print" Buddhist and Taoist books and heterodox writings and "various national chronicles" which were associated with "profligacy."[49] The result was the growth of a very strong tradition, in Vietnamese villages, of the oral circulation of poetry, history, and soothsayings of all kinds. This tradition, which often harbored utopian visions and political subversion, continues to dominate Vietnamese rural politics in the revolutionary twentieth century. After 1820 the Nguyễn court renewed the Lê policy of centralizing the printing of books at its capital. All the printing blocks for the Chinese classics which had previously been stored at the Lê Temple of Literature (*Văn Miếu*) in Hanoi were now brought by junk to Huế, and deposited at the National College.[50] Officials in the provinces who had manufactured their own printing blocks in the decentralized Gia-long era, like the energetic Trần Công Hiến in Hải Dương, were compelled to send them also to Huế.[51] One of the duties of students at the National College was to examine the printing blocks of the empire and to extract the ones that had deteriorated from the collection.[52]

The court's control of the production of Vietnamese literature benefited from the failure of many centers of printing activity to flourish outside Huế. Scholars who wished to print their own private texts had to take their own paper and ink and report to officials at the Huế Historical Institute (*Quốc sử quán*), where their wishes might or might not be granted.[53] Of course printed books did circulate in the provinces. Textbooks like the Four Books and the Five Classics and Chinese histories, as well as compilations of model examination answers and the latest editions of the emperor's poems, were even liberally distributed periodically to provincial schools by the court. Yet classical books (*quan thư*) were so much rarer in quantity in Vietnam than in China that they were often treated by provincial educational officials more as precious artifacts than as educational tools. Vietnamese provincial scholars, denied the academies of their Chinese and even their Korean contemporaries, were sometimes also denied access to official school libraries. Minh-mạng's edict of 1837 declared: "Previously I have heard that educational officials, because they considered that government books were to be heavily respected, merely cherished them and stored them. None of the scholars under their jurisdiction were able to read them or to transcribe materials from them. Surely this was not the purpose of the court's distributing the books . . . [Educational officials] must allow the scholars under them to come by themselves and copy materials and study, in order to broaden their experience. If . . . the books that were originally supplied become worn out and cracked it does not matter."[54]

What this constriction of literature meant was that those Vietnamese scholars who were genuinely devoted to the Chinese classical tradition—and not all were, as will be shown—were more conservative and less intellectually innovative than Chinese classicists. The textual transmission of the Confucian legacy in Vietnam was so much more arduous and more fragile that there was a greater fear of change in the transmitted tradition itself. Transmission of this heritage from one Vietnamese generation to another, being less massively certain than in China, had to be almost unnaturally pure and completely uninfluenced by the events of the day. This was just one consequence; another was the undermining of social mobility.

It was a consequence which was more meaningful at the intermediate levels of Vietnamese education than in the villages. Village education acknowledged the almost invulnerable sovereignty of the private schoolteacher, unassociated in any way with the bureaucracy, who did his job thoroughly. French observers like Pasquier later in the century recalled encountering five-year old children who could recite without a flaw the elementary texts they had memorized.[55] Village school classes in the vicinity of Huế "were not difficult to discover, for the discordant cries which the pupils uttered in them [learning Chinese characters out loud by rote] and which one heard from far afield were a certain indication of their existence."[56] Teachers customarily grouped children around them and traced selected Chinese characters, with a ruler, on a board that was covered with soil or clay. After the teachers had ingeminated the names of the characters and their meanings, the children would repeat what they had been taught in loud voices and then learn how to trace the characters themselves.[57] Later, when such teachers introduced the children to the Four Books and the Five Classics—here literacy became linked to ideology for the first time—they lectured "with their eyes shut," in the sardonic words of a modern Vietnamese writer, being afraid only that they would violate the interpretative glosses of the Sung philosophers.[58]

Girls remained at home. Special primers written by great Vietnamese scholars of the past, like Nguyễn Trãi and Lê Quí Đôn, were read to them. These primers taught them "the four virtues" (*tứ đức*) of Sino-Vietnamese feminine behavior. The "four virtues" included the proper way to stand and sit (*dung*), the proper way to speak respectfully (*ngôn*), the importance of cooking and sewing (*công*), and the proper way to be virtuous and gentle (*hạnh*). Boys were supposed to begin their schooling at the age of seven, the age of eight by Sino-Vietnamese reckoning. At the age of eleven they first applied themselves to the *Analects* of Confucius (*Luận ngữ*), *Mencius* (*Mạnh tử*), the *Doctrine of the Mean* (*Trung dung*), and the *Great Learning* (*Đại Học*). At the age of fourteen, having finished the Four Books, they read the *Classic of Songs* (*Thi kinh*), the *Classic of Documents* (*Thư kinh*), the *Classic of Changes* (*Dịch kinh*), the *Record of Rituals* (*Lễ ký*), the *Spring and Autumn Annals* (*Xuân thu*), and the earlier Chinese dynastic histories.[59]

Superimposed upon this predictable schedule after 1834 was the need to inculcate Minh-mạng's ten moral maxims or exhortations, which concerned life in the villages. Each village, and every provincial educational official, was supposed to possess one copy of the maxims. They were expounded twice a year, in the first and seventh lunar months, at all provincial, prefectural, and district offices; four times a year, on the first day of the second month of every season, at all local schools; and four times a year, in the third, sixth, ninth, and twelfth lunar months, in every village. The provincial offices of the bureaucracy, the provincial schools, and the *đình* of every village in this way became the three foci of the indoctrination system.

The actual composition of ten moral maxims by the emperor himself was an obvious requirement of the Sino-Vietnamese monarchy. This requirement was based upon precedents set by Ch'ing emperors like K'ang-hsi (or Ming emperors like Hung-wu) in China. It dramatized the emperor's idealized position as the moral arbiter of his society. Yet the promulgation of the maxims merely confirmed the values of the Sino-Vietnamese bureaucracy, which the emperors more or less served.

Of Minh-mạng's ten maxims of 1834, the first was "esteem the human relationships" (*đôn nhân luân*), the hierarchically determined proprieties of behavior between sovereign and minister, father and son, husband and wife, and older brother and younger brother. "Rectify the calculations of the heart" (*chính tâm thuật*) was the second, a maxim directed chiefly against class war in the villages. It warned the rich not to be arrogant and the poor not to be seditious. "Devote attention to your original calling" (*vụ bản nghiệp*), the third maxim, upheld the Confucian four-class hierarchy of scholar, peasant, artisan, and merchant and charted the ideal behavior for members of each of these four classes. The fourth, "esteem frugality" (*thượng tiết kiệm*), attacked the wearing of extravagant clothes, the building of dwellings that were too ornamental, the expenditure of too much money upon weddings and funerals, and the smoking of opium. The fifth, "enrich moral customs" (*hậu phong tục*), addressed the peasant directly in impeccable Sino-Vietnamese classical phrases that he only dimly understood. It told him to avoid strife in his family, lineage, and village. The sixth, "teach your children" (*huấn tử đệ*), suggested that filial piety must be inculcated early. It quoted Mencius to the effect that "he who lives idly and is without education leads a life akin to that of the wild birds and animals."

But education meant indoctrination only. The seventh maxim, "reverence orthodox studies" (*sùng chính học*), stated quite candidly that no one outside the scholar class had the slightest need for literacy: "As for soldiers, peasants, artisans and traders, surely they do not all have to be able to read books and recognize characters?" The eighth maxim preached sexual restraint, asking villagers to "abstain from dissoluteness and wickedness" (*giới dâm nặc*). The ninth demanded that laws be obeyed (*thận pháp thủ*). The tenth and final maxim recommended "the broadening of good conduct" (*quảng thiện hạnh*). Good conduct was defined as being filial piety, brotherly submission, loyalty, trustworthiness, humaneness, right conduct, politeness, and knowledgability.[60] The purpose of these ten maxims of 1834 was to reinforce Sino-Vietnamese cultural stability, especially outside Huế. Their more immediate background was the alarming spread of Christianity, both in the central and in the southern provinces. Partly outmoded as socio-political dogma for the Vietnamese peasant even in the 1830's, they enjoyed an ironically persistent influence in the minds of Vietnamese elites. This influence has still not faded, at least in southern Vietnam, in the second half of the twentieth century.[61]

Villages chose their own teachers. The teachers might be scholars who had failed the civil service examinations, scholars who had passed the examinations but who had no desire to be officials (Lê dynasty loyalists in the north after 1802), or scholars who had served as officials and had then returned to their villages for purposes of rest or retirement. Teachers might open schools in their own homes. If they could not afford to do this, they would request rich men with large homes to "build partitions" or "hang curtains" (*thiết trướng*) in theirs, in order to create classrooms. Teachers might live with their newly found landlord hosts, even receiving their keep. If the teachers' instruction became famous, many people would bring their sons to enroll under them. The teachers would ask the family heads under whose roofs they were staying for approval of their increased enrollment. The latter would usually agree, because the teachers' popularity added to their prestige as well.

A father would bring his son, impeccably dressed, to the place where the teacher was staying, carrying with him gifts for the teacher, like wine and cooked chicken. The father, the teacher, and the household head who sponsored the teacher would then sit down to sample the food and wine and to discuss education. The teacher would indulge in astrology in order to determine the future success of his new pupil. The three men together might even confer about the creation of a new and auspicious name for the boy. To maintain discipline over his students, a teacher might select two assistants from his bigger students. An "elder brother inside the school" (*anh trưởng trường nội*) was the more important one, as a solver of disputes and as a trustworthy servant of the teacher. A less important "elder brother outside the school" (*anh trưởng trường ngoại*) bore responsibility for the students' behavior outside the classroom. This division of "inner" and "outer" assistants was in some respects reminiscent in a prosaic way of the division between inner and outer ministers at court.

The village teacher received no payment from the official bureaucracy. This would actually have lowered his prestige in the village. It would have implied that he had not earned rapport with, or support from, his social environment. (But low payment for primary school teachers in southern Vietnam, a legacy of this tradition, was producing great tensions there after 1954.) Instead, his students formed class associations (*hội đồng môn*), which visited the homes of all the villagers, soliciting contributions for the teacher's livelihood. Significantly, evasion of the regular imperial tax collections decreed from Huế was considered almost respectable in some nineteenth-century Vietnamese villages, but failure to pay "alumni money" (*tiền đồng môn*) for the local teacher's expenses was dangerous. Social ostracization, and even the loss of furniture and livestock, which the zealous student committees sometimes confiscated in compensation, might result. A student was compelled to give his teacher a special subvention at every lunar New Year to allow him to return to his native village. At least one student had to accompany the teacher and serve him while he was making this annual journey. If the teacher (or his wife) died, his students had to mourn him for three years. He was like a father. And in their first few months at school, students were taught, not Chinese characters, but rather, more of the rites and the discipline of the Sino-Vietnamese elite status culture: how to fold their hands (*khoanh tay*), how to bow their heads (*cúi đầu*), how to report to superiors (*bẩm báo*) and how to converse with superiors in a respectful way (*thưa gửi*).[62]

The sense of priorities in nineteenth-century village education was actually summarized by an austere Sino-Vietnamese commonplace which said: "First one studies the rites of conduct, later one studies literature" (*tiên học lễ, hậu học văn*). Books that made up the literature of elementary education in Nguyễn Vietnam, when literature rather than rites was studied, might be imported from China. Otherwise they were Sino-Vietnamese textbooks which had been written, with variations, in imitation of Chinese prototypes. The redoubtable *Three Character Classic* (*San tzu ching*) of Sung times was one of the most popular Chinese textbooks in Vietnam. The more ancient *Classic of Filial Piety* (*Hsiao ching*) and *Classic of Loyalty* (*Chung ching*) were also read, along with the *Family Exhortations of Ming Tao* (*Ming Tao chia-hsün*). This last book was a collection of Confucian strictures by the Sung philosopher Ch'eng Hao (known to the Vietnamese as Trình Hiệu). Yet in fact Sino-Vietnamese textbooks, which had been written in Vietnam itself, played a far more important role.

The Sino-Vietnamese *Thousand Character Litany* (*Nhất thiên tự*) was the cornerstone of village learning. It actually amounted to 1,015 characters, and should not be confused with the Chinese *Thousand Character Classic*. It was designed to help Vietnamese schoolchildren make the transition from their own language, with its very different words and word order, to classical Chinese. In it, Chinese characters (*chữ Nho*, "Confucian scholars' words," in Vietnamese) appeared in an alternating rhythm of three to the first line and four to the second. But after the Vietnamese student had given each character its Sino-

Vietnamese pronunciation, he then enunciated the native non-Sinic Vietnamese word whose meaning corresponded to that of the cited character. Thus the student read out loud six words in the first line and eight words in the second—in a pattern intended to suit the famous Vietnamese six-eight meter poetry form. In this way the rhythms of Southeast Asian poetry were skilfully employed to disseminate the Sino-Vietnamese written language. A sample two lines from the *Thousand Character Litany* juxtaposed the Sino-Vietnamese and the indigenous words for "heaven," "earth," "clouds," "rain," "wind," "day," and "night":

> Thiên trời, địa đất, vân mây,
> Vũ mưa, phong gió, trú ngày, dạ đêm.[63]

Another Sino-Vietnamese primer which was familiar to children in ambitious, scholarship-dominated families was one called *Asking the Way in Elementary Studies* (*Sơ học vấn tân*). It consisted of 270 four-character phrases, which were divided into three parts. One part (130 phrases) dealt with Chinese history from its mythical beginnings to the nineteenth century. A second part (64 phrases) described the history of Vietnam from its mythical beginnings down to the Nguyễn dynasty. A third part (76 phrases) contained sober words of advice upon studying and upon life in general. An eight-phrase section from the second part underlined Vietnam's high position, by virtue of having been ruled by the relative of a Chinese sage-emperor, in the Chinese classical world: "The ancient name of the nation at its founding was *Việt-thường*. The T'ang changed it to Annam, the Han called it *Nam-Việt*. Of the Heavenly Farmer's four descendants, the second one was enfeoffed to rule us. He was called the *Kinh-dương* king, and his reign title was *Hồng Bàng*."

Still another Sino-Vietnamese primer which did its work of strengthening elite culture in the villages was the book of *Five Word Poems for Youthful Studies* (*Ấu học ngũ ngôn thi*). Its 278 lines of five-word poetry descanted upon the rewards of studying classical Chinese (it compared instruction in the Chinese classics to possession of a fortune in money, an echo of a simile in Chinese primers in China) and suggested the immense prestige that lay in wait for graduates of the examination system. Because of this it was also called *Poems of the Highest*

Graduates (*Trạng-nguyên thi*). Often in Vietnamese local schools in the nineteenth century the tendency was to read these Sino-Vietnamese primers first but then study the major Chinese classics directly, ignoring more elementary Chinese texts as being superfluous. Tôn Thọ Đức, then financial commissioner of Hanoi province, memorialized in 1837: "Today's students in large numbers skip over [texts]. From their youth they have already practiced writing essays, and do not know how to progress gradually in the proper sequence. In teaching children of seven and eight years of age, please let them be taught to read the [Chinese] *Classics of Loyalty and Filial Piety* first, as well as the Four Books which belong to primary studies. Only afterwards let lecturing on the Five Classics and philosophy and history be continued."[64]

In the battles of the Minh-mạng period over school curricula, Đức's views were those of a typical conservative. In reality the ideological burdens of Chinese and Sino-Vietnamese primers were hardly dissimilar. The environments rather than the texts diverged.

The Bureaucratic Organization of the Examination System

In the first half of the 1800's the number of sites for regional examinations in Vietnam was usually either five or six. Ordinarily there was one southern site, in Gia Định (Saigon); one central site, in Thừa Thiên (Huế); one or two north central sites, in Nghệ An and Thanh Hóa; and two northern sites, at Hanoi and in Nam Định province. Scholar candidates in all the provinces from Khánh Hòa south went to Saigon. Those living in provinces from Quảng Bình south to Phú Yên went to Huế. Nghệ An and Hà Tĩnh scholars competed at the Nghệ An site, and Thanh Hóa and Ninh Bình scholars competed in Thanh Hóa. Scholars from eight provinces—Hanoi, Sơn Tây, Bắc Ninh, Tuyên Quang, Hưng Hóa, Thái Nguyên, Lạng Sơn, and Cao Bằng—swarmed to Hanoi for the regional examinations. Those from four other northern provinces—Nam Định, Hưng Yên, Hải Dương, and Quảng Yên—came to Nam Định.[65] In late 1834 the Thanh Hóa site was abolished. Thanh Hóa candidates had to attend the Nghệ An site and Ninh Bình candidates had to swell the numbers of the competitors at Nam Định. In 1834 also, Lê Văn

Khôi's rebellion and a Siamese invasion forced the cancellation of the Saigon examinations. Gia Định site scholars had to go to Huế if they wished to compete.[66]

Hence arrangements fluctuated. But what stood out was the existence of several convenient sites in underpopulated central Vietnam and the lack of enough sites in the more densely populated north. Obvious to historians today, this uneven pattern of site location (relative to population) was even more obvious to the nineteenth-century elite. In the north, it constituted a major source of grievances against the dynasty.

As in China (where regional examinations were commonly held in the eighth lunar month) the Vietnamese regional examinations were held in the late summer or in the fall. Before 1840, examinations in Nghệ An, Huế, and Saigon occurred in the seventh lunar month. Those at more northern sites took place in the ninth or tenth lunar months. This meant that Huế officials who were appointed to serve as examiners in Saigon had to leave the capital in the first ten days of the sixth lunar month in order to arrive at the site in time. The malarial summer heat in the south was soon able to take a deadly toll of these officials. Eventually in 1840 Saigon regional examinations were transferred from the seventh to the ninth lunar month—to the dry season.[67] Candidates began the first stage of the examinations on the first day of the month, the second stage on the sixth day, and the third stage on the twelfth day. The list of winners was supposedly issued ten days later, on the twenty-second day of the month. In 1843 this schedule was expanded to permit examiners increased time for marking the papers (specifically, to allow second examiners time to scrutinize papers which the preliminary examiners had failed). Now the candidates entered the second stage of the examinations on the ninth day of the month and the third stage on the eighteenth day. The list of winners was not promulgated until the first day of the next month. Significantly, this 1843 reform did not apply to the Saigon site, which continued to adhere to the old schedule. The number of competing candidates at Saigon was usually so much smaller that examiners there hardly required the extra time.[68]

In China, even at provincial sites, the institutional preeminence of the examination system expressed itself in large complexes of walls, buildings, and roads which were called *kung-yüan*. Of the 16 or so *kung-yüan* in China, many had permanent accommodations for more than 10,000 candidates. In fact, the walls of some of them, like the massive Kiangnan ("south of the Yangtze," Kiangsu and Anhwei) site at Nanking in the eighteenth century, were continually being torn down in order to permit the annexation of whole nearby streets or lanes of buildings for purposes of additional space.[69] Basically, the Chinese regional examination site or *kung-yüan* consisted of long rows of roofed solitary cells. The cells were situated on alleys which opened off a main site thoroughfare or raised road (*yung-tao*), which traversed the *kung-yüan*. The huts or cells themselves (known as *hao-she*) were roofed and were walled on three sides by brick. But they had no doors and no furniture and their floors were earthen. Candidates, who had to spend three days and two nights in these tiny prisons, had to make three planks serve as bed, bench, table, and bookshelf. Because these spacious brick sites were used only once every three years, weeds, fungus, and mildew thrived in them. At night deserted *kung-yüan* were believed to be haunted by ghosts.[70] Nonetheless, with their kitchens, granaries, copying rooms, offices, towers, huts, and pools with elaborate stone bridges over them ("crossing the pool" was Chinese elite slang for winning a degree), these sites were intricate and solid structures. They were both symbols of dynastic emphasis upon the importance of the examination system everywhere in China and monuments to local "gentry" contributions for their upkeep. These contributions were solicited without difficulty by enterprising Ch'ing provincial officials like Juan Yüan in Canton.[71]

Vietnamese examination sites were rarely so elaborate or so permanent. Evidence suggests that even the vital Hanoi regional site existed upon a primitive, makeshift basis before 1831. In the middle of 1831, the walls of the former government mint there were razed (the mint having been moved to Huế) and its lands were appropriated for the new Hanoi site.[72] Examination sites in Vietnam were typically great rectangular fields with bamboo fences around them. They were divided into two parts, separated by a long wall (*liêm*). The "inner wall" part (*nội liêm*) was reserved for examination officials and markers. The "outer wall" part (*ngoại liêm*) was the place where the candidates assembled, the place where they raised their own tents and their own bamboo beds. (*Lều chõng*, "tents and bamboo beds," became a fashionable synonym for the whole system as a consequence.) In fact, the "outer wall" area where "the battle of the writing brushes" took place was further subdivided into four fenced enclosures (*tứ vi*) separated by two crisscrossing lanes. At the intersection of these lanes there stood a watchtower (*thập đạo đường*).

Until 1840 the bamboo walls of these sites, and the activities which went on behind them, were guarded and inspected by soldiers mounted upon elephants. But in 1840 Minh-mạng's Sino-Vietnamese orthodoxy prevailed and the elephants were banished,[73] to be employed from then on only in war and in court receptions of diplomatic envoys from elsewhere in Southeast Asia—two realms of Vietnamese life where Chinese cultural influences could be subdued. If there were 1,000 or 2,000 competing candidates at a regional site there were usually about 300 or 400 soldiers on duty maintaining order.[74]

In 1843 a more durable, Chinese-style examination site was planned at Huế, inside the citadel in Ninh Bắc ward. Before 1843 regional examinations at Huế had been held in Nguyệt Biêu village on the south bank of the Perfume River. Metropolitan examinations had taken place in front of the Zenith Gate in the Imperial City. Now, however, the thatched huts and bamboo fences disappeared, in favor of a new site of brick walls, permanent buildings, half-moon gates, and a roofed kitchen.[75] But Vietnamese provincial sites were much slower to imitate such sinicized (and such expensive) site architecture. This grandiose change of styles at Huế in 1843 really suggested that the dynastic capital enjoyed a greater hegemony in the Vietnamese educational world than Peking enjoyed in China.

With or without brick edifices as settings for examinations, the stresses of the examination life for Vietnamese scholars were just as acute as they were for Chinese ones. In both countries candidates underwent what the Chinese novelist P'u Sung-ling (1640–1715), himself an unsuccessful candidate, was reported to have satirized as the "seven metamorphoses" of the regional examination competitor: a beggar (candidates had to carry their own luggage as they arrived at the sites); a convict (candidates had to have their bodies inspected for concealed writings by jeering attendants and shouting soldiers); a member of a swarm of bees (thousands of candidates crawled in and out of the brick cubicles where they wrote their examinations); a sick bird which had just been released from a cage (candidates tottered dizzily out of their huts into the fresh air after having written their examinations); a monkey (candidates fidgeted and moved about erratically waiting for the proclamation of the results of the examinations); a dead fly (candidates who learned that they had failed were physically exhausted and threw themselves on the ground, unable to move); and finally, a pigeon crushing its own eggs (once candidates who had failed recovered from the initial shock, they smashed the furnishings of their huts, and personal possessions, in demonstrations of fury against the examiners).[76]

At each Vietnamese regional site, examinations were conducted by one master examiner (*chủ khảo*), one associate master examiner (*phó chủ khạo*), one or two invigilators (*giám khảo*), one or two proctors (*đê điều*), one or two assistant proctors (*phó đê điều*), one or two special examiners (*phân khảo*), second examiners (*phúc khảo*; ranging from eight at sites like Hanoi and Huế to two at Saigon), preliminary examiners (*sơ khảo*; ranging from sixteen at Hanoi and Huế to four at Saigon), two censors, and a corps of military investigators (*thể sát*) and inspectors (*mật sát*). Copyists, sealers, proofreaders, ordinary subbureaucrats and soldiers were also present. In other words, a miniature bureaucracy resided at each site. It spanned at least eleven different types of commissions, ran from the second grade to the ninth grade of the bureaucratic hierarchy, and was not inconsiderable in numbers. There might be 48 different ranking officials at large sites like Hanoi and Huế and 18 at the smallest site, Saigon.[77]

Although the titles of these site officials were mostly Sino-Vietnamese equivalents of the names of corresponding officials at Chinese examination sites, Vietnamese examiners were not quite so intricately subdivided into marking specialists as Chinese examiners were. Chinese regional sites possessed "examiner fellows" (*t'ung-k'ao-kuan*). These men were usually higher degree holders, resident in districts and prefectures, who had passed tests at their provincial capitals after having been recommended for duty and had then been sent to examination sites in "neighboring provinces." As of 1738 at the big Kiangnan regional site in China, of the 22 "examiner fellows" serving at the site, 7 specialized in the *Classic of Changes*, 4 in the *Classic of Documents*, 7 in the *Classic of Songs*, 2 in the *Spring and Autumn Annals*, and 2 in the *Record of Rituals*.[78] Vietnamese examiners, on the other hand, do not appear to have been differentiated on the basis of special textual attention to one of the Five Classics in this way.

But the holding of the examinations, in Vietnam as in China, represented an important vested interest for bureaucrats who had already received their own degrees. At the outset, of course, this vested interest was economic. The master examiner at a regional examination site in Vietnam in the 1840's received more payment for his month of work than a provincial educational commissioner received in a year.[79] The salary of the master examiner at the metropolitan examinations was much higher. Lesser posts at the sites were less well paid but not undesirable. They were competed for by doctoral degree holders, regional graduates, and secretaries and records keepers serving under provincial financial and judicial commissioners.[80]

More important—especially in Vietnam—was the fact that this vested interest was cultural. The whole examination system was a process of professional acculturation, of social and cultural change, for the individual Vietnamese student. He had to prove that he excelled, not merely in writing Chinese-style poetry but also in wearing specific types of clothing and in conforming to specific behavioral demands, like those associated with the proper Chinese-style methods of bowing, meditating, and using honorific words in encounters with equals and superiors. The higher his place became on the social and occupational scale as a result of the examinations, the more rigidly his behavioral patterns were prescribed for him and the more numerous these obligatory patterns became. The point was that these patterns were explicitly Chinese.

Profound differential acculturation symbolized and governed the gulf between the elite and the ruled in Vietnam. The Vietnamese bureaucrat looked Chinese; the Vietnamese peasant looked Southeast Asian. The bureaucrat had to write Chinese, wear Chinese-style gowns, live in a Chinese-style house, ride in a Chinese-style sedan chair, and even follow Chinese-style idiosyncrasies of conspicuous consumption, like keeping a goldfish pond in his Southeast Asian garden.[81] In one sense he was less free than the Vietnamese peasant was to make cultural choices. The peasant's circumscription was more a matter of a lack of knowledge of alternatives than of socio-occupational determinism. On the other hand, an important empirical basis for the stimulation of peasant rebellions in traditional Vietnam was always offered by this strange omnipresence of the culturally semi-alien or alien trappings and attributes of the Vietnamese elite.

In the late eighteenth century, the peasant-born Tây-sơn Quang-trung emperor attempted to minimize the use of classical Chinese at his court in favor of *nôm*. And as early as the 1860's, intellectual but Christian reformers at the court of Tự-đức like Nguyễn Trường Tộ, dismayed by the weakness of Vietnamese society in the face of Western aggression, could plausibly demand the permanent renunciation of the use of the Chinese script. Thanks to its two thousand years of elitist homage to a foreign culture, in no country in the world is differential acculturation more psychologically invidious and politically dangerous than in Vietnam, once social instability becomes pervasive.

This progressive cultural sinicization of the Vietnamese scholar as he rose through the examination system, together with the strong personal relationships he eventually developed with his examiners and with other students, bound him socially, intellectually, and emotionally to the values and interests of the bureaucratic ruling class. But this meant that the dynasty could only maintain its own power over this class by preventing informal organizations, based upon personal friendships, from appearing within the formal bureaucratic organization, which was based upon the prestige of statuses.

Statuses were easily controlled and manipulated from the top. But private personal friendships were not. The holding of examinations demonstrated the dynasty's power, its ability to grant and withdraw favored degrees and positions without much regard for the existing places in society of the contenders seeking these privileges. Yet at the same time, recurrent mass gatherings of like-minded examiners and students at examination sites geographically remote from the capital created problems. For these sites now became the ideal environments for the exercise of those personal relationships which the court could not control—and even for the emergence of intrigues and cliques. As a consequence of the fact that the examinations maximized the maintenance and growth of personal links among the scholars, who already shared a definitive status culture, melees of degree candidates at the sites could even crystallize into "pressure groups" demanding changes in court policies. This actually occurred at Vietnamese examinations in the 1860's and at the Chinese metropolitan examinations in Peking in 1895. In both episodes, chagrin at military defeat by a foreign power was the background influence.

In Ch'ing China, "laws of avoidance," which were designed to prevent collusion of all kinds among examiners and between examiners and students, were extensively developed. All children of officials serving at Chinese examination sites, and in fact all members of those officials' lineages, as well as the husbands of the officials' sisters and the elder and younger brothers of their wives were prohibited from competing at sites where those officials were stationed. (Actually, avoidance laws were elaborated in other sectors of the Ch'ing bureaucracy first and then were applied to the examinations. An examiner had to avoid his wife's brothers and his sisters' husbands at Chinese examination sites, for example, only after 1762. And avoidance laws at Chinese sites historically were applied to high examiners first. Later they were broadened to include proctors, sealers, copyists, and proofreaders.)[82] Only occasionally, allowance was made for the sons of the examiners. They were given special examinations of their own, as in 1724.[83]

Indeed an important if little studied feature of the mid-Ch'ing bureaucracy was its creation of a series of complex avoidance laws, both for examinations and for other bureaucratic activities, which restricted the involvement in bureaucrats' public lives of matrilineal kinsmen (*ch'in-ch'i*) and the male relatives of their wives. These laws were added to older ones which had already dealt with agnatic kinsmen (*ch'in-tsu*). And they came into being despite the fact that in Chinese society men owed no formal obligations to matrilineal relatives. After 1803 the nephews of a site official who were the children of his wife's brother could not compete at any examination he was conducting. A new rule of 1821 even forbade such relatives as the sons of an examiner's mother's sister (matrilineal cousins) from appearing at his site.[84] Only when a lineage had dissolved to the point where various branches were living scattered in separate provinces, lacking even a periodic geographical focal point, were "laws of avoidance" waived.

Ch'ing officials in Peking who had been chosen to serve as examiners at provincial examinations were required to leave the capital within five days of being selected. In this way "favor seekers" would have little opportunity to communicate with them before they departed. Until 1819, the names of the examiners who had been chosen to preside at the Peking regional and metropolitan examinations had been proclaimed at the Zenith Gate. A crowd of court officials habitually loitered in front of the gate, "exchanging talk" and speculating about the emperor's choices. The stakes were high. In 1819 these informal discussions were prohibited; the list of examiners' names became a sealed and secret document handled by special couriers, Grand Secretaries, and censors. Loitering bureaucrats at the gate were warned that they risked impeachment.[85]

More important as an index of imperial concern was the fact that the movements of candidates traveling between the provinces and Peking in search of doctoral degrees were also tightly controlled. Provincial educational officials who came to Peking to compete in the examinations were ordered to leave again (if they had failed) within five days of the posting of the names list of successful candidates. From 1771, their return journeys to their provincial posts were bureaucratically timed. To prevent them from visiting friends or nursing their resentments in their home districts, they received certificates from the Peking Board of Rites with the dates of their departures written upon them. At the other ends of their journeys, provincial governors collected their certificates, wrote the dates of their arrivals on them, and returned them to the board. An official from Soochow or Hangchow was allowed a maximum of 50 days to resume his duties in Soochow or Hangchow. A man from Taiwan was given 110 days, one from Canton received 90 days, and one from Foochow or Ch'eng-tu got 80 days.[86] Inevitably, early in the second half of the nineteenth century this system collapsed.

In Vietnam, dynastically sponsored bureaucratic control of civil service examinations was far less comprehensive. The timing of the movements of examiners and candidates was not as complete. Vietnamese educational officials traveling back and forth between Huế and the provinces do not appear to have received certificates and journey time limits like their Chinese counterparts. It was true that the behavior of Huế officials who were sent to regional sites to serve as master examiners was very carefully watched. When a prospective master examiner arrived in a provincial capital and was received by high provincial officials, he had to sit on one side of the room while they sat on the other, in what was called, in Sino-Vietnamese, the official "etiquette of confrontations" (địch thể lễ). In conversation, the provincial officials were allowed to ask him innocuous questions about the health of court officials. But "private items" were not to be broached. And after this initial meeting, "face-to-face discussions" (*diện thương*) between the examiner and his provincial hosts were forbidden, unless urgent public business arose which required joint management.[87] It was apparently necessary to take these measures in order to keep communal gossip within the bureaucracy at a low ebb.

Laws of avoidance at Vietnamese sites were relatively weak, and sometimes worked differently from those in China. In China, the sons and relatives of examiners were forbidden to enter the sites where those examiners were stationed. In Vietnam, examiners who had relatives wishing to enter examinations were allowed to "avoid" the sites where their relatives might compete. This bureaucratic inversion of Chinese avoidance practices reflected a Vietnamese awareness that the flow of good candidates to Vietnamese examination sites was not as dependable or as inevitable as the similar triennial flow in China. Avoidance laws in Vietnam also largely ignored the mid-Ch'ing emphasis on matrilineal kinsmen and wives' male relatives. They extended mainly to such obvious relatives as children, brothers, patrilineal uncles and nephews. Sub-bureaucrats toiling at Nguyễn sites were required (after 1834) to supply certificates stating that they possessed no relatives among the candidates competing at their site, before they could assume their posts.[88]

This was as far as Vietnamese avoidance laws went. In some respects, bureaucratic control measures were more rigid in the northern provinces than they were in the south. They seemed to decay as the examination system moved deeper into the recently colonized tropics. Sub-bureaucrats serving at the Hanoi examination site were recruited from Hưng Yên, Nam Định, and Hải Dương. Those working at the Nam Định site came from Hanoi, Sơn Tây, and Bắc Ninh. At the Saigon site, on the other hand, sub-bureaucrats were not required to "avoid" the site of their home province and could actually be recruited from the Gia Định area.[89] Nowhere in Vietnam did rules appear, even for a moment, like the short-lived proviso of 1727 in China that doctoral degree holders who served as site officials could not do so in provinces whose borders were 300 li or less from their native villages.[90]

Although laws of avoidance were weak, the candidates' geographic and academic backgrounds were not ignored. From 1807 to 1825, at

Vietnamese regional sites, candidates were segregated by districts and prefectures. Each of the four enclosures within the "outer wall" part of the regional site represented different administrative areas within the region.[91] This segregation by locality lasted only eighteen years. By a more permanent principle, the reputation of the district educational official under whose auspices a certain candidate had studied was at stake not only in the candidate's academic performance but also in his deportment at the site. If the candidate were quarrelsome or loud-mouthed, other men suffered as well as he.

Vietnamese methods of marking the papers themselves were cumbrous but grew more sinicized each year. Before the master examiners saw the examination papers which had been written at a site, these papers had already been marked and signed by the preliminary and the second examiners, whose headquarters at the sites were inaccessible to most other site officials. Papers which they passed, they further had to categorize as being excellent, average or above average, or sub-standard. If two of a candidate's examination books were excellent and one was average, for example, he belonged to the "above average" category. The third stage of the examinations was considered the most important one for these purposes. The first stage was the least important.[92] But only after 1825 at Vietnamese sites were all the examination books of each candidate strung together (*xuyên quyển số*) and considered as a unit by master examiners and by Huế officials, as well as by the emperor. In 1825, also, effective precautions were finally taken to disguise the identities of candidates' writings from examiners. Each candidate was given a series of designations (one of the Eight Diagrams, from the Chinese *Classic of Changes*, combined with a number) under which he wrote his successive tests.

However, even the marking formulas of the Vietnamese examination system suggest that a mixture of particularistic and universalistic criteria determined the selection of degree holders. After 1847 regional examiners were compelled to notify the court, at the end of the examinations, if any of the new regional graduates possessed fathers who had served in the bureaucracy. Such data was apparently available to the examiners at these local sites at short notice. This indicates that they were probably aware of the backgrounds of candidates.[93]

Again, the generalization that emerges is related to the effect Vietnam's smallness had upon Chinese institutions. A recruitment system that worked relatively impartially in the vast Ch'ing empire encountered difficulties in a smaller country. In Vietnam it was harder, especially in small provincial villages, for examiners and candidates not to know about each other. Here, lack of size made universalistic criteria more difficult to enforce. In 1834 at the Nghệ An regional site, examiners at first denied regional graduate status to two of the candidates. Suddenly they discovered that the two men whom they had rejected enjoyed a considerable local reputation as scholars. Bowing to public opinion, the examiners immediately altered their previous comments on the examination books, allowing these two men to pass. (The examiners were punished.)[94]

The absence in Vietnamese provinces of printing centers, academies, and libraries—and merchant wealth that could support such institutions—has been noted. It meant, perhaps even more than in China, that talent tended to cluster in a select number of families whose traditions of success in the examinations were firmly established. Fathers passed on their expertise to sons. In the 1843 regional examinations at Nam Định, two brothers who were simultaneously competing for degrees were failed because the compositions they had written for the second stage of the examinations seemed identical. But Thiệu-trị himself set aside their failures on the grounds that both of them were dutiful sons enthralled by the literary influence and methods of their common father. Older and younger brothers, fathers and sons, or uncles and nephews, were allowed to win degrees together at the same sites. If they did so, examiners were required to note in their post-examination memorials merely (1) the specific nature of their family connection, (2) whether or not they had entered the same site enclosures together, (3) whether or not their compositions were similar.[95]

The type of scandal the Vietnamese examination system would not accept occurred at the Nghệ An site in 1825. Before the examinations were even held, the examiner gathered together the relevant provincial (protectorate) educational commissioners and prefectural and district officials and ordered them to recommend to him the names of competing scholars whom they knew. Armed with a list of such names, he then proceeded to select, according to the court's subsequent estimate, six licentiates who otherwise would have failed and ten regional graduates who did not deserve their status. The circumstance that he did not personally know these men hardly abated Minh-mạng's wrath. The precedent of a centrally appointed official accepting the preconceived verdicts of local power holders was ruinous.[96] At this same site in 1825, the provincial educational commissioner allowed eligible candidates to enter the site improperly by letting them pretend they were his attendants. When more than one hundred students who had failed the first stage of the examinations then stood outside the gates of the site making "piteous accusations," he let them reenter the site and continue the examinations.[97]

Possibly the Chinese system was less likely to permit irregularities, if only because its settings, the brick *kung-yüan*, lacked the extemporization of Vietnamese candidates' self-supplied "tents and bamboo beds." Enough has been said to show that examiners in the provinces, being unmistakable agents of the central civil administration, were also peculiarly vulnerable to local pressures. To combat these local pressures, the court tried to ensure that the examinations would be impartial. With impartial examinations, the court could prevent the devolution into regional hands of control over the composition of the bureaucracy.

The Chinese court was confronted by a much greater, more far-flung array of regional and social vested interests than the Vietnamese court. Thus its antidotes—like the laws of avoidance—were correspondingly more aggressive. But both courts plotted the moves of each different type of examination site official in advance, as if the examination sites were gigantic bureaucratic chessboards. Something of the flavor of this kind of traditional bureaucratic politics emerges from a long memorial of Vũ Đức Khuê to Minh-mạng in 1840. Khuê proposed new restrictions upon the behavior of examination site censors (themselves there to spy upon other officials):

> Up until now, censors who have been sent out to examination sites have ignored the distinction between inner and outer sites and have all been able to go and come in turns, day and night. The censors know all the records of names and native places of the competing scholars which are kept in the proctors' hall. It has even got to the point where censors sometimes come outside the site

gates, roaming around looking at things and meeting the scholars, at the time when names are being chanted at the site gates allowing the scholars to enter. When the scholars' papers are handed in, the censors have priority seating at the crossroads watchtower. They grasp and examine the papers . . . Of the censors who are sent to serve at examination sites, please from now on have one man especially [charged with] investigating the inner site and one man especially [charged with] supervising the outer site. They must definitely not be allowed to go in and out [of the other site] without authority . . . With regard to the chanting of names at the site gates, censors must not go outside the sites and meet with the scholars. In the evening, when papers are handed in, censors must sit together with the outer site officials in the crossroads watchtower. They must not without authority take the scholars' examination papers and grasp them and examine them. They must also not have foreknowledge of the names—native place records in the proctors' hall.[98]

The Contents of the Examinations and Their Purpose

The number of stages (*trường*) at Vietnamese regional and metropolitan examinations fluctuated confusingly throughout the nineteenth century. In brief, four stages were the rule between 1807 and 1832; between 1850 and 1858; and after 1884. Three stages prevailed in the times when the system was at the peak of its importance, in the 1830's, the 1840's, and during most of the Tự-đức period.

The literature which candidates were required to write for each of these three stages observed a predetermined tyranny of forms which rarely tolerated cultural divagation. Because Vietnamese poetry was the only existing literary medium which seemed regularly able to free itself of the Chinese influence, Vietnam's nineteenth-century "literature of protest," implicit and explicit, against the Chinese model is, for the most part, poetry. But even indigenous poetry had to struggle against the impregnable domination of Chinese prose poems and regulated verse, enshrined as they were by the examination system, which imposed Chinese-style topics and conventions upon Vietnamese literary minds. As Nguyễn Văn Vĩnh (1882–1936), the brilliant and penetrating early translator of European works into Vietnamese (Hugo, Balzac, Molière, Swift), was to write in 1913: "If our people write poetry they chant about the landscape of Mount T'ai and the Yellow River, the skies that are high and the seas that are broad. As for the Tản Viên mountains [on the border of Sơn Tây province in northern Vietnam] and the Red River, which are obvious and right in front of their noses, these are landscapes to which they never respond."[99]

In the first stage of the examinations the candidates wrote exegetical elaborations of aspects of the Four Books and the Five Classics, based upon their Sung neo-Confucian commentaries. This classical exegesis was, of course, known by its Sino-Vietnamese name *kinh nghĩa*. The ghosts of the twelfth-century Chinese Sung neo-Confucian philosopher Chu Hsi and his followers hovered over Nguyễn examination sites as much as they did over Ch'ing ones. The instructions the Nguyễn court had issued to Vietnamese examiners stated:

As to marking the examination papers, when interpretations of the Five Classics are involved, take as your central authority for the *Classic of Changes* what the Ch'eng brothers and Chu Hsi have transmitted. For the *Classic of Documents*, take as your central authority what Ts'ai [Ts'ai Ch'en, a Sung scholar] has transmitted. For the *Classic of Songs*, take as your central authority the assembled transmissions of Chu Hsi. For the *Spring and Autumn Annals*, take the original account of Tso as your central authority, and use, comparatively, the Kung-yang and Ku-liang commentaries and sometimes the statements in the tradition of Hu [Hu An-kuo, a twelfth-century Chinese scholar of the *Annals* who had rescued them from relative neglect as classical writings]. For the *Record of Rituals*, take as your central authority the collected statements of Ch'en [Ch'en Hao, a Chinese Yüan dynasty scholar of this text]. When interpretations of the Four Books are involved, take as your central authority the assembled annotations of Chu Hsi.[100]

In the second stage of the examinations Chinese-style poetry was the subject. Candidates were required to write prose poems (*phú*) and, at the regional examinations, seven-word regulated verse (*thất ngôn luật*). Seven-word regulated verse was, of course, written in seven-word lines and possessed an eight-line stanza. It obeyed a strict rhyme scheme and strict rules of verbal parallelism. At the metropolitan examinations, five-word regulated verse was substituted for it. Regulated verse in general required perfect rhymes. It had been an established poetry form in China for more than 1,000 years. It constituted what the Nguyễn dynasty regarded as the ideal Sino-Vietnamese literary discipline. As if its technical rigidities of composition were not formidable enough, Vietnamese examination candidates after 1832 knew that they faced a range of about five possible types of topic which they could attempt to transmute into such poems. These types of subject material included "political matters" (*chính sự*), "classical historical episodes and occasions" (*điển cố*), "original texts of the classics and histories" (*kinh sử chính văn*), "established phrases of past writers" (*cổ nhân thành cú*), and "views of the countryside" (*sơn xuyên cảnh vật*).[101]

In practice, poems written at Vietnamese examinations tended to revolve around such sterilized themes as the activities of the founder of the Han dynasty in China and the recovery of classical Chinese books from the Ch'in holocaust. Specifically Vietnamese themes which were allowed included "narrations of this court's extensions of excellence and beauty."[102] In writing prose poems, candidates had to construct their poems upon the basis of "upper" and "lower" Sino-Vietnamese rhyme words which were announced to them only at the outset of the examinations, like "east" and "winter" (*đông* and *đông*) or "branch" and "small" (*chi* and *vi*).[103] This meant that students had to memorize a host of suitable corresponding rhyme-words before they entered the examinations. The bane of the students (and of the court) was the examiner who constantly issued conflicting rhyme-words which did not harmonize. In 1829 Minh-mạng gave orders that such examiners were to be summarily dismissed.[104]

These tortuous, history-bound and ideology-bound frameworks of literary composition looked more impressive than they were. The traditional Vietnamese literary world was far too fertile and too diversified to maintain itself as two completely separate stagnating spheres. The forms of Sino-Vietnamese bureaucratic literature often gained new magic when they were absorbed into the world of non-

Sinic indigenous literature. The contents and patterns of the two spheres intermingled.

The prose poem, for example, was an archetypal Sino-Vietnamese literary genre which nonetheless flourished on its own away from the examination sites. From the sixteenth century on, at least, two types of prose poetry had existed side by side in Vietnam. The serious examination system *phú* drew upon the Chinese classics. The playful style (*lối chơi*) of *phú*, which was written with many Vietnamese *nôm* characters, incorporated many native proverbs and idioms and often mocked the Sino-Vietnamese order. When a master of the playful prose poem like Nguyễn Bá Lân (1701–1775) practiced his art it was unlike any poetry ever written in China.

Thus even more than in China, the Vietnamese examination system's intellectual controls challenged its environment. At the Thanh Hóa regional site in 1825 one scholar even ignored the issued topics completely. He chose instead to use the space in his examination book to write a diatribe against them: "If examinations and their topics are for choosing scholars, you ought to revive the elegance of good literature and abolish the vulgarities of learning for the purpose of government service."[105]

The celebrated Sino-Vietnamese "policy question" or *sách văn* confronted candidates in the third stage of the examinations. *Sách* meant stratagems or plans. The whole question was an exercise, basically, in replying to certain questions at the head of the exercise as cleverly as possible in order to demonstrate virtuosity. Rhymes were not required, but couplets (*đối*) were frequently used. The topics of the "policy question" at regional examinations were 300 words in length. Those of the metropolitan examinations at Huế were 500 words. Written answers to these topics could not be less than 1,000 words at regional sites and 1,600 words at the metropolitan examinations. Before 1835, Vietnamese candidates were even compelled to copy out the entire question before beginning to answer it. But a reform of 1835 partly ended this time-consuming ordeal by allowing the preliminary distribution of "topic papers" to the candidates.[106] (Usually topics were announced at the sites by being published upon elevated signboards, of which there might be four to an enclosure. These signboards reminded Pasquier, later in the century, of the postings boards at a European race track.)[107]

In effect, the "policy questions" took the form of artificial conversations between a Confucian ruler and his ministers. At the end of his examination book the candidate would write the Sino-Vietnamese expression "your scholar respectfully replies" (*sĩ cẩn đối*) or "your student respectfully replies" (*sinh cẩn đối*). Yet the stuff these conversations were made of was usually—not always—harmless banalities and generalities about Chinese antiquity, King Wen of Chou, the difficulties of stimulating orthodox scholarship, and the sayings of a host of Chinese philosophers of a period no later than the Sung.

On the whole, the subject matter of Vietnamese examinations conformed to Ch'ing usages. Poetry was possibly emphasized more in Vietnam. In both societies the emperors themselves took pride in scrutinizing both topics and examination books. In 1783 the aging Ch'ien-lung emperor in Peking was still astute enough to discover that a Kwangtung master examiner had improperly inserted two words from the biography of a Han dynasty philosopher, recorded in the Han History, into a "policy question" which dealt with the Sung scholar Ou-yang Hsiu.[108] What was interesting was that Minh-mạng and other Vietnamese rulers constantly read the collections of model Chinese examination papers which were published in Peking, in order to compare them with Vietnamese examination scholarship. In the eyes of the Nguyễn emperors the fate of the whole Vietnamese classical bureaucracy hung upon the ability of its future members to answer the most trivial questions that might be inspired by Chinese texts. Private fears existed that Vietnamese standards might not match those of the "Northern Court." Examination answers were therefore considered portents of history. Would Sino-Vietnamese civilization prevail in Southeast Asia? After the 1835 palace examinations, Minh-mạng said:

"Issuing question topics is easy, writing the answers is difficult. Now the site officials who issue the themes have books that they can examine, but the scholars who write the answers merely depend upon their memories and nothing else. [At the examinations] yesterday the question was asked, What phenomenon is described by the term *phục nê trưởng ly*? But those who answered it did not know what thing it was." Previously the regional graduate Cao Bá Quát was tested. The theme topic was, What phenomenon is described by the term *phục nê trưởng ly*? Quát was unable to answer *phục nê trưởng ly* is the name of a star which comes from the [Chinese] book on the strange names of natural phenomena. [The emperor said] "The books of our country are very few. Although we possess vast, extensive talent, we lack breadth of perspective. Subsequently when we send expeditions to the Ch'ing country we must purchase a great number of books and distribute them among our scholars."[109]

But imperial chagrin at the discrepancy between court scholarship and provincial reading habits in Vietnam, which was far more marked there than in China, could sometimes turn to self-satisfaction. The much greater control measures which Chinese courts had devised for ensuring the impartiality of their examiners made Chinese examination system questions more stereotyped. Topics from the Four Books and the Five Classics, for example, might often be chosen in China only after each classic had been divided into labeled sections before the examinations. The master examiner, in a public lot-drawing ceremony, then had to make blind, unpremeditated choices of the sections from which examination themes were to be taken.[110]

Furthermore, Vietnamese relative lack of breadth or depth in classical learning had the happy result, in Minh-mạng's opinion, of reducing the amount of obscure classical minutiae in Vietnamese examination questions. Vietnamese scholars were not as well able to fathom it. Once after he had some Ch'ing Chinese examination essays read to him in the 1830's, Minh-mạng said of them: "In their examination themes, why must they demand such strangely recondite things? I regard the issuing of policy questions as being like asking questions about the Territorial Leader of the West [Hsi Po, King Wen of Chou, an ancient Chinese warrior ruler] conquering Li [an ancient state, situated in modern Shansi in China]. Sometimes we ask about such matters as King Wen serving the Yin dynasty and King Wu attacking the Yin dynasty. Questions like these have some bearing on the meanings of names and terms. Only then can one examine the scholars' mental and moral idiosyncrasies. If one emptily asks questions which use strange, eccentric phraseology, then those most prolific at repeating things from memory are able to answer them on their own. Truly, what is the advantage of choosing men by means like these?"[111]

In fact, the rather desiccated antiquarianism of these examination topics was highly deceiving. They were deadlier than they looked. The content of the questions that were asked at regional and metropolitan examination sites could be controversial. Attempting to make the content of such questions as innocuous as possible in advance was only one more aspect of the struggle by Chinese and Vietnamese courts to prevent their bureaucrats from gaining a disproportionate leverage over official recruitment.

The courts were especially afraid of the "policy questions" which master examiners might ask at remote sites. In both China and Vietnam the lengths of the "policy questions" were officially limited. The Ch'ing 300-word limit dated from 1687. It was probably attributable, as Miyazaki has suggested, to the fear that anti-Manchu sentiments might come to life during the writing of the "policy" examination in the Chinese provinces.[112] In other words, veiled allusions could be made, within the contexts of "policy" questions and answers, to current events—and to the behavior of current emperors.

In 1732 the battle of the "policy question" had a crisis in China. A master examiner in Shensi province suggested in his question that water conservancy opportunities in Shensi were many. He then asked the Shensi site candidates to list in detail the dike-building achievements of officials of the Han, Sung, and Ming dynasties in Shensi. In case dull-witted scholars at the site had missed his implication, his question also contained an oblique reference to more contemporary water control activities which had been carried out recently—not in Shensi but in the neighborhood of Peking. This topic was, of course, a bold challenge to the Ch'ing court, one which the Ch'ing Yung-cheng emperor had no difficulty in recognizing. After embarking on an eloquent defense of dike repairs in Shensi under his reign and asserting that the province was prospering, he then said: "If Wu Wen-huan and his colleagues were going to use water conservancy as a policy question with which to examine the scholars, then they ought to have used as a subject what is currently happening in that province and have commanded that they set forth in their answers such things as what relief might be prepared and adopted, or what might constitute reconstruction plans. To ignore the present and adduce the past as an example, to reject the near and seek the far in time . . . is gross. And to bring forward out of nowhere the example of the Peking area as evidence of recent revived construction of water works, while not having a single word about the crucial profits and shortcomings of public works in the home province, is to suggest the idea that the various ditches that have been dredged in Shensi have brought no benefit at all to the people's livelihood . . . Politically and academically this is disastrous."[113]

Yet examiners were forbidden, by other rules, to refer to the Ch'ing dynasty or to its officials in "policy questions." Both the past and the present were dangerous. Treason could lurk under the surface, either way; the "policy questions" were fearsome weapons. By 1788 scholars at Chinese regional sites had been forbidden to discuss possible "policy question" topics before their examinations, which indicates that political speculation before 1788 had habitually run high. In 1792 a censor even suggested that all the question topics be devised in Peking beforehand and then sent to the regional examiners. But this would have caused too much trouble.[114]

In Vietnam, once again, fewer regional sites made the control of examiners easier. Consequently, not as many rules were created to circumscribe their autonomy in setting questions. Ironically, political discontent most obviously raised its head in Vietnam during the writing of the "policy question" at the stormy metropolitan examinations of 1862 in Huế. Under the pretext of commenting on "current events," a scholar from the north accused the Nguyễn court of favoring scholars and bureaucrats from central Vietnam at the expense of northerners. This accusation was so politically explosive that Tự-đức, like Yung-cheng in 1732, was compelled to defend himself publicly.

If the content of examination questions and answers was sometimes unsettling to sensitive dynasts, it was, nonetheless, their form rather than their content that was important. By writing such Sino-Vietnamese formulas as "your scholar respectfully replies" in the "policy questions" over and over again in different sets of examinations, the Vietnamese student learned, and became familiar with, a specific written system of political signals. This system in turn taught him his place in the Sino-Vietnamese social and bureaucratic structure.

The nature of the bureaucracy was communicated to him through the recurrent patterns of the examination system's written codes. For these codes overemphasized, like transmitted documents in the bureaucracy itself, the status aspects of social relationships and the application of ideologically talismanic sayings from the classics, and underemphasized, again like bureaucratic documents, the possibilities of presenting new information through formal written channels. These written codes were narrow and restricted, in the interests of encouraging predictable behavior. Individual discretion and originality were reduced in the process. The scholar from Hải Dương or Gia Định was to be converted into an agent of Sino-Vietnamese bureaucratic culture.

Because the famous Chinese "eight-legged essay" (*pa-ku wen* in Chinese, *bát cổ văn* in Sino-Vietnamese) had its place in this bureaucratic scheme, it was imported from China too. It appeared in the first stages of Vietnamese examinations, as the mandatory form of answering questions which demanded expositions of the Chinese classics. In its celebrated exaltation of a finical writing style which depended upon the use of antithetical couplets ("legs"), it was a form which tested technical virtuosity rather than intellectual brilliance, right from its beginning (*phá đề*), which was most important, to its conclusion (*kết thúc*). It standardized examination answers. In China, this was especially important. Changes in the contents of the examinations could not be made too often without undermining the curricula of thousands of district teachers and the expectations of thousands of candidates. The very size of the participation in the Chinese system, and the number of local schools which fed candidates into it, probably made inevitable the appearance of such stereotyped forms in the Ming and Ch'ing periods. Far from coincidentally these were also the periods of the greatest mass extension of the Chinese examination system and of the greatest sub-system utilization of local schools and academies.

In Nguyễn Vietnam the "eight-legged essay" may have survived more for a different reason. The intricacies of the "eight-legged essay" were meaningful because they were incomprehensible to men outside the system. Initiation into the mysteries of so esoteric a literary form could thus be highly valued; the high valuation of esoteric literary forms was in the interests of social stratification. And the fact that Nguyễn examination topics and contents were usually carefully divorced from Vietnamese subjects and personalities and confined to ancient Chinese history only made more stark this socio-cultural stratification line which the examination system drew across traditional Vietnamese society.

Regional Vicissitudes of the Vietnamese Examination System

It would be naive to assume that success in the examinations and upward social mobility were one and the same thing in either nineteenth-century China or Vietnam. Vietnamese society was too complex for this generalization to be true. And the targets of the ambitious were too diverse. Office, status, landed property, other types of financial resources, artistic or religious or intellectual or literary eminence, and legal privileges were some of them.

Nonetheless, it was true that success in the examinations did lead to the acquisition of status and office and legal privileges and did place men in a better position to acquire the remaining symbols and substances of grandeur. Moreover, it was unlikely that the fish vendor's son could very easily become a mandarin. He lacked property, and he lacked personal contacts with bureaucrats and scholars. But above all he lacked a family tradition of Sino-Vietnamese classical education and the leisure to set about continuing such a tradition himself. Family constellations of degree holders were notable in eighteenth- and nineteenth-century Vietnam for the zeal with which they expanded themselves. Phan Huy Chú, for example, a licentiate of 1807 who presented a vital work on Vietnamese institutions to Minh-mạng in 1821, could look back upon numerous patrilineal relatives who had won doctoral degrees, including his father (in 1775), his father's brother (in 1780), and his grandfather (in 1754). Family as much as individual prestige was at stake in the examinations.

"New talent" was not always prized even by the Nguyễn court so much as the development, in hundreds of Vietnamese villages, of family traditions of service to the bureaucracy. A large, recently arrived class of officials who were innocent of such traditions might be volatile and unstable. Generational continuity in competing for and winning degrees was deliberately stressed. A family which had regularly won doctoral degrees for at least three generations back was entitled to hang a silk banner from its door with the Sino-Vietnamese slogan *thể khoa liên đăng* (roughly, "uninterrupted advancements in several generations of examinations") emblazoned upon it. One which had intermittently won degrees for from two to five generations back could still raise a less conspicuous flag, bearing a truncated version of this slogan—*thể khoa*.[115]

It is safe to say that the fear of downward mobility among the Vietnamese elite was greater than any corresponding desire for upward mobility among the peasantry. Nguyễn Công Trứ, the powerful official and famous poet of the Minh-mạng, Thiệu-trị, and early Tự-đức periods, has been accused by modern Vietnamese scholars of having had a "superiority complex" because of his family background.[116] His father had been a high Lê official and his mother had been the daughter of a high Lê official. But after 1802, "mounting the elephant" (*lên voi*) in official life was difficult and dangerous without patrons and friends, even for a man with these antecedents. Forced to battle for recognition on his own in the examination system, Trứ entered the 1813 examinations and was able to win merely the status of a licentiate. Chagrined at his failure to outshine the other candidates, Trứ viewed the future with pessimism, in a stylized pronouncement to some singing girls which expresses this elitist fear of declining fortunes: "You young girls! After thirty-six years, I am notorious everywhere in Heaven's four directions of east, west, south, and north as the mortally poor son of a mandarin. O Heaven and Earth, if I falter one time more, I shall put away my bow, my sword, my lute, and my books [the properties of a gentleman in nineteenth-century Vietnam] and so expose myself as a good-for-nothing man."[117] However, the mandarin's son eventually redeemed his inheritance at the 1819 examinations.

No doubt downward mobility was feared especially because of the social stigma which attached itself to the son of a scholarly family who betrayed his ancestors' legacy of "the spirit of making something out of himself" (*chi xuất thân*). Although Nguyễn Công Trứ complained about the economic poverty to which failure in the examinations had condemned him, he used the concept of "poverty" in a relative sense. The style of life of even the poorest members of the scholar class remained higher, in substance and expectations, than that of illiterate peasants. In his long study of "the manners and tastes of the poor scholar," which began by cursing the humiliations of poverty, Nguyễn Công Trứ painted a picture of faded gentility, not of the loss of gentility itself: "An antique painting hangs above the poor scholar's wall, smudged by smoke, the hues of its water colors blurred . . . book volumes in the attic are nibbled by cockroaches, who expose their cheap clay-red seals . . . A coffinwood chessboard has been stored in his ghost house for seven existences, its characters for 'sun' and 'field' having become deformed. A salary of rice from his own personal rice field fills up one small box; an abstinence regimen of sweet potatoes fills up one market basket."[118]

Thus there was not a very generous inter-generational turnover of personnel between the civil bureaucratic elite and the population at large. Other more interesting factors, related to the difference in scale of imperial power in China and Vietnam, frustrated upward mobility through the Vietnamese examinations.

Nguyễn rulers were less aware of the need to promote regional equitability in recruiting a bureaucracy. Chinese emperors took pains to make sure that their future officials came from Yünnan as well as from Szechwan, from Kansu as well as from Kwangtung. By upholding social mobility through geographical space in this way, they expressed their own power against that of the bureaucracy itself, by preventing the growth of a civil administration with a narrow, homogeneous regional base.

The Vietnamese emperor ruled a much smaller bureaucracy. Such techniques of imperial self-assertion were proportionately less necessary. In nineteenth-century China men from provinces like Kansu and Hopei may well have enjoyed disproportionate opportunities for social mobility through the examinations, at the expense of men from culturally and economically more advanced southeastern provinces like Kiangsu and Anhwei.[119] But in Nguyễn Vietnam, the provinces from Phú Yên south—those of southern Vietnam, the most recently colonized area of the empire—came within the compass of the examination system only barely. Just one southerner, Phan

Thanh Giản (1796–1867), won a doctoral degree, out of the 56 that were given at Huế, between the years 1822 and 1840. Just three southerners had won doctoral degrees when French imperialists seized south Vietnam in the 1860's.

Once again, it might be underlined that the examination system was not the sole road to power. A southerner like Nguyễn Văn Hiếu, the Định Tường laborer who raised irregulars for Gia-long's cause against the Tây-sơns, was later rewarded with the Hanoi governor-general's post in 1831. Nguyễn Tâm, another southern general, received the same post in 1840 for having aided the repression of the Lê Văn Khôi revolt in the south in the 1830's. There was also a small stratum of court sinecure-holders, more prestigious than powerful, which constituted a kind of non-imperial hereditary nobility. Members of this stratum were drawn from the descendants of soldiers who had supported Gia-long when he was living in exile in Bangkok, in the late 1700's, and who were known in the Gia-long period as "Bangkok merit ministers" (*Vọng Các công thần*). Finally, the sons of high officials could receive "shade" appointments to the National College and as clerks at the Hanlin Academy. As of 1844, all the sons of first, second, third, and fourth grade civil officials serving in Huế, and one of the sons of a fifth grade official, could receive admission, with stipends but without having to pass examinations, into the National College. All the sons of first to third grade civil officials serving in the provinces, and one of the sons of a fourth grade official, were similarly favored. Vietnamese proverbs therefore took a skeptical view of the opportunities of the poor and the unknown for self-advancement. "The son of the emperor will become emperor, the son of the pagoda watchman will sweep the leaves of the *bo* tree."[120] But social mobility in Vietnam suffered more from the limited growth of literacy and of literary facilities than it did from "shade."

To return to the essential point: the failure of southerners to win doctoral degrees in the Nguyễn examination system was startling. In China men of all provinces, even the backward ones, regularly won degrees. In Vietnam, fortune, which was manipulated by the court and its examiners, rarely smiled on men from the Mekong delta. If southern candidates for doctoral degrees had not existed, the situation would not have been so remarkable. But the surviving records of various Vietnamese regional examinations indicate that the Saigon examination site did indeed produce periodic crops of eligible regional graduates (see Table 5).[121]

Nguyễn records reveal, therefore, that the progress of southerners in the Nguyễn examination system was not blocked at the regional examinations. It was blocked, if anywhere, at the metropolitan and palace examinations at Huế. And it was at these higher examinations, especially at the palace examinations, that emperors personally were most inclined, and able, to influence the results. The inference is that the court was not decisively alarmed by the failure of the south to participate in the system, although Giản, the one southern *tiến-sĩ* before 1840, did owe his degree to Minh-mạng's personal intervention in 1826.

The south, of course, was not really culturally backward. Rather, it was culturally different. It was more Cambodian, more Buddhist, less Confucian, less Sino-Vietnamese than the center and the north. There were reasons for lack of southern interest in the examinations. Actively commissioned civil bureaucrats who could demonstrate the practical career advantages of having read the Chinese classics to southerners were few in number in the southern provinces before the late 1830's, thanks to Lê Văn Duyệt's personal military regime there in the 1820's and the rise of rebellion in the 1830's. As a result, southerners were less exposed to Sino-Vietnamese elite culture. The one successful southern doctoral degree holder of the Minh-mạng era, Giản, who came from Vĩnh Long, was of Chinese ancestry. Yet even he had received his schooling when he was young from a Buddhist monk. It has been suggested that southern scholarly culture in the 1800's was more pragmatic, more concerned with geography, medicine, fortune telling, and astrology than that of the rest of Vietnam.

Table 5. Winners (*cử nhân*) at Regional Examinations.

Year	Hanoi	Nam Định	Thanh Hóa	Nghệ An	Huế	Saigon
1813	16	28	9	12	9	8
1821	23	34	19	15	25	16
1825	28	27	17	33	10	15
1840	14	12	—[a]	20	29	6
1843	21	19	—[a]	25	39	15

a. Site discontinued.

Pages of the immortal poem *Lục Vân Tiên*, written by the great southern poet Nguyễn Đình Chiểu, probably about the middle of the century or slightly later, are crowded with the eclectic figments of southern doctors, Buddhist priests, and soothsayers. They reveal some of the priorities of nineteenth-century southern interest. The district schoolteacher in southern frontier areas competed with magicians and soothsayers and himself had to understand the popular healing arts. Local prestige went to the man whose fingers could "aid people and help mankind."[122]

The economic and social power of landlordism has often been associated with academic and bureaucratic achievements in both China and Vietnam. But in the 1800's, while northern Vietnamese landlords may well have spawned degree-winning sons, south Vietnamese landlords could not and did not. In the southern province of Bình Định, before the 1839 land reforms there, the private estates of landlords are reported to have amounted to more than 70,000 *mou*, whereas the public lands of Bình Định villages are said to have totalled no more than 7,000 *mou*. (The 1839 reforms attempted to convert half the acreage that was "private" back into public lands. In the court's view, 5 *mou* was all that one landowner should have. Some of them, before 1839, possessed estates of 100 or 200 *mou*.)[123] Bình Định landlordism was considered to be the worst in the empire.

Yet no doctoral degree holders came from Bình Định before 1835. In fact, southern Vietnam in the early 1800's was expanding both in population and in areas of settlement. The consequence of a growing population moving into thinly settled areas was instability both of local and of familial units. Men kept moving from one community to another. Furthermore, a severe conflict existed in the south between the potentialities for the accumulation of landed property (which were far greater than in the north) and the Sino-Vietnamese Confucian emphasis upon suppression of class struggle, acquisitiveness, and individualistic behavior in the villages. The old landlord families of the north were stable, inward-looking nurseries of scholar-bureaucrats. The new landlord families of the south looked outward. They were less concerned with family academic traditions, more concerned with land.

Contemporaries saw another regional bias in the Nguyễn examination system equally clearly. Scholarship clustered about the capital, and it was meant to. Scholarly families who remained at Hanoi, rather than migrating after 1802 to Huế, saw their sons' opportunities for success in the examinations steadily decline as the century wore on. In 1813 the numerical quota of regional graduates who were allowed to receive degrees at the Hanoi regional examinations was 16, and that for the Huế regional site was 9. In 1819 the quotas for these two sites were 23 and 17 respectively. Northerners dominated examinations in the Gia-long reign. This period was, not so coincidentally, a time when soldiers, mainly from the south and the center, predominated in influential administrative posts. After 1820, examinations became more important. And at the same time, despite the fact that the central Huế area was far less populous than the Red River basin, the quotas of *cử nhân* for the Huế regional site began to surpass those of the northern sites. For the 1813 and 1819 examinations, Hanoi had been allowed 39 regional graduates to Huế's 26. But for the five sets of regional examinations held in the Thiệu-trị period in the 1840's (1841, 1842, 1843, 1845, 1846) the situation had been so revolutionized in the preceding twenty years that Huế was allowed 213 *cử nhân* to Hanoi's 107. (Saigon was allowed 87.)[124]

The lack of enough good libraries outside the dynastic capital, the lack of an indigenous merchant class outside the capital which could finance its sons' ways into the system, the pressure of families residing in Huế's environs who already had members serving in the bureaucracy, and the suspicions entertained by a new, central Vietnamese dynastic house of the ancient northern heartland of Vietnamese culture, all combined to deny the Nguyễn examination system the better regional balance of its Chinese archetype. Residential agglomerations of pro-Nguyễn scholarly and military families at Huế increased rapidly, especially as these families withdrew from other regions, like the Gia Định frontier in the south, where their immediate ancestors had fled to escape the Tây-sơns. Proximity to the new capital so improved their sons' educational prospects that those who received degrees at the Huế regional site were not only more numerous but also were younger than winning candidates at other sites. Thiệu-trị said in 1843: "Many of the men who have been chosen at the Thừa Thiên site [Huế] are quite young. At first I was suspicious of their abundance, to the point where I read their examination papers. There were those who had struggled to gain licentiate status, those whose ancestors had been officials, and those who were young in years but literarily mature. Only then I began to realize that the study of literature has been advancing daily recently, and that Quảng Nam is especially prospering [literarily]."[125]

The dynasty made Quang Nắm's literary prosperity conspicuous. By the 1840's the quotas of degree winners at the Huế regional site were higher than at the other sites. The architecture of the site itself was more permanent, more Chinese and more imposing than that of the other sites. And as a final touch, the poems of the newly hatched regional graduates at Huế were collected, presented to the emperor, and disseminated throughout the court.[126] In this way the regional graduates of central Vietnam received special ceremonial and literary recognition from influential power holders which other regional graduates did not receive.

It should be noted that the sons of civil and military officials who had helped Gia-long found the dynasty in 1802 were allowed to participate in regional examinations at any one of the five or six regional sites, no matter where in Vietnam they were originally registered. This was a privilege, known as "adopting examinations" (*phụ thí*), forbidden to most scholars, who were compelled to be examined in their home provinces.[127] Men who could take advantage of it naturally preferred to become *cử-nhân* at Huế. By 1846 more than 1,000 candidates competed in the Huế regional examinations, an unnaturally high number for the thinly populated central region.[128]

The Nature of Vietnamese Confucianism and the Alienation of Cao Bá Quát

In traditional China there was a profusion of novels, operas, and plays which contained allusions or discussions, admiring or satirical, concerning the examination system. The examination system had caught hold of the Chinese imagination. It dominated the minds of creative writers as well as those of hopeful bureaucrats. In the famous opera *Tale of the P'i-P'a* (*P'i p'a chi*), for example, the author, who lived in late Yüan and early Ming times, made his hero a "highest graduate" (*chuang-yüan*) of examinations of the Later Han dynasty. This was an anachronism, because the title had not been created until the T'ang dynasty. In the Ming play *Tale of the Dream of Han-tan*

(*Han tan meng-chi*), the hero, a poor youth, received a magic pillow. He dreamed, under its guidance, that he had become a "highest graduate," the most lofty goal of which he could conceive. More celebrated in China than these plays were major novels satirizing the examination system, like Wu Ching-tzu's *Ju-lin wai-shih* (An unofficial history of the scholar class).

In Vietnam, however, folk stories, poems, and plays may not have customarily revealed quite as much concern with the trappings and the titles of the examination system. And in the nineteenth century, Vietnamese expectations of social mobility were troubled by pessimistic undertones. The first two lines of Vietnam's greatest poem, *The Story of Kiều* (*Truyện Kiều*), written by Nguyễn Du (1765–1820), stated that within the past hundred years the words "talent" (*tài*) and "destiny" (*mệnh*) had hated each other. By "destiny" the poet appears to have meant not the fates foretold by fortune tellers or the heavenly destiny or "mandate" which the upright ruler was supposed to possess but rather the ways in which individual human lives interacted with the visible and invisible limitations and dictates of their environment. A man who lived long possessed a "longevity destiny." One who died young possessed a "short-life destiny." Destiny dominated talent, which could not be freely exercised. This formulation of conflict between freedom and fate was influential. Du, who died in 1820 on the eve of being sent to Peking as a Nguyễn envoy, was the literary titan of the century in his country.

A variation of this deep-rooted belief that academic and political success was predestined as much as earned was expressed, perhaps, by a popular book, *Tang Thương Ngẫu Lục* (Random recordings of great changes), which was first published by Phạm Đình Hổ (1768–1839) and Nguyễn Án (1770–1815; a regional graduate of 1807) in 1806. It described with vividness how a famous Vietnamese empress dowager had recognized a certain scholar at the palace examinations of 1463 as being the man she had dreamed had been appointed in heaven to be her son's chief minister and how this scholar had in fact subsequently received a high post in Lê officialdom.[129]

Even at the top of Nguyễn society the efficacy and mystique of the examination system never went completely unchallenged. Minh-mạng may well have been the first man in the East Asian classical world to observe that the examination system could not prepare Chinese or Vietnamese societies for their looming confrontation with the military powers of Europe. In early 1838, a year or more before the Opium War, he had told his high officials: "Now we have the *Classic of Songs* and the *Classic of Documents* with which to test many scholars, and the military classics with which to teach warfare . . . Only naval warfare has not yet had books written about it that people can be made to study. I indeed have a cursory knowledge of one or two of the tactics of the Western countries, but I want you all to examine them and become familiar with them . . . and make [your findings and calculations] into books. We will order soldiers to study them day and night."[130]

Yet the emperor's misgivings may also have been caused by his sensitivity to certain domestic countervailing winds which had been blowing for some time against his Sino-Vietnamese cultural and political orthodoxy. Nguyễn society had its alienated intellectuals. Typically enough they were supplied not by the most downtrodden social elements in Vietnam but rather by men who were successful but not too successful. One of the more interesting disaffected intellectuals is worth describing.

Cao Bá Quát (?–1854) was the son of a prominent scholar-teacher-official family in Bắc Ninh province. He was a brilliant, precocious student. Once, when he was young, he wrote self-confidently of his own abilities: "In the whole world there are four bamboo bins [to be filled with] literary skill. My own [talent] fills two of them, that of my brother Bá Đạt and my friend Nguyễn Văn Siêu fills another, and there is one more to be offered to all the [remaining] scholars."[131] (The image of the literary talent of the empire filling four bamboo bins [*bốn bồ chữ*]— four, that is, the four directions, suggests a completeness of possibilities in Vietnamese—was a typically northern one.) In 1831 he became a regional graduate at the Hanoi regional examinations. But after 1831 the imported scholasticism of the examination system defeated him. Although he tried the metropolitan examinations at Huế repeatedly, he failed every time, largely because of his insolent wit and his skeptical individualism, which made his examination books both recognizable and unacceptable.

As a result, by the 1840's he had become an interesting anomaly. He was a professionally unsuccessful scholar who was still considered by everyone in Huế society, including the emperor, as being possibly the most radiant literary star in the Vietnamese horizons. He was even invited to join a select Huế poetry society which included several imperial princes as well as high officials; he declined, suggesting that the effects of his superiors' poetry were comparable to the odor of the junks which carried salted fish and rotting shrimps from Nghệ An: "Oh, how bored I am with this unlucky nose of mine [which has to endure] both the poems of the poetry society and the Nghệ An junks."[132]

Disillusioned with the court and the bureaucracy, Quát turned his immense talents to the writing of satirical verses. These poems, which are difficult to translate into English, possessed a ferocity and an earthiness for which few parallels could be found in the nineteenth-century Chinese literary tradition. Life as a Sino-Vietnamese official was found to be valueless:

> A day of waiting at court is a day of boredom . . .
> If you have just acquired a certain degree of status,
>   you are bored to the same degree
> With a little more status, how many lives of boredom will
>   you have to live?

In Quát's hands, the rich Vietnamese tradition of skepticism of the activities of power holders—even of corrupt village chiefs who stole village funds, satirized by Quát in the following poem—could be extended this far in the first half of the nineteenth century:

> Praise to him who so skillfully constructed the elephant,
> Complete with head, complete with tail, and complete with trunk.
> But I wonder why there is one thing it wasn't given,
> Or perhaps the village chief has already castrated it?[133]

More important, Quát was one of the court opponents most skillful at using the literary form of the parable to attack abuses. In some respects, Quát was a social mystic. But one of the more palpable strands of his philosophy of discontent was his belief that the Chinese-style capital of Huế was concentrating the country's resources within itself at the expense of the villages. He dramatized this theme of the capital-against-the-village by writing a story about a starving apothecary who could find no business in Huế because there was so much food stored there that no one ever became ill. Such simple parables were dangerous because they could conquer and enter the parochial frame of reference of the peasant, who often faced famine. Thus the story-telling methods which Quát commanded were potentially revolutionary:

A staggering, reeling man,
His shirt was torn, his conical hat was battered!
Suddenly came toward me from the south,
And muttered importunate, insistent words to me.
I asked, uncle, what's the cause of your sadness?
He replied, "My situation
"Is that my household is impoverished and I am a physician,
"I went up to the capital city expecting to make some money.
"But in the capital city there was no one who was sick,
"And they had so many physicians there they were stacked
    up like mountains!
"At my wit's end I had to turn back home . . .
"The second day, I tried the begging bowl,
"The third day, I abstained from eating and starved.
"If I met anyone who was still merry,
"I wanted to speak but I couldn't utter a word."
Oh, stop it, uncle, don't weep. Please have a meal with me.
One hundred years in the inn of life: is there anyone who
    takes life calmly?
Be leisurely and do not swallow rapidly.[134]

Quát became one of the gigantic prophets of that discursive iconoclasm which always ran with such artistic violence just below the surface in Vietnamese intellectual life, searching for weaknesses in the Sino-Vietnamese bureaucratic order. To put the matter more abstractly, the truth of the cultural assumptions upon which court institutions rested in China was regularly self-validated by the strong consensus in Chinese society itself that these assumptions were true. The value of an examination system based upon ancient literature depended upon a consensus that this literature was socially relevant and upon recurrent actions in the Chinese community which conceded it such relevance. In Vietnam, such a consensus existed but was weaker than it was in China. There was tension in traditional Vietnam, of a kind unlike any in China, between the borrowed institutional patterns of the Vietnamese court, which demanded orthodoxy and conformity as they did in China, and a weaker general acceptance of Chinese cultural assumptions by the Vietnamese community, which meant that such assumptions were not self-validated by community support as comprehensively or as frequently as they were in China. Although Cao Bá Quát competed in the Nguyễn examination system, a trace of this curious tension is visible in his attack upon the Chinese literature which the Vietnamese examination system enshrined: "If the prose poems of Yang Hsiung [a Han dynasty philosopher] are [really so] majestically expressed, then please send this poor devil out to the region of the Eastern Sea, so that I can carry my books and my sword [in freedom] and determine to convert residences of mean people back into great homesteads. If [you think that] the literature of Han Yǔ [a T'ang dynasty writer] is [so] spiritually powerful, then please exile this humble soul to Poulo Condore, so that I can shoulder the problems of the nation and determine to throw away my examination system degree in exchange for the beauties of nature."[135]

The ideological premises of the Sino-Vietnamese bureaucracy were more likely to be assailed in Vietnam than they were in China. Yet they were often assailed, ironically, by Chinese literary references, which writers like Quát employed as political variables independent of, and outside, their usual narrowly orthodox contexts. His reference to "residences of mean people" (more literally "white houses," *bạch ốc*), for example, was drawn from Chinese classical history. Furthermore, the style of the whole passage is influenced by the individualistic idealism of Chinese Taoism in its Vietnamese form. (In some respects Cao Bá Quát is the outstanding literary Taoist of early nineteenth-century Vietnam.) Yet the passage and its metaphors as Quát used them hinted at rebellion against Vietnam's nineteenth-century court.

Just as often, Quát might paradoxically combine the serious use of genuinely Sino-Vietnamese themes with the subversive use of highly mocking caricatures of Sino-Vietnamese stylistic conventions. In the following passage he is serious in his description of the hardships of the unsuccessful scholarly life. But at the same time, his mercurial genius may very well be attacking the affectations of orthodox Sino-Vietnamese literary society by referring absurdly to "frost and snow," which never appeared in Vietnam: "One's hut is very tiny, and its over-long thatch roof drags upon the ground. The days are dreary, and raindrops fall with a stony heaviness. One's lamp is dim, and there is only one scruffy sleeping mat. A lustrous moon illuminates the quiet night. One's badly faded poor scholar's garment must go through both spring and autumn, to the point where it becomes imbued with the color of hard labor. One's Mother Phiếu's rice is old and stale, and life in general must savor the taste of bitterness . . . Frost and snow blow lightly, making the *nhạn* bird lean. Taking one's poor bag of supplies, one travels up and down away from home. There are many roads, and time flies, as fast as spiders weave their webs. One's cold lamp awakens and flickers in the southern nook of one's hut, and several yellow flames spring up feebly."[136]

Quát, in fact, was early nineteenth-century Vietnam's literary master of the art of superimposing Sino-Vietnamese cultural characteristics upon a strong implicit background of Southeast Asian cultural resistance. His philosophy of subversion of Sino-Vietnamese institutions also belonged unmistakably to the romantic tradition in Vietnamese political literature. This tradition was possibly stronger in Vietnamese literature than in Chinese. The romantic strain was strong in Quát's unforgettable idealized portrait of what the true iconoclast should be like in Nguyễn Vietnam: "There is a man: his appearance is wretched but he belongs to a noble family. . . . His mouth still smells of milk [from his mother] and he still has a splash of blood upon his head [this conceit invoked the Vietnamese belief that all new babies were born this way] . . . The freshness of his student's countenance is apparent; he opens his eyes, recognizes the world, and [just dares to] kick the doors of his masters. Shamelessly summoning up the courage of the vagabond, he stretches out the hand created for him to change the direction of destiny."[137]

Such writings as these did their deadly work in falsifying the attractions of unquestioning loyalty to the examination system. They also undermined slavish dedication to the narrow forms of literature the examination system demanded. "Kicking the doors of one's masters" (*đạp cửa phú đồ*) might mean young men indiscreetly vying against older teachers who were more experienced than their students. But it might also mean disillusioned middle-aged men vying against the dynasty and its bureaucracy as a whole. Quát himself eventually chose the latter course. Appointed to the post of prefectural educational official in a prefecture in Sơn Tây province, he suggested then what his plans would be, in a bitter delineation of the life he was leading at his prefectural school in mid-nineteenth century Vietnam:

> I, the model for a handful of pallid-faced students
> One and a half pieces of gold in salary is all [I
>   can expect]
> An empty house with three partitions, a master, a
>   servant girl, and a bitch dog.
> Several students who look part men, part idiots,
>   and part monkeys.
> I bind up my adventurous legs and put myself in
>   a fish trap
> I quell my reluctance [literally "pull back my guts,"
>   *rút ruột*] and go out into the world in order
>   to pay off my rice debts.[138]

By saying that he would put himself in a fish trap (*tra vào rọ*) he symbolized his anticipated sacrificing of his freedom. By saying that he would pay off his rice debts (*trả nợ cơm*) he symbolized his determination to rebel. This he did, in 1854. But he was abruptly captured and summarily executed. In the last analysis he had been more memorable as an apostle of rebellion than as a rebel himself.

Significantly, it would be hard to find a counterpart of Quát in early nineteenth-century Chinese society. Of course there were disaffected scholars in Ch'ing China, men like Kung Tzu-chen (1792–1841), who, as one of the advocates of the New Text school in Chinese scholarship, was an intellectual forerunner of the two great Chinese polemicists of the end of the century, K'ang Yu-wei and Liang Ch'i-ch'ao. Like Quát, Kung was born into a family which had produced high officials for several generations. Like Quát, Kung had witnessed agrarian unrest in the countryside in his youth and had recognized that social decay was widespread in his society. Like Quát, Kung was less than completely successful at winning degrees in the examination system. When he was in his twenties he wrote a dramatic tract, *Ming-liang lun* (On elucidating excellence), in which he attacked the Chinese bureaucratic class for its materialism and its lack of idealism, declaring, "Of the scholars of recent times whom I have seen in the course of my life, those who have still preserved a sense of shame from the day they memorialized the throne and the year they began to advance are few. The longer officials remain officials the more their spirit becomes self-indulgent, the more reverently they are respected, the more an atmosphere of flattery is confirmed."[139] Kung, like Quát, was also an accomplished writer of provocative satires. He proved this, for example, in his 1834 "author's preface" to a "new book on the seeking of official rewards" in which he elaborated a litany of mind-numbing technical trivialities which examination system candidates had to observe in writing their examinations.

But Chinese Confucian scholasticism was so richly multi-faceted that dissatisfied intellectuals like Kung could choose from a variety of options within the Confucian tradition if they wanted means to express their dissatisfaction. If they rejected the Sung neo-Confucian orthodoxy of the Peking court, they could easily adopt different textual and scholastic positions and then become dedicated reformers. Kung himself, as a peaceful would-be reformer of a political situation which alarmed him, became a spokesman for the famous New Text school. This school argued, among other things, that Confucius had been a prophet rather than a mere transmitter of the institutions of the past. It argued that the *Kung-yang Commentary* (*Kung-yang chuan*) of the *Spring and Autumn Annals*, one of the Five Classics, had conveyed the possibility that evolutionary changes could be introduced into institutions.

This was a luxury alienated Vietnamese scholars like Quát were denied. In Vietnam, iconoclasm (aimed at Sino-Vietnamese institutions) was more destructive. Such an abundance of theoretical vantage points for constructive reform did not exist in Vietnamese Confucianism. Because there were fewer peaceful alternatives in Vietnamese society for intellectuals like Cao Bá Quát, who could not accept court Confucian orthodoxy, rebellion, the violent alternative, became intellectually less remote and eccentric an act, although it was just as hazardous as in China.

Chinese Confucian culture rarely presented its full face to the Vietnamese. Only by accident did the tidings of deliberations in private Chinese academies, of controversies like those among Chinese advocates of the New Text school, the Old Text school, Sung-Han eclecticism or the School of Empirical Research, come to Vietnam. Confucian learning was transmitted to Vietnam from China as part of the intercultural communication between the two societies. But much of the time this communication was specifically channeled to the Vietnamese court, rather than being diffusely channeled to a large number of Vietnamese scholars. As a consequence, the range of Confucian learning that was presented to Huế elites by the books they purchased in China tended to be narrower and more orthodox than its Chinese reality. Occasionally, but only occasionally, Vietnamese courts unintentionally imported heterodox materials from China. At the end of the nineteenth century, Vietnamese revolutionaries and reformers like Phan Bội Châu would learn about the existence of K'ang Yu-wei and Liang Ch'i-ch'ao when the Huế court purchased their books and first allowed scholars at the Vietnamese metropolitan examinations to see them.

At the same time, why did Vietnamese scholars not formulate competing theoretical positions within the one broad Confucian tradition on their own? Their own literary culture was extraordinarily rich and sophisticated. They were well versed in all the Confucian classics and their commentaries. Intellectual inspiration from China was not necessarily indispensable to them. Even the court's control of printing, which has been described, was not an insuperable obstacle. It did not prevent non-conformists and rebels like Quát from publishing their clever attacks.

Any explanation for the failure of Vietnamese Confucianism to exhibit much variation in form must probably begin with the fact that Confucianism was simply less focal to the interests of the Vietnamese people than it was to those of the Chinese people. This was purely a question of degree. Enough has been written to show that Confucian values and scholarship were nonetheless well entrenched in traditional Vietnam. But because the Confucian tradition was slightly less important to the Vietnamese, they were less inclined to discuss it, synthesize its elements in new ways, or canvass it for all its possibilities. The result was that prospects for intellectual realignment within the tradition never really emerged as clearly in Vietnam as they did in China. And resistance to the very idea of introducing variations itself was never decisively undermined. Chinese Confucian scholasticism exhibited a greater complexity not merely because there were far more Chinese scholars to add accretions and reinterpretations to it but also because it dominated Chinese life more. It was more of a cultural focus.

In this sense, ironically, the Vietnamese court-sponsored examination system was probably more central to Vietnamese Confucian scholarship than the Chinese system was to scholarship in China. Not much genuinely independent Sino-Vietnamese classical scholarship flourished very far outside the ambit of the system. And until the end, for sharp-eyed, insanely proud, prophetic, self-tormented writers like Cao Bá Quát who had been fully trained in the Chinese classics but who defied almost all their pretensions, there was little outside the system but isolation—and the beckonings of the non-Sinic Vietnamese folk world.

This conflict between iconoclastic poets like Cao Bá Quát, who regarded the institutionalized culture of the Nguyễn examination system as being inappropriate and constraining, and a dynastic court which depended upon the hegemony of orthodox Sino-Viet-namese culture for its own survival was just one facet of a larger situation in the 1800's. Another facet of the same situation was reveal-ed in the dilemmas of the court's adjustments to the changing interna-tional scene around it. The ideological nature of these adjustments was important. It governed the history of Vietnam's early interaction with an irrepressibly expansive Western civilization.

The Vietnamese Court's Creation of a Tributary System

Essentially, the Sino-Vietnamese court could not adopt and use Chinese institutions without adopting and using the Chinese world view as well. The Nguyễn emperor could not call himself a Son of Heaven and rule his country through a Confucian bureaucracy without main-taining publicly that his own political virtue in the world was unchal-lengeable, that he had no true competitors for "the mandate of heaven," and that he attracted the respect of foreigners. Shorn of such classical ideological apparatus, he would not have been believ-able in the eyes of Vietnamese bureaucrats and the "pale-faced stu-dents" (bạch diện thư sinh) who were being educated in Vietnam, generation after generation, in the Chinese classics.

In their romantic imaginations, these bureaucrats and students actually affected to see themselves as Chinese players on a Chinese historical stage. Đặng Trân Thường (1759–1816), a high official who fell from power in the Gia-long period, wrote a poem (*Hàn vương tôn phú*), after Gia-long sent him to prison, in which he compared himself with the Chinese general Han Hsin, who had rebelled against the founder of the Chinese Han dynasty. And Nguyễn Công Trứ compared his father, a Lê official who had refused to serve the Tây-sơns, with Shang loyalists who had refused to serve the Chou. On such a stage, the Vietnamese ruler's own part had to be dramatically convincing. His own life and style of power had to be interchangeable with the Chinese emperor's, any Chinese emperor's. In international relations this was impossible unless his court were made the focus of a tributary system of dependent nations, all of which would send him periodic envoys and gifts in acknowledgment of their cultural homage. His rule could be justified only by its association with the symbols and formulas of a Chinese-style tributary system.

At this point, however, in Vietnamese hands, the Chinese model threatened to get out of control. China was a universal empire, whose tributary system only reflected, with ponderous exaggeration, China's very real cultural and economic dominance and magnetism in East and Southeast Asia. Vietnam, on the other hand, was not a universal empire at all. Rather, it was one of a number of competing domains in the genuine if vaguely defined multi-kingdom political environment of mainland Southeast Asia. The fact that Huế was really no more than an equal of the Siamese and Burmese courts in the 1800's produced an acute tension in Vietnam, of a kind rarely known in Peking, between the hierarchical Sino-Vietnamese ceremonial forms for diplomacy and actual Southeast Asian diplomatic exigencies. It was the emperor who had to exorcise this tension.

The Vietnamese court was most successful at maintaining the internal consistency of the Chinese model in its use of geographical terminology. Its method was to give most of Vietnam's major Southeast Asian neighbors impeccable Sino-Vietnamese variants of their contemporary Chinese names. Burma was known to the nineteenth-century Vietnamese as *Miến-Điện* (Chinese, *Mien-tien*), Siam as *Xiêm La* (Chinese, *Hsien-lo*), Vientiane as *Vạn Tượng*, and Luang Prabang as *Nam Chưởng* (Chinese, *Nan-chang*). Occasionally all of

Laos was still given separate consideration as Ai Lao (Chinese, *Ai-lao*). This term had probably first appeared in China in Later Han texts, as a designation for non-Chinese peoples, resident in Yŭnnan, who had previously been known during the Early Han empire as the Kunming barbarians.[1] However, proof that this term for Laos was more fashionable in Vietnam in the Lê period than in the 1800's was afforded by the fact that in 1842 Thiệu-trị had to ask his officials what it meant and where it was.[2]

More generally, Western countries, goods, and ships were identified, as in China, by the Sino-Vietnamese adjective *dương* (overseas). All aspects of neighboring Cambodia's civilization were described as being those of "border barbarians" (*phiên;* this term, which goes back to the Chou period in China, indicated the non-Chinese minorities of Yŭnnan, Kweichow, Sinkiang, and Taiwan in the Ch'ing period). And when the court made alterations in its inherited Chinese geographical terminology, it often did so merely to increase the force of the cultural stratification of kingdoms this terminology was inclined to suggest. Cambodia was regularly called "the country of the upper barbarians" (*Cao Man*). The effect of such an official appellation was hardly altered by unofficial but eminent scholar-geographers like Phạm Đình Hồ (1768–1839), who published a famous atlas of Cambodia entitled *Đại Man quốc địa đồ* (A geography of the great barbarian country).[3]

In developing this rather parasitic geographical terminology, Sino-Vietnamese orthodoxy was inspired and strengthened by the hold that Chinese classical histories exercised over the minds of court literati. Another pioneering geographer-scholar of the early 1800's, Nguyễn Siêu (1799–1872), gathered information about countries outside Vietnam by reading the "biographies" of such exotic places in the Chinese *Ming History* (*Ming shih*). The official compendium of biographies of the Nguyễn dynasty itself, the *Đại Nam liệt truyện*, summarized the early history of Luang Prabang by borrowing observations more than ten centuries old from Chinese texts which had been written during the T'ang dynasty.[4] Such deference to the traditional viewpoints of Chinese historians on Southeast Asia portended less than deference to neighboring Southeast Asian societies themselves. It was, rather, an expression of a highly aggressive Vietnamese cultural self-definition, directed against the very different cultural backgrounds of Siam, Burma, Cambodia, and Laos.

What was the next step? The sinicization of Vietnamese geographical terminology was only a beginning. Once Vietnamese geographical consciousness was given a Sino-Vietnamese cultural framework, other countries (with the exception of China) were ranked according to a hierarchy of values, all of them being placed below Confucian Vietnam. This meant that diplomatic intercourse with them could only be carried out at the Vietnamese court if their envoys to Huế followed the ritualized behavior of vassals. If such ritual were removed, the Vietnamese emperor would look uncomfortably like an incompetent imitator of his Chinese archetype. If he were unable to attract vassals to his court, Chinese fashion, his prestige would begin to unravel.

Thus in 1815 Gia-long published a list of 13 countries which he claimed were vassals (*viễn phương chư quốc lai cống*) of Vietnam. This list included Luang Prabang, Vientiane, Burma, France, England, Trấn Ninh (a plateau in eastern Laos), and two countries which the Vietnamese called "Water Haven" (*Thủy Xả Quốc*) and "Fire Haven" (*Hỏa Xả Quốc*). Gia-long claimed that these countries conceded the legitimacy of Sino-Vietnamese diplomatic laws. Such laws in turn were an important theoretical complex, borrowed from China, which the Nguyễn court called "the harmonious management of distant peoples" (*nhu viễn;* more literally, "accommodate the distant"). They governed the presentation of tribute by such countries to the Vietnamese court, their participation in ceremonies at Huế at the New Year and on the emperor's birthday, their receiving of uniforms and other gifts from the Vietnamese ruler, their agreeing to visit Vietnam only by certain routes and only with a certain number of men, their agreeing to obey all ordinances and admonitions the Vietnamese ruler gave them. The principle behind the laws was that superior culture, combined with largesse, could usually ensure compliance.

The nature of these "vassals" was diverse. "Water Haven" and "Fire Haven" actually stood for several groups of warlike Malayo-Polynesian highland villagers known as the Jarai, who lived in a mountainous zone between Indianized Cambodia and sinicized

Vietnam, chiefly in what is known today as the Vietnamese province of Pleiku. The Jarai resisted supra-village organization. They were ruled by two sorcerers, one of whom was considered to be the master of water (and thus of floods and rain), the other of fire. The two sorcerers lived apart from each other. But both of them were traditional vassals of the Cambodian rulers as well as of the Vietnamese.[5]

Jarai-occupied areas were important to Huế because, as potential cultural transition zones, they could be used to filter Vietnamese influence into Cambodia. But interpreters at the Vietnamese court could not distinguish between their two "countries" or branches. In 1831, when "Water Haven" sent tribute to Huế for the first time after a long hiatus, it was mistakenly identified as "Fire Haven," which was actually a branch of the Jarai farther west.[6] In 1834, hoping to sinicize the Jarai sorcerers, Minh-mạng conferred the Sino-Vietnamese name Vĩnh Bảo upon the sorcerer of "Water Haven." Even more significantly, however, he upgraded his rank in the Vietnamese tributary system to that of "king" (*quốc vương*)—the same rank Minh-mạng himself occupied in Peking's eyes in the Chinese tributary system—on the grounds that there were few rebellions among the Jarai, the ruler-subject distinction was clear among them, and their customs were "pure and honest."[7] In reality, of course, the Jarai sorcerer's importance was artificially inflated in this way in order to meet the political needs of the Vietnamese Son of Heaven. The more client kings there were who sent envoys to Huế, the more the man who ruled in Huế could regard himself as a successful Southeast Asian version of the Chinese emperor. Quantity was important; European merchants, neighboring Southeast Asian countries, and highland populations within Vietnam's own borders were all classed equally as tributary states. All of them played a part, whether they were aware of it or not, in the construction of this Sino-Vietnamese dream-fabric.

It must be borne in mind that the maintenance of a tributary system was by no means alien to Southeast Asian political procedures. Nineteenth-century Siam, for example, presided over an array of vassals, which included, at different times, Malay sultans, western and eastern Laotian princes, and the rulers of Cambodia. What were striking in the purely Southeast Asian context were the cultural as well as the political pretensions which supported the Vietnamese tributary system. The Siamese court, lacking Vietnam's cultural evangelism, rarely attempted to transform the institutions and customs of the peoples who paid it homage.

Pretensions led to fictions. Few of Vietnam's Southeast Asian neighbors actually sent tribute to Huế regularly, for example, every three years. The real pattern the Burmese, Siamese, Laotians, and Cambodians observed was to send gift-laden envoys to Vietnam whenever they needed a Vietnamese military counterweight to one of the other Southeast Asian courts. This pattern was more suggestive of continental European diplomacy in the age of "the balance of power" than it was of the Chinese diplomatic system.

Burma appeared on Gia-long's 1815 list as one of Vietnam's vassals. But direct contact between Ava and Huế in the 1800's appears to have been non-existent before 1822–23, when a capricious sea wind precipitated it. Lê Văn Duyệt, the Saigon overlord, sent out one of his subordinates on a merchant ship to explore the buying of arms from English merchants. Wind and current took the ship of Duyệt's agent to Burma, where he was arrested, suspected of being a Siamese spy, and interrogated exhaustively. When he finally established the fact that he came from Vietnam, not Siam, he was given a belatedly warm reception, and the Burmese court sent a "return" mission to Saigon and Huế. The purpose of the return mission was to request that Minh-mạng break relations with Siam, Burma's traditional enemy. This was hardly the kind of message that a humble vassal state would have addressed to its suzerain.[8] Minh-mạng rejected the request, because war with Siam at that time might have jeopardized Vietnam's hegemony in Cambodia, won under Gia-long. Yet in 1813, when that precarious hegemony had not yet been established, a northern Vietnamese scholar had proposed to Gia-long that he contract an alliance with Burma against the Siamese.[9]

Thus cultural symbols were opposed by political realities. The asymmetrical, hierarchical Sino-Vietnamese tributary system had to accommodate the need or prospective need for more equal, symmetrical dealings and even alliances among a number of Southeast Asian courts. As a consequence, in 1802–1847 the relatively weaker courts of Luang Prabang, Vientiane, and Phnom Penh were the only ones which could be called true vassals of Vietnam's. Vientiane envoys, bringing tribute gifts, were received in audience at the Hall of Supreme Harmony in Huế as early as 1805. They were escorted to and from the capital by elephant guards, elephants being the symbols of military pomp everywhere in mainland Southeast Asia. But they performed the "five obeisances" (*ngũ bái*) while they were presenting their gifts.[10] The Cambodian ruler Nak Ong Chan (*Nặc Ông Chân* in Sino-Vietnamese), dominated by Siam and faced with the task of suppressing the three ambitious pro-Siamese brothers in his own family who threatened to destroy him, requested Vietnamese investiture in 1807. He received a gilded seal from Gia-long, similar to the one Gia-long received from China. He was also promised Vietnamese protection against Siam. In return he undertook to send tribute (elephants, elephant tusks, rhinoceros horns, waxes, medicines, and sapan wood) to Huế once every four years.

Yet it would be unfair to conclude that the Nguyễn court's less than completely successful imitation of the Chinese tributary system was motivated solely by the dynastic need to demonstrate the Vietnamese emperor's cultural superiority in Southeast Asia. It was not even completely motivated by the desire to control non-Vietnamese territory in Cambodia and eastern Laos. Importation of the language of the Chinese tributary system was part of the process of importing Chinese bureaucratic language in general. As the Vietnamese people expanded south along the eastern periphery of Southeast Asia, they found that the familiar categories of the Chinese tributary system's language offered a convenient means for reducing the empirical complexity of the new environment they were encountering. Knowledge of distant, unvisited places in Burma and Malaya could be acquired and organized by Vietnamese pioneers more rapidly through the symbolic mediation of Chinese concepts of the non-Chinese. Occasionally, it is true, the imposition of innately Chinese categories upon Southeast Asia created semantic confusion. The word *Man* was used by Nguyễn bureaucrats both to classify the "barbarian" Cambodians, in the Chinese fashion, and to refer to the actual Man highlanders who lived in the mountainous areas north of Hanoi. But this confusion seemed a minor problem.

Moreover, Vietnamese use of the language of the Chinese tributary system merely confirmed the Chinese influence in Vietnamese perceptions of time and space. These perceptions were, of course, intimately related to the Sino-Vietnamese social system, which gave its own emphasis to different aspects of time and space. Most of the temporal frames of reference of the Vietnamese elite were Chinese-inspired. They ranged from the "watches" (*canh, keng*) which defined time in Vietnamese cities and on Vietnamese junks, to the court's official agricultural calendars, to the device of keeping historical records of the reign years of past dynasties. Spatial frames of reference were often Chinese too, like those purveyed by the maps of Chinese merchants and sailors which circulated in Saigon. Chinese classical folklore was often borrowed by Vietnamese writers. They disguised it and wove it into literary schemes which centered upon the unique enchantments of the Vietnamese, not the Chinese, homeland. In a famous poem, whose aesthetic effects some Vietnamese historians have compared to those of an ancient Chinese painting, the poetess Bà Huyện Thanh Quan wrote in the early 1800's:

[As I] arrive at the Đèo Ngang,[11] the light of
    the sun is sinking,
Grass and trees struggle through the rocks, and
    leaves struggle with flowers.
Bent down below the mountains, a few old wood-
    cutters [appear],
Scattered along the river, several families of
    savages [are seen].
When it remembers its country, the heart of the
    "country-country" bird aches,
When it calls of its love for its family, the
    mouth of the "family-family" bird tires.
I stop and look around: sky, mountains, and water.
A private package of feelings: I share them with
    myself.[12]

The original Chinese folktale upon which this emotional poem depends is, of course that of Tu Yü. Tu Yü was a prince of the state of Shu (in Szechwan) during the decadent last days of the Chou dynasty. His soul was believed to have assumed the form of a goatsucker or nightjar after he had died. The bird's plaintive song was explained as being the melancholy prince's calling out for his country after he had left it. Inspired by this legend, Vietnamese writers attached it to a Vietnamese bird. In this nineteenth-century poem, the bird which sings out "country country" (*con quốc quốc*, "country-country" bird) is a migrant from the romantic imagination of ancient Chinese storytellers. But its moral has become exclusively Vietnamese: the sanctity of the Vietnamese "sky, mountains, and water."

Hence Chinese influences abounded as psychological integrating forces in the Vietnamese elite's view of its environment, at home and abroad. In one sense, the consciously imported fictions of the Nguyễn tributary system were merely awkward diplomatic extensions of these influences.

Whatever the difficulties were for a smaller court manipulating a Chinese-style tributary system in Southeast Asia, the Vietnamese attempt to do so had two important consequences. One was that the Vietnamese court had no love for a relationship with Peking that was more intimate than necessary. The monarchy of the Nguyễn "Sons of Heaven" could maintain its theocentric pose in its own theater of activities only in conditions of relative isolation from China. Paradoxically, it needed conditions both of contact—in order to study Chinese institutions—and of lack of contact. Had the Kwangsi judicial commissioner, or some other Ch'ing envoy, visited Hanoi frequently for inter-state ceremonies, instead of descending upon the Vietnamese once a reign, he would have become a rival rather than a guest. He would not have been a rival in the sense of directly challenging the Vietnamese emperor's political control. No Chinese could have done that without a large army. Rather, he would have been a rival in the sense of challenging the Vietnamese ruler's uniqueness as a teacher-ruler in his own carefully selected milieu.

This paradox was demonstrated in a variety of ways during the early 1800's. One example of its workings occurred in 1843. Thiệu-trị received a communication from the Peking Board of Rites notifying him of an impending lunar eclipse. Because his own court astronomers had failed to predict this eclipse before the "Ch'ing country forwarded a report," the Vietnamese emperor's independent dignity as the arbiter between nature and man in his own environment was shaken. At the same time, he had only lost face when the efficiency of his own astronomers had accidentally been compared with that of their more skillful Chinese counterparts. This was the real implication of the episode.[13] An even more remarkable revelation of the paradox had come several years earlier, at the end of 1840. Minh-mạng accused the Peking court of incompetence in managing the etiquette of its own tributary system: "Up until this year the Board of Rites of the Ch'ing country has been mistaken in its hierarchical arrangements. Surely they should not have a rule that our envoys rank after those from Korea, Luang Prabang, Siam, and the Ryukyus? Korea as a country of literature and worthy men is definitely not worth discussing. As for Luang Prabang, it receives status as a tributary from us, and Siam and the Ryukyus are both barbarian countries . . . If they rank envoys this way again, I would prefer to abandon their audiences altogether and receive their censure and punishment, rather than stand below those several countries."[14]

What was at issue here was the fact that the international protocol of the Chinese court was contradicting the international protocol of the Chinese court's closest imitator, the Huế court. This undermined the latter's prestige. Vietnamese envoys from Peking had returned with the dangerous insight that the sense of hierarchy of their own smaller tributary system in Southeast Asia was not reflected in the same ways in the greater Chinese tributary system. Confronted with the hard choice of modifying his own diplomatic policies or attenuating still further his periodic links with the Chinese emperor, Minh-mạng left little doubt what his decision would be. But the Vietnamese tributary system, inevitable as it was, was built on quicksand. It faced daily controversion from the Chinese, as well as from Southeast Asian rivals.

A second consequence of the Vietnamese tributary system was, strangely enough, its magnification of the Vietnamese court's tendency to isolate minority peoples, while sinicizing them, and to erect barriers between different peoples within Vietnam itself. In borrowing the hierarchical categories of the vast Chinese tributary system, Vietnamese rulers applied them to a much smaller world. Thus small highland groups like the Jarai, as has been shown, could take on the significance that whole nations did in the Chinese diplomatic code. This meant, to some extent, that the barriers between such groups had to be preserved, because they had almost the same import that barriers between nations did to the Chinese.

What is certain, at least, is that the appreciation of ethnic differentiation and stratification was more finely developed in the Vietnamese imperial outlook than it was in the political outlook of Vietnam's Southeast Asian neighbors. In appointing a protector for the southern border province of Hà Tiên in 1811, Gia-long told him that his duty would be to build schools, clear land, regulate markets, and "distinguish and separate people of Chinese descent, Chinese merchants, Cambodians, and Malays."[15] Minh-mạng never ceased to marvel at the fact that the overseas Chinese community in Bangkok was permitted to live among the Siamese people. He predicted in 1840 that Siamese failure to segregate the overseas Chinese more effectively would lead to Siam's downfall: "Nowadays within Siam the Malay and Chinese [minorities] reside confusedly and are not restrained and controlled. If there are foreign instabilities, how can [the Siamese] be certain that people who are not of their race will remain unalienated?"[16]

The Vietnamese framework of ethnic administrative separation (combined, paradoxically, with cultural proselytization) was so much a part of the court's approach to its environment that it survived even when it crippled political control rather than consolidating it. In the northern provinces the Thổ, the Nùng, the Man, and the Mèo highlanders all lived under their own local chiefs. On occasion, these chiefs presented tribute to Huế. Here arrangements were quasi-tributary, quasi-bureaucratic. Sometimes hill peoples, like the Mường in 1833, presented requests and tribute indirectly through their Laotian patrons in Luang Prabang.[17] At other times, like the Nùng, they paid annual taxes in silver, together with the Chinese minority in the north, although the Nùng taxes were only half as much as those the Chinese paid: Nùng "slash and burn" agriculture (đao canh hỏa nậu, "scythe-plough fire-hoe") was considered unproductive.[18] Two lower officials proposed in 1836 that the northern highlanders be ruled directly by the Vietnamese, that their own chiefs be transferred to remote provinces, that roads be built into their mountains, and that their communities be organized into Vietnamese-style villages with village chiefs.[19] This proposal, although expensive, would have extended the court's power. But it would also have torn down ethnic political barriers. With their downfall, administrative diversification and hierarchy in Vietnam similar to that in the larger Chinese world might have suffered. The proposal was not received with enthusiasm.

The Vietnamese tributary system was a frame of reference for mediating Vietnamese adaptation to the external world. But it was a culturally borrowed frame of reference. As such it was characterized by the feature that its own internal and external adaptiveness was often slower and more cumbersome than that of its Chinese model.

This is best illustrated by the fate of some of its vocabulary. The term for Penang Island, which Vietnamese junks knew and visited in the early 1800's, was written *Pin-lang-yǔ* in classical Chinese. This Chinese term *Pin-lang* was a serviceable approximation of the sound of the name "Penang," but it also conveyed an idea: "Palm Island." In borrowing this term, Vietnamese officials first converted it into Sino-Vietnamese: *Tân lang dữ*. The Sino-Vietnamese expression still managed to capture much of the sound of the original name but also retained the adventitious meaning of its Chinese equivalent. At this point, however, a further change occurred. Vietnamese junks were sailed by men who received orders from the Huế bureaucracy but who were themselves unfamiliar with classical Chinese. As a result, in the *Xiêm La Quốc lô-trình tập lục* (Collected records of travel itineraries to Siam), a book of documents compiled at Huế in 1810 which contained the accumulated lore of Vietnamese sailors, monks, interpreters, and petty soldiers about land and sea routes all over Southeast Asia, "Penang" was no longer written in Sino-Vietnamese.

Instead, it had been transformed into a non-Sinic Vietnamese term written in *nôm: Cù lao cau*. Because *Cù lao cau* meant "Palm Island" in Vietnamese, what had happened was that the end product of all these linguistic conversions had preserved the irrelevant decorative meaning of the Chinese transcript of the name but had sacrificed the all-important transcription of its sound. The end product was more parochial and less serviceable internationally; not being Chinese, it was better understood by uneducated Vietnamese junk captains, but its new sound would not suggest "Penang" to anybody but a Vietnamese. Chinese geographers could absorb the name of a remote port of call by making only one change: "Penang" to "Pin-lang-yǔ." Vietnamese geographers who were conditioned by the Chinese example were eventually compelled to make three: "Penang" to "Pinlang-yǔ" to "Tân-lang-dữ" to "Cù lao cau."

Wherever geographical terminology exercised an immediate bearing on political and military strategy, the court attempted to evade the cultural dictates of its borrowed frame of reference. In 1834 Minh-mạng ordered that all Cambodian documents that arrived in Huế be translated directly into *quốc âm* (that is, into Vietnamese, not classical Chinese). He formally forbade their additional translation into Chinese characters and classical Chinese.[20] Furthermore, the Vietnamese tributary system was never self-sufficient or ideologically strong enough to resist the cultural influence of the rest of Southeast Asia. For example, the word for "island," *cù lao* in "Cù lao cau," was a Vietnamization of the Malay word "pulau"; it was employed more commonly in early nineteenth-century Nguyễn documents than the Sino-Vietnamese word for "island," *đảo*. Europe was often designated in these same documents as *Hoa-lang quốc* (the *Hoa-lang* country), *Hoa-lang* being a Vietnamization of the Siamese word for white men, *farang*.[21] The fact that the Vietnamese could borrow terminology at both ends of their tributary system, from Southeast Asia as well as from China, reveals once again the inner uncertainty of their diplomacy's cultural pretensions. These pretensions and their vicissitudes were demonstrated in the Nguyễn court's attempts to annex Cambodia.

Model versus Realities: The Nguyễn Duel with Siam over Cambodia and Laos

The Vietnamese first began to encroach upon Cambodia in the seventeenth century. At that time the Cambodian court still ruled the Mekong delta. Its fertile, underpopulated expanses were unusually tempting to the landowners of central Vietnam, faced as these landowners were with frequent bad harvests and the ravages of Trịnh-Nguyễn civil war. Vietnamese settlers began to move south, forming communities at Mô-xoài (now Bà-rịa) and at Đồng-nai (in modern Biên Hoà).

Another pattern of the future first asserted itself in 1658. The Cambodian king died, and two claimants disputed his throne. When they appealed to the Nguyễn court of central Vietnam to help them, the Nguyễn ruler sent an army of 3,000 men as far south as Biên Hòa and eventually imposed his own choice upon the Cambodian throne. The new Cambodian ruler promised to become a Nguyễn vassal. In 1674, however, a Cambodian prince imported Siamese troops to fight another Cambodian prince, and the latter appealed to the Nguyễns for help. This time Vietnamese troops marched all the way south to the Cambodian outpost at Saì-gòn (Saigon, a Vietnamization of a Cambodian name). Then they marched upon Phnom Penh (known to the Vietnamese as Nam Vang) itself. The Siamese-supported prince fled into the jungle, and the Vietnamese established two Cambodian kings, one at Long-úc and one at Saigon. Both of them had to send tribute.

From this point on Vietnamese armies began to intervene regularly in Cambodian politics, in 1699, 1705, 1714, 1747, 1753–1755, and 1771–1772. On most of these occasions, too, the theme of the intervention was the same: the need to supply military support to the current Vietnamese candidate for the Cambodian throne, in his struggles against a rival candidate favored by Siam.

A number of factors made these recurrent "wars of the Cambodian succession," as they might be termed, increasingly explosive. Cambodian demographic anemia created a weakly populated power vacuum between Siam and Vietnam. The lack of cohesion of the Cambodian royal family, the crystallization of an obsessive inter-state rivalry between Siam and Vietnam, and, last but not least, the pressure of new Chinese and Vietnamese settlements in the Mekong delta, also played their part. As early as 1679, when a Ming loyalist navy of 50 ships and 3,000 Chinese soldiers arrived on Nguyễn shores and asked permission to live in Vietnam, Nguyễn rulers decided to use Chinese refugees as pawns in their campaign to occupy and develop Cambodian territory. Thus Ming loyalist settlements grew up in modern Gia Định, Biên Hoà, and Định Tường in the late 1600's. A Cantonese adventurer, Mo Chiu, founded another Chinese colony in Hà Tiên about 1700. When a Siam-backed Cambodian king at Phnom Penh overplayed his hand in the 1750's by attempting to rig an alliance with the Trịnh rulers at Hanoi against the Nguyễns—a politically divided Vietnam has often had a fatal appeal for Cambodians—Nguyễn troops drove him out of his kingdom. They allowed him to return only when he had ceded Vietnam more Cambodian territory. Such a policy of slow territorial absorption of Cambodia, one Nguyễn general described at the time as "the policy of slowly eating silkworms" (*chính sách tàm thực*). Vietnam's present-day six southern provinces were eaten away from the Cambodians in this manner roughly during this century from 1650 to 1750.

The remarkable if typical length of this train of historic causes and consequences across Asia should be noted in passing. In a minor way, the rise of the Manchus in China had contributed to the downfall of the Cambodians in the Mekong delta. But what is of real concern to this study is the way in which Southeast Asian international politics, of the kind that have just been described, were twisted and distorted by Vietnamese rulers to fit Sino-Vietnamese cultural formulations, and the way in which Vietnam's use of the Chinese model in managing diplomatic relations affected Southeast Asia. The ascendancy of the Chinese model of diplomatic relations in Vietnam was, of course, just one aspect of the basic polarization of mainland Southeast Asia into two different social and political worlds, one Indianized, one sinicized.

Siamese domination of Cambodian politics was unopposed by the Vietnamese during the Tây-sơn rebellion. In 1807, however, the Cambodian ruler Nak Ong Chan, who had been crowned in Bangkok and given a Siamese royal name, became tired of Siamese pressures and offered to make himself Gia-long's vassal. When Siamese armies later invaded Cambodia, he fled to Saigon. In 1813 the Saigon overlord Lê Văn Duyệt escorted him back to Cambodia at the head of more than 13,000 Vietnamese troops.[22] From this moment Cambodia became a Vietnamese protectorate.

Nonetheless, in 1813 (in contrast to 1834) there is no doubt that the Nguyễn court preferred an indirect influence in Phnom Penh to direct rule itself. When evidence arrived at Huế in 1814 that the two senior Vietnamese officials in Cambodia were monopolizing decisions and making the Cambodian vassal king a virtual prisoner, Gia-long, acting upon the advice of a memorial by Nguyễn Văn Thành that "the purpose of the institution of the protectorate is to strengthen the preservation" of Cambodia, ordered these officials to give the Cambodian court more autonomy.[23] A major motive behind this order was a desire to curb the power of Lê Văn Duyệt (an enemy of Thành's), whose bailiwick at Saigon possessed very ambivalent geographical and cultural loyalties, having once been the site of a Cambodian town. In 1815 Gia-long forbade Duyệt to visit the Cambodian king in his capital.[24] In 1827, when Duyệt artfully proposed that his army at Saigon be built up for the sake of a surprise attack against Siam, Minh-mạng commanded him to "remember . . . the dangers of war."[25]

In the 1820's another Siamese vassal, Anu (A Nộ in Sino-Vietnamese), the ruler of Vientiane, rebelled and invaded Siam itself. When Siamese forces recovered from their initial panic and then seized Vientiane, Anu requested Vietnamese help. Vietnamese armies failed to win back his kingdom for him. But they did seize the Laotian plateau of Trấn Ninh, after a conflict with the Siamese-supported ruler of Luang Prabang (1827).[26] The Vietnamese military absorption of Sầm Nứa, Cam Môn, and Savannakhet as well as Trấn Ninh followed. (Sầm Nứa and Trấn Ninh are just across the border from the province of Nghệ An. The Vietnamese-supported Pathet Lao guerrilla movement is strong today in those border areas of Laos which Minh-mạng annexed.) One of the historian's best indications of how Vietnam's acquisition of this Laotian territory was viewed by ordinary Vietnamese—as a cultural as well as a military triumph—is to be found in a popular song which celebrated the event:

> Ai Lao engirdles mountains and jungles,
> The petty prince of Luang Prabang was conniving
>   with Siam . . .
> The isolated barbarian chieftain [of Trấn Ninh]
>   was disturbed
> And offered as tribute to the court of the
>   Southern Country his seven districts . . .
> The sympathies of Cam Môn, Sầm Nứa and Sa-van
>   [Savannakhet]
> Gradually surrender to [the influence of] our
>   country.[27]

In 1833, a Vietnamese rebel, Lê Văn Khôi, seized Gia Định and requested Siamese help against the armies of Huế. Hoping at least to bring Vietnamese penetration of Cambodia and Laos to an end, Rama III accepted the invitation by attacking Vietnamese positions in Cambodia, Châu Đốc, and An Giang, Hà Tiên, Trấn Ninh, and other parts of Laos in the winter of 1833–34. But by the early summer of 1834 the tide had turned against the Siamese. The Nguyễn court repelled them on the Laotian border, recovered Châu Đốc and Hà Tiên, and reinvaded Cambodia. Led by Trương Minh Giảng, a central Vietnamese general,[28] Vietnamese forces drove the Siamese out of Cambodia and reestablished Gia-long's old protectorate. This time, however, there was to be a difference.

When Nak Ong Chan, the Vietnamese vassal king since 1807, died at the end of 1834, the Vietnamese converted Cambodia into "the overlordship of the pacified west" (*Trấn tây thành*). They divided it into more than thirty Sino-Vietnamese prefectures and districts. In effect, it had become another southern Vietnamese province. Cambodian puppet officials were given Sino-Vietnamese bureaucratic titles and grades. Sino-Vietnamese taxation categories were introduced. Vietnamese military officials even attempted to tax shipping on the upper reaches of the Mekong. Cambodian peasants were conscripted for extensive public works, the building of roads and the draining of canals. Twenty secretaries and unranked underlings of the Six Boards in Huế were hastily promoted in early 1835 and sent to staff the new Vietnamese administration in Cambodia;[29] later in the same year 10 prefectural and district educational officers, 9 middle level board officials, and 68 low level or unranked board underlings followed them.[30] The educational officers' task was to teach the Cambodians Chinese characters.

Vietnamese documents also reveal that such officials did well in their new Cambodian province. Giảng himself lost three months' salary when the emperor's attention was attracted by the large number of postal station attendants whom members of his official entourage deputed to carry back spoils from Cambodia.[31] Apart from the movement of Vietnamese officials into Cambodia in the 1830's, poor Chinese of southern Vietnam and the most recent Chinese immigrants (*đáp khách*, "passengers") to the Saigon area on Chinese merchant junks were methodically encouraged to move to Cambodia. Here they were supposed to clear the jungle, develop villages, and farm with government-supplied agricultural tools.[32] Remnants of the Cham minority in southern Vietnam were similarly channeled into primitive frontier settlements along the Cambodian border.[33] Chinese merchants who had been resident in Cambodia before the Vietnamese conquest were now organized into government-controlled "congregations."[34]

Not surprisingly, by 1841 revolts had broken out all over Cambodia. They spread immediately to southern Vietnam. There substantial enclaves of Cambodians existed in provinces like Vĩnh Long, An Giang, and Hà Tiên. The revolts were led by a group of Cambodian Buddhist monks and by a former Cambodian puppet bureaucrat (sixth grade) turned revolutionary visionary, Lâm Sâm as he is known in Vietnamese records.[35] Revolt among the Cambodians of southern Vietnam was stimulated by a quite specific process of sinicization called *cải thổ qui lưu*, "changing from [hereditary] aboriginal [chieftains] back to [appointed] circulating [bureaucrats]." What this process, borrowed from China, entailed in Vietnamese hands was the replacement of more independent-minded Cambodian leaders in southern communities that were ethnically Cambodian by regularly appointed Vietnamese officials. (In China this famous policy of substituting direct rule by court-appointed circulating officials for indirect rule through the leaders of a given minority people had originated in the Ming period, in reaction to misrule by the hereditary chieftains of such southwestern peoples as the Miao and the Yao. In the Ch'ing period it was applied to minority peoples in provinces close to Vietnam like Kwangsi and Kweichow.) Although, as has been shown, preservation of ethnic administrative (but not cultural) barriers was normal in Vietnam, in Cambodian-settled southern areas it was considered dangerous. Cambodian rebels against Vietnam in 1841 were joined by a floating population of Chinese immigrants in the south. The court had customarily sent branded criminals like the notorious Yang Erh-ti, a Chinese who originally came from Nam Định, to the southern frontier to serve on hard labor details.[36] South Vietnam's rebel population was ready-made.

The revolts of 1841 spelled the end of the Nguyễn regime in Cambodia. After the Vietnamese withdrew from Phnom Penh, the Siamese invaded. From 1841 to 1845 it was Siam's turn to exploit the Cambodians, who sent the usual emissaries to Saigon asking for assistance. In 1845 another war broke out between Vietnam and Siam over Cambodia. But this time peace talks were held which finally seemed to stabilize the Cambodian throne. It became an official tributary of both Bangkok and Huế, its condition of dual vassalage being recognized by both its suzerains. This was to last until 1863, when the newly arrived French colonialists at Saigon, inheriting the Nguyễn determination to control the Mekong River and thus Cambodia, installed their own protectorate over the Cambodians.

In examining the background of this continuing Vietnamese adventure in Cambodia, it would of course be quite possible to point to important military and economic vested interests which reigned behind the scenes. For example, the need for war elephants dominated mainland Southeast Asian courts in the early 1800's. The court which possessed the most effective and most numerous elephant brigades was considered to have seized an important military advantage over its neighbors. Cambodia was a major supplier of elephants. In the two years 1812 and 1813 alone it had "presented" Gia-long with 127 elephants, being repaid on the basis of a three-category classification of the elephants' heights: elephants over six feet (Chinese) high were worth fifty silver taels, those of medium height earned forty silver taels, and smaller ones earned thirty silver taels each.[37] Because Nguyễn military statistics of the 1830's reveal that the total number of war elephants in the Vietnamese army usually remained at slightly under 400, of which more than 100 were usually stationed at Huế itself, the magnitude of these two Cambodian contributions of 1812 and 1813 is obvious.[38] Further evidence which underlined the nature of the court's interest in Cambodia emerged in early 1835. Minh-mạng, receiving twenty-one more elephants from Phnom Penh as tribute, offered lavish rewards for Cambodian donations of elephants to the Vietnamese army. More significant, the emperor conspicuously failed to ban the private maintenance of elephants by Cambodians themselves, although in Vietnam it had long been illegal to raise large elephants privately outside the ambit of the army.[39] Apparently it was feared that the extension of this restriction to Cambodia would reduce the Cambodian elephant market. Yet the risk of abandoning such a restriction could not have been taken lightly at the Vietnamese court. In 1832 it had been discovered that the Saigon overlord Lê Văn Duyệt, a potential rival of the court's and the prime manager of Vietnamese infiltration into Cambodia until his death, had been secretly accumulating his own personal herd of war elephants.[40]

On any evaluation, however, the economic and military costs of the short-lived Nguyễn conquest of Cambodia far outstripped the gains. This must have been clear to contemporaries. Vietnamese garrisons in Cambodia were far from self-sufficient. Provisions for them and for the Cambodians had to be found in the granaries of southern Vietnamese provinces like Vĩnh Long.[41] In fact, one Saigon memorial of 1832 reveals that the Cambodian ruler Nak Ong Chan habitually used his conquered status as a means of extracting such valuable commodities as salt on favorable terms from areas like Ba Thác (Sóc Trang, in modern Ba Xuyên province) in southern Vietnam. On his behalf, Saigon officials would request Huế to prevent Vietnamese military officers from blocking shipments of their own stores to Phnom Penh.[42] Another clear sign of the Cambodian economic drain on Nguyễn resources came in 1835. Minh-mạng was forced to relax a ban on the export of Vietnamese rice and salt by private Chinese merchant junks. They were now to be allowed to develop a one-way carrying trade in rice from south Vietnam to Cambodia, "but no farther."[43] Trương Minh Giảng himself, the protector of Cambodia, had requested this move.

It is the thesis of this study that one of the main explanations of the Vietnamese attempt to dominate Cambodia in the early 1800's lies in the subtle change the values, procedures, and working conditions of the Chinese tributary system underwent when they were transposed to a smaller Southeast Asian society. In remaining true to the Chinese system of political organization, the Vietnamese emperor and his bureaucracy were compelled to believe that they were the cultural cynosures of a society surrounded by subversive "barbarians." As has been shown, they even called themselves "the central kingdom," borrowing the Chinese term for China. In a sense, they could see their mission in the world as constituting a continuation of that culture-spreading process in which the Chinese had indulged from the central Asian steppes to the Kwangsi wilderness and which they themselves had later extended south to the Gulf of Siam and now to Cambodia. But the point of contrast is that by the 1800's, Chinese-style cultural egocentricity was profoundly defensive in its institutional arrangements in China. When it was translated into Vietnamese terms, it often generated expansionist impulses. Force transcended the classical ideal of influence through passive moral rectitude (*vô vi nhi trị*). The Vietnamese court's cultural pretensions were as great as those of its Chinese archetype but less appropriate to its situation. Its own territory and potency in its Southeast Asian context were smaller, and it was surrounded by antithetical ethnic and cultural diversities—above all, by the proximity of its neighboring "Indian-ized" rulers—which were unprecedented in China. Southeast Asia's balance of cultures—a more relevant term than the European phrase balance of power—thus denied Vietnamese rulers the self-confidence of their Chinese prototypes. The result was tension and insecurity, not harmony.

Thus the Vietnamese conquerors of Cambodia attempted to change Cambodian clothing, the Cambodian language, Cambodian political administration, and even Cambodian agriculture. (Viet-namese crops were imported and systematically planted in the late 1830's.)[44] They even hoped that Sino-Vietnamese (and Mahayana) forms of worship would permeate the Cambodian (Theravada) Buddhist church. At times when Siamese kings had enjoyed hegemony in Cambodia, on the other hand, they had usually preferred the discreetly patronized preservation of Cambodian institutions—which were not, culturally, too much unlike their own. In late 1834 Minh-mạng even sent an edict to the Cambodian "barbarian king" (*phiên vương*) imposing a reform of military practices upon Cambodian soldiers. They were now to be trained according to the Vietnamese "law of battle array," rather than adhere to the "lax" military formations of pre-conquest Cambodia.[45]

Of all the episodes of cultural conflict associated with the Vietnamese conquest of Cambodia whose data have survived, perhaps none illustrates Minh-mạng's self-aggrandizing Confucianism better than the Phnom Penh funeral crisis of early 1835. When Nak Ong Chan, his Cambodian vassal, died, Minh-mạng said to his Huế Privy Council:

"Among the customs of the country of Cambodia, there is a law that one shaves one's head in going into mourning. Now many barbarian [Cambodian] officials have already received the bureaucratic commissions of this court. All the Cambodian soldiers have already been enrolled into ranks in our army . . . "

[The emperor gave orders to Trương Minh Giảng, the protector of Cambodia, saying] "You must secretly and personally investigate if [this custom] can be stopped. At your leisure you ought to tell the barbarian bureaucrats in a casual way, but with the conviction of logic, that 'Your barbarian king has unfortunately passed away. All the requirements of mourning—an escorted funeral to the grave, the wearing of mourning garments, and cremation— should all be allowed to be performed according to your country's customs. Only when it comes to this one matter of shaving the head, during this period of frontier defense this ought not necessarily be carried out.' If they must consider this custom as one which repays the kindness [of their king] . . . then give way to what they wish."[46]

Once his influence had been extended over Cambodia by force of arms, Minh-mạng, as a supposedly charismatic Sino-Vietnamese Son of Heaven, required testimony that it was achieving results. Proof that he was an authentic culture hero whose example was inspiring to the peoples who knew him could hardly be found in a reformed Cambodian bureaucracy, serving under his aegis, which still preserved shaved heads. Even appearances must no longer be "Indianized."

In dealing with the weaker Cambodians, the Nguyễn court thus adopted the Chinese scheme of tributary relations—but added its own aggressive elaborations to it. The consequence was cultural as well as military aggression, which may well have tried to compensate for the fact that the real gap in sophistication between Vietnam and Cambodia was not as great as that between China and, say, the Mongols. In dealing with the stronger Siamese, however, the Vietnamese were forced to do the opposite—to dilute the manners and forms of their adopted Chinese scheme. Thus in neither instance did Chinese concepts and practices of international relations remain unchanged in substance after the Vietnamese had borrowed them. Great dexterity was required even to salvage all the ingrained continuity of their terminology.

In sum, in order to understand Vietnamese-Thai diplomacy in the early 1800's, it is necessary to remember the dominance, on both sides, of four interrelated features of Southeast Asian history which had exercised no influence at all upon the genesis of Vietnam's borrowed principles of Chinese Confucian statecraft. First, the coexisting

cultural models which Southeast Asian societies had domesticated—Chinese, Indian, Islamic—were heterogeneous in nature, having lit-
② tle in common with each other. Second, these diverse cultural models nonetheless all required absolute loyalty to their own ideological premises and mythologies in the political relationships they antici-
③ pated. Third, this requirement of ideological conformity in political relationships was almost artificially exaggerated by the fact that Southeast Asian courts, with long frontiers, numerically small ruling elites, and an alien merchant class dominating their commerce, could not afford the cultural and political self-confidence that the truly ego-
④ centric Peking rulers exhibited. But fourth, these diverse models' requirements of conformity were unlikely to be satisfied even symbolically in diplomatic relations. Few of the culturally dissimilar courts could successfully impose projections of the inner structure of their institutions upon their neighbors.

As a consequence, normal features of the interaction between the Vietnamese Confucian Son of Heaven and the Siamese Indian-style divine king in the 1700's and 1800's included (1) recurrent wars, (2) a volume of inter-court communications, often of the "messages to the unenlightened" category, that seemed heavy by Chinese standards, (3) a double view of the opposite court designed to accommodate both ideological and practical needs, and (4) certain tacit techniques of compromise. This brief sketch of episodes in Huế-Bangkok relations in the early 1800's which follows may suggest certain themes that any future historical theories of traditional Southeast Asian international relations should consider.

First of all, the Vietnamese court's double view of Siam should be considered. The first Vietnamese image of Siam in the early 1800's was the official one, required to buttress the Vietnamese domestication of the hierarchical Chinese world view. Its tenor was perhaps best expressed in the "biography" of Siam which appeared in one of the court's major historical compilations. This proposed: "This country's customs and disposition are strong and violent, and cunning and deceitful as well. [The Siamese] are experienced in sea warfare . . . Many men and women become monks and nuns, and eat only vegetables and do penance . . . Their climate is uneven, alternating between vapors and heat, and their land is low-lying and damp. All the people live in two-storey houses without beds or chairs. The men cut their hair and let it grow."[47]

Thus the nearby Siamese had to be depicted officially as being uncultured, irrational, and exotic. Even their climate had to be described the way the Chinese would describe it, distantly, although it was no different from Vietnam's own. Tendencies like these reached their height when Minh-mạng told his startled officials, in 1839, that centuries back the Siamese had required the Cambodians to send them a yearly tribute of twenty human bowels.[48] And in late 1826, the emperor, in the best Chinese fashion, had read a group of visiting Siamese envoys to Huế moral lessons about how to govern their country. Vietnamese documents record, Chinese fashion, that the Siamese envoys "sighingly acquiesced." When the envoys informed Minh-mạng that the purpose of their visit was to report the death of the Siamese king's grandmother (hardly the real purpose), Minh-mạng replied, "Up until now your country has been partly harmonized by the principles of propriety but partly not harmonized by the principles of propriety. Giving thanks for the favor of superiors is a principle of [inter-state] propriety, but reporting mourning is not."[49]

The other image of Siam, the unofficial but more serious one, was of course more complex. As early as 1810, Nguyễn envoys to Bangkok had codified geographical and military information about Siam. They had drawn a map of Siam (no longer extant) and had described six separate travel routes in use between south Vietnam and Siam. These travel routes also encompassed Siamese-ruled parts of the Malay peninsula, coastal islands of the Gulf of Siam, and islands of the west coast of Malaya. In their work the envoys recorded that Chiangmai in north Siam (*Xương mại mương*) was garrisoned by about 5,000 Vientiane troops. They described Bangkok (*Vọng Các*) as being a southwest-facing, tortoise-shaped city about two li long and one li broad, with many temples and merchants. But they made little mention of its Chinese population being allowed to live among the Siamese. This was of interest to the culturally sensitive Minh-mạng two decades later. It was not of interest to Gia-long's military men or their lower class informants.[50]

The first Nguyễn image of Siam, the Sino-Vietnamese one, was ideologically sponsored and remained stable and unchanging throughout the early 1800's. If it had not remained stable, the court might have lost much of its artificially cultivated sense of identity.

But the existence of this first picture of Siam permitted only a very murky crystallization of the second image, which was more concerned with presenting information about the Siamese as they actually were. Thus, although the Huế bureaucracy received a continuing stream of data about Siam, little attempt was made to organize this data or to accumulate intelligence. Sometimes information about Siam was supplied by Vietnamese who lived in Hà Tiên, which was then almost a cultural no-man's-land on the Siamese and Cambodian borders. (Siamese ships frequently came to Hà Tiên. The court exempted from all taxation those whose cargoes were 80 percent or more rice.)[51] One native of Hà Tiên, the enterprising Nguyễn Văn Xung, for example, had lived in Siam for more than thirty years. He returned to Vietnam in 1838. When he was desperately questioned by the Nguyễn court, he described the Siamese king, the people of Bangkok, the arsenals of Bangkok, the markets of Bangkok, Siamese geography ("about 15 days' travel" from Chiangmai to the sea coast), Siamese trade with the West, and Christianity in Siam. In 1838 Xung estimated that more than two thousand Chinese in Siam were Christians. But the depth of the Nguyễn court's ignorance about its greatest Southeast Asian rival was revealed by the questions it asked him. For example: "[Question:] Does the Siamese government employ Siamese people exclusively, or a mixture of races, including people of Chinese descent and actual Chinese? At the moment, who is chief official?" "[Answer:] Of the major Siamese government posts, most are filled by Siamese. Among them there are Chinese and people of Chinese descent who merely occupy subordinate positions. Of the Siamese officials, I only know Phạt Lăng [the Chaophraya Phrakhlang, an official who was in charge of both the department of the south and the department of foreign affairs at Bangkok; he had led a Siamese naval force against Hà Tiên in 1833]. He is the most intractable and possesses the most authority. The Buddha king believes in him and loves him."[52]

On the whole, the Sino-Vietnamese court's need, based on its domestication of the Chinese model, publicly to exaggerate the importance of its own position in international politics, led not so much to the distortion of Vietnamese information about Siam as to the retardation of its acquisition. Privately, Siam was regarded more realistically as an equal. The formulas of the written diplomatic correspondence that was exchanged between the Vietnamese and Siamese rulers suggested equality. Yet Vietnamese Confucian historians copied such correspondence into the dynasty's official records. According to the letters in the Nguyễn archives which have survived, the Siamese ruler addressed the Vietnamese Confucian emperor as "the Buddha king of the Vietnam country" (*Việt Nam Quốc Phật vương* when transcribed).[53] The Huế court accepted this term. Another indication of Huế's practical determination to preserve good relations came in 1809. Gia-long received a letter in classical Chinese from the Bangkok court. The letter, being unusually arrogant (in Vietnamese eyes), deserved to be rejected. But Gia-long was agile enough to invoke an attitude of cultural superiority as a means of accepting the letter and maintaining the peace. The Siamese, he said, could not write Chinese characters. Therefore the letter must have been composed by Bangkok Chinese.[54]

Finding a framework for diplomatic relations which would accommodate the cultural differences between the tensely balanced "Indianized" world of Bangkok and the "sinicized" world of Huế was never easy. In 1820 Minh-mạng sent an embassy to Bangkok to announce Gia-long's death and his own succession. The mission was led by Bùi Đức Mân, an official of the Board of Rites, who took with him cinnamon, sugar, cloth, and gems as gifts for Rama II. Thus it was Mân's task to uphold, far from the citadel walls of Huế, some of the pretensions of the Vietnamese Son of Heaven as a universal monarch. At the same time he had to adjust to his Siamese hosts. On this occasion Rama II received him warmly and informed him (according to Vietnamese records) that it was a Siamese custom to make a generous gift of gold to the bereaved—namely, Minh-mạng himself. In Bangkok Mân was pressed into accepting this principle. When he returned to Huế, however, he had to face Minh-mạng's fury.[55]

Siamese envoys ultimately came to Saigon and Huế in the same year with their promised gift of gold. They also brought with them a miscellany of other presents, including gold spittoons and gold opium pipes. These were intercepted by Lê Văn Duyệt at Saigon. He noti-

fied the Nguyễn court that (1) the presents were of the kind which
Siamese kings gave to their own nobles, (2) a Siamese court docu-
ment had accompanied the presents, declaring that Rama II was
Minh-mạng's senior as a ruler. The question of rejection or accep-
tance of the Siamese gifts now precipitated a hot debate at Huế. In
Peking, such a debate could have had only one outcome. In Huế, it
resulted in a deadlock of opinions, among high officials like Nguyễn
Văn Nhân and Lê Bá Phẩm. Minh-mạng therefore returned the
issue unresolved to Duyệt in Saigon. Duyệt sent the presents back to
Bangkok, together with a letter to the Chaophraya Phrakhlang
scolding him for violating protocol in claiming Rama II's seniority.
All these maneuvers between the representatives of the two courts
had taken place at Saigon, not Huế. But once the crisis was ended
the Siamese envoys journeyed to Huế. There they were cordially
received by the emperor as if nothing had happened.[56] The very
existence of these bicultural intrigues, which undermined the court's
prestige, had had to be kept at arm's length from the capital.

Rama II died in 1824. When Siamese envoys arrived in Vietnam
to announce this fact, Minh-mạng suspended the business of the
Vietnamese court for three days of formal mourning. His real motive
was that of one Southeast Asian ruler among several. Unless he
performed such ceremonies, Siamese courts would not reciprocate
when Vietnamese emperors died. But he was careful to find a rationalization for this deed that was unimpeachably Sino-Vietnamese.
The Chinese Sung court, he told his officials, had once suspended its
business when a ruler of the Hsi Hsia, "a small country," had passed
away.[57]

In brief, the Southeast Asian pattern of substantively equal multicourt diplomacy and the Sino-Vietnamese tradition of hierarchical
tributary relations intermingled in Vietnam in a thousand complicated ways. Disentangling and identifying their many elements is
one of the prerequisites for understanding the Nguyễn court's outlook
upon the world. By the 1840's, Vietnamese politicians had entered a
period of painful encounters with the wholly alien civilization of
western Europe. It is just possible that enough subterranean deviations from Sino-Vietnamese norms of statesmanship were present in
this outlook to give Vietnamese diplomacy an inner dynamic that in
time—if the deviations had accumulated—might have produced

profound change. Time was never granted. Through military weakness independence was to be lost as soon as the 1870's. But it was noteworthy that Minh-mạng sent a diplomatic mission to France in 1840. It was also noteworthy that the Vietnamese Confucian official of the 1840's who affected to condemn Siam on Chinese-style cultural grounds was easily replaced in the 1860's by men like the Catholic Vietnamese scholar, Nguyễn Trường Tộ, who admired Siam, not China, as a model for Vietnam: "Let us look at the example of Siam, which is indeed no larger and no stronger than our own country. However, when it engaged in contact with Westerners, that country knew how to wake up to reality immediately . . . That country does not have to defend its borders and rights and still is able to be respected as though it were a world power . . . Siam merely relies upon foreign relations and nothing else, but foreign relations further allow that country to become daily stronger and more prosperous . . . When they [the Siamese] have reached an extremely high level of development, we have come to our senses extremely slowly."[58]

The ambivalences of the traditional Nguyễn diplomatic system had provided a background for such an exhortation. They made it less revolutionary in Vietnam than it would have been in the mouth of a Chinese official of the same decade.

The Nguyễn Court's Approaches to Foreign Trade

Actually, the Western threat to Sino-Vietnamese complacency in external relations had been foreshadowed for centuries. The Portuguese were probably the first Europeans to visit central Vietnam in significant numbers. They set up shops at Hội-an (Faifo) in Quảng Nam in the sixteenth century, and their entrepot subsequently attracted Chinese, Japanese, and Dutch traders.[59] In 1614, apparently, the Portuguese built a gun-casting foundry for the Nguyễn rulers in the vicinity of nineteenth-century Huế. In northern Vietnam, the Dutch were the dominant Europeans of this early period of contact. In 1637 the Trịnh rulers invited them to open an entrepot at Phố-hiến (near the heart of modern Hưng Yên). Japanese, Chinese, and Siamese merchants flocked to Phố-hiến, forming an international trading center of two thousand "rooftops" or more which inspired the proverb, "the capital is number one, Phố-hiến is number two." With the spread of civil war in Vietnam between the north and the center, the Dutch supported the Trịnh while their rivals, the Portuguese, supported the Nguyễns.

What was considered to be the subversive behavior of the European missionaries who followed the merchants to Vietnam eventually doomed this early commercial interaction. Christianity was banned by the Nguyễn court in 1631, by the Trịnh court in 1663. Missionaries were executed at Đà Nẵng as early as 1644. In 1696 a Trịnh ruler burned Christian texts, and in 1712 another Trịnh ruler seized Vietnamese Christians in the north and carved the words "student of Dutch religion" on their foreheads. Remarkably, despite these executions and bans, underground Christianity flourished. Although Alexandre de Rhodes, the Avignon Jesuit who served in Vietnam in 1624–1630 and 1640–1645, commented that Vietnamese peasants would blame "the new sorcerers" (the Christian priests) for such things as unexpected droughts which ruined harvests,[60] Vietnamese still split into two camps, "the good and the religious" (*bên lương bên giáo*) as a result of the tenacity of Christianity. Vietnamese rulers' desire for European trade diminished as Vietnamese Christianity grew.

European pressures began to make themselves felt again under Gia-long. Several times, beginning in 1803, English missions visited Huế and requested the establishment of a trading entrepot at Trà-sơn in Quảng Nam. They were rebuffed. A French warship visited Đà Nẵng in 1817. It requested that Gia-long implement a treaty of 1787 (concluded when he needed French military aid against the Tây-sơns) allowing France privileges at Đà Nẵng and Poulo Condore. Because France had never observed its role in this treaty, Gia-long rejected it, despite the presence of French advisers at his court. Of these French advisers, none was closer to the emperor than J. B. Chaigneau. When Louis XVIII appointed Chaigneau France's first consul in Vietnam in 1820, he ordered him to secure a commercial treaty between Paris and Huế. But Chaigneau's very effectiveness as an adviser to the Nguyễn court sprang from the fact that he had married a Vietnamese wife and had personally succumbed to Vietnamese culture. Consequently, a French naturalist, Diard, who visited the Far East at this time, wrote that Chaigneau was "very timid," an apostle of "Cochinchinese etiquette," too much of a mandarin to advance France's interests.[61] No commercial treaty was forthcoming.

It is necessary to examine the Vietnamese attitudes and institutions which lay behind the vicissitudes of European commerce in Vietnam. The Vietnamese emperor, in ruling through a Chinese-style bureaucracy, was forced to borrow and domesticate the Chinese world view. Perhaps his imitation of it was initially purer and more consistent when he dealt with remote European countries than it was when he dealt with closer, more familiar Southeast Asian rivals. Borrowing the concepts of the Chinese tributary system, he also borrowed its terminology. Thus most of the inadequate, exotic Chinese terms for European countries had a second vogue, this time in Sino-Vietnamese dress, at the Huế court. France was called *Phú-lăng-sa*, a variant of the Chinese *Fo-lang-hsi*. England, on the other hand, was often represented in Vietnamese court records as *Anh-cát-lợi-mao quốc*. This was a fantastically piebald concoction which actually linked two common Chinese terms for the English together; it offered a good example of Vietnam's determinedly composite cultural borrowing from China. *Anh-cát-lợi* was a Vietnamization of the Chinese phonetic equivalent for "English," *Ying-chi-li*. *Mao* was the second half of the pejorative term for the English in use in both Peking and Huế, *Hồng-mao*, "Red Hairs." Thus the general effect of the formal Nguyễn term for England was "English-hairs country."[62]

Side by side with such a use of borrowed Chinese terminology at the Vietnamese court, there ran a Chinese-style suspicion of the culture and the motives of the Europeans. As early as 1804, Gia-long privately informed his court that the English were cunning and deceitful, that they "are not of our race," and that they could not be allowed to reside in Vietnam.[63] Furthermore, recurrent European requests for commercial treaties were regarded with deep suspicion. In the Sino-Vietnamese outlook, it was not credible that trade could ever constitute a diplomatic end in itself. In 1830, the court believed that the English were planning to invade Kwangtung. And it quite gratuitously interpreted overt English requests for trade with Vietnam at this time as covert attempts to persuade the Vietnamese not to aid the Chinese in any Anglo-Chinese war.[64]

There was, however, this difference between the Chinese and Vietnamese courts: the Vietnamese court definitely desired trade with Europeans, provided it could manage such trade on its own terms. It had no Chinese-style illusions that Vietnam was economically self-sufficient or that trade was merely a favor conferred upon deserving barbarians. Its own terms meant, of course, a narrowly limited number of ports for the trade, heavy bureaucratic taxation of the trade, and prohibitions of the export of basic Vietnamese commodities like rice, silk, and metals used for imperial coinages. Nonetheless, any reader of Vietnamese documents of 1820 will find Minh-mạng publicly gloating over Vietnam's bountiful sugar crops, declaring that "Westerners are fond of" sugar and that it is useful in trade, because sugar is not essential to warding off famine or clothing the people when they are cold.[65]

Direct court control of trade with Western merchant ships took shape with the creation of a Merchant Superintendency (*Thương bạc ty*), at Huế. In name it was a Vietnamese version of similar institutions which had existed in China for centuries and which had been introduced into Vietnam by the Ming conquerors of 1406. Until 1830, at the end of every year the Nguyễn Merchant Superintendency sent its officials to Hanoi, Saigon, and Quảng Nam to check the merchant taxes which had been collected there by local officials. After 1830, however, its officials remained in the capital. Local officials were required to transmit annual statistical reports.[66] In the 1830's, domestic rebellions and an increasingly vigorous repression of Christianity led, against the dynasty's wishes, to a drying up of trade. The result was the bureaucratic eclipse of the Merchant Superintendency. Its greater importance in the previous decades had been indicated by the fact that the most illustrious high officials at court had managed it. After 1832 local officials and the Board of Finance were charged with the administration of the tax collections accruing from external trade, and underlings at the Merchant Superintendency were reassigned to other offices.[67]

But although the Merchant Superintendency was eclipsed, other trends in the bureaucracy pointed the other way, toward a growth in emphasis of contacts with the West. Three Western missionaries, Gabelin, Taberd, and Odorico, were employed at Huế from 1826 to

1828 as interpreters and translators. A fourth, Father Jaccard (executed 1838), worked at Huế from 1829 to 1833. He apparently supplied Minh-mạng with translated accounts of the French Revolution, Napoleon, and the English conquest of India.[68] In 1827 the court formed its own corps of Vietnamese interpreters. It ordered them to study Cantonese, Siamese and Lao as well as Western languages. They were known as the "Office of traveling deputies" (*Hành nhân ty*).[69] In 1835 the major diplomatic hostel at Huế was converted into a new Translation Office (*Tứ dịch quán*). It represented both an expansion and a consolidation of previous attempts to foster the development of interpreters, but it emphasized Western languages and Cambodian. In discussing its purpose with one of his officials, Minh-mạng commented that he wanted multilingual specialists "simply for the purpose of preparing our replies to foreign countries, but nothing else." He suggested that overly impressionable students at the Office be warned that "Our country basically follows the teachings of Confucius and Mencius."[70]

The dynasty, in other words, wanted and expected intercourse with the West but simultaneously feared Western military aggression and religious proselytization. More receptive than the Ch'ing court to the benefits of Western commerce, it was perhaps far less certain that it could withstand the undesired pressures that accompanied them. Hence it moved inconclusively between the two extremes of a closed country policy (*chính sách bế môn tỏa cảng*, more literally, "close the gates and lock the harbor") and what were later to be called "bread and milk studies" (*học bánh tây sữa bò*)—that is, the study of the culture of Westerners, renowned for their milk drinking. It never really fully espoused either. Its uncertainty was especially demonstrated in the autumn of 1835, when the Board of War sent instructions to the provinces of Quảng Nam, Bình Định, Khánh Hòa, Bình Thuận, Biên Hòa, and Gia Định about "large Western ships." The moment one anchored in Vietnamese waters, the instructions read, seaport officials were to board it with an interpreter or "a Chinese who is well versed in Western languages." They were to ascertain the ship's port of origin, its architectural style, its national flag, the size of its crew, and whether it was a merchant ship or a warship. If it was a merchant ship it was to be "managed as usual" and taxed. If it was a warship it was to be surrounded by war junks, while "flying communications" were sent to neighboring provinces to alert them to the need for defensive preparations.[71]

But ship identification was a new and difficult art. In 1825 a Vietnamese government junk in the capital city anchorage was mistaken by harbor officials for a Western ship.[72] Ten years later local officials along the coast falsely identified a government grain junk as a French merchant ship.[73] One cause of this confusion was the failure of coastal officials to obey Minh-mạng's decree that they use the new telescopes with which the court had supplied them. Despite these errors, cultural familiarity with the behavior of Western ships and their crews undoubtedly grew in Vietnam in the 1820's and 1830's. When Minh-mạng made an imperial tour of Quảng Nam in 1825, he received a 21-gun salute from a Western merchant ship. Although this strange Western custom was notorious for scandalizing officials in Ch'ing China, Minh-mạng understood the significance of it perfectly. He ordered "oxen and wine" to be supplied to the ship which had greeted him.[74] In fact, by 1837 the firing of cannon as salutes had become so comprehensively adopted in Vietnam that a code had evolved for regulating such rituals when government junks entered and left Đà Nẵng and Thuận An (at Huế). A junk that was entering Thuận An would now fire a three-cannon salute and receive an answering one from the shore.[75]

It has been said that the Nguyễn court was receptive to trade. But it did not adopt a merely passive role, waiting for Western ships to come to Vietnam. During the colonial period it was common for French students of Vietnamese history to assert that Vietnamese had not been allowed to leave their country in Minh-mạng's reign in order to participate in international trade.[76] French eyewitnesses of the reign itself knew better. Eugène Chaigneau, who was posted to Vietnam in 1825 and 1830 in two unsuccessful attempts to become French consul there, observed in 1832 that Vietnamese junks regularly visited Singapore, Malacca, and Penang and even rarely sailed as far as India.[77] Nguyễn records suggest as much. In 1836, four officials who had been sent on missions by government junk to the Indonesian archipelago were disgraced when they returned to Đà Nẵng with opium and Christian texts. But this offense was a common one in the 1830's. After 1836, when government junks returned to

Đà Nẵng, the Boards of Finance and Public Works and the Censorate were all required to have representatives in the port who could "jointly confer and investigate" the junks. Crews were not allowed ashore until the junks had been inspected.[78]

More legislation of the Minh-mạng period exemplifying the court's concern with its own overseas trading excursions came in 1840–41. A system was set up which rigidly defined time limits for capital city officials to leave and return to their regular bureaucratic positions, if they were being sent on a sea voyage. A capital city bureaucrat who was being sent to India, for example, could leave his position twenty days before the start of his trip and was given fifteen days to resume his post after he had returned. One who was being sent to the Philippines or to France (considered to be equally distant from Huế) was only allowed an interregnum of fifteen days before the voyage and ten days after it. A Huế bureaucrat who was sailing to and from Singapore was merely given ten days and five days leave respectively.[79] Such bureaucratization of travel leaves is revealing. Overseas travel had become almost commonplace by 1840.

What, however, happened to the commodities which the government junks imported? By and large, these commodities were regarded as elite luxury goods. Most of them were destined immediately for the court itself. There they were stored in the treasuries of the Office of Household Affairs (*Nội vụ phủ*) of the emperor. In name and function this office imitated a similar one (Chinese, *Nei-wu-fu*) which had been created at Peking under the Manchus. Its purpose was to control the income and expenditures of the imperial family. In Vietnam it was subdivided into nine treasuries or storehouses. In them, varieties of textiles, gold and silver, wax (for candles), porcelain, glass, and drugs were deposited and accumulated separately.[80] Primitive hoarding was not the real purpose of such accumulations. Rather, it was a policy of maintaining reserve savings of elite goods at the capital. In this way, the emperor could dispense such goods as rewards, gifts, or remuneration to officials and tributary envoys. With such goods he could also finance the needs of provincial administrations. In 1838, for example, the office issued 900 rolls of satin to the treasuries of twenty-one provinces and thousands of rolls of white cloth to fourteen more provinces.[81] The initial centralization of such goods represented fiscal and therefore political power.

Trade with the West allowed Minh-mạng to elaborate and diversify these reserve holdings of elite articles of conspicuous consumption. This, of course, meant that such trade buttressed his power. An 1837 inventory of some of the possessions of his nine household treasuries at Huế has survived. It describes varieties of blue and gold and silver "Western" satins and cottons, gives their precise dimensions, and cites plans for making uniforms out of them.[82] In fact, by 1837 these household treasuries had been ordered to store and evaluate "Western silver," especially Philippine dollars, and to work out a rate of exchange for it with Vietnamese coinages.[83] One expression of the heightened power of patronage the Vietnamese court gained with its importation of Western goods was also offered in this same year, 1837, when Minh-mạng rewarded Nguyễn army officers serving in Cambodia with "Western" cotton shirts.[84] In this atmosphere, the cultivation of a taste for Western products spread slowly downward through Nguyễn society from the throne itself. It was Minh-mạng who set the example in 1835 when he proudly introduced his court officials to "Western anti-cold liquor," probably French brandy. Earlier, in the Gia-long period, J. B. Chaigneau had characteristically written to French friends of his in India, requesting them to send him wines which he could present to certain Huế mandarins.[85]

Above all, Vietnamese trade with the West, although never more than a trickle, fitted smoothly into an interesting if historically elusive Southeast Asian trading network. In this network, the seaboard country (Vietnam) exchanged maritime imports (like Western goods) which the landlocked inner kingdoms in Laos and Cambodia could not get, for products of the Southeast Asian interior (especially Laotian elephants) which were less plentiful or non-existent in Vietnam. The exchange itself often took place as reciprocal "gift-giving" within the context of Vietnam's fragile tributary system. Thus in 1833 Minh-mạng was found bestowing "Western" bowls, plates, and cups upon some Cambodian envoys to Huế. In 1834 the sorcerers of the Jarai received Western porcelain tea dishes, and in 1846 Thiệu-trị gave them "Western" red and white cotton narrow-sleeved jackets.[86] There was even a discernible historical trend. In the 1820's, Chinese commodities had predominated in the "gifts" the Huế court made to its clients and friends, but in the 1830's Western goods became more prominent. This was not a clear-cut change. Minh-mạng had been giving Western muskets to the ruler of Vientiane, Anu, as early as 1821.[87]

Essentially, then, the pattern in Minh-mạng's Vietnam was experimental adoption of selected items of Western culture without recourse to more direct Western contact than was necessary. This was a contradiction. But it was one that revealed a quality of response to the West which was lacking in China of the 1830's, where Ch'ing emperors usually more consistently declined both adoption and contact. And the slightly different Vietnamese response, like almost everything else in the Nguyễn world of the early 1800's, was produced by conflict between Chinese-type cultural determinism (Westerners were "barbarians") and the Southeast Asian environment. For centuries mainland Southeast Asia had been a meetingplace of merchants and travelers. Its geographical barriers and its lack of ethnic and cultural homogeneity had prevented the formation of one or two strong indigenous states sufficiently able to keep foreigners and foreign ideas out of its coastal entrepots. Here there could be no Nagasaki or Canton one-port trade systems, despite the Vietnamese court's attempt to confine Westerners and their trade to Đà Nẵng. Under Minh-mạng, even the most culturally orthodox Vietnamese officials were less perfect seclusionists than their Peking contemporaries. As inveterate cultural borrowers, they had to admire certain Western commodities, although they also found them meretricious. The xenophobic Vũ Đức Khuê commented in 1840: "Of all the Western products, for sheer beauty of appearance nothing is better than their glass. But it is a substance which rapidly is ruined, and one cannot use it for a long time."[88]

Even opium was never linked exclusively to the malevolence of Westerners. It is true that some court officials believed that the great plague epidemic of 1820 had come to Vietnam from the West. But when Minh-mạng renewed the ban on the consumption, hoarding, or sale of opium in Vietnam in the autumn of this year, stipulating even that sons and younger brothers who did not report opium-smoking fathers and older brothers would be punished, he classified opium merely as "a poisonous substance that comes from foreign countries."[89] The reason for Vietnam's failure to infer Western aggression from the spread of opium as readily as the Ch'ing court inferred it was simple. In Southeast Asia, Chinese merchants rather than British and American ones were the pernicious opium carriers of the budding "age of imperialism." Before 1839, for example, one established practice of "Ch'ing junks" in northern Vietnam was to sail up the Red River to Hanoi. Because Nguyễn tax inspectors did not board the junks at Nam Định, their first port of call, but waited for them in Hanoi, they were able surreptitiously to unload profitable cargoes of opium in the countryside as they went from Nam Định to Hanoi. Only at the end of Minh-mạng's reign were all incoming Chinese junks intercepted at Nam Định first and forced to produce written itemized lists of their cargoes.[90] But the activities of Chinese retailers of opium in Vietnam continued elsewhere and in different guises.

In the last analysis, the court found it impossible to suppress this Chinese-dominated opium traffic. And the reason was extremely instructive. The overseas Chinese merchant community in Vietnam constituted one of the foundations of the court's whole structure of foreign trade. As has been shown, this community was divided formally and informally into two groups, partly assimilated Chinese who were known as Minh-hương or "Ming loyalists" and unassimilated Chinese who lived in "congregations" (*bang*) of their own with their own headmen (*bang trưởng*). Before 1802, Minh-hương villages could be found in Quảng Nam (Hội An), Biên Hoà, and Gia Định. After 1802, they spread to the north. The more autonomous Chinese "congregations," usually differentiated by Chinese provincial origin, were found in the northern border provinces, in Hanoi, and in the south. In a Tự-đức era survey of seven districts of the province of Biên Hoà, for example, the Vietnamese geographer Nguyễn Siêu found 408 Vietnamese villages and 7 Chinese "congregations."[91] Neither the Chinese "congregations" nor the Minh-hương villages were as culturally introverted and as residentially stable as they might have seemed. Following the southern rebellions of 1840–41 and the Vietnamese military withdrawal from Cambodia, a bureaucratic census of these settlements in the province of Hà Tiên revealed that only 62 of the original 315 inhabitants of 6 Chinese "congregations" had "returned" to their homes following the disturbances, and only 86 Minh-hương of a recorded original population of 330 in 4 Minh-hương villages.[92]

Sons and grandsons of "congregation" Chinese who had been born in Vietnam, who were adult, and who did not shave their heads and wear queues could become Minh-hương. If there were no Minh-hương villages in the provinces where they lived, if there were five or more of them wishing to become Minh-hương they could form their own village. Otherwise they continued to live in the "congregation" but were separately recorded in the court's Chinese-style tax registers as Minh-hương. This meant that they could enter the Vietnamese examination system and become bureaucrats. Moreover, crews or Chinese passengers of Chinese junks in Saigon or other ports who wished to emigrate to Vietnam had to be formally guaranteed both by "congregation" headmen and by Minh-hương village leaders.

To the Vietnamese peasant, the overseas Chinese merchant who lived in Vietnam but still followed Ch'ing China clothing styles seemed a mystifying oddity, a figure of fun. He neither wore a sash nor admired and wore long hair, two prerequisites for maintaining self-decency in traditional Vietnamese society. A southern folksong dating from this period satirically criticized the Vietnamese woman who married a Chinese merchant: "Her lover disdains her long hair which touches all the way to the ground. And she must caress a Chinaman (*thằng Chệt*) whose skull is blank on all four sides. On the top of his head he braids his hair as if it were the tail of a lizard. His shining white teeth have never chewed betel. When you think about the Chinaman it makes you all the sadder, he only has one head but he doesn't leave it as nature intended. If his hair grows he shaves it off immediately . . . He wears trousers that lack a sash and a jacket that only goes half-way down and looks as awkward as the tail of a water buffalo."[93]

Nonetheless, this folk song betrayed uneasiness as well as scorn. Historically it is important to realize that it was the Vietnamese court, almost as much as Chinese parochialism, that fostered Chinese separateness in south Vietnam. The contrast with the Chinese in Siam is obvious. The Siamese, further removed themselves from Chinese culture, had less reason to fear being completely sinicized by the living examples and influences of the Chinese among them. Thus they lacked the need to discriminate as much against their overseas Chinese community as did the Vietnamese. The Siamese also, ironically, lacked some of the means of discrimination. For the Vietnamese court very skillfully applied the borrowed techniques of Chinese bureaucratism to the purpose of keeping Chinese in Vietnam segregated.

The Chinese merchant class in Vietnam was a formidable pillar of the Vietnamese trading economy. Chinese merchant and fishing fleets swarmed into Vietnamese waters. The court was accustomed to the alien-dominated shipping world at its doorstep. Diplomatic tributary relations between Peking and Huế were never involved with this maritime trade. Vietnamese bureaucrats freely inflicted the most severe taxation upon Chinese junks without a word of protest from Ch'ing officials; trade and politics were never integrated. Chinese junks from different Chinese provinces were even often identified by local officials at Vietnamese ports as coming from various "countries" (*quốc*) because their dialects and cargoes differed. There was no consciousness either on their part or on the Vietnamese part of any association of theirs with the Peking court. Below the elite, court level there were a number of fragmentary Chinas in Vietnamese eyes; and it was only the court and its scholars who commanded diplomatic respect. Meanwhile, Chinese traders living in "congregations" in Vietnam had to retain organic connections with Chinese merchants in south China if the Sino-Southeast Asian trade they controlled was to thrive. Thus they could never allow themselves to become completely assimilated by or completely alienated from either of the two groups, Chinese and Vietnamese, with whom they traded. They required ties with both. It was here that the motives of Vietnam-based Chinese for remaining separate from the Vietnamese came into play: if they even became Minh-hương, their function as practicing commercial middlemen was threatened.

To make one final theoretical generalization about the role of overseas Chinese in Nguyễn trade, in China itself much of the merchant class was socially transitional. Merchants invested in land, and used their wealth to see that their sons or grandsons became, not merchants, but scholar-officials. It is at least a tenable working hypothesis, however, that many Chinese merchant families in Vietnam may have constituted a more formidable permanent social class there than they would have in China. As aliens, their sons were denied access to the Nguyễn bureaucracy, unless they became Minh-hương. Many did so. But the process was difficult. Entrenched Chinese merchant houses in Vietnam, denied the customary Chinese alternatives to commercial success as ways in which to win vocational and status advancement, thus gave weaker indigenous Vietnamese merchants (who also lacked their connections in south China) overwhelming competition.

The system of taxation which the Vietnamese court applied to Western merchant ships visiting Vietnam after 1802 had actually been created bureaucratically with Chinese shipping in mind, not Western. The miscellany of taxes which foreign ships had to pay included both harbor taxes (*cảng thuế*) and "proprieties money" (*lẽ-tiền*). If foreign ships wanted to buy and carry away Vietnamese "precious commodities," like ivory, cinnamon, pepper, or sapanwood, they also had to pay a "goods tax" (*hoá thuế*) as well as the buying price. Gold, silver, rice, copper, salt, and certain kinds of textiles were "forbidden commodities" which could not be legally carried away at all.[94] Chinese junks from Kwangtung, Fukien, and Shanghai, along with Western merchant ships, paid the largest assessments of harbor taxes and proprieties money. But junks from Ch'ao-chou prefecture in Kwangtung province were required to pay only 75 percent of the taxes other Kwangtung junks paid. This bureaucratic patchwork was made even more elaborate with the inclusion of special categories for Hainan Island junks. They paid the smallest taxes of all.[95] Sometimes Vietnamese calculations ostensibly took Chinese internal affairs into account, taxing junks on the basis of conditions in the province where they originated. In 1833, for example, the tax on Fukien junks was lowered, on the grounds that "their people are poor, commodities are expensive, and their ships that come here are few."[96]

Another feature of Vietnamese maritime trade taxation which confounded Westerners but was accepted by Chinese in the 1800's was its regional variations in Vietnam itself. A ship which called at Saigon was required to pay more taxes than one which called farther north at Quảng Nam. One which visited Quảng Nam paid more taxes than one which went even farther north to Nghệ An or Thanh Hóa. Furthermore, large junks were taxed far more heavily than small junks, regardless of cargo. It became increasingly disadvantageous to trade along the Vietnamese coast in large junks, which may have been discriminated against because of their military and piratical capabilities. Nguyễn tax officials who boarded a junk would measure it (using the official copper foot as a standard) from its bow to its stern. Standing at the median point of this measurement, they would then measure the width of the junk's hull. Its width decided its tax category.[97]

To enforce this complicated taxation, court officials who boarded Chinese junks were often accompanied by Minh-hương interpreters. Assimilated enough to be loyal to Huế but still Chinese enough to understand the language and customs of south Chinese junk crews, the Minh-hương interpreters were in fact charged with finding out if Hainan junks were really Hainan junks. Chinese junk captains from provincial ports in China susceptible to higher Vietnamese taxation knew Nguyễn regulations so well that they frequently pretended to come from Hainan or Ch'ao-chou when they did not.[98] The interpreters made out two clearance documents for each ship. One of them was attached to the ship's badge of origin, and the second one was sent to Huế. Two statements of the tax revenues accruing in the Huế area and three statements of the tax revenues of northern and southern ports were prepared and submitted to the throne in the tenth lunar month of every year. Disposition of these annual trade tax revenues was complicated. Ten percent went to the supervisor of shipping (*cai tào quan*), who was ultimately responsible for their collection. The remaining 90 percent was distributed among the princes and descendants of the imperial family, palace concubines, high military and civil officials, and even among the wives of former officials. Significantly, at least in the Gia-long period, military officials received twice as large a share of these revenues as civil officials.[99]

But the most important facet of the Vietnamese court's relationship with Chinese traders has yet to be stated. Westerners of the later 1800's conceived of China as a limitless market for their exports. Vietnamese rulers of the 1800's regarded China in just the opposite way. They saw it as a limitless cornucopia of desirable goods which they sought to import. But they were careful to import these goods indirectly. In the first and second lunar months of every year, Vietnamese local officials, under instructions from the Board of Finance, made formal visits to the Chinese junks trading in their administrative jurisdictions. They asked their captains if they wished to be placed under contract to the Nguyễn court. Those junk captains who were willing signed written agreements. These agreements, in turn, were certified and insured by the collective guarantees (*liên danh bảo kết*) of Chinese "congregation" headmen and Minh-hương leaders permanently resident in Vietnam.

After the Board of Finance had approved these agreements, the Chinese junk captains involved were given government funds (which did not exceed 20,000 *mân* in any instance) and lists of Chinese goods the Nguyễn court wished to import. They then sailed back to China, purchased the goods, and transported them to Vietnam. Their invoices, which they had to preserve, were immediately sent to Huế for inspection. The goods themselves were divided into two categories, "light" or fragile goods like silks and fresh fruits and "ordinary" goods like teas, drugs, incense, paper, dried fruits, bamboo chairs, and even bricks and tiles.[100] If any Chinese junk which had been commissioned by the court to import such Chinese goods defaulted or failed to return to Vietnam by the deadline of its commission, the "congregation" headmen and Minh-hương, who had formally guaranteed it, were forced to indemnify the court. This way, government funds were less often embezzled.[101]

Here was an impressive demonstration of the remarkable capacity for subterranean paradoxes in the relationship between China and Vietnam. The Vietnamese bureaucracy used Chinese-style contractual forms to harness the omnipresent Chinese shipping world at its doorstep and to induce Chinese ships to supply it with Chinese goods. That way, it could expand its commercial relations with China without actually entering into too suffocatingly close an interaction with the Chinese political order. Such an interaction might have undermined the independent position of the Huế Son of Heaven. Chinese bureaucratic forms, in brief, allowed the Nguyễn court to keep clear of the Chinese. They offered decisively valuable techniques for maintaining a measure of aloofness from China while simultaneously exploiting and enjoying the Chinese cultural and economic heritage. All that was required was the application of these techniques—mutual guarantees, bureaucratic inventories, and other documentation—to the alien Chinese merchant class living in Vietnam. Chinese officials in Peking believed that their "vassal kingdoms" were dependent upon them. Because they were unaware that Vietnamese tributary missions were only the surface expression of this dependence or that south Chinese junk captains could often be the actual commissioned agents of a Southeast Asian ruler, in some respects they may have underestimated the dependence of their Vietnamese "vassal."

In Vietnam, this pattern of indirect trade with China influenced the Sino-Vietnamese conduct of international relations. It ensured that the Nguyễn court's whole view of foreign trade would be dominated by the idea of employing bureaucratically controlled Chinese middlemen. This was exactly what happened. When Westerners arrived by ship in south Vietnam, for example, the Chinese "congregation" headmen were made responsible for them. They were allowed to live in Chinese overseas communities in Vietnam but not to leave them.[102] Thus the Chinese "congregations" were used to insulate Vietnamese from too extensive an acquaintance with Westerners. Eventually, however, it became a question of who controlled the middlemen. Western ships themselves were allowed to trade only at Đà Nẵng. Consequently, English merchants and their products began to travel to Vietnam regularly on Chinese junks. The merchants used Chinese services in this way in the obvious hope of eluding Nguyễn regulations about Western trade.[103]

As of the 1840's, therefore, it was the rigidity of the Nguyễn court's bureaucratic preconceptions about how foreign trade should be conducted, not its disinterest or lack of desire for it, that made Vietnam's adjustment to Western commercial penetration more difficult.

The Vietnamese Reaction to the Opium War

The outbreak of the hostilities of the Opium War between British and Chinese forces in Kwangtung in the autumn of 1839 had ramifications in Vietnam. In fact, Vietnamese documents suggest that historians should not persist in regarding this war or its background solely as a confrontation between the West and China alone. Certainly the Vietnamese part of classical East Asia was affected. But the cause of Vietnam's vulnerability to this war lay not in its overt vassalage to Peking so much as in its more covert bureaucratic and economic integration into the south Chinese commercial world, aspects of which have just been described.

In eighteenth-century Vietnam, copper and lead coins were the normal official media of commercial exchange. But there seems to have been a serious shortage of cash. This shortage became more acute after the Tây-sơn rebellion. The Tây-sơn emperors were accused in retrospect by the Nguyễn court of having minted coins "only at their convenience," rather than "without rest," like the Lê court, and of having allowed money in general to become dangerously scarce.[104] Such anti-Tây-sơn propaganda was, of course, predictable. But it is a historic fact that one of the phenomena of the Gia-long reign was a vast increase in the official circulation of silver, sponsored by the court and caused by the lack of enough regular copper and lead coins. In the Gia-long period, the market price of silver was probably lower than the officially fixed price.[105] The dynasty minted "Flying Dragon" silver coins (*Phi Long ngân tiền*; actually 80 percent silver, 20 percent lead) and used silver lavishly in the payment of salaries, the rewarding of soldiers, and the financing of official buying missions to Canton.[106]

But the market price of silver began to rise dramatically and inexorably in Vietnam in the Minh-mạng period. At the end of the Gia-long period, the official price of one silver tael had been less than three *mân* in dynastic currency. The market price of one silver tael in southern provinces in the early Thiệu-trị period had risen to nine *mân*. In other words, it was more than three times what the official price of one silver tael had been just twenty years before and nearly twice what the market price had been in the late 1820's.[107] Rising prices of most commodities were a feature of Vietnamese history after 1820. Yet the price of rice rose less fast than the prices of metals, and the prices of metals other than gold and silver rose less fast than the prices of gold and silver themselves.

Vietnamese silver production was concentrated in the mining heartland north of Hanoi, in provinces like Thái Nguyên. Usually the mines were developed by Chinese entrepreneurs. They paid taxes to Huế and occasionally sublet their mines to other Chinese. In official documents they were known as *khách trường*, "guest leaders." The Vietnamese court smiled on the revenues they supplied it, but its civil bureaucrats disliked these alien Chinese mining communities in the north. Evidence of local antagonism to the Chinese miners is found in a long 1834 memorial written by none other than Nguyễn Công Trứ, at that time a high provincial official in the north. Describing Chinese miners in northern provinces like Tuyên Quang, he declared that they owed debts, provoked quarrels, gathered to eat together in large groups of 700 or 800 men, violated geomantic sanctities by "boring through the earth's arteries," and went completely uncontrolled: "The numbers that enter [our country] have no relationship with there being or not being gold mines in every place."[108] But when he requested that Minh-mạng deport them to China, he was refused.

Partly because of its political and cultural organization, the Vietnamese economy depended upon alien miners. The governor-general of Sơn Tây, Hưng Hoá, and Tuyên Quang reported in 1832 that there was a shortage of Vietnamese mining artisans in his jurisdiction. He requested that Minh-mạng allow him to recruit such artisans from among those living in neighboring provinces. Instead, he was told to conscript inexperienced peasants from his own jurisdiction. Trans-provincial movements of indigenous labor were forbidden.[109] One invisible source of the costs of silver production in Vietnam in the 1830's, in other words, was the fact that the stability of the dynasty's tax registers, as well as the attachment of Vietnamese to their native villages, required the conscription of non-specialists within one small administrative area to meet that area's labor demands, rather than a flow of more specialized labor from other areas. Alien Chinese miners in Vietnam were popular with the court because, as a special temporary population, they were less subject to the rigid considerations of local tax registers and native villages.

Chinese domination of Vietnamese silver mines, both by entrepreneurs and by laborers, had important consequences. At least from the middle of the 1700's, when the Ch'ing historian Chao I documented it, China itself imported silver bullion extensively both from northern Vietnam and from Burma. China's own silver mines were becoming exhausted. By the 1800's, China may have been draining away more than two million taels of Vietnamese silver annually.[110] By the 1830's, the acute inflation of silver prices in Vietnam obviously stemmed from the fact that the demand for the metal was increasing far faster than its supply. Falling production of silver was one factor behind this. The court's extraordinary need to finance the pacification of the rebellions of the 1830's, as well as the conquest of Cambodia, was undoubtedly another. A third factor, however, was what produced a sense of economic crisis at the Nguyễn court. The rising value of silver in China was caused, among other things, by an outflow of silver to pay for Chinese opium imports from the British. It shifted the attention of Chinese merchants in Vietnam away from the Vietnamese commodities (ivory, lacquer, betel nuts, incense) they had traditionally exported back to China. Now they began illicitly to accumulate and export Vietnamese silver. Vietnamese silver in turn helped to pay for Chinese opium imports. In sum, Gia-long's attempt to reconstruct Vietnamese coinage, by increasing the use of silver in the payment of taxes and as a medium of exchange, had coincided fatally with the opium crisis in China. The result of this historic accident was the onset of inflation in Vietnam. The link between the two situations had been provided by the indispensable roles the alien Chinese mining and merchant classes had been allowed to play in the Vietnamese economy and its foreign trade.

The dynasty blamed the people for hoarding silver and for selling it "secretly" to non-Western "foreign merchants."[111] It attempted to extract more silver in taxes from the Chinese "congregations" and the Minh-hương settlements. The innocent suffered. By 1841 Minh-hương communities in the south were petitioning to pay their taxes in ordinary currency instead of silver. They were allowed to do so, but their silver tax was commuted at the high, unofficial market rate of exchange.[112] In 1847 court tax collectors were warned to "verify" the content of the "local" silver paid in taxes by Chinese communities in the northern border provinces. It was noticed that privately made ingots were becoming increasingly diluted in value. Ten years earlier, however, Minh-mạng had recognized the spread of rumors among the people that the dynasty's own silver coins were not as high in silver content as the court claimed but contained increasingly large admixtures of copper and lead.[113] Gone, perhaps, were the times when Minh-hương tax inspectors could readily collect 1,500 silver taels a year in "dwelling taxes" from Chinese merchants in Hanoi—as in 1815.[114]

Thus the Opium War and the circumstances which produced it undermined more than one East Asian court. Deteriorating fiscal circumstances made the Huế bureaucracy their prisoner. They forced it to look inward when it should have been looking outward.

Politically, the Nguyễn court quite characteristically gave the Opium War itself a Southeast Asian historical background. It regarded it as a variation of the tactics the British had first applied "in years previous" in Burma and then "transferred" to the "Ch'ing country."[115] In one sense, the independent-minded Minh-mạng was almost pleased by the war's humbling of the Chinese court's pretensions: "The Ch'ing people are weak and lack energy. We know them. Last year the Red Hairs went to and fro for ages among the large and small islands of Kwangtung, but we did not hear of [the Chinese] making a single plan or sailing a single junk in order to attack them."[116]

What is certain, however, is that this war's impact took the form of a loss of economic confidence in Vietnam. Alarm at the continuing inflation of silver was just one feature of this depression of mood. More generally, there was a pervasive fear that the presence of the British in the Far East would bring the entire traditional structure of Vietnam's commercial interaction with south China tumbling down. This was ironic. In Vietnamese eyes, the British were seen as the harbingers of an end to international trade, not (as the British thought) the harbingers of its rationalization and expansion. Minh-mạng's own words best explain this reaction: "Although this affair [the Opium War] is taking place in another country, still I cannot fail to bear in mind that our country's boundaries adjoin those of the Ch'ing country. Up until now, trade in hundreds of goods and commodities has circulated [between the two countries]. Now the Red Hairs are making an obstruction. Consequently the sea routes are not open. Where shall we obtain by transactions the commodities that are habitually in use among our people, like drugs and Northern teas? Since this [episode] makes commerce sick it also makes the people sick."[117]

Too much has, perhaps, been made in these pages of the elitist nature of the trade between Vietnam and China, of the fact that so many of the Chinese goods that the Vietnamese imported were in use only at the court or among scholar-officials. This must be qualified. It should be remembered that the Vietnamese Buddhist church depended upon the China trade for many articles of worship, ranging from books of liturgies to candles. Also, as Chaigneau noticed, Vietnamese druggists scorned pharmaceutical self-sufficiency, which was within their reach, in favor of buying their drugs only from China.[118] Some of the best transcripts historians possess of the daily life of the early nineteenth-century Vietnamese people are found in the richly colloquial poems of the eccentric poetess Hồ Xuân Hương. In one poem, "Laughing at the Wife of an Apothecary Who Is Weeping for Her [Dead] Husband," Hồ Xuân Hương satirized, through the words of this fickle widow, the wide village-level circulation and use of Chinese drugs on the traditional Vietnamese market:

> In sweet times, I remember the taste of your *cam-thảo*
>   [a Chinese preparation of licorice],
> And in bitter times, oh husband, the taste of your *quế chi*
>   [a Chinese preparation of cinnamon twigs].
> Why did you leave behind you your *thạch-nhũ* and
>   your *trần-bì* [bitter Chinese medicines]?
> You took with you [in your coffin] your *qui-thân* and
>   your *liên-nhục* [sweeter Chinese medicines].
> I wonder to whom I will entrust your knife for slicing
>   up herbs?
> Life is so temporary, oh husband, and dying means
>   going back [to a more permanent other world].[119]

The economic alarm of 1840 inevitably colored the Nguyễn court's response to Western civilization and its Far Eastern representatives, both of whose natures had become more discernible to the Vietnamese by the end of the Minh-mạng reign.

The Invasion of Western Culture

The Nguyễn Court's Admiration of Western Technology. Compared to the Chinese court of the 1830's, the Vietnamese court was much more extensively informed about Western culture. It was also more receptive to the idea of borrowing certain of the technological and military strengths of that culture. One reason for this, no doubt, was the fact that the Vietnamese possessed an explicit, bureaucratically recognized tradition of cultural borrowing. In addition, no Southeast Asian country, and certainly not Vietnam, with its long, exposed coastline, could luxuriate in the sense of cultural and economic self-sufficiency and massive geographic self-centeredness that characterized the Ch'ing empire. Yet most modern Vietnamese scholars would undoubtedly claim, with justice, that the Vietnamese court of the 1830's and 1840's was not nearly receptive enough to Western culture. Western ideas were accepted in the Minh-mạng and Thiệu-trị eras. But they were accepted only in those areas of Vietnamese life where there were no well-defined Confucian prototypes of behavior to resist and distort them. Also, the court was aware of the need for innovation in its military institutions. But it was aware as well of the concomitant need, three decades after the Tây-sơn Rebellion, for consolidation of its civil bureaucracy's social control; inertia was thus buttressed by the recent memory of how costly in time and effort the evolution of the Nguyễn bureaucracy had been. In the 1830's, Minh-mạng attempted to accommodate both these needs, which balanced each other, simultaneously.

Minh-mạng himself read Western (presumably British) plans of battle for naval warfare. He showed them to his court. The moral he drew from them was that if Western ships had the advantage of the wind, Vietnamese war junks should simulate defeat and attempt to entice them within range of Vietnamese shore cannon. If Vietnamese war junks enjoyed the wind advantage, on the other hand, they should attempt to nudge the Western ships out of Vietnamese waters, without coming close enough to the Western ships to allow them to open fire.[120] Minh-mạng had less respect for Western charts of astronomy, to which he also had access. One such Western chart, he claimed, made the Milky Way look like a real river, although it was obvious that in fact the Milky Way merely had the appearance, but not the properties, of a true river.[121]

To some extent the court's familiarity with Western maps and theories must have come from its experiences with Gia-long's French military advisers. Most of these had left Vietnam by 1820. Yet, at the end of 1838, the Huế Board of Works published a handbook on coastal defense, *An Investigation of Collected Naval Itineraries* (*Hải trình tập nghiêm sách*). This book discussed and set forth expertise about naval weather prognostication and the building and the sailing of ships. Because its compilers searched for data on these subjects in Vietnamese maritime records no earlier than 1820, it is clear that the French influence of Gia-long times had lost its appeal by the late 1830's.[122] In fact, England was the Western country which seized

Minh-mạng's imagination in the 1830's. There was a distinct if very minor cult of things English at Minh-mạng's court. Observing in 1833 that England's army did "not exceed 50,000 or 60,000 soldiers," Minh-mạng decided to reduce the number of soldiers on his own rolls in Vietnam, as soon as certain public works were finished; he also drastically reduced the number of flag bearers in the Vietnamese army.[123] By 1836 Vietnam was purchasing English gunpowder, which court officials declared was the best in the world.[124] Vietnamese artisans at the Huế Board of Works completed in the same year (1836) an imitation of an English merchantman's longboat.[125] Imperial cannoneers often wore Western rather than Vietnamese clothes, and in 1843 Thiệu-trị issued Western muskets to his ministers, ordering them to learn how to use them.[126]

None of these ventures matched the passion the court developed in the late 1830's for Western steamships. Some time during the decade the Vietnamese actually purchased a Western steamship, acknowledging that with a steamship there was "no question of the favor of wind and water." The engine of this steamship was removed and closely guarded. Vietnamese artisans attempted to copy it. A factory was even built for this purpose in 1839 outside the *Chính Nam* Gate of the capital city. No Western experts were invited to advise the artisans, however, any more than Chinese bureaucrats would have been permitted to advise Minh-mạng when he created his Privy Council— in imitation of the Ch'ing Grand Council—in 1834. Unfortunately, Western steam engines and their blueprints were not as easily imitated as Chinese bureaucratic institutions and their statutes. The general heritage of cultural reflexes and predispositions which Vietnamese imitators shared with Chinese administrative innovators they did not share with Western scientific ones. By 1840, according to the records of the Board of Works, the Nguyễn court had three small steamships in service. Only one of them was seaworthy enough to voyage to the north. All of them had been purchased from the West.[127] Minh-mạng had failed in his attempt to build a Vietnamese steamship.

In sum, Vietnamese officials were far more enthusiastic about Western technology in 1840 than Chinese officials were. But enthusiasm was not enough. They proved unable to make a technological breakthrough on their own. The reason, not unnaturally, was that they were inclined to imitate the products of Western science in the same mechanical way that they imitated Chinese institutions. The traditional forms of acculturation and institutional transposition which their relations with China had encouraged proved to be false precedents which blocked true modernization. It did not occur to the Vietnamese in the 1830's that they needed to study the principles, the theories, or the culture that lay behind Western science.

The Nguyễn Court's Dislike of Christianity. It would require a separate monograph even to outline the spread of Christianity in late traditional Vietnam. Here the subject can be very briefly appraised only as it is related to the theme of this study, the effect of the domestication of Chinese cultural patterns upon the outlook of a Southeast Asian society. In general, Vietnam's cultural membership in the East Asian classical world, combined with its situation in the much more open, less self-contained environment of Southeast Asia, meant two things.

First, Sino-Vietnamese resistance to Christian "heterodoxy" was bound to approximate the resistance to Christianity of scholar-officials in China. The traditional Vietnamese order could not tolerate French Catholic religious evangelism because Vietnamese political institutions were predicated, not upon the modern Western concept of the separation of church and state, but upon the concept of the state as the expression of the residual elite religion. If Catholicism made inroads among the elite, it would threaten to change the nature of elite beliefs, and if it changed the nature of the elite religion then the nature of the state, which expressed it, would also have to change. Even if only a minority of the intelligentsia became Catholics, the traditional Vietnamese state also lacked adequate mechanisms of institutionalized dissent to regulate the unprecedented political and ideolcgical conflict that would result. To this very general situation were added historical accidents like the Vietnamese succession controversy of 1816. At this time Gia-long had chosen the future Minh-mạng as his political heir, passing over an immature candidate more in the direct line of succession who was championed by Lê Văn Duyệt. After 1820, in other words, Vietnam was ruled by a man who knew that he would not have become emperor if Duyệt's intrigues had triumphed. Minh-mạng also knew that Duyệt, at Saigon, enjoyed close, friendly relations with French missionaries, whom Duyệt hoped might obtain European weapons for him as a means toward his domination of Vietnamese politics.

Second, because of Vietnam's position in Southeast Asia, the penetration of foreign books, goods, and ideas along the extended seaboard of the narrow Nguyễn kingdom was accomplished more easily than it was in China, and the bulwarks of the Confucian world in the Vietnamese provinces proved weaker than they were in the Chinese provinces. Because of Christianity's greater penetration in Vietnam, Sino-Vietnamese resistance to it was vehement but was based upon a slightly greater acquaintance with its ideas.

The Vietnamese elite could remember Gia-long's use of French missionaries as his emissaries to sources of French military power, like Pondicherry in India and France itself. This had been in the 1780's, before he was emperor, when he had needed help against the Tây-sơns. Gia-long had entrusted his eldest son to the keeping of Pigneau de Behaine, who took the boy on a visit to France in 1787. By 1792 it had come to the point where this prince refused to prostrate himself before the altar of his ancestors. (Had he lived to succeed Gia-long, Vietnamese history might have been different.) Frightened, the future Gia-long warned Pigneau de Behaine that unless Christianity accommodated ancestor worship, it would not appeal to his court. He also complained that if too many of his officials became Christians, he would be forced to perform state ceremonies almost alone. This would weaken the Sino-Vietnamese throne.[128] With variations, this was an echo of the earlier "rites controversy" in Peking and Rome.

Gia-long's flirtation with Christianity was a momentary aberration, based upon diplomatic need. But in the Vietnamese villages, Christianity flourished remarkably. One eighteenth-century Roman Catholic missionary in Vietnam, Bertrand Reydellet, estimated in 1756 that there were about 300,000 Vietnamese Christians, perhaps one Vietnamese out of every twenty.[129] Whether or not there was much truth in this, the movement was more conspicuous in Vietnam in the early 1800's than it was in China. Chaigneau could describe a so-called "Christian village" that he had seen, in the Gia-long period when he was a boy, near Huế.[130] Minh-mạng was informed in

1832 that one Thừa Thiên village near Huế (a different one from Chaigneau's) possessed both a church and a Western priest and that there was not a single peasant in it who wished to recant.[131] In 1838 the governor-general of Nam Định and Hưng Yên and the governor of Hưng Yên were both degraded because they had been unable to prevent Christian proselytization and the dissemination of Western books in their areas. Hưng Yên's Christian movement had a Vietnamese Christian leader.[132] Vietnamese records show the execution in 1833 of Western missionaries who had been active in the provinces of Quảng Nghĩa, Bình Định, and Phú Yên, the execution in 1838 of Vietnamese Christian leaders in Quảng Bình, and the execution less than a year later of Vietnamese Christian leaders in Nam Định.[133]

The vigor of Vietnamese Christianity requires an explanation. It may have stemmed both from socio-economic decline and from the fact that the Confucian cultural infrastructures of Vietnamese villages, as well as the presence in those villages of a Confucian gentry class, were not as strong as they were in Chinese villages. Yet generalization is difficult. Some Vietnamese Christians of the Minh-mạng era mixed Christianity with the traditional culture and actually defended their adherence to Christianity on Confucian grounds. In 1839, for example, a delegation of soldiers from Nam Định province, led by Phạm Nhật Huy, came to Huế. These soldiers declared that their grandfathers and fathers had been Christians, that Christianity ran in their families, but that provincial officials were now forcing them to walk upon the cross—as a public gesture of recanting their faith. They petitioned Minh-mạng to allow them to remain Christians for the sake of filial piety to their Christian ancestors.[134]

Such a demonstration that Christianity was winning converts in his army alarmed Minh-mạng. The army was not as subject to the process of cultural borrowing from China as the civil bureaucracy was. It was more vulnerable to Western influences. Moreover, a Western missionary, Marchand (Mã-song), had fought against the dynasty in the Lê Văn Khôi rebellion, which had racked the southern provinces in the early 1830's. These rebels had even invited Siamese aid. The link between Christianity and sedition seemed incontrovertible. Marchand was captured and executed by a slow process of mutilation. The grisly nature of his execution was then described by imperial edict to all the villages, partly as a means of destroying the superstition (as it was regarded) that Christians could ascend intact to heaven after death.[135]

The scholar class itself examined the precepts and practices of Christianity through a veil of Confucian rationalism. It was even less disposed than Minh-mạng to treat Christians leniently. Phan Bá Đạt, a high-ranking censor from Nghệ An who had won a doctoral degree in 1822, memorialized in 1835–36: "Western heterodox teachings . . . command one male and one female to live in the same house and occupy it for a long time as neighbors. If they want to release their passions for each other, they are repressed. They fetch water and combine to make wafers. Every time they preach their doctrine, they universally command people to eat them. They are caused to be bewitched by their doctrines and cannot refuse . . . At the time that a male and female [Christian] are to be married, their priest takes the female into a secret apartment [a confessional?]. In name this is preaching the doctrine, in fact it is vile and licentious."[136]

Usually, Christian writings and rituals were taken as literal demonstrations of Christian belief and behavior. To the extent that the hidden spiritual sense of Christian rituals was appreciated, Vietnamese intellectuals associated it with the subversive symbolism of soothsayers. Ordinary people concerned themselves with philosophy and history. Only eccentrics or megalomaniacs indulged in cosmological fantasies, anagogical pronouncements, or even the public discussion of dreams. This attitude was best summarized by Nguyễn Huy Hổ (1783–1841), in the preface he wrote, probably about the year 1809, to his beautiful 298 line poem *Chronicle of the Dream of Mai Đình* (*Mai Đình mộng ký*): "Big things like the beginning and the end of the universe . . . remote things like the changes of the past into the present, are all sensations that are found in dreams. Therefore only people who are called visionary, worldly, vagabonds, or travelers may talk about dreams."[137]

But one primary feature of this Sino-Vietnamese cultural examination of Christianity must be restated. The ventilation of Christian ideas, sometimes in highly distorted forms, was far more advanced in Vietnam than it was in China in the 1830's. Unlike Peking rulers of this era, Minh-mạng himself could recount stories from the Old

Testament—like those of Noah's Ark and the Tower of Babel—to his officials at court. In 1839, he did so:

> This Western book says that in the age of Yao there was a flood. Their country's prince used one great ship and took all the people and birds and animals within the country and fled to occupy the inaccessible top of a high mountain. [The book] also says that at the time of this flood within their country there only existed seven people. Later the people daily increased but all of them stemmed from the ancestry of these seven people. Such a theory is truly unfounded! [The book] also says that their country had one prince who led the people of the country to manufacture and erect a heavenly pagoda. Its height was goodness knows how many thousands of *trượng* and he wanted to climb it and roam the heavenly palace in order to examine conditions in heaven. The emperor of heaven was afraid and immediately ordered heavenly bureaucrats to come down and change their tones [languages], causing them to be unable mutually to work together. Hence they were unable to complete their pagoda. That every place in their country now has different languages and customs is attributed to this. This theory is even more irrational.[138]

The Vietnamese court, like the Chinese court, possessed its own myth system, its own collection of value-impregnated beliefs about the past that could not be historically or empirically verified. The idealized stories about the exemplary political acts of the Chinese sage emperors Yao and Shun were an example. In confronting an alien myth system, however, the Nguyễn court applied abnormally rigorous standards of evaluation—in much the same way that Western missionaries in Vietnam (or China) were more likely to recognize quaint, irrational patterns in Vietnamese (or Chinese) culture than they were to see them, although their existence was incontestable, in their own.

In Minh-mạng's version of these Old Testament stories, for example, the flood was a random event, not the divine punishment of evil. Noah was merely a prince, not the only good man who deserved to survive on earth. In other words, as ethical allegories, these stories failed to establish themselves in Vietnam. They were disguised by unfamiliar cultural symbolism, and they lacked the centuries of social authority which had buttressed them in Europe. Minh-mạng plainly regarded them as pretentious Western equivalents of Vietnamese dynastic historical chronicles. As such he found them badly wanting. He treated them as a highly implausible collection of value-free, supposed historical facts, whose implausibility only mirrored the lack of reason of Westerners.

Christianity's seeming lack of reason only gave the Chinese model of political and social ideology greater prestige. And Minh-mạng paid a magnificent negative compliment to the hegemony of the Chinese scholar class in East Asia, as a force for cultural transmission, when he warned that Christianity would triumph in East Asia only if, like Buddhism in its heyday, it converted Chinese scholars. They, in turn, would then convert the world.

Minh-Mạng Versus Vũ Đức Khuê: The Policy Debate of 1840. By the end of Minh-mạng's reign, controversy was rampant in the Vietnamese bureaucracy over the future of Vietnam's relations with the West. This controversy came to a head in 1840 with a debate between the emperor himself and Vũ Đức Khuê. Khuê was a Hải Dương scholar official in his late forties who had won a doctoral degree in 1822. It is, perhaps, suitable to bring this study to an end with a summary of this debate, because the course of its arguments demonstrated a feature of Vietnam's relationship to the Chinese model which has already been discussed. The Vietnamese emperor, who had never visited China and never passed classical civil service examinations, could often look at that model with greater freedom than his more intensely indoctrinated officials could.

To put it another way, in searching for a suitable response to Western pressures, Vietnamese bureaucrats were disinclined to change the bureaucracy's structure, purposes, or rules. By 1840, it is certain, a greater number of formal rules governing circumstances of official involvement with Westerners had been developed in the Vietnamese bureaucracy than had been developed in China by Chinese officials. Some of them have been mentioned: official leaves for bureaucrats' overseas voyages, bureaucratic language study curricula, procedures for the control and treatment of Western shipping, procedures for the high level disposition of imported Western goods. The Vietnamese bureaucracy was not to enjoy this small lead over the Chinese bureaucracy for long, but it did possess it in 1840. Its existence merely reflected the fact that the Nguyễn bureaucracy had encountered such circumstances of involvement and interaction more often—often enough to develop rules for their recurrence. No Cantonese hong merchants had stood between it and European commerce. Vietnamese officials were aware in 1840 that their external environment was changing. They were also uneasily unaware that this changing environment, combined with the fact that functions and responsibilities were broadly and vaguely defined in their bureaucracy, encouraged an increasing diversity of actions and ideas among bureaucrats themselves.

Yet the Nguyễn bureaucracy needed a strong internal goal consensus badly; increasing diversity was dangerous. It did not require this consensus merely for the sake of maintaining the coordination of its vast hierarchy, which was by no means as vast as that of Chinese officialdom. There was another reason. The Nguyễn bureaucracy was a Sino-Vietnamese bureaucracy located in the culturally and ethnically heterogeneous environment of Southeast Asia. It needed to maintain and conserve its own Confucian identity, by every means possible, in order to carry out the work of cultural integration it considered was its mission in this heterogeneous milieu. Some of its members feared that it would lose its goal consensus—the collective, ideologically pure agreement among its members about its style and purposes—if outside influences were allowed to play upon it too strongly. Isolation from these outside influences seemed a logical corrective device. Isolation was what Vũ Đức Khuê proposed in 1840.

In the memorial which set forth his position, Khuê attacked Westerners as being dangerous barbarians who should be uniformly repelled by Vietnam. Then, in the most perfectly orthodox fashion, he enumerated successive episodes in Chinese history of Chinese interaction with barbarians of various kinds, all of which were intended to prove his point that such interaction was harmful. For example, he mentioned the Japanese pirates of the Ming dynasty and their contribution to the erosion of that dynasty's finances. He also mentioned the Opium War and concluded that the British now sought to occupy Taiwan, Kwangtung, and Fukien. Finally, he proposed that Vietnam should end its international trade altogether. It should send out no more junks of its own "in order to stop completely other peoples' coming to our shores." In his eyes, such a scheme would have only one drawback: Vietnam would be cut off from gaining information about the West. Even Khuê could not believe in complete self-sufficiency. To remedy this drawback, he suggested that Chinese junks calling at Vietnamese ports have their taxes reduced and be supplied with government funds. Under contract to the court, they could then be sent to the Western countries to trade and spy out conditions there.

Thus, in Khuê's memorial, the Nguyễn dynasty's system of developing multiple trading networks indirectly, through controlled Chinese middlemen, now became apotheosized. Chinese middlemen were the solution to the problem of contact with the West. This advice was the joint product of Chinese-style cultural xenophobia and Southeast Asian determination to manipulate an alien Chinese merchant class.

Minh-mạng's reply to Khuê was one of the longest answers to a memorialist of his entire reign. Its length was an indication, perhaps, that he was aware of great sympathy among his officials in 1840 for Khuê's point of view. First of all, Minh-mạng asserted that Vietnam could not live without foreign trade. A loss of such trade would bankrupt Vietnamese sugar producers, who exported sugar and imported rice. It would also deprive Vietnam of imported military necessities like muskets, gunpowder, and textiles. Secondly, the emperor argued that a cessation of the voyages by government junks would prevent Vietnamese sailors from becoming familiar with navigation.

Looking at Khuê's recitation of the outrages barbarians had inflicted upon the Chinese, Minh-mạng coolly declared that the Chinese had brought these indignities upon themselves. In his opinion, the Chinese court had made two errors. It had allowed barbarians to live on Chinese soil as well as trade there. It had also allowed local Chinese vested interests like "the thirteen hongs" of Canton to spring up. These local vested interests had profited from trade with the West but had also hamstrung Peking's initiatives in attempting to control it. As Minh-mạng put it: "The Ming people allowed [the barbarians] to live at random in various places. All the places that the barbarians came to, they sketched maps of. Of the strategic points of the entire sea coast of the Ming country [China under the Ming] there were none that the barbarians did not know . . . As to our court's relationship with Westerners, we do not resist their coming and do not chase them away . . . When transactions are finished, we immediately order them to sail away. We have never allowed them to live in residence ashore. Our [ordinary] people everywhere are not permitted to enter into private reciprocal trading relations with them."

Minh-mạng believed in 1840 that Vietnamese naval defenses were adequate. He told Khuê that Vietnam's desisting from trade with other countries would not cause Westerners to stop coming to Vietnam. Also he asserted that he preferred that Vietnamese junks "not yield to the strong points of others" but sail the seas as effectively as those Western ships which "boastfully make impressions on the various countries."

Finally, he remarked: "If we merely deputize Chinese people to go abroad to make inquiries, then the Chinese are already inadequately trustworthy. Moreover, the things that they hear and know do not amount to anything more than 'gossip heard on the road' . . . How can we possibly become conversant with the various barbarians' true conditions?"[139]

Tragically for the Vietnamese people, Minh-mạng failed to appreciate the enormity of the gulf in military technology between his own civilization and that of the West. In this failure his own example hardly differed from that of the Ch'ing emperors in Peking. And yet, as I have attempted to show in this chapter, qualitative differences in Chinese and Vietnamese reactions to European pressures had appeared, even though it was also true that they failed to define the end results of their societies' confrontation with Europe differently. A summary of some of these differences is instructive.

First, Minh-mạng was at pains to differentiate from Chinese procedures the Vietnamese court's tradition of direct dealings between itself and Western ships. It can be argued, however, that this tradition was ultimately costlier, because it allowed the Vietnamese ruler little room to maneuver; he had no way of blaming local plenipotentiaries or hong merchants or provincial dissidents for anti-Western incidents the way his Chinese counterpart could.

Second, the Vietnamese bureaucracy was smaller than the Chinese bureaucracy and had been renewed more recently (1802). It lacked the Ch'ing bureaucracy's organizational conservatism of several centuries' growth. Also, because it had fewer members, the costs of its adopting and disseminating new behavioral patterns did not seem as extreme. Unfortunately, however, it needed ideological cohesion to resist what it regarded as the hostile pressures of its multicultural environment. Furthermore, the bureaucracy could not escape its borrowed Confucian heritage. Because it required its members to exemplify Confucian behavior in all aspects of their lives, to participate in their official roles in a "total" fashion rather than segmentally, it could risk changes in its ideological patterns, at short notice, no more comfortably than could its Chinese prototype. Thus although the Nguyễn civil service developed programs for studying Western languages before the Chinese bureaucracy did and sent its members on ocean voyages to live and study in foreign countries before this practice was accepted in Peking, in the last analysis these innovations were only of minor importance.

Third, the Vietnamese court cherished no delusions of economic self-sufficiency but welcomed Western trade. The court was undone not by its disinterest in commerce but by the false precedent of its manipulative relationship to Chinese merchants in Vietnam, which encouraged it to try to constrict such trade within a profitable Chinese-style bureaucratic mold. Another feature of its interaction with China, its imitation of Chinese institutions by examining Chinese blueprints at long distance, also played it false when it attempted to construct Western steamships without even the indirect advice of Westerners. But its determination to bureaucratize Western trade, combined with its fear of French missionaries, eventually gave the Nguyễn court a posture misleadingly similar to that of the Ch'ing court. In fact, no Vietnamese Lin Tse-hsű would ever have informed a European ruler, even in bluff, that Vietnam exported indispensable products and depended upon no imports in return.

These differences, which were almost to disappear from human memory in the deluge of history after 1847, take their place in the inexhaustible story of Vietnam's relationship to China. Whether or not they were representative of developments in other Southeast Asian societies, Sino-Vietnamese culture and politics constituted something of a mosaic of adjustments and surprises. Only some of the individual pieces of this mosaic have been examined in the preceding pages of this book: the dualism of the Vietnamese monarchy, tensions between the environment and imported institutions, certain recurrent divergences in social structure (merchants) and social ideology (women), the impact of differences in scale upon institutional borrowing (the lesser Vietnamese interest in the *pao-chia* system), the impact of a historicist methodology upon institutional borrowing (Minh-mạng's Grand Secretariat), the impact of centuries of narrowly channeled Confucian acculturation upon the political options of disenchanted intellectuals like Cao Bá Quát, the impact of Chinese-style hierarchical structures upon local government, the differences in examination systems, the influence of Vietnam's lack of China's material wealth upon the transfer of bureaucratic and familial institutions, and the influence of Southeast Asian multicourt intercourse and multicultural competition upon a Chinese-style tributary system. Other pieces of this mosaic remain to be discovered.

Burdened as he was by a Chinese-style world view in an environment which daily contradicted it, it was amazing that the Vietnamese ruler maneuvered as much as he did. If it was true that Vietnam never completely conquered the difficulties of domesticating the Chinese institutional model, it was also true that the Chinese model's influence never completely stifled Vietnamese ingenuity. That, perhaps, was the most important recurrent moral of early nineteenth-century Vietnamese history.

Notes, Bibliography and Glossary

ABBREVIATIONS USED IN THE NOTES

BAVH   *Bulletin des Amis du Vieux Huế* (Huế)
BEFEO   *Bulletin de l'École Francaise d'Extreme Orient* (Hanoi and Paris)
BSEI   *Bulletin de la Société des Études Indochinoises* (Saigon)
CHTSL   *Ch'in-ting Ta-Ch'ing hui-tien shih li*
DLTY   *Đại Nam điển lệ toát yếu*
DNTL   *Đại Nam thực lục chính biên, đệ nhất, nhị, tam kỳ*
HDSL   *Khâm Định Đại Nam hội điển sự lệ*
LT   *Đại Nam chính biên liệt truyện sơ tập*
NCLS   *Nghiên cứu lịch sử*
NTC   *Đại Nam nhất thống chí*
NTCB   *Nguyễn triều châu bản*
QSDB   *Phan Thúc Trực, Quốc sử di biên*
TCHT   *Ta Ch'ing hui-tien*

1. Vietnam and China

1. Henri Maspero, "Etudes d'histoire d'Annam: L'Expédition de Ma Yŭan," *BEFEO*, 18. 3: 27–28 (1918). Not without justice, some scholars like John Whitmore are inclined to question Maspero's assurance that sinicization was so wide-ranging in Vietnam before the end of the T'ang. But sinicization was certainly more extensive in Vietnam in this period than it was in southwest China, and the consequences of the process for Vietnamese history cannot be doubted, even if its effects were more belated than Maspero believed.

2. Nguyễn Phương, "Đà lịch sử,' *Sử Địa*, 1: 33 (Saigon, 1966). He quotes from one of his own works.

3. See the *Đại Việt lịch triều đăng khoa lục*, trans. into modern Vietnamese by Tạ Thúc Khai. (Saigon, 1962), quyển 1. Originally an eighteenth-century compilation.

4. Cited by Phương on behalf of his own argument that it is easy for Chinese to become Vietnamese because of racial and cultural similarities. Nguyễn Phương, "Đà lịch sử," p. 25.

5. G. William Skinner, *Chinese Society in Thailand* (Ithaca, 1957), pp. 20ff.

6. Quoted in Lê Văn Hảo, "Mấy nét về hội sống Việt Nam giữa thế kỷ thứ XIX," in Trương Bá Cần et al., *Kỷ niệm 100 năm ngày Pháp chiếm Nam Kỳ* (Saigon, 1967), p. 70.

7. Hsŭ Chi-yŭ, *Ying-huan chih-lŭeh*, preface dated 1848, 1: 24b.

8. Michel Duc Chaigneau, *Souvenirs de Huế* (Paris, 1867), pp. 110–112.

9. Cf. *Chính Luận*, Saigon, November 20–21, 1966, pp. 4–5: the article by Mẫn Chính on the possible need to tolerate the existence of French schools in south Vietnam.

10. Lý Tế Xuyên, *Việt Điện U Linh Tập*, trans. into modern Vietnamese by Lê Hữu Mục (Saigon, 1961), pp. 49, 222.

11. Higo Kazuo, *Tennōshi* (Tokyo, 1950), pp. 61–66.

12. *DNTL*, II, 90:23ff; *DNTL*, II, 40:30.

13. *DNTL*, II, 219:29bff.

14. *DNTL*, II, 138:23ff.

15. *DNTL*, II, 217:3.

16. L. Cadière, "Les Français au service de Gia-long," *BAVH*, 13.1: 21 (January–March 1926).

17. Phạm Việt Tuyền, "Một vài ý kiến về sự nghiệp Gia-long," *Đại Học*, 8:58ff. (Huế, March 1959).

18. For a description of the history of the Bắc Ninh provincial capital, built by Vietnamese who had been taught by French engineers like Olivier de Puymanel, see Ardant du Picq, *Histoire d'une citadelle annamite: Bắc Ninh* (Hanoi, 1935).

19. Nguyễn Phương has attempted to dispose of this argument in an article, "Ai đã thống nhất Việt Nam: Nguyễn Huệ hay Nguyễn Anh, trả lời Ô. Văn Tân, Hà-nội," *Đại Học*, 6:667–695 (October-December 1963). Phương's article is one of the later salvos fired in a hot controversy between northern and southern Vietnamese historians.

20. G. Aubaret's translation of Trịnh Hoài Đức's gazetteer of south Vietnam of the early nineteenth century *Gia Định thông chí* in G. Aubaret, *Histoire et description de la Basse Cochinchine* (Paris, 1863), failed to include the vital monograph on cities and towns in southern Vietnam. Ch'en Ching-ho came to the rescue of scholars everywhere by reprinting this monograph in 1956, from a manuscript owned by Henri Maspero, in *Nan-yang hsüeh-pao* 12.2:1–31 (December 1956). Data for early Saigon come from this version.

21. *LT*, 28:1ff. and 28:7ff.

22. For an excellent brief outline of territorial administration in Vietnam as it was initially arranged under Gia-long in 1803, see *QSDB*, I, 27. The city of Hanoi (or what I call the city of Hanoi for convenience, because many cities have risen and fallen on the one site and Hanoi—Hà-nội—is a relatively new name) was known then as Thăng-long. The second character in the name was altered in 1804 from "dragon" to "eminence," in time for Gia-long's investiture as Vietnamese ruler in the city by Ch'ing envoys.

23. *DNTL*, I, 26:22. Actually Vietnamese practices were not completely consistent. Rare references to Ch'ing China as the "middle kingdom" do appear in Nguyễn archives. Cf. *DNTL*, II, 33:5. Other societies in the East Asian classical world were also not above appropriating the Chinese term for China, "middle kingdom," for their own use. For a Japanese example, see R. Tsunoda et al., *Sources of the Japanese Tradition* (New York, 1958), p. 602.

24. Ngô Sĩ Liên, *Đại Việt sử ký toàn thư, đệ nhất sách* (book 1), *ngoại ký* (preliminary remarks), p. 1. I cite the Japanese edition of 1884, con-

sulted at the Tōyō Bunkō, Tokyo, Japan. The *ngoại ký* of this work was supposedly written by Liên himself in 1479.

25. Nguyễn Phương, "Phương pháp sử của Lê Văn Hưu và Ngô Sĩ Liên," *Đại Học*, 6:876ff. (December 1962).

26. Ngô Sĩ Liên, *Đại Việt sử ký toàn thư*, book 2, 1:1. Liên suggests that the Vietnamese kingdom was on the southwestern outskirts of the society known in classical Chinese times as the Hundred Yüeh (*Pai Yüeh*). Very briefly, *Yüeh* was the name of a rather heterogeneous non-Chinese people who were considered by the Chinese (in the days of the north China city states) to inhabit a large area of south China ranging from present-day north Vietnam to present-day Chekiang. They were called the Hundred Yüeh because they were fragmented into a number of small political units, like the *Yü-Yüeh* (roughly, in modern Chekiang), the *Min-Yüeh* (roughly, in modern Fukien), the *Nan-Yüeh* (Kwangtung), and the *Lo-Yüeh* (southwest China and northern Vietnam). Whatever Vietnamese historians thought about Vietnam's origins, the Chinese were convinced in classical times that the *Lo-Yüeh* people in particular tended to exhibit gross and offensive animal habits; the character *lo* meant "camel"; and the seal of authority which Ch'ing emperors bestowed upon their Nguyễn "vassals" three times in the period 1802–1847 was a gilded camel seal. More interestingly, both the original Vietnamese people and the original Cantonese people (as opposed to Chinese who later migrated south) probably felt the initial impress of the sinicization process at about the same time.

27. As the redoubtable iconoclast Nguyễn Phương has asserted in his "Đà lịch sử," pp. 24ff. For an exploration of some of the reasons why Chinese invasions of Vietnam were unsuccessful, see A. B. Woodside, "Early Ming Expansionism, 1406–1427: China's Abortive Conquest of Vietnam," *Papers on China*, 17:1–37 (1963) Harvard University, East Asian Research Center.

28. From the *Lam-sơn thực lục*, quoted and translated into modern Vietnamese in Hải Thu, "Bàn Thêm về thái độ của Nguyễn Trãi đối với nhân dân lao động," *NCLS*, 85:24–29 (April 1966). The identity of the author of the *Lam-sơn thực lục* is uncertain. There are several candidates. It is worth pointing out that many scholars of the early 1800's had no hesitation in ascribing it to Lê Lợi himself.

29. *Đại Việt sử ký toàn thư, bản kỷ thực lục* (the first Lê chronicle), 1:41.

30. For an analysis of how such a thing could happen in another non-Chinese East Asian society, pre-modern Japan, consult Yoshikawa Kojiro, *Shinajin no koten to sono seikatsu* (rev. ed., Tokyo, 1965), pp. 159ff.

31. Nghiêm Thẩm, "Sự tồn tại của bản chất Anh-đô-nê-diêng trong nền văn-hóa Việt-Nam," *Quê Hương* (Saigon, June 1962), pp. 133–173.

32. Lê Quý Đôn, *Vân đài loại ngữ*, author's preface dated 1773, *quyển* 9. I read the manuscript at the Tōyō Bunkō, Tokyo. Topically this important eighteenth-century text is divided into nine different sections under three general headings, which reflect the author's avowedly Sung neo-

Confucian world view: heaven, man, and earth.

33. Trương Quốc Dụng, *Công hạ ký văn*, 1 :80b. This work, of the Tōyō Bunkō collection, is undated but was written about the middle of the nineteenth century. Dụng came originally from Hà Tĩnh province in the north, won his doctoral degree under Minh-mạng, and eventually rose to become president of the Board of Justice. He died in the early 1860's.

34. Ibid., 1 :102b.

35. As Georges Azambre has pointed out. Georges Azambre, "Hanoi: Notes de géographie urbaine," *BSEI*, 30.4:355ff. (1955).

36. A brief examination of these similarities is made by Vũ Lang, "Cổ tích Chàm và Cổ tích Việt-Nam," *Văn Hóa Á Châu* 15:58ff. (Saigon, June 1959).

37. Bửu Cầm, "Văn hóa Việt-Nam dưới hai triều Lý và Trần," *Văn hóa nguyệt san* 11.12:1341ff. (Saigon, 1962).

38. Võ Văn Lập, comp., *Dã sử hạt biên*, 1 :55. This text, also of the Tōyō Bunkō collection, is also undated. It probably dates from the Gia-long period, Gia-long's court being mentioned as "this court" by the author.

39. *DNTL*, II, 198:9b.

40. *DNTL*, II, 3:17–17b.

41. *DNTL*, II, 152:14.

42. Hoa Bằng, "Nguyễn Hữu Cầu với cuộc khởi nghĩa nông dân giữa thế kỷ XVIII," *NCLS*, 75:23ff. (June 1965).

43. *DNTL*, II, 31:10.

44. Trần Quốc Vượng and Đinh Xuân Lâm, "Về nguồn gốc và lịch sử tuồng chèo Việt-Nam," *Tạp chí văn học* (Hanoi, April 1966), pp. 99ff. It is only fair to mention that although modern Vietnamese scholars, especially in the north, currently tend to emphasize the non-Chinese origins of much of Vietnamese culture, the older tradition, alive at least in colonial days, was to conclude that everything had come from China. For a different view of the origins of the *chèo* and the *tuồng*, this time underlining Chinese influences, see Nguyễn Đình Lai, "Etude sur la musique Sino-Vietnamienne et les chants populaires du Viet-Nam," *BSEI*, 31.1:1ff. (1956).

45. *DNTL*, II, 213:1ff.

46. *HDSL*, 100:5–5b.

47. *DTLY*, item 196 and after, pp. 338–342.

48. A. B. Woodside, "Vietnamese Buddhism: The Vietnamese Court and China in the Early 1800's," unpub. ms., 1968.

49. *Tam Giáo chính độ thực lục*, 17b–18. No. A–33 of the Sino-Vietnamese texts of the Bibliothèque Nationale, Paris, dated 1817.

50. Nguyễn Tường Minh, *Khảo luận về Nguyễn Công Trứ* (Saigon, 196?), p. 78.

51. *NTC*, 9:27b–28.

52. *DNTL*, II, 194:35ff.

53. John Crawfurd, *Journal of an Embassy from the Governor-General of*

India to the Courts of Siam and Cochinchina (London, 1830), I, 405.

54. George Finlayson, *Mission to Siam and Hué, The Capital of Cochin-china, in the Years 1821–1822* (London, 1826), p. 305.

55. Finlayson, *Mission*, p. 365.

56. Finlayson, *Mission*, p. 366.

57. Finlayson, *Mission*, p. 312.

58. Đào Duy Anh, *Việt Nam văn hóa sử cương* (Saigon, 1938), p. 64. For a sample of the difficulties such villages encountered in remitting their taxes, see *NTCB: Chư bộ nha tấu chiếp*, Minh-mạng 14:10:15 (1833), microfilm roll F 1608.

59. *DNTL*, II, 203:3bff. For background on my generalizations about Japan, see especially Miyamoto Mataji, *Nihon shōgyō shi* (Tokyo, 1943), pp. 176, 333ff.

60. *DNTL*, II, 174:8–10.

61. Translated from the *quốc ngữ* text in Nguyễn Tường Minh, *Nguyễn Công Trứ*, pp. 80–81.

62. For an essay on the culture of China south of the Yangtze before it became a part of the Chinese empire, by an anthropologist who has been a pioneer in the study of Vietnamese history, see Matsumoto Nobuhiro, *Indo-Shina no minzoku to bunka* (Tokyo, 1942), pp. 295–313.

63. Ch'ü Ta-chün et al., comps., *Kuang-tung hsin-yü*, 7:13. Published in 1700, this work was compiled earlier in the seventeenth century.

64. Li Tiao-yüan, *Nan-Yüeh pi chi*, author's preface undated. Li was a doctoral degree holder of 1763. He wrote this book perhaps in the late 1700's. It is a mine of information for any comparative socio-cultural history of south China and Vietnam. See chüan 6 for the entry quoted. Much of the betel consumed in Kwangtung came by junk from Vietnam and Siam. The importance of the junk trade in fostering common cultural trait-complexes along the south Chinese and Vietnamese coasts cannot be ignored.

65. Tsung Ping, *Ching-Ch'u sui shih chi*, p. 8, in Ch'en Yün-jung, comp., *Lu-shan ching-she ts'ung-shu*, 1900 ed. For an excellent modern study of "Dragonboat Day" see Huang Shih, *Tuan-wu li tsu shih* (Hong Kong, 1963).

66. *NTC*, 14:17.

67. *NTC*, 9:9.

68. *HDSL*, 69:22–23b; *DNTL*, III, 31:2.

69. *DNTL*, II, 70:17b.

70. *DNTL*, II, 6:18b.

71. To invoke the epigram of Kuwabara Jitsuzō, *Shina hōsei shi ronsō* (Tokyo, 1937), p. 13.

72. *Một người làm quan, cả họ được nhờ.* Only one of these eight words (*quan*) can be written with a Chinese character.

73. *DNTL*, II, 58:19.

74. *DNTL*, I, 49:3.

75. *QSDB*, I, 73–74.

76. *QSDB*, I, 23.
77. *LT*, 10:1–2b (biography of Nguyễn Bảo Trí).
78. *DNTL*, II, 207:30.
79. *DNTL*, III, 34:11ff.
80. *HDSL*, 37:17b.
81. *HDSL*, 100:26–26b.
82. *CHTSL*, 405:12b.
83. *CHTSL*, 406:1b.
84. *HDSL*, 123:25–25b. The example of the Long Phúc temple in 1824 is a good one.
85. *DNTL*, II, 167:2b–3.
86. L. Cadière, "La Famille et la religion en pays annamite," *BAVH*, 17. 4:353ff. (October–December 1930).
87. Nguyễn Văn Siêu, *Phương Đình văn loại*, 3:63ff. The date in the introduction to the text is 1856, but Siêu's use of administrative terms like "northern citadel" for Hanoi—terms that were anachronistic by the 1850's—suggests that most of the pieces were written before the Tự-Đức reign. Of the Tōyō Bunkō collection.
88. *Ibid.*, 3:75ff.
89. Hsü, *Ying-huan chih-lüeh*, 1:24b.
90. Pierre Gourou, *Les Paysans du delta tonkinois: Etude de geographie humaine* (Paris, 1936), pp. 124ff.
91. *DNTL*, II, 57:11. Officials' complaints often came from Nghệ An, as in this instance of 1828–29.
92. For an excellent survey of medieval Vietnamese family law, which draws upon his own research as well as upon that of French scholars like Deloustal, see Makino Tatsumi, *Shina kazoku kenkyū* (Tokyo, 1944), pp. 687–724.
93. Hoa Bằng, "Nhà Tây-sơn đối với hai nữ anh hùng Nguyệt Thai và Nguyệt Độ," *NCLS*, 86:35ff. (May 1966).
94. Translated from the *quốc ngữ* text in Đỗ Thúc Vịnh, *Hồ Xuân Hương: tác giả thế kỷ XIX* (Saigon, 1956), p. 66. Other treatments of Hồ Xuân Hương which are worth reading include Phạm Văn Diêu, "Khảo luận về Hồ Xuân Hương," *Văn hóa nguyệt san*, 11.69:247ff.; (March–April 1962) and Thái Bạch, *Thơ Hồ Xuân Hương* (Saigon, 1968).
95. Translated from the *quốc ngữ* text in Vịnh, *Hồ Xuân Hương*, p. 55.
96. Translated from the *quốc ngữ* text in Vịnh, *Hồ Xuân Hương*, p. 54; the romanized Vietnamese version is also given in Nguyễn Sỹ Tế, *Hồ Xuân Hương* (Saigon, 1956), p. 118. The poem has eight lines in all. It is extraordinarily difficult to translate because of its word plays, which of course create ambiguities. Literature on Hồ Xuân Hương is expanding in Vietnam, if not in the West. But her original poems were in *nôm*, subsequent generations of compilers meddled with them, and it could almost be said that no one is really entirely certain now in some of her poems what is original and what is not.
97. A famous study of the language is Henri Maspero, "Etudes sur la

phonetique historique de la langue annamite," *BEFEO*, 1:1–118 (1912). But many linguists now might challenge Maspero's linking of Vietnamese to Thai.

98. Chaigneau, *Souvenirs*, pp. 250–251.

99. *DNTL*, II, 170:15b.

100. *HDSL*, 132:29–29b.

101. An important article on the linguistic significance of *nôm* within the East Asian classical world is that of Wen Yu, "Lun Tzu-nan chih tsu-chih chi ch'i yü Han-tzu chih kuan-she," *Yen-ching hsüeh-pao*, 14:201–239 (Peking, December 1933).

102. Dương Quảng Hàm, *Việt-Nam văn học sử yếu* (Hanoi, 1951), p. 46.

103. Nguyễn Đình Hòa, "*Chữ Nôm*: The Demotic System of Writing in Vietnam," *Journal of the American Oriental Society*, 79.4:270ff. (1959). *Nôm* was undeniably inadequate for expressing certain things. Significantly, *nôm* forms for numbers from one to ten occur infrequently even in documents otherwise heavily laden with *nôm*.

104. The theories are reviewed by Bửu Cầm, "Nguồn gốc chữ nôm," *Văn hóa nguyệt san*, 50:347–355 (May 1960).

105. Võ Văn Lập, *Dã sử hạt biên*, 5:2.

106. Bửu Cầm, "Hai bức thư chữ nôm mở màn cuộc phân-tranh Trịnh-Nguyễn," *Văn hóa nguyệt san*, 85:1387–1393 (September 1963).

107. Đôn is at least the putative author of this text. See Phạm Văn Diêu, *Văn học Việt-Nam* (Saigon, 1960), pp. 633ff.

108. Đông Hồ, "Tương-quan giữa thơ hán và thơ nôm của thi phái Chiêu-anh-các," *Văn hóa nguyệt san* (May 1965), pp. 773–779.

109. *HDSL*, 17:12.

110. *QSDB*, II, 105.

111. *HDSL*, 106:8b–9b.

112. *Sơ Học Vấn Tân*, p. 3 of the text consulted, no. B–26 of the collection of *nôm* texts in the Bibliothèque Nationale, Paris, France. This version was printed in Vietnam in 1882 but was essentially unchanged from the primer in use in the earlier part of the century.

113. Bửu Cầm, "Thử tìm nguồn gốc văn-thể Lục-Bát," *Văn hóa nguyệt san*, 69: 189 ff. (March-April 1962).

114. *Tống Chí Truyền*, 8 *quyển* in all, no. B–30 of the Bibliothèque Nationale's collection of *nôm* texts. Date unknown—possibly the seventeenth century. From a brief examination of it, its quantity of *nôm* characters does not seem extraordinarily high. (The *nôm* texts which appeared in the 1890's in Vietnam, as part of a nativist literary resurgence, like Trương Minh Ký's celebrated *Như Tây Nhật Trình* (Day by day journey to the west) are, in contrast, almost surfeited with obscure *nôm* characters.) This text deserves comparison with Chinese historical novels by specialists in comparative literature.

115. The rebellion is discussed, on the strength of a wide range of oral and written evidence, by Đặng Huy Vận, Nguyễn Phan Quang and Chu Thiên, "Cuộc khởi nghĩa Phan Bá Vành," *NCLS*, 86: 21ff. (May 1966).

116. *Bản triều bạn nghịch liệt truyện*, trans. into modern Vietnamese by Trân Khải Văn (Saigon, 1963 ed.), p. 41 (p. 10b, old pagination).

117. *Thánh giáo yêu lý quốc ngữ*, no. B-5 of the Bibliothèque Nationale's collection of *nôm* texts. Dated 1837 (p. 4b, end of preface; the date is deliberately subversive, because it is written in Western terms).

118. *HDSL*, 99: 34ff.

2. *Nguyễn and Ch'ing Central Civil Administration*

1. Nguyễn Tường Minh, *Khảo Luận Nguyễn Công Trứ* (Saigon, 196?), pp. 50-51.

2. For a summary of the two different systems of bureaucratic grades which prevailed historically in Nguyễn Vietnam, the system of 1804–1821 and the system instituted by Minh-mạng, see *QSDB*, II, 117-126. Alfred Schreiner (in *Les Institutions annamites en Basse-Cochinchine avant la conquête française*, Saigon, 1900, I, 261) has argued that a civil bureaucrat could not rise beyond 3A in the Nguyễn mandarinate without passing military examinations. This is quite untrue, although Minh-mạng did encourage civil officials to acquire military skills, and men could certainly hold high positions in both military and civil hierarchies simultaneously. Schreiner's work is an interesting, colorful, but inaccurate pioneering French interpretation of Nguyễn Vietnam.

3. *DNTL*, II, 23: 13b-14b.

4. *DNTL*, II, 2: 21b.

5. *DNTL*, II, 194: 21ff.

6. *DNTL*, II, 159: 3bff.

7. A memorial from the Vietnamese Board of Appointments to Minh-mạng in 1838 declares, "We have examined previous histories. In the Sung they had information cards (*cha-tzu*) and in the Ming they had personal handbooks (*shou-pen*). Although these systems are not the same, in general they seek to cause officials to adopt a way of showing their honesty." *DNTL*, II, 194: 21ff.

8. *DNTL*, II, 32: 21b.

9. *DNTL*, II, 67: 14b.

10. *DNTL*, II, 57: 10.

11. *DNTL*, II, 164: 17.

12. *DNTL*, II, 191: 11.

13. *QSDB*, III, 389-390.

14. Phan Huy Chú, *Lịch triều hiến-chương loại-chí*, trans. into modern Vietnamese by Lường Thân and Cao Nãi Quang (Saigon, 1957), *quyển* 4, sec. 43.

15. *HDSL*, 234: 1ff.

16. *DNTL*, II, 205: 15b.

17. *DNTL*, II, 142: 28.

18. *DNTL*, II, 40: 22b.

19. *HDSL*, 8: 1ff; *CHTSL*, 19-20.

20. *DNTL*, II, 190: 19ff.

21. *HDSL*, 227: 1ff.

22. *DNTL*, II, 183: 38b.

23. For the elaborate prefecture-by-prefecture list of time limits, cited within the section of the Ch'ing statutes specifically dealing with the Censorate, see *TCHT*, 69: 4b-7b.

24. *HDSL*, 229: 4b.

25. Thiệu-trị riposted: "According to the acting supervising secretary at the office of scrutiny of justice, Giang Văn Hiến, my self-indulgent abandonment of myself to reciting and chanting successive works of poetry . . . is a distressing expenditure of energy. He requests that in my leisure from my duties I should read widely in the classics and histories in order to seek the essence of the principles of right conduct and the successes and failures of government . . . Diligently from day to day I have obliged myself to seek what ought to be done, sometimes considering and investigating masses of arguments, sometimes holding face-to-face discussions with great ministers . . . Has it ever happened that in the depths of the palace I have written the odd song . . . and forthwith indulged irresponsibly in what he points out as self-indulgent chanting and reciting? Merely in the leisure that remains from affairs of state to grasp a brush and record something in order to test myself, surely such diligent labor is more worthy than idly confronting my wives and servants!" *HDSL*, 228: 1-3. But the censor escaped immediate destruction. The imperial style, in Huế as in Peking, more usually favored a written refutation than vengeful, morally self-damaging demonstrations of power.

26. *DNTL*, II, 87: 11b-12b.

27. Miyazaki Ichisada, "Nihon no kan-i-ryō to Tō no kampin-ryō," *Tōhōgaku*, 18: 45ff. (June 1959).

28. Translated from the *quốc ngữ* text of the poem supplied in Phạm Văn Diêu, *Việt-Nam văn học giảng bình* (Saigon, 1961), p. 117.

29. I. e., *HDSL*, 18: 1-1b.

30. *DNTL*, II, 174: 8-9b.

31. *DNTL*, II, 156: 15. Oral terms of address within the bureaucracy were, for the most part, non-Sinic Vietnamese. High officials were usually saluted as *quan lớn*. (*Quan* is Sino-Vietnamese and means "official." *Lớn* is non-Sinic Vietnamese and means "great.") French colonial administrators later were to translate this phrase, not inaptly, as "your eminence." Cf. Pierre Pasquier, *L'Annam d'autrefois* (Paris, 1907), p. 153. Gia-long appears to have addressed Chaigneau, his French adviser, as *ông lớn* (Chaigneau, *Souvenirs de Huế*, p. 112); *ông*, which specifically means "grandfather" but is a normal, polite word for "you" (to males) in modern Vietnamese, was also applied to the emperor, who was known colloquially as *ông vua*, "grandfather ruler."

32. The details and motives of this land distribution program are set forth in the emperor's legislation in *DNTL*, I, 24: 9ff.

33. *HDSL*, 38: 29-33.

34.   For a sample of the controversies over Nguyễn land policy which enliven the research of scholars in north Vietnam, see Nguyễn Khắc Đạm, "Vài Ý Kiến góp cùng Ông Hồ Hữu Phước về Vấn Đề Ruộng Tư," *NCLS*, 74: 35ff. (May 1965). Was the situation in the south, where private estates were dominant, a peculiar regional one (Đạm) or a more general one (Phước)? Did Nguyễn emperors make some effort to circumscribe predatory landlords (Đạm) or no effort (Phước)? Nineteenth-century cadastral records, presently in the Viện Văn Khố in Đàlạt, await serious research.

35.   Trương Quốc Dụng, *Công hạ ký văn*, I, 15-16.

36.   *DNTL*, I, 46: 15b.

37.   *DNTL*, I, 47: 17.

38.   *DNTL*, I, 49: 11bff.

39.   *DNTL*, II, 35: 3.

40.   *DNTL*, II, 207: 2.

41.   *DNTL*, II, 75: 19b-20.

42.   *DNTL*, II, 193: 3b.

43.   *QSDB*, I, 49.

44.   See Đỗ Thúc Vịnh, *Hồ Xuân Hương*, pp. 58-59, for the modern Vietnamese text of the poem.

45.   *DNTL*, I, 25: 1.

46.   *DNTL*, II, 1: 23b-24.

47.   *DNTL*, II, 87: 35bff.

48.   *DNTL*, II, 6: 16b-17.

49.   *CHTSL*, 47: 2ff.

50.   *DLTY*, sec. 97, pp. 122-125.

51.   *DNTL*, I, 26: 8.

52.   Note the language of Gia-long's legislation in 1816 establishing the *triều hội điều lệ* (regulations for court audiences). *DNTL*, I, 52: 9b.

53.   *DNTL*, II, 38: 27.

54.   *DNTL*, II, 4: 12.

55.   *DNTL*, II, 3: 9; *DNTL*, II, 28: 2b.

56.   *DNTL*, II, 54: 19b.

57.   *HDSL*, 224: 6b-8.

58.   *CHTSL*, 19: 1ff.

59.   *HDSL*, 224: 8-8b.

60.   *HDSL*, 224: 5-11b.

61.   S. Y. Teng and J. K. Fairbank, *Ch'ing Administration: Three Studies* (Cambridge, Mass., 1960), pp. 36-106. See also Silas Wu, "The Memorial Systems of the Ch'ing Dynasty," *Harvard Journal of Asiatic Studies*, 27 (1967).

62.   *TCHT*, 2: 4b-5.

63.   *DNTL*, II, 64: 3bff.

64.   *DNTL*, II, 201: 18ff.

65.   *HDSL*, 231: 1ff.

66.   *HDSL*, 226: 5-5b.

67. *DNTL*, II, 3: 18b.
68. *HDSL*, 226: 3b-4.
69. *HDSL*, 224: 15b-16.
70. *HDSL*, 226: 5b-6b.
71. *HDSL*, 226: 7b.
72. *DNTL*, III, 23: 14bff.
73. *HDSL*, 226: 23b.
74. *CHTSL*, 14: 4b-5.
75. *TCHT*, 2: 7b; *CHTSL*, 14: 7-7b.
76. This cliche originates in the *Record of Rituals*, the *Li chi* or *Lễ Ký*.
77. *HDSL*, 224: 16.
78. *DNTL*, III, 58: 11b.
79. *DNTL*, II, 1: 10.
80. *DNTL*, II, 36: 23b.
81. *DNTL*, II, 40: 13.
82. *DNTL*, II, 1: 25b.
83. *DNTL*, II, 192: 9b.
84. *HDSL*, 5: 11ff.
85. *HDSL*, 5: 14.
86. *HDSL*, 40: 23b-25. Without descending at this moment into the kaleidoscopic complexities of Nguyễn currency and its domestic values, which kept changing, there were 60 *văn* to one *mạch*, and 10 *mạch* to one *mân*. As of 1823, a median year in this study, the official value of the *mân* was that 3 of them equalled one silver tael. (*DNTL*, II, 23: 15b.) The real price of silver kept rising in nineteenth-century Vietnam and is a subject in itself. By 1841 in Saigon one silver tael was worth 9 *mân*. The causes and consequences of this will be treated later in this study.
87. *HDSL*, 40: 27b.
88. *LT*, 7: 8b.
89. *DNTL*, II, 87: 12b-13.
90. Chao I, *Yen-p'u tsa-chi*, in *Ou-pei ch'üan-chi* (Shanghai, 1877 ed.) 1:1.
91. Liang Chang-chü et al., *Shu-yüan chi-lüeh* (1875 ed., author's preface dated 1823), 1: 17.
92. *TCHT*, 3: 3.
93. Teng Chih-ch'eng, "T'an Chün-chi-ch'u" given at Yen-ching University in 1937 and republished recently in Wang Chung-han, *Ch'ing-shih tsa-k'ao* (Peking, 1957), pp. 272-278.
94. *TCHT*, 3: 4.
95. *TCHT*, 3: 11b.
96. Liang, *Shu-yüan chi-lüeh*, 1: 18ff, recounts this interesting administrative *cause célèbre* of 1819.
97. Chao I, *Yen-p'u tsa-chi*, 1: 6ff.
98. Chao I, *Yen-p'u tsa-chi*, 1: 8.
99. Liang, *Shu-yüan chi-lüeh*, 13: 9b-10.
100. *HDSL*, 5: 1.
101. *DNTL*, III, 22: 22b.

102. *HDSL,* 5: 7-7b.
103. *HDSL,* 5: 9.
104. *DNTL,* II, 149: 16-17.
105. See the revealing fifteen benefits of a Chinese-style provincial system which Minh-mạng lists in creating such a system in 1831. *QSDB,* II, 208-209. For a concise summary of the Nguyễn Văn Thành affair, see Phạm Văn Sơn, *Việt-Sử tân biên: Từ Tây-sơn mạt-diệp đến Nguyễn sơ* (Saigon, 1961), pp. 292-293. The "Ái-châu" which is cited both in the original poem and in Sơn's modern Vietnamese version is an old name for Thanh-hóa province.
106. *DNTL,* II, 36: 13; *DNTL,* II, 54: 31.
107. *LT,* 16: 18ff. and 16: 12ff. respectively.
108. *DNTL,* II, 58: 14bff.
109. *DNTL,* II, 203: 18b-19.
110. *HDSL,* 18: 27b.
111. *DNTL,* II, 7: 4b.
112. *DNTL,* II, 13: 9.
113. *DNTL,* II, 33: 5b.
114. *HDSL,* 118: 1ff.
115. Teng and Fairbank, *Ch'ing Administration,* pp. 77, 104.
116. *HDSL,* 19: 8ff. For definitions of credentials types, see *HDSL,* 18: 1-27b.
117. *CHTSL,* 13: 18b.
118. *TCHT,* 11: 8ff.
119. *DNTL,* I, 25: 7.
120. *DNTL,* I, 42: 20b-21.
121. *DNTL,* II, 38: 2bff.
122. *DNTL,* II, 58: 18b.
123. *DNTL,* II, 1: 15b-17b.
124. *HDSL,* 22: 9.
125. *HDSL,* 22: 12b-13.
126. *HDSL,* 22: 15-15b.
127. *CHTSL,* 78: 9-10b.
128. *CHTSL,* 78: 8-8b.
129. For Ch'ien-lung's edict announcing the quotas system, *CHTSL,* 80: 24b-27. For the quotas themselves, *TCHT,* 11: 13-14.
130. For a brilliant discussion of the problems surrounding the meaning of this word, see Tezuka Ryōdō, *Jukyō dōtoku ni okeru kunshin shisō* (Tokyo, 1934), pp. 385-392.
131. *Bảo phù lại có quý quan, ắt là bình phục, trị hoàn như xưa.*

3. Borrowing Ideals and Practical Problems

1. In the mid-twentieth century it is considered that the minority peoples occupy about 13 percent of Vietnam's population of more than thirty million. For a discussion of the role of the minorities in Vietnamese his-

tory—and a sample of the new north Vietnamese historiography which stresses their historical integration—see Lã Văn Lô, "Thử bàn Về việc viết lịch sử các dân tộc thiểu số anh em," *NCLS*, 91: 39-42 (October 1966).

2. *DNTL*, III, 22: 16ff.

3. *DNTL*, II, 218: 33ff.

4. Tân Việt Điêu, "Kỳ-thoại về bang-giao và nghi-lễ giao-hiếu của nước Việt thời xưa," *Văn hóa nguyệt san*, 11. 75: 1219ff. (November 1965).

5. *DNTL*, II, 218: 33.

6. *HDSL*, 128: 1ff.

7. Ch'en Ching-ho, *Ch'eng-t'ien Ming-hsiang she Ch'en shih cheng p'u* (Hong Kong, 1964), p. 31. The character of the second word in Minh-hương was changed in 1827.

8. For the rules governing the transition from the congregations to the Minh-hương communities, as of 1842, see *HDSL*, 44: 8-8b.

9. For Đức's official biography, see *LT*, 11: 3bff; for Tịnh's, see *LT*, 11: 12ff.

10. Trịnh Hoài Đức, *Cấn Trai Thi Thập* (New Asia Research Institute reprint, Hong Kong, 1962), pp. 126, 104.

11. *DNTL*, II, 217: 32ff.

12. *QSDB*, III, 346.

13. Nguyễn Văn Siêu, *Phương Đình vạn lý tập* (dated 1851), pp. 58b-59. Consulted at the Tōyō Bunkō, Tokyo.

14. *DNTL*, II, 79: 17-18.

15. *Đại Việt sử ký toàn thư, sách 3, quyển 4*, 7b-8.

16. For Thận's biography, see *LT*, 26: 6. See also *DNTL*, I, 40: 20b.

17. *QSDB*, II, 107.

18. *DNTL*, II, 2: 20.

19. *HDSL*, 128: 2-2b.

20. *HDSL*, 128: 21-21b.

21. For the decree of 1838 announcing the official use of the term Đại Nam from 1839 on, see *DNTL*, II, 190: 1ff. For Minh-mạng's justification of the name change, see *DNTL*, II, 200: 7bff.

22. Chin Chao-feng, *Ch'ing-shih ta-kang* (Hong Kong, 1963), p. 302.

23. *DNTL*, II, 159: 29b.

24. *DNTL*, II, 208: 28ff.

25. *DNTL*, II, 207: 42.

26. *DNTL*, II, 26: 22.

27. *DNTL*, II, 116: 25b-26b.

28. *DNTL*, II, 1: 21.

29. *DNTL*, II, 72: 1.

30. *DNTL*, I, 38: 9.

31. See Đức's early nineteenth-century monograph on the cities and towns of south Vietnam, already cited, as reprinted in *Nan-yang hsüeh-pao*, 12. 2: 17ff. (December 1956).

32. Like Vietnamese gazetteers, in style Tokugawa gazetteers imitated the model of the Chinese *Ta Ming i-t'ung-chih* (Gazetteer of the Imperial

Ming). For a fascinating article which discusses Yoshimune and which is important to any understanding of classical institutions in East Asia, and their comparative behavior, see Hibino Takeo, "Tokugawa bakufu ni yoru Chugoku chihōshi no shūshū," in *Iwai hakushi koki kinen tenseki ronshū* (Tokyo, 1963), pp. 534ff.

33. *TCHT*, 3: 13.

34. For the edict founding it, see *DNTL*, II, 3: 12b.

35. Chú, *Lịch triều hiến chương, quyển* 15, sec. 80.

36. *DNTL*, II, 200: 3b.

37. *DNTL*, II 216: 21b.

38. Thái Văn Kiểm, "Tìm hiểu kiến trúc Kinh-thành Huế," *Văn hóa nguyệt san*, 12. 85: 1360ff. (September 1963).

39. Phạm Việt Tuyền, "Gia-long," *Đại Học*, 8: 76-77 (March 1959).

40. Nguyễn Sỹ Tế, *Việt-Nam văn học nghị luận* (Saigon, 1962), pp. 109-110.

41. *DNTL*, II, 7: 9b.

42. *DNTL*, II, 6: 9b.

43. *DNTL*, II, 1: 36.

44. *NTC*, 1: 1-6.

45. Thái Văn Kiểm, "Kiến trúc Kinh-thành," pp. 1360ff.

46. *DNTL*, II, 88: 14ff.

47. *DNTL*, II, 88: 15b.

48. *DNTL*, I, 41: 20.

49. *DNTL*, II, 184: 5.

50. *DNTL*, II, 191: 12.

51. *DNTL*, II, 160: 27ff.

52. *NTC*, 3: 58b-59. Minh-mạng was, of course, by the device of these urns, attempting to link his own dynasty to Chinese antiquity. Cadière has suggested this in "Les Urnes dynastiques du palais de Huế: Notice historique," *BAVH*, 1. 1: 39ff. (January–March 1914).

53. *DNTL*, II, 90: 12bff.

54. *DNTL*, II, 90: 12bff.

55. *DNTL*, II, 160: 8ff.

56. *HDSL*, 115: 1ff.

57. Nguyễn Văn Siêu, *Phương Đình vạn lý tập*, p. 68.

58. *NTC*, 5: 10b. For the Cham relics and the *Shui-ching chu*, *NTC*, 9: 23bff. For the double names of markets, see *NTC*, 11: 27b.

59. *NTCB: Chư bộ nha tấu chiếp*, Minh-mạng 8: 5: 7, microfilm roll F 1583.

60. *DNTL*, II, 210: 20.

61. For the edicts of 1828 and 1837 and their situations, *DNTL*, II, 54: 21; *HDSL*, 78: 36-36b. Folksong translated from *quốc ngữ* text in Lê Văn Hảo, "Mấy nét về hội sống Việt-Nam," p. 66.

62. *DNTL*, II, 5: 10.

63. *DNTL*, II, 66: 2b.

64. *DNTL*, II, 80: 13b-14.

65. Nguyễn Phan Quang, Đặng Huy Vận, "Tình hình đấu tranh giai cấp ở thời Gia-long," *NCLS*, 78: 9-23 (September 1965). According to these authors the province of Quảng Nghĩa had the most exciting fever chart in this period, with an average of one uprising a year. This was not a northern province.

66. Bùi Quang Tung, "Cuộc khởi loạn của Công tử Hồng Tập dưới triều Tự-đức," *Văn hóa nguyệt san*, 68: 69 (January–February 1962).

67. *DNTL*, II, 161: 2.

68. For the Vietnamese text of the entire poem, "Vịnh Hà-nội" (A song of Hanoi), see Nguyễn Tường Minh, *Nguyễn Công Trứ*, pp. 91-92. Again, my translation of lines 8 through 15 of this poem captures the meaning (I trust) but not the verbal magic and the rapid transitions of mood.

69. *DNTL*, II, 144: 14b.

70. For an excellent introduction to the question of local dike control in traditional China, seen through the lens of local histories, see Maeda Katsutarō, "Mindai chūki ikō no Fukken ni okeru suiri kikō no hembō ni tsuite," *Tōhōgaku*, 32: 88ff. (June 1966).

71. Hà Ngọc Xuyên, comp. and trans. into modern Vietnamese, *Bắc Kỳ Hà-đê sự-tích* (Saigon, 1963), p. 87. A collection of nineteenth-century Vietnamese texts.

72. *DNTL*, II, 61: 36b-38.

73. *DNTL*, II, 183: 11 and *HDSL*, 205: 6-7.

74. *DNTL*, II, 183: 11b-12b.

75. *LT*, 10: 11.

76. Phan Huy Lê, "Tình hình khai mỏ dưới triều Nguyễn," *NCLS*, 51: 40-49 (June 1963).

77. Chu Thiên, "Vài nét về công thương nghiệp triều Nguyễn," *NCLS*, 33: 47-62 (December 1961).

78. *DNTL*, II, 36: 26.

79. These estimates must be regarded with some caution, however. Nguyễn Phan Quang and Đặng Huy Vận, "Tìm hiểu chế độ lao dịch và binh dịch dưới triều Gia-long," *NCLS*, 80: 15-25 (November 1965).

80. *DNTL*, II, 206: 25bff. One *hộc* was worth slightly less than two *phương* of rice, slightly more than two *phương* of grain; this was confusing for the harassed local official because, at least until 1834, all crops were measured together rather than separately. (*DNTL*, II, 121: 15.)

81. *DNTL*, II, 169: 15-15b.

82. *DNTL*, II, 169: 3-4.

83. *DNTL*, I, 50: 6ff.

84. *DNTL*, III, 24: 1b.

85. *DNTL*, II, 169: 15-15b.

86. *QSDB*, I, 27.

87. *DNTL*, I, 46: 5.

88. These are, roughly, the statistics supplied at two different places in the dynasty's statutes: *HDSL*, 13: 1–14: 21 (the section on territorial ad-

ministration) and *HDSL*, 36: 12ff. (the Board of Finance section).

89. Trương Quốc Dụng, *Công hạ ký văn*, p. 91.

90. *DNTL*, II, 75: 6ff.

91. *DNTL*, II, 118: 18bff.

92. Phan Húy Chú, *Lịch triều hiến chương, quyển* 14, sec. 71.

93. *LT*, 19: 10b-11.

94. *HDSL*, 11: 6ff.

95. *DNTL*, II, 205: 18bff.

96. *HDSL*, 11: 11b-13.

97. *HDSL*, 14: 21-22.

98. *NTCB: Chư bộ nha tấu chiếp*, Minh-mạng 1: 11: 26 (1820), micro-film roll F 1561.

99. *DNTL*, II, 190: 5bff.

100. *DNTL*, III, 5: 17b-18.

101. *DNTL*, II, 155: 2.

102. *HDSL*, 205: 5b.

103. *DNTL*, II, 57: 4ff; *DNTL*, II, 197: 21.

104. Phan Khoang, "Lược Sử chế độ xã-thôn ở Việt-Nam," *Sử Địa*, 1: 34-51 (1966).

105. *NTCB: Chư bộ nha tấu chiếp*, Minh-mạng 11: 9-10 (1830), micro-film roll F 1603.

106. *QSDB*, II, 314.

107. *DNTL*, II, 57: 37ff.

108. *DNTL*, I, 38: 10b.

109. *HDSL*, 63: 26.

110. *HDSL*, 104: 14.

111. *DNTL*, II, 101: 25-25b.

112. *DNTL*, II, 116: 25b. *HDSL*, 38: 29b.

113. *HDSL*, 38: 32b-33.

114. *QSDB*, I, 29; *DNTL*, II, 6: 20-20b; *DNTL*, II, 220: 36. For a discussion of Vietnamese population statistics and related problems of the Nguyễn economy, see an excellent article by Nguyễn Thế Anh, "Vấn đề lúa gạo ở Việt-Nam trong tiền bán thế kỷ XIX," *Sử Địa*, 6 (1967) esp. p. 11.

115. *DNTL*, II, 31: 30b.

116. John White, an American sea captain, claimed that it might be as high as 14 million in 1820. John White, *A History of a Voyage to the China Sea* (Boston, 1823), p. 283. And Chaigneau's son suggested in his reminiscences that it was between 20 and 25 million. Chaigneau, *Souvenirs de Huế*, preface. Writing in the 1880's, Silvestre put the population of Huế at about 100,000 people, the population of Hanoi at 130,000 or 140,000. J. Silvestre, *L'Empire d'Annam et le peuple Annamite* (Paris, 1889), pp. 26-28. Pasquier pointed out that it was an absolute principle in Vietnam that the numbers of the "registered" should never decline. Pierre Pasquier, *L'Annam d'autrefois* (Paris, 1907), p. 48. However, in 1840 the recorded adult male population was 970,516, but in 1841 it did decline drastically to 925,184.

(*DNTL*, III, 14: 4.) This decline, an important example, reflected instability in the south and the collapse of the Vietnamese province in Cambodia.

117. *DNTL*, II, 178: 2-2b.

118. *DNTL*, II, 183: 38.

119. *DNTL*, II, 216: 7.

120. Feng Kuei-fen, *Chiao-pin lü k'ang-i* (Shanghai, 1884; author's preface dated 1860-1861), 1: 13.

121. *DNTL*, II, 12: 19b.

122. *DNTL*, II, 12: 7.

123. *DNTL*, II, 121: 8.

124. *DNTL*, III, 13: 5-5b.

125. *DNTL*, III, 22: 18b-20.

126. *DNTL*, III, 22: 17b-18b.

127. *DNTL*, II, 171: 24.

128. *DNTL*, II, 182: 2-2b. "Hsia" is here used of course as a classical synonym for Chinese culture.

129. *NTCB: Chư bộ nha tấu chiếp*, Gia-long 17: 6: 10 (1818), microfilm roll F 1556.

4. Education and Examinations

1. Dương Quảng Hàm, *Việt-Nam văn học sử yếu* (Hanoi, 1951), p. 78.

2. *DNTL*, I, 40: 21.

3. Ngô Tất Tố, *Lều Chõng* (Saigon reprint, 1958), pp. 17-21.

4. Trương Quốc Dụng, *Công hạ ký văn*, I, 20b.

5. *HDSL*, 108: 16-17.

6. Phạm Thế Ngũ, *Việt-Nam văn học sử giản ước tân biên: Văn học lịch triều: Việt văn* (Saigon, 1963), p. 436, footnote.

7. Wang Chieh et al., *Ch'in-ting k'o-ch'ang t'iao li* (dated Ch'ien-lung 54-55; 1789-1790), 22: 1-3b.

8. *HDSL*, 108: 16-17.

9. *HDSL*, 107: 9b-10.

10. *DNTL*, III, 31: 1ff.

11. *HDSL*, 17: 14b-15.

12. *DNTL*, II, 199: 6b.

13. *HDSL*, 15: 5 and 15: 8; *HDSL*, 15: 9-9b.

14. *DNTL*, II, 173: 19b-20.

15. *DNTL*, II, 200: 14b.

16. Miyazaki Ichisada, *Kakyo: Chūgoku no shiken jigoku* (Tokyo, 1963), pp. 21-22.

17. Shang Yen-liu, *Ch'ing tai k'o-chü k'ao-shih shu-lu* (Peking, 1958), p. 3.

18. *TCHT*, 32: 2-3b. And Miyazaki, *Kakyo*, p. 20.

19. This has been pointed out by Takeda Ryōji, "Annan kakyo seido shōkō," *Shigaku*, 37. 1: 14 (1964).

20. *HDSL*, 104: 14.

21. *HDSL*, 104: 16b-18.

22. Ho P'ing-ti, *The Ladder of Success in Imperial China* (New York, 1962), p. 189.

23. Many of the Nguyễn examination lists that have come down to us are the work not of court clerks but of private Vietnamese scholars of the period, like Lê Chỉ Trai, who first compiled the records of the examinations held from 1822 to 1843. The dynasty did engrave the names of all victorious doctoral degree holders upon stone monuments. The statistics I have just presented are derived from the modern *quốc-ngữ* text of Cao Xuân Dục, comp., *Quốc triều đăng khoa lục* (Saigon, 1962 reprint), pp. 13, 26-113. The compiler, who died in 1923, was a regional graduate of 1877.

24. *HDSL*, 108: 16-17. The figure of 8,000 competing regional graduates at Peking is cited by Chang Chung-li in *The Chinese Gentry: Studies on their Role in Nineteenth Century Chinese Society* (Seattle, 1955), p. 126.

25. *DNTL*, II, 32: 27.

26. *CHTSL*, 372: 14b.

27. *DNTL*, III, 6: 13-13b.

28. *DNTL*, II, 174: 14.

29. *HDSL*, 17: 5b-6.

30. For his appointment in 1820, see *DNTL*, II, 1: 37. For his official biography, see *LT*, 26: 11.

31. *DNTL*, III, 36: 19bff. And *HDSL*, 102: 3ff.

32. *QSDB*, I, 26.

33. *NTC*, 1: 45b. See also Nguyễn Văn Trình and Ưng Trình, "Le Quốc-tử-giám," *BAVH*, 4. 1: 38ff. (January-March 1917).

34. For the stipends as of 1825, see *DNTL*, II, 33: 16b.

35. *DNTL*, III, 36: 19b-20.

36. *DNTL*, II, 26: 22.

37. *DNTL*, II, 31: 13bff.

38. *HDSL*, 17: 1b-2.

39. *HDSL*, 15: 11ff.

40. *CHTSL*, 24: 1ff.

41. Pasquier, *L'Annam d'autrefois*, p. 170.

42. *HDSL*, 228: 6ff.

43. *HDSL*, 16: 33-36. *DNTL*, II, 117: 20b.

44. *DNTL*, II, 205: 12.

45. *DNTL*, II, 35: 7ff.

46. *DNTL*, I, 44: 16b.

47. *DNTL*, II, 54: 24b-25.

48. Shang, *Ch'ing tai k'o-chü k'ao-shih shu-lu*, pp. 223-224.

49. Trần Khải Văn, trans. into modern Vietnamese, *Lê triều giáo hóa điều luật* (Saigon, 1962), p. 48, regulation 35.

50. *HDSL*, 102: 8ff.

51. Officials like Trần Công Hiến in Hải Dương, for example: *LT*, 16: 18ff.

52. *DNTL*, II, 65: 8.

53. *HDSL*, 102: 11b.
54. *HDSL*, 102: 12b.
55. Pasquier, *L'Annam d'autrefois*, p. 168.
56. Chaigneau, *Souvenirs de Huế*, p. 73.
57. E. Luro, *Le Pays d'Annam: Etude sur l'organization politique et sociale des annamites* (Paris, 1878), pp. 144-145.
58. Đào Duy Anh, *Việt Nam văn hóa sử cương* (Saigon, 1938), p. 259.
59. *HDSL*, 100: 5ff.
60. *HDSL*, 100: 11-18.
61. As part of its guerrilla pacification program in southern Vietnamese villages, the south Vietnamese army was being enjoined in the year 1967 to practice the five Sino-Vietnamese virtues of humaneness, right conduct, politeness, knowledgability, and trustworthiness. (*Chính Luận*, Saigon, May 6, 1967. Article by Nguyễn Tú). These were, of course, the major qualities Minh-mạng cited in his description of good behavior in 1834.
62. For an idealized picture of elementary Vietnamese schooling in the 1800's, see Nguyễn Duy Diễn, "Việc học và việc thi chữ Nho ngày trước," *Gió Mới* (Saigon, September 1961), pp. 467-470.
63. Hàm, *Việt-Nam văn học sử yếu*, p. 28.
64. *DNTL*, II, 184: 8b.
65. *DNTL*, II, 122: 20-21b.
66. *DNTL*, II, 126: 6ff.
67. *DNTL*, II, 216: 9bff.
68. *DNTL*, III, 35: 6bff.
69. Wang Chieh, *Ch'in-ting k'o-ch'ang t'iao-li*, 26: 5-5b, or *CHTSL*, 343: 3b.
70. Miyazaki, *Kakyo*, pp. 60-61.
71. Shang, *Ch'ing tai k'o-chü k'ao-shih shu-lu*, pp. 50ff.
72. *DNTL*, II, 74: 35.
73. *DNTL*, II, 215: 1ff.
74. *DNTL*, II, 131: 27ff.
75. *DNTL*, III, 34: 5b-6.
76. Quoted with relish by Miyazaki, *Kakyo*, pp. 92-93.
77. *HDSL*, 103: 16ff.
78. *CHTSL*, 334: 7b-8b.
79. *HDSL*, 104: 1ff for the salary scale of officials at examination sites.
80. *HDSL*, 103: 19-19b.
81. Note Chaigneau's description of the style of life of a Vietnamese "mandarin" in *Souvenirs de Huế*, pp. 44-45.
82. Wang Chieh, *Ch'in-ting k'o-ch'ang t'iao-li*, 25: 1; *CHTSL*, 345: 22b-23.
83. *CHTSL*, 345: 18.
84. *CHTSL*, 345: 27b-28.
85. *CHTSL*, 333: 19-19b.
86. *CHTSL*, 352: 15b-19.
87. *HDSL*, 100: 3b-4b.

88. *HDSL*, 103: 31-31b.
89. *HDSL*, 103: 26ff.
90. *CHTSL*, 334: 4bff.
91. *HDSL*, 107: 1-1b.
92. *DNTL*, II, 35: 7ff.
93. *HDSL*, 107: 13b.
94. *DNTL*, II, 137: 1b.
95. *DNTL*, III, 33: 10ff; *HDSL*, 107: 11b-12b.
96. *DNTL*, II, 37: 16b.
97. *DNTL*, II, 35: 5b.
98. *DNTL*, II, 218: 1ff.
99. Phạm Văn Diêu, *Việt-Nam văn học giảng bình* (Saigon, 1961), p. 427.
100. *HDSL*, 106: 1ff.
101. *HDSL*, 106: 9b.
102. *DNTL*, II, 87: 2ff.
103. *DNTL*, II, 122: 20-21b.
104. *DNTL*, II, 57: 33.
105. *DNTL*, II, 35: 1ff.
106. *DNTL*, II, 152: 19ff.
107. Pasquier, *L'Annam d'autrefois*, p. 175.
108. Wang Chieh, *Ch'in-ting k'o-ch'ang t'iao-li*, 14: 11.
109. *DNTL*, II, 154: 6. In fact, while *fu-ni* is listed in the *Shih-wu i-ming lu* as the name of a star, *ch'ang-li* is surely the name of a supernatural bird which appears in the *Han History*.
110. *CHTSL*, 331: 1-1b.
111. *DNTL*, II, 142: 28-28b.
112. *CHTSL*, 331: 3; Miyazaki, *Kakyo*, p. 82.
113. *CHTSL*, 331: 5b-6b.
114. *CHTSL*, 331: 14b-15.
115. Cao Xuân Dục, *Quốc triều đăng khoa lục*, pp. 11-13.
116. Nguyễn Tường Minh, *Khảo luận Nguyễn Công Trứ*, p. 11.
117. Quoted by Kiêm Đạt, *Nguyễn Công Trứ: Luận-đề, nghiên-cứu, khảo luận* (Saigon, 1959), p. 143.
118. Translated from the *quốc-ngữ* text in Nguyễn Tường Minh, *Nguyễn Công Trứ*, pp. 62-63.
119. Ho, *The Ladder of Success in Imperial China*, pp. 222-254.
120. Quoted in Đào Văn Hội, *Phong tục Miền Nam Qua Mấy Vân Ca Dao* (Saigon, 1961), p. 56.
121. Data for the 1813 regional examinations from *DNTL*, I, 46: 8; *DNTL*, I, 47: 1; *DNTL*, I, 47: 7bff. For the 1821 regional examinations, *DNTL*, II, 10: 1ff. and *DNTL*, II, 11: 1ff. For the 1825 regional examinations, *DNTL*, II, 34: 1b and *DNTL*, II, 35: 1ff. For the 1840 regional examinations, *DNTL*, II, 215: 1ff. and *DNTL*, II, 218: 1ff. For the 1843 regional examinations, *DNTL*, III, 32: 1ff. and *DNTL*, III, 33: 10ff.
122. Phạm Thế Ngũ, *Việt-Nam văn học: Việt văn*, p. 463.
123. *DNTL*, II, 207: 40; *DNTL*, II, 200: 7bff; *HDSL*, 37: 14ff.

124. *HDSL*, 108: 1ff.
125. *DNTL*, III, 32: 2b.
126. *DNTL*, II, 183: 5ff.
127. *HDSL*, 104: 16b-17.
128. *HDSL*, 107: 13.
129. Phạm Đình Hổ and Nguyễn Án, *Tang thương ngẫu lục*, trans. into modern Vietnamese by Đạm Nguyện (Saigon, 1961 ed.), I, 50: 232-234. *Tang thương* has the connotation of change that is very sad, and might better be translated as "vicissitudes."
130. *DNTL*, II, 192: 5bff.
131. Phạm Văn Diêu, *Việt-Nam văn học giảng bình*, p. 157.
132. Ibid., p. 158.
133. Phạm Thế Ngũ, *Việt-Nam văn học: Việt văn*, p. 440. The word that is used for "castrate" in this poem—*bớt*—is also used to mean "squeezing" public funds (*ăn bớt*) in Vietnamese, the pun being intentional, of course.
134. Trans. from the *quốc ngữ* text in Trịnh Vân Thanh, *Giảng luận Việt văn* (Saigon, 1963), p. 243.
135. Phạm Văn Diêu, *Việt-Nam văn học giảng bình*, p. 162.
136. Ibid., p. 161. "Mother Phiếu's rice" (*cơm Phiếu Mẫu*) refers to a long-suffering woman who cooked rice for poor scholars, although the story, which comes from Han China, seems to have developed variations in Vietnam. Something like "the rice of hardship" is roughly the idea the expression suggests in Vietnamese.
137. Phạm Thế Ngũ, *Việt-Nam văn học: Việt văn*, p. 439.
138. Ibid., p. 441.
139. *Kung Ting-an wen-chi* (Shanghai, 1908 ed.); *Ming-liang lun*, p. 2.

5.   The Emperor, the Bureaucacy, and the World outside Vietnam

1. Cf. Y. Fujisawa, "Unnan kodai no Dairi bunka," *Shichō* 82-83: 11-29 (March 1963).
2. *DNTL*, III, 20: 2b.
3. Phạm Văn Diêu, *Văn học Việt Nam*, p. 686.
4. *LT*, 33: 8ff.
5. Cf. Bernard Bourotte, "Essai d'histoire des populations montagnardes du Sud-Indochinois jusqu'à 1945," *BSEI*, 30. 1 (1955). For the list of vassals of 1815, *QSDB*, I, 88.
6. *DNTL*, III, 5: 6b-7.
7. *HDSL*, 134: 3.
8. *LT*, 23: 4bff. Some of the documents associated with this Burmese diplomatic mission of the 1820's, which appears to have been headed by a man of Anglo-Indian parentage, G. Gibson, are presented in translation by Suzanne Karpeles, "Notules sur un manuscrit relatif à une ambassade birmane en Cochinchine," *BSEI*, 24.1:37ff. 1 (1949).
9. *DNTL*, I, 47:11bff.
10. For a description of some of the ceremonies which occurred at the

Nguyễn court during its reception of tributary envoys, see *HDSL*, 132:5bff. Books 132–133 of the *HDSL* have been translated into modern Vietnamese by Tạ Quang Phát (and rev. and ed. by Bửu Câm), *Nhu Viễn* (Saigon, 1965).

11. The Đèo Ngang was the name of a mountain pass in a branch of the Trường-sơn range in central Vietnam. This particular branch stretched out to the coast and formed a rough boundary between the two provinces of Hà Tĩnh and Quảng Bình. In the early 1800's strangers traveling by land from northern to central and southern Vietnam had to cross this pass, through which the one public road led.

12. The text upon which I have based my translation is that given in Phạm Văn Diêu, *Việt Nam văn học giảng bình*, p. 120, "Qua Đèo Ngang." Actually the word *rợ* in line 4 may refer not to racially non-Vietnamese "savage" or "barbarian" people at all, but rather to Vietnamese "slave" families, i.e., those who are so poor and who have to work so hard that they are considered unfree. I have, perhaps improvidently, clung to the usual meaning of this word, which is applied in Vietnam to the Mọi highlanders.

13. *DNTL*, III, 33:13ff.

14. *DNTL*, II, 220:8.

15. *DNTL*, I, 43:5.

16. *DNTL*, II, 210:31b.

17. *DNTL*, II, 97:1ff.

18. *DNTL*, II, 70:24.

19. *DNTL*, II, 170:13b–14.

20. *HDSL*, 132:27–27b.

21. For speculation on the origins of this word in Siam, see Chula Chakrabongse, *Lords of Life: The Paternal Monarchy of Bangkok, 1782–1932* (London, 1960), p. 36.

22. *LT*, 22:15b.

23. *DNTL*, I, 48:17bff.

24. *DNTL*, I, 50:5.

25. *LT*, 23:9–10b.

26. For the Siamese side of these complicated wars, see Walter F. Vella, *Siam under Rama III, 1824–1851* (Locust Valley, N.Y., 1957). Cf. also David K. Wyatt, "Siam and Laos, 1767–1827," *Journal of Southeast Asian History*, 4. 2:27ff. (September 1963).

27. Huỳnh Thiên Kim, *Cận đại Việt sử diễn ca* (Saigon, 1962), p. 67.

28. For a biography of Giảng, see, among others, Nguyễn Huyền Anh, *Việt Nam danh nhân tự điển* (Saigon, 1960), pp. 360–361.

29. *DNTL*, II, 142:18b.

30. *DNTL*, II, 160:20.

31. *DNTL*, II, 153:24ff.

32. *DNTL*, II, 176:12–12b.

33. *DNTL*, II, 121:28.

34. *DNTL*, II, 156:16.

35. *DNTL*, III, 6:8ff.

36. *NTCB*: *Chư bộ nha tấu chiếp*, Minh-mạng 18:7:17 (1837), microfilm roll F 1616.

37. *DNTL*, I, 44:18; *DNTL*, I, 47:3b.

38. *DNTL*, II, 197:30; *DNTL*, II, 199:4ff. The 343 war elephants reported on the rolls in 1838–39 were divided among 43 brigades which comprised 1,577 soldiers. Every male elephant at Huế required 10 herders and riders, but in the provinces, where ceremonial was not so important, the number was reduced to 4 apiece.

39. *DNTL*, II, 142:23b.

40. *DNTL*, II, 87:9b–10.

41. *DNTL*, II, 118:34b.

42. *DNTL*, II, 78:33bff.

43. *DNTL*, II, 149:19b.

44. *DNTL*, II, 138:27.

45. *DNTL*, II, 131:20b.

46. *DNTL*, II, 145:23bff.

47. *LT*, 32:32b–33.

48. *DNTL*, II, 203:14b.

49. *DNTL*, II, 40:10.

50. Tống Phúc Ngoạn and Dương Văn Châu, comps., *Xiêm La Quốc lộ trình tập lục* (Hong Kong, New Asia Research Institute reprint, 1966), pp. 81, 76.

51. *DNTL*, II, 34:7b.

52. *DNTL*, II, 198:2ff.

53. Cf. *NTCB*: *Ngoại quốc thư trát* (Foreign Correspondence), Gia-long 15–16 (1816–1817), microfilm roll F 1558. These documents of the Gia-long reign are of great value, of course, because they were not tampered with by the more Confucian court historians of later reigns. The gulf between pre–1820 and post–1820 Vietnamese documents must be borne in mind. If it is reversed in its sense of sequence, the implication of the eighteenth-century Chinese historian Chang Hsüeh-ch'eng's famous warning against employing Ch'in-Han costumes in painting likenesses of Ming Chinese is relevant here. (Chang Hsüeh-ch'eng, *Wen-shih t'ung-i*, Peking, 1956 ed., p. 65). Later nineteenth-century copyists were inclined to rewrite Gia-long period materials according to more orthodox documentary styles.

54. *DNTL*, I, 39:19ff.

55. *DNTL*, II, 1:23–23b.

56. *DNTL*, II, 4:17–19b.

57. *DNTL*, II, 28:17b.

58. Trans. from the text in Dương Quảng Hàm, *Việt Nam văn học sử yếu*, pp. 336–337.

59. Historic Faifo, which was actually slightly southeast of nineteenth-century Hội An, has puzzled Vietnamese scholars. Its name appears to have been a Western distortion of a Vietnamese geographical name, a distortion that survived after the local word it distorted had vanished. But

what was the local word? Although some writers have suggested Phải-phố, a more plausible suggestion possibly is the Sino-Vietnamese word Hải-phố, meaning "walled city on the seacoast." See the interesting correspondence on this subject by Nguyễn Bội Liên in *Sử Địa*, 7–8:249–252 (1967).

60. Georges Taboulet, *La Geste française en Indochine: Histoire par les textes de la France en Indochine des origines à 1914* (Paris, 1955), I, 10–12.

61. Taboulet, *La Geste française*, I, 308–309.

62. *HDSL*, 48:5.

63. *DNTL*, I, 24:16b.

64. *DNTL*, II, 70:18.

65. *DNTL*, II, 4:8b.

66. *DNTL*, II, 70:16.

67. *DNTL*, II, 79:14b–15.

68. Taboulet, *La Geste française*, I, 326.

69. *HDSL*, 10:33ff.

70. *DNTL*, II, 159:17ff.

71. *DNTL*, II, 159:28b.

72. *DNTL*, II, 31:15.

73. *DNTL*, II, 151:12.

74. *DNTL*, II, 33:10.

75. *DNTL*, II, 182:4–6b.

76. For example, Silvestre, *L'Empire d'Annam et le peuple annamite*, pp. 196–199.

77. Taboulet, *La Geste française*, I, 319.

78. *DNTL*, II, 170:10–10b.

79. *DNTL*, II, 219:13b.

80. *DNTL*, II, 3:9 and *DNTL*, II, 34:19b.

81. *DNTL*, II, 193:3 and *DNTL*, II, 194:23b.

82. *NTCB: Chư bộ nha tấu chiếp*, Minh-mạng 18:7:17 (1837), microfilm roll F 1616.

83. *DNTL*, II, 182:22b.

84. *NTCB: Chư bộ nha tấu chiếp*, Minh-mạng 18:7:15 (1837), microfilm roll F 1616.

85. *DNTL*, II, 155:2b; L. Cadière, "Les Français au service de Gia-long: Leur correspondance," *BAVH*, 13. 4:421–422 (October–December 1926).

86. *HDSL*, 133:13–19b.

87. *DNTL*, II, 8:6.

88. *DNTL*, II, 218:19ff.

89. *DNTL*, II, 4:3–3b; *DNTL*, II, 4:6b.

90. *DNTL*, II, 207:16.

91. Nguyễn Siêu, *Phương Đình dư địa chí*, trans. into modern Vietnamese by Ngô Mạnh Nghinh (Saigon, 1959), pp. 167–170.

92. *HDSL*, 38:21b–22.

93. Trans. from the Vietnamese text given in Cửu Long Giang and Toan Ánh, *Người Việt Đất Việt* (Saigon, 1967), p. 247. The Vietnamese

term I have translated as "Chinaman," *thằng Chệt*, might more accurately if impolitely be rendered as "Chink." The word *Chệt*, a Vietnamese term of abuse for the Chinese, both reminds the Vietnamese listener of the word for "rat" (*chuột*) and satirizes Chinese inability to pronounce Vietnamese words like *chuột* correctly.

94. *HDSL*, 48:37b.

95. *HDSL*, 48:1–1b. Merchant ships from Malacca and points in Malaya also paid the Hainan rates. Students of the evolution of the south Chinese shipping world in the Ch'ing period may gain a truer appreciation of its far-flung enterprises from Vietnamese archives than from Chinese ones, because the junk trade was a far greater concern to rulers in Huế than it was to the Manchu emperors.

96. *DNTL*, II, 88:5.

97. *HDSL*, 48:21.

98. *HDSL*, 48:26ff.

99. *HDSL*, 48:23b–24.

100. *HDSL*, 64:9b–10.

101. *HDSL*, 64:9.

102. *HDSL*, 48:31.

103. *DNTL*, II, 160:2b–3.

104. *DNTL*, I, 42:14b.

105. I am indebted for much of this analysis to a very fine pioneering article by a leading economic historian of Nguyễn Vietnam, Fujiwara Riichirō, "Gen-chō chika ni okeru kinginka no mondai," *Shisō*, 17–18:35ff. (1960).

106. Gia-long sent Chinese agents to Canton in 1814 with 10,000 silver taels to purchase various commodities. (*DNTL*, I, 48:19bff.) Earlier, in 1810, he had given 20,000 gold taels to several Minh-hương from Gia Định to go to Canton to buy goods. (*DNTL*, I, 40:14b.)

107. In his article Fujiwara supplies the relevant documentation from the *DNTL* for these price changes.

108. *DNTL*, II, 121:9b–12b.

109. *DNTL*, II, 80:7bff.

110. This problem has been explored and documented by Wada Hironori, "Shindai no Uetonamu-Biruma Gin," *Shigaku*, 33.3–4:119ff. (1961).

111. *DNTL*, II, 193:12.

112. *HDSL*, 44:3b.

113. *HDSL*, 44:8b–9; *DNTL*, II, 181:8bff.

114. *DNTL*, I, 50:10b.

115. *DNTL*, II, 217:32ff.

116. *DNTL*, II, 212:32ff.

117. *DNTL*, II, 209:6ff.

118. Chaigneau, *Souvenirs de Huế*, pp. 169–170.

119. Translated from the Vietnamese *quốc-ngữ* text furnished in Đỗ Thúc Vịnh, *Hồ Xuân Hương*, pp. 65–66. The words for "knife for slicing

up herbs" in the second last line—*dao cầu*—also suggest the idea of the ball—*cầu*—which a highly placed woman threw out of her window as a fatalistic way of making a marriage choice. She married the man who caught the ball. The apothecary's wife in the poem, in other words, is suggesting that she will remarry very shortly—"I wonder to whom I will entrust the ball of my marriage choice?"

120. *DNTL*, II, 206:2.

121. *DNTL*, II, 204:25.

122. *DNTL*, II, 197:21b.

123. *DNTL*, II, 88:19b–20.

124. *NTCB*: *Chư bộ nha tấu chiếp*, Minh-mạng 17:2:1 (1836), microfilm roll F 1614.

125. *NTCB*, ibid.

126. *DNTL*, II, 9:6b; *DNTL*, III, 33:8b.

127. *HDSL*, 217:30–38b.

128. L. Cadière, "Documents relatifs à l'époque de Gia-long," *BEFEO*, 12. 7:20–23 (1912).

129. Taboulet, *La Geste française*, I, 105–107.

130. Chaigneau, *Souvenirs de Huế*, pp. 84ff.

131. *DNTL*, II, 80:11b.

132. *DNTL*, II, 191:24ff.

133. *DNTL*, II, 109:22b; *DNTL*, II, 193:22; *DNTL*, II, 207:2b.

134. *DNTL*, II, 202:2b.

135. *DNTL*, II, 205:12bff for Minh-mạng's discussions with provincial officials of the best ways of dealing with Christianity, and Minh-mạng's views on Marchand.

136. *DNTL*, II, 164:1ff.

137. Cited in Phạm Thế Ngũ, *Việt Nam văn học sử: Việt văn*, p. 322.

138. *DNTL*, II, 202:6bff. The book from which the emperor read was Chinese, not Western. Minh-mạng believed that it had been written by a Westernized Chinese.

139. *HDSL*, 227:19–21b.

Note on Major Primary Sources

This book has sprung from what I hope can be called a comprehensive reading of the primary Vietnamese documentary and literary sources for early nineteenth-century Vietnamese history. The reading of nineteenth-century Chinese documents—above all, the *Ta Ch'ing hui-tien*, the *hui-tien shih-li*, and the private writings of eighteenth- and nineteenth-century Chinese officials like Liang Chang-chü—has also been an integral part of my research, although my work here has naturally not been as exhaustive. This is true also of my reading of secondary French literature, famous or obscure, on nineteenth-century Vietnam, although obviously I am greatly indebted to the reminiscences of Chaigneau and the brilliant scholarship of Maspero, Cadière, Durand, and others. Limitations of time and space, combined with the need to allow the basic Vietnamese documentation, which is immensely stimulating and surprisingly varied, to come into its own, imposed this bibliographical pattern upon me.

In Saigon the historian's most rewarding haven is the Viện Khảo Cổ (Institute of the Study of the Past). Of importance also are the Thư Viện Quốc Gia (National Library) and the Viện Bảo Tàng (Museum) of the Thảo Cầm Viện (Botanical Gardens). In Japan the historian may consult, as I did, some invaluable nineteenth-century Vietnamese texts at the Tōyō Bunkō (Oriental Library) in Tokyo. In Paris, the baffling riches of the fascinating collection of *nôm* texts at the Bibliothèque Nationale are a challenge to any scholar.

On any evaluation, the single most important source for early nineteenth-century Vietnamese history is the *Đại Nam thực lục chính biên*, the *Veritable Records of Imperial Vietnam*. Formal compilation of this work was begun in the summer of 1821 in Huế, under the aegis of the project's chief editor, the general Nguyễn Văn Nhân, who directed an initial staff of two assistant editors, nine senior collectors of materials, twenty-five compilers, five officials to inspect and collate, twelve secretarial managers, and eight copyists. Long before 1821 the project had been a focus of concern at the court, however. In 1811 Gia-long ordered bureaucrats serving in southern Vietnam to summarize all the written data and oral traditions in their region which dealt with the history of the dynasty for future inclusion in the *Records*, proof that he had had the concept in mind for some time (*DNTL*, I, 42:19ff.) By 1835 the chief editorship of the *Records* had gravitated into the hands of Trương Đăng Quế, at that time the president of the Board of War. In 1842, when Thiệu-trị asked Quế why the *Records* for earlier reigns had not yet been completed, he replied that court historians were working hard but that court archives were difficult to sort and "thread together." The emperor replied by commending to him the terse literary style of the Chinese *Ming shih* (Ming history; *DNTL*, III, 23:5b.) Because of such delays the two hundred and twenty books of *Records* for the Minh-mạng reign, for example, did not emerge in their final form, with signed prefaces, until after 1860.

Essentially, the *Veritable Records* transcribe the day-to-day business of the Vietnamese court. Their contents range from the daily conversations of the emperors, to imperial appointments lists, to detailed anatomies of diplomatic crises or of provincial economic, social, and political problems, received in Huế but written by bureaucrats serving on the scene. In reading these records, the modern analyst need not fear extensive suppression of the evidence. On the whole this was rare. The *Veritable Records* were propaganda. But they were propaganda of a peculiar kind, designed more for a small lineal audience of future courts than for a mass popular audience of the present. The key to the potency of historiographical propaganda in traditional Vietnam was not considered to be manipulation of factual content. Rather, it was considered to be demonstration of imperial form. Therefore, communications from the provinces which described every manner of social and political evil were faithfully recorded. The emperor was supposed to reveal his worth not by suppressing them but by publishing them, answering them, acting upon them and thus transcending them. He had the last word, or, to invoke a more appropriately Sino-Vietnamese coinage, he left the final image on the "mirror." For the modern analyst, omission of evidence—because it did not interest the scholars of the time—is rather the central problem in using such documents.

Another documentary cornerstone of research on nineteenth-century Vietnam is the *Đại Nam hội điển sự lệ* or *Compendium of Institutions and Institutional Cases of Imperial Vietnam*. When he first ordered it compiled in 1843, Thiệu-trị traced the historiographical principles behind its creation back to the bamboo slip archives of the Chinese sage-emperors Yao and Shun (*DNTL*, III, 31:18b.) But when it was initially printed in 1851 it turned out to be so vast an agglomeration of documents that its printers required nearly 8,000 wood blocks. It is the major primary source for the study of the traditional Vietnamese government. Containing all the important statutes and administrative occurrences of Vietnamese history from 1802 to 1851, its topical framework reflects the functional divisions of the Nguyễn bureaucracy itself into Six Boards dealing with bureaucratic commissions, finance, education and foreign affairs, military problems, judicial matters, and public works.

Still another basic source is the *châu bản*, the *Vermilion Books* of the Nguyễn dynasty, the original court documents which Vietnamese emperors had personally perused and signed with their vermilion writing brushes. The *Vermilion Books* which have survived the ravages of an interminable civil war offer the historian fascinating but disorganized data, and especially the raw materials for an analysis of important aspects of traditional Vietnamese socio-economic life. Inventories of the Huế imperial treasuries, lists of the cargoes of Western ships calling at Đà Nẵng in the 1830's, synopses of bureaucratic judicial cases, reconstructions of *causes célèbres* of village government, and above all, "rice price reports" from numerous provinces of the country for given years like 1829, are some of the types of documents occasionally included in their contents. So far only a few scholars, like Fujiwara Riichirō of Japan, have made much of an effort to appraise the problems of nineteenth-century Vietnamese socio-economic history.

The early nineteenth-century elite itself may be studied through its own writings. These may range from the numerous but sometimes faintly materialistic poems of Nguyễn Công Trứ, a few of which have been presented in translation in this book, to ponderous memoir-histories like Trương Quốc Dụng's *Công hạ ký văn* (Things recorded and heard on duty and in leisure), a copy of which the Tōyō Bunkō preserves. The elite may also be studied through biographies of individual bureaucrats, like those of the court-sponsored *Đại Nam liệt truyện* (Biographies of imperial Vietnam). This work also contains, Chinese-style, imitatively ethnocentric essays on foreign countries. I have found Cao Xuân Dục's list of examination system winners, with its attendant biographical data, useful for examining upward and downward social mobility purely within the context of bureaucratic recruitment.

But what broods over this documentation, for modern analysts, is the ghost of an old Tolstoyan paradox. The higher officials are in the pyramid of authority at any given time, the farther removed they are from its base, the ordinary people, whose lives are the real stuff of history. Vietnamese historians have only recently begun to put the historical pieces of nineteenth-century peasant rebellions together. Sometimes they gather these pieces from relatively subterranean sources, even exploring the memories of certain aged villagers who may recollect the extravagant oral traditions that famous rebellions left in their wake. This was actually done by Chu Thiên and his associates in their exciting reconstruction of the Phan Bá Vành rebellion of the 1820's (*Nghiên cứu lịch sử*, May 1966).

This book, I do not need to point out, has merely scratched the surface of the body of Vietnamese historical materials, the variegated body of materials, which the early 1800's have bequeathed us. Some of these materials—for example, the bundles of Nguyễn land registers (*địa bộ*) stored at the present time (1970) in a library on the Avenue Yersin in Đàlạt—still remain uncatalogued. Unused and forgotten, they are highly vulnerable to the deadly vicissitudes of the current civil war.

In deference to the linguistic revolution in modern Vietnam, which has discarded the use of Chinese characters, such characters are not supplied for the names of twentieth-century Vietnamese authors and publications.

Aubaret, G. *Histoire et description de la Basse Cochinchine.* Paris, 1863.

Azambre, Georges. "Hanoi: Notes de geographie urbaine," *Bulletin de la Societé des Études Indochinoises,* vol. 30, no. 4 (1955).

Bắc Kỳ hà đê sự tích 北圻河堤事跡 (Historical materials concerning the river dikes of the north). Comp. and trans. into modern Vietnamese by Hà Ngọc Xuyên. Saigon, 1963.

Bản triều bạn nghịch liệt truyện 本朝叛逆列傳 (Biographies of rebels of this dynasty). Trans. into modern Vietnamese by Trần Khải Văn. Saigon, 1963.

Bourotte, Bernard. "Essai d'histoire des populations montagnardes du Sud-Indochinois jusqu'à 1945," *Bulletin de la Société des Etudes Indochinoises,* vol. 30, no. 1 (1955).

Bùi Quang Tung. "Cuộc khởi loạn của Công tử Hồng Tập dưới triều Tự-đức" (The Hồng Tập rebellion in the Tự-đức reign), *Văn Hóa Nguyệt San* (Culture monthly), nos. 1–2 (Saigon, 1962).

Bửu Cầm. "Nguồn gốc chữ nôm" (The origins of the *nôm* script), *Văn Hóa Nguyệt San,* no. 5 (Saigon, 1960).

——"Thử tìm nguồn gốc văn thê lục bát" (An attempted search for the origins of the *lục bát* literary style), *Văn Hóa Nguyệt San,* nos. 3–4 (Saigon, 1962).

——"Văn hóa Việt-Nam dưới hai triều Lý và Trần" (Vietnamese culture under the two Lý and Trần courts), *Văn Hóa Nguyệt San,* no. 12 (Saigon, 1962).

——"Hai bức thư chữ nôm mở màn cuộc phân tranh Trịnh-Nguyễn" (Two *nôm* letters opening the Trịnh-Nguyễn hostilities), *Văn Hóa Nguyệt San,* no. 9 (Saigon, 1963).

Cadière, L. "Documents relatifs à l'époque de Gia-long," *Bulletin de L'École Française d'Extreme Orient,* vol. 12, no. 7 (1912).

——"Les Urnes dynastiques du Palais de Huế: Notice historique," *Bulletin des Amis du Vieux Huế,* vol. 1, no. 1 (January–March 1914).

——"Les Français au service de Gia-long," *Bulletin des Amis du Vieux Huế,* vol. 13, no. 1 (January–March 1926).

————"Les Français au service de Gia-long: Leur correspondance," *Bulletin des Amis du Vieux Huế,* vol. 13, no. 4 (October–December 1926).

————"La Famille et la religion en pays annamite," *Bulletin des Amis du Vieux Huế,* vol. 17, no. 4 (October–December 1930).

Cao Xuân Dục 高春育, comp. *Quốc triều đăng khoa lục* 國朝登科錄 (A list of successful examination candidates of this dynasty). Trans. into modern Vietnamese by Lê Mạnh Liêu. Saigon, 1962.

Chaigneau, Michel Duc. *Souvenirs de Huế.* Paris, 1867.

Chang Chung-li. *The Chinese Gentry: Studies on Their Role in Nineteenth-Century Chinese Society.* Seattle, University of Washington Press, 1955.

Chang Hsüeh-ch'eng 章學誠. *Wen-shih t'ung-i* 文史通義 (A comprehensive exposition of literature and history). 1956 ed. Peking.

Chao I 趙翼. *Yen-p'u tsa-chi* 簷曝雜記 (Miscellaneous notes), in *Ou-pei ch'üan-chi* 歐北全集 (Collected writings of Ou-pei). 1877 ed. Shanghai.

Ch'en Ching-ho 陳荊和. *Ch'eng-t'ien Ming-hsiang she Ch'en shih cheng-p'u* 承天明鄉社陳氏正譜 (The family register of the Trần lineage of the Minh-hương villages of Thừa Thiên). Hong Kong, 1964.

Chin Chao-feng 金兆豐. *Ch'ing-shih ta-kang* 清史大綱 (A summary of Ch'ing history). Hong Kong, 1963.

Ch'in-ting Ta Ch'ing hui-tien shih-li 欽定大清會典事例 (Official compendium of institutions and usages of the Imperial Ch'ing). 1899 ed.

Ch'ü Ta-chün 屈大均 et al., comp. *Kuang-tung hsin-yü* 廣東新語 (New terms of Kwangtung). Pub. in 1700 but comp. in the 1600's.

Chu Thiên. "Vài nét về công thương nghiệp triều Nguyễn" (Some points about the industry and commerce of the Nguyễn court), *Nghiên cứu lịch sử* (Historical researches), no. 33 (Hanoi, December 1961).

Chula Chakrabongse. *Lords of Life: The Paternal Monarchy of Bangkok, 1782-1932.* London, Redman, 1960.

Crawfurd, John. *Journal of an Embassy from the Governor-General of India to the Courts of Siam and Cochinchina.* London, 1830.

Đại Nam chính biên liệt truyện sơ tập 大南正編列傳初集 (First collection of the primary compilation of biographies of Imperial Vietnam). 1841; reprint, Tokyo, 1961.

Đại Nam điển lệ toát yếu 大南典例撮要 (A summary of the statutes of Imperial Vietnam). 1909 ed. Trans. into modern Vietnamese by Nguyễn Sĩ Giác. Saigon, 1962.

Đại Nam nhất thống chí 大南一統志 (Gazetteer of Imperial Vietnam). Cao Xuân Dục 高春育 et al., comp. 1909 ed.

Đại Nam thực lục chính biên, đệ nhất, nhị, tam kỷ 大南實錄正編, 第一, 二, 三紀 (Primary compilation of the Veritable Records of the first three reigns of Imperial Vietnam). Formal organization and compilation from 1821.

Đại Việt lịch triều đăng khoa lục 大越歷朝登科錄 (Chronicles of successful examination candidates of successive Vietnamese courts). Trans. into modern Vietnamese by Tạ Thúc Khải. Vol. 1. Saigon, 1962.

Đặng Huy Vận. Nguyễn Phan Quang, and Chu Thiên. "Cuộc khởi nghĩa Phan Bá Vành" (The Uprising of Phan Bá Vành), *Nghiên cứu lịch sử* (Historical researches), no. 86 (Hanoi, May 1966).

Đào Duy Anh. *Việt-Nam văn hóa sử cương* (A general history of Vietnamese culture). Saigon, 1938.

Đào Văn Hội. *Phong tục Miền Nam Qua Mấy Vần Ca Dao* (Southern customs expressed in folk songs). Saigon, 1961.

Đỗ Thúc Vịnh. *Hồ Xuân Hương: Tác giả thế kỷ XIX* (Hồ Xuân Hương: nineteenth-century writer). Saigon, 1956.

Đông Hồ. "Tương-quan giữa thơ hán và thơ nôm của thi phái Chiêu-anh-các" (Relationships among the poems in Chinese and Vietnamese characters of the *Chiêu-anh-các* group of poets), *Văn hóa nguyệt san*, no. 5 (Saigon, 1965).

Dương Quảng Hàm. *Việt-Nam văn học sử yếu* (A historical summary of Vietnamese literature). Hanoi, 1951.

DuPicq, Ardant. *Histoire d'une citadelle annamite: Bắc Ninh*. Hanoi, 1935.

Feng Kuei-fen 馮桂芬. *Chiao-pin lü k'ang-i* 校邠廬抗議 (Remonstrances from the studio of Chiao-pin). Author's preface dated 1860–61. 1884 ed. Shanghai.

Finlayson, George. *Mission to Siam and Hue, The Capital of Cochinchina in the Years 1821–1822*. London, 1826.

Fujisawa, Y. 藤澤義美. "Unnan kodai no Dairi bunka" 雲南古代の大理文化 (The Tali culture of ancient Yunnan), *Shichō* 史潮 (The historical tide), nos. 82–83 (Tokyo, March 1963).

Fujiwara Riichirō 藤原利一郎. "Gen-chō chika ni okeru kinginka no mondai" 阮朝治下における金銀價の問題 (The problem of gold and silver prices under the rule of the Nguyễn court), *Shisō* 史窓 (Historical windows), nos. 17–18 (Kyoto, 1960).

Gourou, Pierre. *Les Paysans du delta Tonkinois: Etude de geographie humaine*. Paris, Les Editions d'art et d'histoire, 1936.

Hải Thu. "Bàn thêm về thái độ của Nguyễn Trãi đối với nhân dân lao động" (Supplementary notes on Nguyễn Trãi's attitudes toward the working people), *Nghiên cứu lịch sử*, no. 85 (Hanoi, April 1966).

Hibino Takeo 日比野丈夫. "Tokugawa bakufu ni yoru Chūgoku chihōshi no shūshū" 德川幕府による中國地方志の蒐集 (The accumulation of Chinese gazetteers by the Tokugawa shogunate), in *Iwai hakushi koki kinen tenseki ronshū* 岩井博士の古稀記念典籍論集 (A Festschrift collection for Dr. Iwai on his seventieth birthday). Tokyo, 1963.

Higo Kazuo 肥後和男. *Tennōshi* 天皇史 (A history of the emperor). Tokyo, 1950.

Ho P'ing-ti. *The Ladder of Success in Imperial China*. New York, Columbia University Press, 1962.

Hoa Bằng, "Nguyễn Hữu Cầu với cuộc khởi nghĩa nông dân giữa thế kỷ XVIII" (Nguyễn Hữu Cầu and the peasant uprisings of the mid-eighteenth century), *Nghiên cứu lịch sử*, no. 75 (Hanoi, June 1965).

Hoa Bằng, "Nhà Tây-sơn đới với hai nữanh hùng Nguyệt Thai và Nguyệt Độ" (The Tây-sơns' attitude toward the two heroines Nguyệt Thai and Nguyệt Đô), *Nghiên cứu lịch sử*, no. 86 (Hanoi, May 1966).

Hsü Chi-yü 徐繼畬. *Ying-huan chih-lüeh* 瀛環志略 (A world gazetteer). Preface dated 1848.

Huang Shih 黄石. *Tuan-wu li-tsu shih* 端午禮俗史 (A history of the rites and customs of the fifth day of the fifth month). Hong Kong, 1963.

Huỳnh Thiên Kim. *Cận đại Việt sử diễn ca* (Versifications of modern Vietnamese history). Saigon, 1962.

Karpeles, Suzanne. "Notules sur un manuscrit relatif à une ambassade birmane en Cochinchine," *Bulletin de la Société des Etudes Indochinoises*, vol. 24, no. 1 (1949).

Khâm định Đại Nam hội điển sự lệ 欽定大南會典事例 (Official compendium of institutions and usages of Imperial Vietnam), comp. at Huế 1842–1851. Deposited in the Tōyō Bunkō, Tokyo.

Kiêm Đạt. *Nguyễn Công Trứ: Luận đề, nghiên cứu, khảo luận* (Nguyễn Công Trứ: A presentation, research, an examination). Saigon, 1959.

Kung Tzu-chen 龔自珍. *Kung Ting-an wen-chi* 龔定盦文集 (Collected writings of Kung Ting-an). 1908 ed., Shanghai.

Kuwabara Jitsuzō 桑原隲藏. *Shina hōsei-shi ronsō* 支那法制史論叢 (Collected discussions on the history of the Chinese legal system). Tokyo, 1937.

Lã Văn Lô. "Thử bàn về việc viết lịch sử các dân tộc thiểu số anh em" (On the task of writing the history of our brotherly minority peoples), *Nghiên cứu lịch sử*, no. 91 (Hanoi, October 1966).

Lê Quý Đôn 黎貴惇. *Vân đài loại ngữ* 藝臺類語 (Classified talk from the study). Author's preface dated 1773, in the Tōyō Bunkō.

Lê triều giáo hóa điều luật 黎朝教化條律 (Moral catechism rules of the Lê dynasty). Trans. into modern Vietnamese by Trần Khải Văn. Saigon, 1962.

Lê Văn Hảo. "Mấy nét về hội sống Việt-Nam giữa thế kỷ thứ XIX" (A few points about Vietnamese life in the nineteenth century), in Trương Bá Cần et al., *Kỷ niệm 100 năm ngày Pháp chiếm Nam kỳ* (The hundredth anniversary of the French occupation of southern Vietnam). Saigon, 1967.

Li Tiao-yüan 李調元. *Nan-Yüeh pi-chi* 南越筆記 (Writings on Nan Yüeh). Author's preface undated, but written in the late 1700's.

Liang Chang-chü 梁章鉅 et al. *Shu-yüan chi-lüeh* 樞垣記略 (A summary account of the inner government). Author's preface dated 1823; 1875 ed.

Luro, E. *Le pays d'Annam: Etude sur l'organization politique et sociale des Annamites*. Paris, 1878.

Lý Tế Xuyên 李濟川. *Việt điện u linh tập* 越甸幽靈集 (Anthology of the spirits of the departed of the Vietnamese domain). Trans. into modern Vietnamese by Lê Hữu Mục. Saigon, 1961.

Maeda Katsutarō 前田勝太郎. "Mindai chūki ikō no Fukken ni okeru suiri kikō no hembō ni tsuite" 明代中期以降の福建における水利機構の變貌について (The change in features of irrigation organization in Fukien from the middle of the Ming dynasty), *Tōhōgaku* 東方學 (Eastern studies), no. 32 (Tokyo, June 1966).

Makino Tatsumi 牧野巽. *Shina kazoku kenkyū* 支那家族研究 (Researches on the Chinese family). Tokyo, 1944.

Maspero, Henri. "Études d'histoire d'Annam: l'Expedition de Ma Yüan," *Bulletin de l'Ecole Française d'Extreme Orient*, vol. 18, no. 3 (1918).

———"Études sur la phonetique historique de la langue Annamite," *Bulletin de l'Ecole Française d'Extreme Orient*, vol. 12, no. 1 (1912).

Matsumoto Nobuhiro 松本信廣. *Indo-Shina no minzoku to bunka* 印度支那の民族と文化 (The peoples and cultures of Indochina). Tokyo, 1942.

Miyamoto Mataji 宮本又次. *Nihon shōgyō shi* 日本商業史 (A history of Japanese commerce). Tokyo, 1943.

Miyazaki Ichisada 宮崎市定. *Kakyo: Chūgoku no shiken jigoku* 科擧：中國の試驗地獄 (Tests and preferment: China's examination hell). Tokyo, 1963.

Miyazaki Ichisada 宮崎市定. "Nihon no kan-i-ryō to Tō no kampin-ryō" 日本の官位令と唐の官品令 (Japanese administrative laws of official positions and T'ang administrative laws of bureaucratic grades). *Tōhōgaku*, no. 18 (Tokyo, June 1959).

Nghiêm Thẩm. "Sự tồn tại của bản chất Anh-đô-nê-diêng trong nền văn-hóa Việt-Nam" (The survival of an Indonesian fundamental substance in Vietnamese culture), *Quê Hương* (Fatherland, Saigon, June 1962).

Ngô Sĩ Liên 吳士連. *Đại Việt sử ký toàn thư* 大越史記全書 (A complete history of Imperial Vietnam). Comp. 15th century. Japanese ed. deposited at Tōyō Bunkō, 1884.

Ngô Tất Tố. *Lều chõng* (Tent and bamboo bed). 1958 ed. Saigon.

Nguyễn Đình Hòa. "*Chữ Nôm*: The Demotic System of Writing in Vietnam," *Journal of the American Oriental Society*, vol. 79, no. 4 (1959).

Nguyễn Đình Lai. "Etude sur la musique Sino-Vietnamienne et les chants populaires du Viet-Nam," *Bulletin de la Société des Etudes Indochinoises*, vol. 31, no. 1 (1956).

Nguyễn Duy Diễn. "Việc học và việc thi chữ Nho ngày trước" (Learning and Confucian examinations of bygone days), *Gió Mới* (New wind) (Saigon, September 1961).

Nguyễn Huyền Anh. *Việt Nam danh nhân tự điển* (A dictionary of famous Vietnamese people). Saigon, 1960.

Nguyễn Khắc Đạm. "Vài ý kiến góp cùng Ông Hồ Hữu Phước về vấn đề ruộng tư" (Matching a few opinions with Mr. Ho Huu Phuoc on the problem of private estates), *Nghiên cứu lịch sử*, no. 74 (Hanoi, May 1965).

Nguyễn Phan Quang and Đặng Huy Vận. "Tìm hiểu chế độ lao dịch và binh dịch dưới triều Gia-long" (Toward an understanding of the corvee and compulsory military service systems under the Gia-long court), *Nghiên cứu lịch sử*, no. 80 (Hanoi, November 1965).

Nguyễn Phan Quang and Đặng Huy Vận. "Tình hình đấu tranh giai cấp ở thời Gia-long" (The situation of social conflict in the Gia-long period), *Nghiên cứu lịch sử*, no. 78 (Hanoi, September 1965).

Nguyễn Phương. "Ai đã thống nhất Việt-Nam: Nguyễn Huệ hay Nguyễn Ánh, trả lời Ông Vân Tân, Hà-Nội" (Who unified Vietnam, Nguyễn Huệ or Nguyễn Ánh, a reply to Mr. Vân Tân in Hanoi), *Đại Học* (Higher learning), no. 6 (Huế, October-December 1963).

Nguyễn Phương. "Đà lịch sử" (Historical impulsions), *Sử Địa* (History and geography), no. 1 (Saigon, 1966).

Nguyễn Phương. "Phương pháp sử của Lê Văn Hưu và Ngô Sĩ Liên" (The historical methods of Lê Văn Hưu and Ngô Sĩ Liên), *Đại Học*, no. 6 (Huế, December 1962).

Nguyễn Sỹ Tế. *Hồ Xuân Hương* (Hồ Xuân Hương). Saigon, 1956.

Nguyễn Sỹ Tế, *Việt-Nam văn học nghị luận* (A discussion of Vietnamese literature). Saigon, 1962.

Nguyễn Thế Anh. *Bibliographie critique sur les relations entre le Viet-Nam et l'occident.* Paris, Maisonneuve et Larose, 1967.

Nguyễn Thế Anh, *Kinh tế và xã hội Việt-nam dưới các vua triều Nguyễn* (The Vietnamese economy and society under the Nguyễn rulers). Saigon, 1968.

Nguyễn Thế Anh, "Vấn đề lúa gạo ở Việt-Nam trong tiền bán thế kỷ XIX" (The rice problem in Vietnam in the first half of the nineteenth century), *Sử Địa*, no. 6 (Saigon, 1967).

Nguyễn triều châu bản 阮朝硃本 (Vermillion Books of the Nguyễn Dynasty). *Chư bộ nha tấu chiếp* 諸部衙奏摺 (Memorials of the various offices) and *Ngoại quốc thư trát* 外國書札 (Foreign correspondence) of the Gia-long and Minh-mạng reigns (to 1838). On microfilm at the Harvard-Yenching Chinese-Japanese Library, Cambridge, Mass.

Nguyễn Tường Minh, *Khảo luận về Nguyễn Công Trứ* (A study of Nguyễn Công Trứ). Saigon, 196?

Nguyễn Văn Siêu 阮文超. *Phương Đình dư địa chí* 方亭輿地志 (The geographical chronicles of Phương Đình). Trans. into modern Vietnamese by Ngô Mạnh Nghinh. Saigon, 1959.

Nguyễn Văn Siêu 阮文超. *Phương Đình văn loại* 方亭文類 (The writings of Phương Đình). 1856 and earlier. In Tōyō Bunko.

Nguyễn Văn Siêu 阮文超. *Phương Đình vạn lý tập* 方亭萬里集 (Phương Đình's collection on his 10,000 li of travels). Dated 1851. In Tōyō Bunkō.

Nguyễn Văn Trình and U'ng Trình, "Le Quốc-tử-giám," *Bulletin des Amis du Vieux Huế,* vol. 4, no. 1 (January-March 1917).

Nhu Viễn 柔遠 (The harmonious management of distant peoples). Trans. into modern Vietnamese by Tạ Quang Phát. Rev. and ed. by Bửu Cầm. Saigon, 1965.

Pasquier, Pierre. *L'Annam d'autrefois*. Paris, 1907.

Phạm Đình Hổ 范廷琥 and Nguyễn Án 阮案. *Tang thương ngẫu lục* 桑滄偶錄 (Random recordings of great changes). 1806. Trans. into modern Vietnamese by Đạm Nguyên. Saigon, 1961.

Phạm Thế Ngũ. *Việt Nam văn học sử giản ước tân biên: văn học lịch triều: Việt văn* (A new concise history of Vietnamese literature: literature of successive courts in Vietnamese). Saigon, 1963.

Phạm Văn Diêu. "Khảo luận về Hồ Xuân Hương" (A Study of Hồ Xuân Hương), *Văn hóa nguyệt san*, nos. 3–4 (Saigon, 1962).

Phạm Văn Diêu. *Văn học Việt Nam* (Vietnamese literature). Saigon, 1960.

Phạm Văn Diêu. *Việt Nam văn học giảng bình* (Critical lectures on Vietnamese literature). Saigon, 1961.

Phạm Văn Sơn. *Việt sử tân biên: Từ Tây-sơn mạt-diệp đến Nguyễn sơ* (A new history of Vietnam: From the end of the Tây-sơn to the early Nguyễn period). Saigon, 1961.

Phạm Việt Tuyền. "Một vài ý kiến về sự-nghiệp Gia-long" (A few opinions on the career of Gia-long), *Đại Học*, no. 8 (Huế, March 1959).

Phan Huy Chú 潘輝注. *Lịch triều hiến chương loại chí* 歷朝憲章類誌 (A reference book of the institutions of successive dynasties). Presented to Minh-mạng in 1821. Trans. into modern Vietnamese by Lưỡng Thần and Cao Nãi Quang. Saigon, 1957.

Phan Huy Lê. "Tình hình khai mỏ dưới triều Nguyễn" (The mine development situation under the Nguyễn court), *Nghiên cứu lịch sử*, no. 51 (Hanoi, June 1963).

Phan Khoang. "Lược sử chế độ xã-thôn ở Việt-Nam" (A summary history of the system of villages and hamlets in Vietnam), *Sử Địa*, no. 1 (Saigon, 1966).

Phan Thúc Trực 潘叔直. *Quốc sử di biên* 國史遺編 (A transmitted compilation of the dynasty's history), 1851–52. Hong Kong New Asia Research Institute reprint, 1965.

Schreiner, Alfred. *Les institutions annamites en Basse-Cochinchine avant la conquête française*. Saigon, 1900.

Shang Yen-liu 商衍鎏. *Ch'ing-tai k'o-chü k'ao-shih shu-lu* 清代科舉考試述錄 (An account of the Ch'ing dynasty examinations). Peking, 1958.

Silvestre, J. *L'empire d'Annam et le peuple annamite*. Paris, 1889.

Skinner, G. William. *Chinese Society in Thailand*. Ithaca, Cornell University Press, 1957.

Sơ Học Vấn Tân 初學問津 (Asking the way in elementary studies). 1882 printed ed., no. B–26 of the collection of *nôm* texts in the Bibliothèque Nationale, Paris.

Ta Ch'ing hui-tien 大清會典 (Imperial Ch'ing compendium of institutions). 1899 ed.

Taboulet, Georges. *La geste française en Indochine: Histoire par les textes de la France en Indochine des origines à 1914.* Paris, Maisonneuve, 1955.

Takeda Ryōji 竹田龍兒. "Annan kakyo seido shōkō" 安南科舉制度小考 (A brief study of Annam's examination system), *Shigaku* 史學 (Historical studies), vol. 37, no. 1 (Tokyo, 1964).

Tam Giáo chính độ thực lục 三敎正度實錄 (The veritable records of the standard law of the three religions). Dated 1817; no. A–33 of the Sino-Vietnamese texts of the Bibliothèque Nationale, Paris.

Tân Việt Điêu. "Kỳ thoại về bang giao và nghi lễ giao-hiếu của nước Việt thời xưa" (Remarkable stories about diplomacy and the ceremonies of state relationships of bygone Vietnam), *Văn hóa nguyệt san*, no. 11 (Saigon, 1965).

Teng Chih-ch'eng 鄧之誠. "T'an Chün-chi-ch'u" 談軍機處 (A lecture on the Grand Council), in Wang Chung-han 王鍾翰, *Ch'ing-shih tsa-k'ao* 清史雜考 (Miscellaneous studies in Ch'ing history). Peking, 1957.

Teng, S. Y. and Fairbank, J. K. *Ch'ing administration: Three studies.* Cambridge, Mass., Harvard University Press, 1960.

Tezuka Ryōdō 手塚良道. *Jukyō dōtoku ni okeru kunshin shisō* 儒敎道德に於ける君臣思想 (Concepts of sovereign and minister in Confucian morality). Tokyo, 1934.

Thái Bạch. *Thơ Hồ Xuân Hương* (The Poetry of Hồ Xuân Hương). Saigon, 1968.

Thái Văn Kiểm. "Tìm hiểu kiến trúc Kinh-thành Huế" (Toward an understanding of the architecture of the capital city of Huế), *Văn hóa nguyệt san*, no. 9 (Saigon, 1963).

Thánh giáo yếu lý quốc ngữ 聖敎要理國語 (Essential principles of Christianity in the national language). Dated 1837; no. B–5 of the collection of *nôm* texts in the Bibliothèque Nationale, Paris.

Tống Chí Truyên 宋志傳 (Chronicles of the Sung). N.d., possibly the 1600's; no. B–30 of the collection of *nôm* texts in the Bibliothèque Nationale, Paris.

Tống Phúc Ngoạn 宋福玩 and Dương Văn Châu 楊文珠. *Xiêm La Quốc lộ trình tập lục* 暹羅國路程集錄 (Collected records of travel itineraries to Siam). Written in 1810. Hong Kong, New Asia Research Institute reprint, 1966.

Trần Quốc Vượng and Đinh Xuân Lâm. "Về nguồn gốc và lịch sử Tuồng Chèo Việt-Nam" (On the origins and history of the Vietnamese *Tuồng* and *Chèo*), *Tạp chí văn học* (Literature magazine) (Hanoi, April 1966).

Trịnh Hoài Đức 鄭懷德. *Cấn Trai thi tập* 艮齋詩集 (The collected poems of Cấn Trai). Hong Kong, New Asia Research Institute reprint, 1962.

Trịnh Hoài Đức 鄭懷德. "Gia Định thông chí: thành trì chí" 嘉定通志城
池志 (Gia Định gazetteer: monograph on towns), in *Nan-yang hsüeh-
pao* 南洋學報 (Nan-yang scholarly journal), vol. 12, no. 2 (Singapore
December 1956).

Trịnh Vân Thanh. *Giảng luận Việt văn* (An exposition of Vietnamese
literature). Saigon, 1963.

Trương Quốc Dụng 張國用. *Công hạ ký văn* 公暇記聞 (Things recorded
and heard on duty and in leisure). N.d., but written about the middle
of the 1800s. In Tōyō Bunkō.

Tsung Ping 宗懍. *Ching-Ch'u sui-shih chi* 荊楚歲時記 (A record of the
times and seasons of Ching-Ch'u), in Ch'en Yün-jung 陳運溶 comp.,
Lu-shan ching-she ts'ung shu 麓山精舍叢書 (Collection of reprinted
works of the Lu-shan library). 1900 ed.

Vella, Walter F. *Siam under Rama III, 1824–1851.* Locust Valley, N.Y.,
Augustin, 1957.

Võ Văn Lập 武文立. *Dã sử hạt biên* 野史轄編 (A compilation of unofficial
history). N.d.; of the Gia-long period. In Tōyō Bunkō.

Vũ Lang. "Cổ tích Chàm và cổ tích Việt-Nam" (Old Cham tales and Old
Vietnamese tales), *Văn Hóa Á Châu* (Asian culture), no. 15 (Saigon,
July 1959).

Wada Hironori 和田博德. "Shindai no Uetonamu-Biruma gin" 清代のヴ
ェトナム―ビルマ銀 (The Vietnam-Burma Silver of the Ch'ing Period), *Shigaku*, vol. 33, nos. 3–4 (Tokyo, 1961).

Wang Chieh 王杰 et al. *Ch'in-ting k'o-ch'ang t'iao-li* 欽定科場條例 (Imperial regulations for examination sites). Dated Ch'ien-lung 54–55
(1789–1790).

Wen Yu 聞宥. "Lun Tzu-nan chih tsu-chih chi ch'i yü Han-tzu chih
kuan-she" 論字喃之組織及其與漢字之關涉 (The organization of *nôm*
and its connection with Chinese writing), *Yen-ching hsüeh-pao* 燕京學報
(Yen-ching scholarly journal), no. 14 (Peking, December 1933).

White, John. *A History of a Voyage to the China Sea.* Boston, 1823.

Woodside, A. B. "Early Ming Expansionism, 1406–1427: China's Abortive Conquest of Vietnam," *Papers on China*, vol. 17 (1963). Harvard
University, East Asian Research Center.

———"Vietnamese Buddhism, the Vietnamese Court and China in the
Early 1800's," unpub. ms., 1968.

Wu, Silas. "The Memorial Systems of the Ch'ing Dynasty," *Harvard
Journal of Asiatic Studies*, no. 27 (1967).

Wyatt, David K., "Siam and Laos, 1767–1827," *Journal of Southeast Asian
History*, vol. 4, no. 2 (September 1963).

Yoshikawa Kōjirō 吉川幸次郎. *Shinajin no koten to sono seikatsu* 支那人の古典
とその生活 (The Chinese people's ancient classics and their way of
life). Tokyo, 1965.

Principal entries in this glossary include Chinese and Japanese words that are used in the text, as well as Vietnamese ones. Where meaningful, romanized Chinese equivalents of Sino-Vietnamese words that parallel Chinese usages are given in parentheses. The reader should note that sometimes the word order of a Sino-Vietnamese phrase may obey non-Sinic Vietnamese grammatical convention, with modifiers following rather than preceding the words they modify.

Many Vietnamese words which appear in the text do not appear in this glossary. The reason, of course, is that these words are non-Chinese and were written in nineteenth-century Vietnam in *nôm* rather than in Chinese characters. The *nôm* script, which was used alongside Chinese characters, was inspired by them at the same time that it diverged from them. Thus the two Chinese characters *t'ien* 天 ("heaven") and *shang* 上 ("above") were combined to form *trời* 圣, the common non-Sinic Vietnamese word for "heaven." The Chinese character *chih* 至 ("to arrive at") combined with the Chinese character *tien* 典 (pronounced *điển* in Sino-Vietnamese, supplying the sound element) to form the *nôm* character for *đến* 至典, "to arrive at." The Chinese character *jen* 人 ("man") combined with an abbreviation which had been squeezed from the Chinese word for "time" (*shih* 時; pronounced *thời* in Sino-Vietnamese) to form the *nôm* character for *người* 𠊛, "man." *Nôm* texts might employ Chinese characters but also give them different meanings: for example, *tsu* 卒 might stand for *tốt*, "good," instead of meaning "soldier" or "to die" as it did in Chinese. Only a small number of *nôm* characters appears in this glossary. Such characters are identified.

A Nộ 阿弩
Ai Lao (Ai-lao) 哀牢
ấm-sinh (yin-sheng) 蔭生
An Biên 安邊
An Giang 安江
An Khánh 安慶
An-ninh 安寧
án sát sứ (an-ch'a-shih) 按察使
Anh-cát-lợi-mao quốc 暎咭唎毛國
Anh Sơn 英山
Ấu học ngũ ngôn thi 幼學五言詩

Bá Đa Lộc 百多祿
Ba Thác 弝式 (*nôm*)
bắc chương kinh (pei chang-
    ching) 北章京
Bắc-kỳ 北圻
bắc-nhân (pei-jen) 北人
Bắc Ninh 北寧
Bắc Thành 北城
Bắc Thành công tư đê tổng sách
    北城公私堤總冊
Bắc Thành tổng trấn 北城總鎮
Bắc Triều (pei-ch'ao) 北朝
bạch diện thư sinh (pai-mien shu-
    sheng) 白面書生
bách hí (pai hsi) 百戲
bạch ốc (pai wu) 白屋
bài chí (p'ai chih) 牌誌
bản chức (pen chih) 本職
bản chương sở (pen chang so)
    本章所
bang (pang) 帮
bang trưởng (pang ch'ang) 帮長
bảo-giáp (pao-chia) 保甲
bát cổ văn (pa-ku wen) 八股文
bát quái thành (pa-kua-ch'eng)
    八卦城
bí thư sở (mi-shu-so) 祕書所
Biện di luận 辨夷論
Biên Hòa 邊和
bình (p'ing) 平
Binh Bộ (Ping Pu) 兵部
Bình Định 平定
Bình Giang 平江
Bình Hoà 平和

bình thiên hạ (p'ing t'ien-hsia)
    平天下
Bình Thuận 平順
bổ (pu) 補
bố-cái đại vương 布蓋大王 (*nôm*
    usage?*)
bố chính sứ (pu-cheng-shih) 布政
    使
Bùi Dức Mân 裴德緡

ca xướng (ko-ch'ang) 歌唱
cách vật (ko-wu) 格物
cải (kai) 改
cai lại (kai-li) 該吏
cai tào quan (kai-ts'ao-kuan) 該艚
    官
cải thổ qui lưu (kai-t'u kuei-liu)
    改土歸流
Cam lộ 甘露
Cần Chính Điện (Ch'in-cheng
    tien) 勤政殿
cảng thuế (kang-shui) 港稅
canh (keng) 更
Cao Bá Quát 高伯适
Cao Bằng 高平
Cao Man 高蠻
cáo cắc (kao-ch'ih) 誥敕
cáo thân (kao-shen) 告身
cấp dưỡng nhất thế (chi-yang
    i-shih) 給養一世
câu (chú) 俱
Chà Bàn 闍槃
cha-tzu 劄子
chang-ching 章京
ch'ang-li 長麗
Chao I 趙翼
Châu (Chu) 朱
châu (chou) 州
châu bản (chu-pen) 硃本
Ch'en Hao 陳澔
Ch'en Ying 陳應
chi-shih-chung 給事中
chia-t'ou 甲頭
chiao-tzu 交子
chiao-yü 教諭
Ch'ien-k'un t'i-i 乾坤體義

chiếu hội (chao-hui) 照会
chiếu văn (chao-wen) 詔文
ch'in-ch'i 親戚
ch'in-tsu 親族
ching-ch'a 京察
chính danh (cheng-ming) 正名
chính kiêm (cheng-ch'ien) 正籤
Chính Nam 正南
chính sách tàm thực (cheng-ts'e ts'an-shih) 政策蚕食
chính sự (cheng-shih) 政事
chính tâm thuật (cheng-hsin shu) 正心術
Chợ Doanh 勢營 (*nôm*)
Ch'u 楚
chủ khảo (chu-k'ao) 主考
chữ nho (ju-tzu) 字儒
chữ nôm 字喃
ch'u-she 鋤社
chủ sự (chu-shih) 主事
Chu-tzu chia-li 朱子家禮
Ch'ủ Yüan 屈原
chuang-yüan 狀元
chức sắc hạng (chih-se-hsiang) 職色項
Chứn-chi-ch'u 軍機處
Chung ching 忠經
chưởng ấn cấp sự trung (chang-yin chi-shih-chung) 掌印給事中
chuyển (chuan) 轉
Cổ Lão 古老
Cơ Mật Viện (Chi-mi-yüan) 機密院
cổ nhân thành cú (ku-jen ch'eng chü) 古人成句
côi (ku) 孤
Côn Lôn Đảo 崑崙島
công (kung) 功
Công Bộ (Kung-pu) 工部
công điền (kung-t'ien) 公田
cống sinh (kung-sheng) 貢生
công tiền (kung-ch'ien) 工錢
cù lao cau 岣嶗楺 (*nôm*)
cử-nhân (chü-jen) 舉人
cung danh (kung-ming) 宮名
cửu đỉnh (chiu-ting) 九鼎

Đà Nẵng 沱㶞
dã sử (yeh-shih) 野史
đại học (ta-hsüeh) 大學
Đại Học (Ta Hsüeh) 大學
đại học sĩ (ta-hsüeh-shih) 大學士
Đại Lý Tự (Ta Li Ssu) 大理寺
Đại Man Quốc Địa Đồ 大蠻國地圖
Đại Nam 大南
Đại Nội (Ta-nei) 大內
đại thần (ta-ch'en) 大臣
đại thử (ta-shu) 大暑
Đại Việt 大越
dân (min) 民
dẫn kiến (yin-chien) 引見
dân sinh (min-sheng) 民生
đang án (tang-an) 檔案
Đặng Trân Thường 鄧陳常
đảo (tao) 島
đạo (tao) 道
đao canh hỏa nậu (tao-keng huo-nou) 刀耕火耨
đáp khách (ta-k'o) 搭客
đê điều (t'i-tiao) 提調
địa bộ (ti-pu) 地簿
Dịch-kinh (I-ching) 易經
địch thể lễ (ti t'i li) 敵體禮
dịch thuyền (i-ch'uan) 役船
Điện Bàn 奠磐
điển cố (tien-ku) 典故
diện thương (mien-shang) 面商
điều (tiao) 調
đinh (ting) 丁
đinh bộ (ting-pu) 丁簿
đình thi (t'ing-shih) 庭試
Định Tường 定祥
Định Viễn 定遠
đô-da 都耶
Đô Sát Viện (Tu-ch'a-yüan) 都察院
doanh (ying) 營
đốc học (tu-hsüeh) 督學
đôn nhân luân (tun jen-lun) 敦人倫
Đông Lâm 東林
Dư (Yü) 余

du học sĩ nhân (yu-hsüeh shih-jen) 遊學士人

đức chủ trời 德主丕 (*nôm*)

dung (jung) 容

dương (yang) 洋

dưỡng liêm (yang-lien) 養廉

Dương Sơn 陽山

Fan-shu-fang 繙書房

feng-chiao 風教

Feng Kuei-fen 馮桂芬

fu-ni 付泥

fu-shih 府試

gia (chia) 家

gia-danh (chia-ming) 嘉名

gia-đình (chia-t'ing) 家庭

Gia Định 嘉定

Gia Định thành tổng trấn 嘉定城總鎮

Gia Hưng 嘉興

Gia-long 嘉隆

giám khảo (chien-k'ao) 監考

giam sát ngự sử (chien-ch'a yü-shih) 監察御史

giám sinh (chien-sheng) 監生

giản (chien) 簡

gian thương (chien-shang) 姦商

giang lộ nhân (chiang-lu jen) 江路人

Giang Văn Hiển 江文顯

giáo thụ (chiao-shou) 教授

giao-tử (chiao-tzu) 交子

giới dâm nặc (chieh yin-ni) 戒淫匿

hà can (ho-kan) 河竿

hạ chí (hsia-chih) 夏至

hạ điền (hsia-t'ien) 夏田

Hà Nội 河內

Hà Quyền 何權

Hà Thanh 河清

hạ thu điền (hsia-ch'iu t'ien) 夏秋田

Hà Tiên 河僊

Hà Tĩnh 河靜

Hải Dương 海陽

Hải trình tập nghiệm sách 海程集驗冊

Hàm Thuận 咸順

hán điền (han t'ien) 旱田

Han Hsin 韓信

Hàn-lâm viện (Han-lin yüan) 翰林院

Han-tan meng-chi 邯鄲夢記

Hán văn (Han-wen) 漢文

Hàn vương tôn phú 韓王孫賦

hạnh (hsing) 行

Hành Nhân Ty (Hsing-jen ssu) 行人司

hành tẩu (hsing-tsou) 行走

hao-she 號舍

hậu điều sách (hou-tiao ts'e) 候調冊

hậu phong tục (hou feng-su) 厚風俗

hậu thăng sách (hou-sheng ts'e) 候陞冊

hiệp trấn (hsieh-chen) 協鎮

hiếu hành khả phong (hsiao-hsing k'o-feng) 孝行可風

hiếu tử (hsiao-tzu) 孝子

Hình Bộ (Hsing-pu) 刑部

hình danh sách (hsing-ming ts'e) 刑名冊

hình danh tối điện sách (hsing-ming tsui-tien ts'e) 刑名最殿冊

Hình thư 刑書

Hộ Bộ (Hu-pu) 戶部

Ho Hsi-wen 何喜文

hộ khoa (hu-k'o) 戶科

Ho-lan 啁嘓

Hồ Xuân Hương 胡春香

Hoa kiều (Hua-ch'iao) 華僑

Hoa-lang quốc 花郎國

hoá thuế (huo-shui) 貨稅

Hỏa Xả Quốc 火舍國

Hoài Đức 懷德

Hoài Nhơn 懷仁

hoàng đế (huang-ti) 皇帝

Hoằng Hóa 弘化

Hoàng Kim Hoán 黃金煥

Hoàng thành (huang-ch'eng) 皇城
hộc (hu) 斛
Hội-an 會安
Hội Đồng Đình thân Công Đồng
  (hui-t'ung t'ing-ch'en kung-
  t'ung) 會同廷臣公同
hội đồng hào mục (hui-t'ung hao-
  mu) 會同豪目
hội đồng môn (t'ung-men hui)
  會同門
hội khảo (hui-k'ao) 會考
hội thi (hui-shih) 會試
hồi t.y (hui-pi) 廻避
Hồng-mao (Hung-mao) 紅毛
Hsi-hsiang chi 西廂記
Hsi Po 西伯
Hsiao-ching 考經
hsien-shih 縣試
Hsű Chi-yű 徐繼畬
Hsűeh-hai t'ang 學海堂
Hu An-kuo 胡安國
huấn đạo (hsűn-tao) 訓導
huấn tử đệ (hsűn tzu-ti) 訓子弟
Huang Ch'ing ching-chieh 皇清經解
hui-tien 會典
Hưng Hóa 興化
Hưng Yên 興安
hương cống (hsiang-kung) 鄉貢
hương đảng điều lệ (hsiang-tang
  t'iao-li) 鄉黨條例
hương hỏa điền (hsiang-hua t'ien)
  香火田
hương thi (hsiang-shih) 鄉試
hữu chiếu (yu chao) 有詔
hữu đô ngự sử (yu tu-yű-shih) 右
  都御史
huyện (hsien) 縣

Juan Yűan 阮元

kan-i-ryō 官位令
K'ang-hsi tzu-tien 康熙字典
kao-ch'ih 誥敕
kế (chi) 繼
kế khóa (chi-k'o) 繼課

kế tứ nguyệt (chi ssu yűeh) 繼四月
kết thúc (chieh-shu) 結束
khách trưởng (k'o-chang) 客長
khanh (ch'ing) 卿
Khánh Hòa 慶和
khảo hạch (k'ao-ho) 考覈
khảo ngữ (k'ao-yű) 考語
khảo tích (k'ao-chi) 考績
khẩu phân điền chế (k'ou-fen
  t'ien-chih) 口分田制
khẩu xứ (k'ou-ch'u) 口處
Khoái Châu 快州
khởi cư chú viên (ch'i-chű chu-
  yűan) 起居注員
khôn (k'un) 坤
Khôn Thái Cung (k'un-t'ai kung)
  坤泰宮
khuyên tiết điền (ch'űan chieh-
  t'ien) 勸節田
kiến (ch'ien) 乾
Kiên An 建安
Kiên Thành Cung (ch'ien-ch'eng
  kung) 乾成宮
Kinh Bắc 京北
kinh lịch (ching-li) 經歷
kinh lược sứ (ching-lűeh shih) 經
  略使
kinh nghĩa (ching-i) 經義
kinh sử chính văn (ching-shih
  cheng-wen) 經史正文
Kinh thành (Ching-ch'eng) 京城
ko-yen ts'e 格眼冊
kuan-p'in-ling 官品令
Kung Tzu-chen 龔自珍
"Kung-yang chuan" 公羊傳
kung-yűan 貢院
Kuo Chű-ching 郭居敬
Kuo-shih kuan 國史館

Lại Bộ (Li pu) 吏部
lại khoa (li-k'o) 吏科
lẫm hý (lin-hsi) 廩餼
Lâm Sâm 林森
Lam Sơn thực lục 藍山實錄
lan nhai (lan-chieh) 欄街

Lạng Sơn 諒山

lang trung (lang-chung) 郎中

Lê Bá Phẩm 黎伯品

Lễ Bộ (Li Pu) 禮部

Lê Chỉ Trai 黎止齋

Lê Đại Cương 黎大綱

Lê Đăng Doanh 黎登瀛

Lê Khiêm Quang 黎謙光

Lễ ký (Li-chi) 禮記

Lê Quý Đôn 黎貴惇

lễ tiền (li-ch'ien) 禮錢

Lê Văn Duyệt 黎文悅

Lê Văn Khôi 黎文傀

Li Tiao-yüan 李調元

Li Tzu-ch'eng 李自成

Liang Chang-chü 梁章鉅

Lịch triều hiến chương loại chí 歷朝憲章類誌

liêm (lien) 簾

liên danh bảo kết (lien-ming pao-chieh) 連名保結

liệt (lieh) 劣

linh đài (ling-t'ai) 靈臺

Linh Giang 靈江

linh mục (ling-mu) 靈牧

Liu Tsung-yüan 柳宗元

lo 駱

Lo-Yüeh 駱越

Long Phúc 隆福

Luận ngữ (Lun-yü) 論語

lục-bát 六八

lục bộ (liu-pu) 六部

lục khoa (liu-k'o) 六科

lục lễ (liu-li) 六禮

Lung-tsung 隆宗

lưỡng quốc trạng nguyên (liang-kuo chuang-yüan) 兩國狀元

Lý 李

lý trưởng (li-chang) 里長

Lý Ưng Lợi 李應利

Lý Văn Phức 李文馥

Mã-song 馬雙

mạch (mai) 陌

Mai Anh Tuấn 枚英俊

Man (Man) 蠻

mân (min) 緡

Mẫn tử Khiện (Min tzu-ch'ien) 閔子騫

Mạnh tử (Meng-tzu) 孟子

mật chiếp (mi-che) 密摺

mật sát (mi-ch'a) 密察

mễ (mi) 米

mei 没

mei-le chang-ching 梅勒章京

mệnh (ming) 命

Miến Điện (Mien-tien) 緬甸

miếu vũ (miao-yü) 廟宇

Min-Yüeh 閩越

Ming-liang lun 明良論

Ming shih 明史

Ming Tao chia-hsün 明道家訓

Minh-hương (Ming-hsiang) 明香 (before 1827) 明鄉 (after 1827)

Minh-mạng 明命

Mo Chiu 莫玖

mộ phu (mu-fu) 墓夫

mộc biểu (mu-piao) 木表

Muro Kyūsō 室鳩巢

Nặc Ông Chân 匿螉禎

Nam Chưởng (Nan-chang) 南掌

nam chương kinh (nan chang-ching) 南章京

Nam Định 南定

Nam-kỳ 南圻

nam mễ (nan-mi) 南米

Nam Vang 南榮

Nam Việt (Nan-yüeh) 南越

Nan-yüeh 南越

Nghệ An 乂安

Ngô Đình Giai 吳廷价

Ngọ Môn (Wu-men) 午門

Ngô Nhân Tịnh 吳仁靜

Ngô Sĩ Liên 吳士連

ngoại khổn (wai k'un) 外閫

ngoại liêm (wai lien) 外簾

ngoại quốc văn tự (wai-kuo wen-tzu) 外國文字

ngôn (yen) 言

ngũ biá (wu-pai) 五拜

ngũ đại đồng đường (wu-tai t'ung-t'ang) 五代同堂

ngụy hiệu (wei hao) 僞號

Nguyễn Án 阮案

Nguyễn Bá Nghi 阮伯儀

Nguyễn Bảo Trí 阮保智

Nguyễn Công Trứ 阮公著

Nguyễn Đăng Giai 阮登楷

Nguyễn Du 阮攸

Nguyễn Hoài Quỳnh 阮懷瓊

Nguyễn Hữu Thận 阮有慎

Nguyễn Khoa Minh 阮科明

Nguyễn Tâm 阮心

Nguyễn Trường Tộ 阮長祚

Nguyễn Văn Hiếu 阮文孝

Nguyễn Văn Nhân 阮文仁

Nguyễn Văn Siêu 阮文超

Nguyễn Văn Thành 阮文誠

Nguyễn Văn Tồn 阮文存

Nguyễn Văn Xung 阮文衝

Nguyệt Biêu 月瓢

Nguyệt Độ 月度

Nguyệt Thai 月臺

Nhạn sơn 雁山

Nhất thiên tự 一千字

nhĩ (erh) 爾

Nhị Thập Tứ Hiếu 二十四孝

nhiêu (jao) 饒

Như Tây Nhật Trình 如西日程

nhu viễn (jou-yűan) 柔遠

niên hiệu (nien-hao) 年號

Ninh Bắc 寧北

Ninh Bình 寧平

no 諾

Nội Các (Nei-ko) 內閣

Nội Hàn Viện (Nei-han yűan) 內翰院

nội liêm (nei-lien) 內簾

Nội vụ phủ (Nei-wu fu) 內務府

p'ai-t'ou 牌頭

Pai-Yűeh 百粵

pao-chang 保長

phá đề (p'o-t'i) 破題

Phạm Đình Hổ 范廷琥

Phạm Nhật Huy 范日徽

Phạm Như Đăng 范如登

phân (fen) 分

Phan Bá Đạt 潘伯達

Phan Bá Vành 潘伯鑅

Phan Huy Chú 潘輝注

Phan Huy Thực 潘輝湜

phân khảo (fen-k'ao) 分考

Phan Thanh Giản 潘清簡

phân trương (fen-chang) 紛張

Phạt Lăng 伐棱

Phi Long ngân tiền 飛龍銀錢

phiên (fan) 番

Phiên An 潘安

phiên vương (fan-wang) 番王

phiêu nghĩ (p'iao-ni) 票擬

phó bảng (fu-pang) 副榜

phó chủ khảo (fu chu-k'ao) 副主考

phó đề điều (fu t'i-tiao) 副提調

phong vũ nhật ký (feng-yű jih-chi) 風雨日記

phú (fu) 賦

phủ (fu) 府

phủ đường (fu-t'ang) 府堂

Phú-lãng-sa 富浪沙

phù lễ (fu-li) 俘禮

phụ thí (fu-shih) 附試

Phú Yên 富安

phúc khảo (fu-k'ao) 覆考

phục nê trưởng ly (fu-ni ch'ang-li) 付泥長麗

Phước Long 福隆

phường (fang) 坊

phượng (fang) 方

P'i-p'a chi 琵琶記

P'i-p'a hsing 琵琶行

p'i-shou 陂首

pi-t'ieh-shih 筆帖式

Pin-lang-yű 檳榔嶼

Po Chű-i 白居易

P'u Sung-ling 浦松齡

quan (kuan) 貫

quan (kuan) 官

quan thư (kuan-shu) 官書
Quảng Bình 廣平
Quảng Điền 廣田
Quảng Đức 廣德
Quảng Nam 廣南
Quảng Nghĩa 廣義
Quảng Oai 廣威
quảng thiện hạnh (kuang shan-hsing) 廣善行
Quảng Trị 廣治
Quang-trung 光中
Quảng Yên 廣安
quốc (kuo) 國
Quốc sử quán (Kuo-shih kuan) 國史館
Quốc triều thông lễ 國朝通禮
Quốc-tử-giám (Kuo-tzu-chien) 國子監
quốc vương (kuo-wang) 國王

sắc thư (ch'ih-shu) 敕書
sắc văn (ch'ih-wen) 敕文
sách văn (ts'e-wen) 策問
Sài-gòn 柴棍 (*nôm* usage)
San-tzu ching 三字經
shan-chang 山長
Shen-nung 神農
sheng-yűan 生員
Shih-wu i-ming lu 事物異名錄
Shu-mi-yűan 樞密院
shu-yűan 書院
Shui Ching Chu 水經注
sĩ cẩn đối (shih chin tui) 士謹対
sĩ nhân danh sách (shih-jen ming-ts'e) 士人名冊
sinh cẩn đối (sheng chin tui) 生謹對
Sơ học vấn tân 初學問津
sơ khảo (ch'u-k'ao) 初考
Sơn-nam-hạ 山南下
Sơn-nam-thượng 山南上
Sơn Tây 山西
sơn xuyên cảnh vật (shan-ch'uan ching-wu) 山川景物
sự tích (ch'u-chi) 儲積

Sứ trình nhật ký (shih-ch'eng jih-chi) 使程日記
sùng chính học (ch'ung-cheng-hsűeh) 崇正學

ta-chi 大計
tả đô ngự sử (tso tu-yű-shih) 左都御史
Ta hsűeh yen-i 大學衍義
Ta Ming i-t'ung chih 大明一統志
tài (ts'ai) 才
T'ai-yeh-ch'ih 太液池
tam cương (san-kang) 三綱
tam đại tiết (san ta chieh) 三大節
tâm thường (hsűn-ch'ang) 尋常
Tân Bình 新平
Tân lang dữ (Pin-lang-yű) 檳榔嶼
Tang Thương Ngẫu Lục 桑滄偶錄
táo chính (ts'ao-cheng) 漕政
Tập thiện đường 集善堂
Tập vận trích yếu 輯韻摘要
tấu (tsou) 奏
tâu báo mễ giá (tsou-pao mi-chia) 奏報米價
Tây-sơn 西山
tê gia (ch'i-chia) 齊家
tế-tửu (chi-chiu) 祭酒
Teng Chih-ch'eng 鄧之誠
tennō (t'ien-huang) 天皇
thạch kiệt (shih-chieh) 石碣
Thái Hòa Điện (T'ai-ho tien) 太和殿
Thái Nguyên 太原
tham-tri (ts'an-chih) 參知
thận pháp thủ (shen fa-shou) 愼法守
thăng (sheng) 升
Thăng-long 昇隆 (after 1804), 昇龍 (before 1804)
Thánh-giáo yếu lý quốc ngữ 聖教要理國語
Thanh-hà-xã 清河社
Thanh Hóa 清化
thành-hoàng (ch'eng-huang) 城隍
thanh-lại-ty (ch'ing-li ssu) 清吏司

Thanh-nhân 清人

Thanh-quốc 清國

·Thanh-quốc ngữ 清國語

thảo kiếm (ts'ao-ch'ien) 草籤

thập đạo đường (shih-tao t'ang) 道堂十

thất ngôn luật (ch'i-yen lü) 七言律

thể (t'i) 體

thể diện (t'i-mien) 體面

thế khoa liên đăng (shih-k'o lien-teng) 世科連登

thể sát (t'i-ch'a) 體察

thị hàn viện (shih-han yüan) 侍翰院

Thi kinh (*Shih-ching*) 詩經

thị-lang (shih-lang) 侍郎

thị thư viện (shih-shu yüan) 侍書院

thị vệ sở (shih-wei so) 侍衞所

thiên-hạ (t'ien-hsia) 天下

Thiên Trường 天長

thiên-tử (t'ien-tzu) 天子

Thiệu Hóa 紹化

Thiệu-trị 紹治

thỉnh an tấu (ch'ing-an tsou) 請安奏

thôn (ts'un) 村

Thông Chính Ty (t'ung-cheng ssu) 通政司

thứ (tz'u) 次

thủ bản (shou-pen) 手本

thu điền (ch'iu-t'ien) 秋田

thủ huyện (shou-hsien) 首縣

Thư kinh (*Shu-ching*) 書經

thủ phủ (shou-fu) 首府

thư tả ty (shu-hsieh ssu) 書寫司

Thừa Thiên 承天

Thuận Hóa 順化

thuận thường (shun-ch'ang) 順常

thuận tôn (shun-sun) 順孫

thuộc viên (shu-yüan) 屬員

Thương Bạc Ty (shang-po ssu) 商舶司

Thượng Bưủ Sở (shang-pao so) 尚寶所

thượng thư (shang-shu) 尚書

thượng tiết kiểm (shang chieh-chien) 尚節儉

Thủy Xả Quốc 水舍國

Ti-chien t'u-shuo 帝鑑圖說

t'i-pen 題本

tiên-chỉ (hsien-chih) 先指

tiên học lễ, hậu học văn (hsien hsüeh li, hou hsüeh wen) 先學禮, 後學文

tiến-sĩ (chin-shih) 進士

tiên-sinh (hsien-sheng) 先生

tiết khí (chieh-ch'i) 節氣

tiết phụ (chieh-fu) 節婦

tiểu học (hsiao-hsüeh) 小學

tính (hsing) 性

tỉnh (sheng) 省

tình cảnh (ch'ing-ching) 情景

tịnh tọa (ching-tso) 靜坐

To-lun-no-erh 多倫諾爾

tộc (tsu) 族

tối yếu (tsui-yao) 最要

tôn-sinh (tsun-sheng) 尊生

Tôn Thọ Đức 尊壽德

tổng (tsung) 總

Tống Chí Truyền 宋志傳

tổng đốc (tsung-tu) 總督

Trà-sơn 茶山

trẫm (chen) 朕

trấn (chen) 鎮

Trần 陳

Trần Công Hiến 陳公憲

Trấn Ninh 鎮寧

Trấn Tây 鎮西

Trấn Tây thành 鎮西城

trấn thủ (chen-shou) 鎮守

Trần triều đại điển 陳朝大典

Trạng-nguyên thi 狀元詩

trào (ch'ao) 嘲

tri huyện (chih-hsien) 知縣

tri phủ (chih-fu) 知府

trị quốc (chih-kuo) 治國

triều hội điều lệ (ch'ao-hui t'iao-li) 朝會條例

Triệu Phong 肇豐

Trịnh 鄭
Trịnh Hoài Đức 鄭懷德
trừ (ch'u) 除
trung (chung) 忠
trúng (chung) 中
Trưng 徵
Trung dung (Chung-yung) 中庸
Trung-quốc (Chung-kuo) 中國
trường (ch'ang) 場
trượng (chang) 丈
Trưởng Khánh 長慶
Trương Minh Giảng 張明講
Trương Minh Ký 張明記
Trương Quốc Dụng 張國用
trưởng tộc (tsu-chang) 長族 (族長)
Ts'ai Ch'en 蔡沈
ts'an-chih cheng-shih 參知政知
tsou-che 奏摺
tử cấm thành (tzu-chin ch'eng) 紫禁城
tư di (tzu-i) 咨移
Tứ Dịch Quán (Ssu-i-kuan) 四譯館
tứ đức (ssu-te) 四德
từ đường (tz'u-t'ang) 祠堂
tứ khuyết (ssu-ch'üeh) 四缺
Từ Sơn 慈山
tú-tài (hsiu-ts'ai) 秀才
tu thân (hsiu-shen) 修身
tự trần (tzu-ch'en) 自陳
tư trình (tzu-ch'eng) 咨呈
từ tự (tz'u-ssu) 祠寺
tứ vi (ssu-wei) 四圍
Tu Yử 杜宇
tuần phủ (hsün-fu) 巡撫
Tuan-wu (Đoan-ngọ) 端午
Tuan-yang (Đoan-dương) 端陽
t'ung-k'ao-kuan 同考官
t'ung-shih 童試
tượng nô (hsiang-nu) 象奴
Tuy An 綏安
Tuy Biên 綏邊
Tuy Viễn 綏遠
Tuyên Quang 宣光
ty (ssu) 司
ty chức (pei-chih) 卑職

ty luân sở (ssu-lun so) 絲綸所
tzu-ch'en 自陳

ưu (yu) 優
uy tín (wei-hsin) 威信
văn (wen) 文

văn dĩ tái đạo (wen i tsai-tao) 文以載道
văn-hóa Việt-Chiêm (Yüeh-Chan wen-hua) 文化越占 (越占文化)
Văn Miếu (Wen-miao) 文廟
văn-thư-phòng (wen-shu-fang) 文書房
Vạn Tượng (Wan-hsiang) 萬象
viên-ngoại-lang (yüan-wai-lang) 員外郎
viễn phương chư quốc lai cống (yüan-fang chu-kuo lai-kung) 遠方諸國來貢
Việt Điện U Linh Tập 越甸幽靈集
Việt Nam (Yüeh-nan) 越南
Việt Nam Quốc Phật vương 越南國佛王
Việt-thường 越裳
Vĩnh Bảo 永保
Vĩnh-điêm thị 永恬市
Vĩnh Long 永隆
Vinh Ma Ly 榮麻離
vinh qui (jung-kuei) 榮歸
Vĩnh Thanh 永清
Võ Văn Lập 武文立
vô vi nhi trị (wu-wei erh chih) 無爲而治
Vọng Các 望閣
Vọng Các công thần 望閣功臣
vụ bản nghiệp (wu pen-yeh) 務本業
Vũ Đức Khuê 武德奎
vua 喭 (*nôm*)
vua bếp 喭忾 (*nôm*)
vương (wang) 王

xã (she) 社
xã quan (she-kuan) 社官
xã thương (she-ts'ang) 社倉

xã trưởng (she-chang) 社長
xích hậu (ch'ih-hou) 斥候
Xiêm La (Hsien-lo) 暹羅
Xuân thu (*Ch'un-ch'iu*) 春秋
Xương mại mương 昌賣茫
xuyển quyển số (ch'uan chứan shu)
　串卷數

Yang Erh-ti 楊貳睇

Yen-shih chia-hsữn 顏氏家訓
yếu (yao) 要
yin-chien 引見
Yoshimune 吉宗
yữ-ying-t'ang 育嬰堂
Yử-Yửeh 於越
yửan-shih 院試
Yửeh-i hui-kuan 越夷會館
yung-tao 甬道

Harvard East Asian Monographs

21. Kwang-Ching Liu, ed., *American Missionaries in China: Papers from Harvard Seminars*

22. George Moseley, *A Sino-Soviet Cultural Frontier: The Ili Kazakh Autonomous Chou*

23. Carl F. Nathan, *Plague Prevention and Politics in Manchuria, 1910–1931*

24. Adrian Arthur Bennett, *John Fryer: The Introduction of Western Science and Technology into Nineteenth-Century China*

25. Donald J. Friedman, *The Road from Isolation: The Campaign of the American Committee for Non-Participation in Japanese Aggression, 1938–1941*

26. Edward Le Fevour, *Western Enterprise in Late Ch'ing China: A Selective Survey of Jardine, Matheson and Company's Operations, 1842–1895*

27. Charles Neuhauser, *Third World Politics: China and the Afro-Asian People's Solidarity Organization, 1957–1967*

28. Kungtu C. Sun, assisted by Ralph W. Huenemann, *The Economic Development of Manchuria in the First Half of the Twentieth Century*

29. Shahid Javed Burki, *A Study of Chinese Communes, 1965*

30. John Carter Vincent, *The Extraterritorial System in China: Final Phase*

31. Madeleine Chi, *China Diplomacy, 1914–1918*

32. Clifton Jackson Phillips, *Protestant America and the Pagan World: The First Half Century of the American Board of Commissioners for Foreign Missions, 1810–1860*

33. James Pusey, *Wu Han: Attacking the Present through the Past*

34. Ying-wan Cheng, *Postal Communication in China and Its Modernization, 1860–1896*

35. Tuvia Blumenthal, *Saving in Postwar Japan*

36. Peter Frost, *The Bakumatsu Currency Crisis*

37. Stephen C. Lockwood, *Augustine Heard and Company, 1858–1862*

38. Robert R. Campbell, *James Duncan Campbell: A Memoir by His Son*

39. Jerome Alan Cohen, ed., *The Dynamics of China's Foreign Relations*

40. V. V. Vishnyakova-Akimova, *Two Years in Revolutionary China, 1925–1927*, tr. Steven I. Levine

41. Meron Medzini, *French Policy in Japan during the Closing Years of the Tokugawa Regime*

42. *The Cultural Revolution in the Provinces*

43. Sidney A. Forsythe, *An American Missionary Community in China, 1895–1905*

44. Benjamin I. Schwartz, ed., *Reflections on the May Fourth Movement: A Symposium*

45. Ching Young Choe, *The Rule of the Taewŏn'gun, 1864–1873: Restoration in Yi Korea*

46. W. P. J. Hall, *A Bibliographical Guide to Japanese Research on the Chinese Economy, 1958-1970*

47. Jack J. Gerson, *Horatio Nelson Lay and Sino-British Relations, 1854-1864*

48. Paul Richard Bohr, *Famine and the Missionary: Timothy Richard as Relief Administrator and Advocate of National Reform*

49. Endymion Wilkinson, *The History of Imperial China: A Research Guide*

50. Britten Dean, *China and Great Britain: The Diplomacy of Commerical Relations, 1860-1864*

51. Ellsworth C. Carlson, *The Foochow Missionaries, 1847-1880*

52. Yeh-chien Wang, *An Estimate of the Land-Tax Collection in China, 1753 and 1908*

53. Richard M. Pfeffer, *Understanding Business Contracts in China, 1949-1963*

54. Han-sheng Chuan and Richard Kraus, *Mid-Ch'ing Rice Markets and Trade, An Essay in Price History*

55. Ranbir Vohra, *Lao She and the Chinese Revolution*

56. Liang-lin Hsiao, *China's Foreign Trade Statistics, 1864-1949*

57. Lee-hsia Hsu Ting, *Government Control of the Press in Modern China, 1900-1949*

58. Edward W. Wagner, *The Literati Purges: Political Conflict in Early Yi Korea*

59. Joungwon A. Kim, *Divided Korea: The Politics of Development, 1945-1972*

60. Noriko Kamachi, John K. Fairbank, and Chūzō Ichiko, *Japanese Studies of Modern China Since 1953: A Bibliographical Guide to Historical and Social-Science Research on the Nineteenth and Twentieth Centuries, Supplementary Volume for 1953-1969*

61. Donald A. Gibbs and Yun-chen Li, *A Bibliography of Studies and Translations of Modern Chinese Literature, 1918-1942*

62. Robert H. Silin, *Leadership and Values: The Organization of Large-Scale Taiwanese Enterprises*

63. David Pong, *A Critical Guide to the Kwangtung Provincial Archives Deposited at the Public Record Office of London*

64. Fred W. Drake, *China Charts the World: Hsu Chi-yü and His Geography of 1848*

65. William A. Brown and Urgunge Onon, translators and annotators, *History of the Mongolian People's Republic*

66. Edward L. Farmer, *Early Ming Government: The Evolution of Dual Capitals*

67. Ralph C. Croizier, *Koxinga and Chinese Nationalism: History, Myth, and the Hero*

68. William J. Tyler, tr., *The Psychological World of Natsume Sōseki*, by Doi Takeo

STUDIES IN THE MODERNIZATION OF THE REPUBLIC OF KOREA: 1945–1975

90. Noel F. McGinn, Donald R. Snodgrass, Yung Bong Kim, Shin-Bok Kim, and Quee-Young Kim, *Education and Development in Korea*

91. Leroy P. Jones and Il SaKong, *Government, Business and Entrepreneurship in Economic Development: The Korean Case*

92. Edward S. Mason, Dwight H. Perkins, Kwang Suk Kim, David C. Cole, Mahn Je Kim, et al., *The Economic and Social Modernization of the Republic of Korea*

93. Robert Repetto, Tai Hwan Kwon, Son-Ung Kim, Dae Young Kim, John E. Sloboda, and Peter J. Donaldson, *Economic Development, Population Policy, and Demographic Transition in the Republic of Korea*

106. David C. Cole and Yung Chul Park, *Financial Development in Korea, 1945-1978*

107. Roy Bahl, Chuk Kyo Kim, and Chong Kee Park, *Public Finances during the Korean Modernization Process*

94. Parks M. Coble, *The Shanghai Capitalists and the Nationalist Government, 1927-1937*

95. Noriko Kamachi, *Reform in China: Huang Tsun-hsien and the Japanese Model*

96. Richard Wich, *Sino-Soviet Crisis Politics: A Study of Political Change and Communication*

97. Lillian M. Li, *China's Silk Trade: Traditional Industry in the Modern World, 1842-1937*

98. R. David Arkush, *Fei Xiaotong and Sociology in Revolutionary China*

99. Kenneth Alan Grossberg, *Japan's Renaissance: The Politics of the Muromachi Bakufu*

100. James Reeve Pusey, *China and Charles Darwin*

101. Hoyt Cleveland Tillman, *Utilitarian Confucianism: Ch'en Liang's Challenge to Chu Hsi*

102. Thomas A. Stanley, *Ōsugi Sakae, Anarchist in Taishō Japan: The Creativity of the Ego*

103. Jonathan K. Ocko, *Bureaucratic Reform in Provincial China: Ting Jih-ch'ang in Restoration Kiangsu, 1867-1870*

104. James Reed, *The Missionary Mind and American East Asia Policy, 1911-1915*

105. Neil L. Waters, *Japan's Local Pragmatists: The Transition from Bakumatsu to Meiji in the Kawasaki Region*

108. William D. Wray, *Mitsubishi and the N.Y.K., 1870-1914: Business Strategy in the Japanese Shipping Industry*

109. Ralph William Huenemann, *The Dragon and the Iron Horse: The Economics of Railroads in China, 1876-1937*